BACKYARD RACEHORSE

**Written by Janet Del Castillo
with Lois Schwartz**

Illustrated by Janet del Castillo

Copyright: 1992 by Janet Del Castillo
               First Edition
Copyright: 1993 by Janet Del Castillo and Lois Schwartz
               Second Edition
Copyright: 1996 by Janet Del Castillo and Lois Schwartz
               Third Edition
               1998 Second Printing
               2000 Third Printing

Published by:
        Prediction Publications & Productions
        3708 Crystal Beach Road
        Winter Haven, FL 33880

Library of Congress Catalog Card No. 93-086831
ISBN No. 1-884475-01-9

ATTENTION

Anyone engaged in training horses, exposes himself to the inherent and associated risks of such actions, including possible personal injury. This manual suggests techniques for training race-horses, but in no way assures or represents that trying these techniques will not result in injury. When you partake in any activity with horses, you do so at your own risk. The authors and publishers disclaim all liability in connection with the use of the information provided in this manual. Seek professional instruction and supervision, before attempting new skills.

TABLE OF CONTENTS

LIST OF ILLUSTRATIONS

A picture is worth a thousand words.

**Flip through the bottom right-hand corner of the book
to see the horses gallop.**

ACKNOWLEDGMENTS

The following people have been a great source of information. I sincerely appreciate the time they have spent with me in person, on the telephone or through correspondence. Communication between those of us in the industry is of utmost importance if we hope to achieve our goal of being informed owners, trainers, and veterinarians.

Tom Ainslie, Writer, *The Racing Form*; Thomas L. Aronson, Racing Resource Group, Inc.; W. Ashbury, DVM, University of Florida, Gainesville, FL; Ann Cain, Mullica Hill, NJ; Albert A. Cirelli, Jr., Professor, University of Nevada; Pat Clark, Circle Resources, Mansfield, TX; Michael Conder, Melbourne, FL; Sharon Creigier, PhD, Prince Edward Island, Canada; Trevor Denman, Track Announcer at Del Mar, Hollywood Park, and Santa Anita, CA; Michael Dickenson, Fair Hill Training Center, Elkton, MD; C. Douglas Donn, General Manager, Gulfstream Racetrack, Miami, FL; C. Kenneth Dunn, President & General Manager, Calder Racetrack, Miami, FL; Gail Emerson, Equine Dental Technician; Cheryl Hall, DVM, Merced, CA; Sue Hengemuehle, DVM, Okemos, MI; Donna Harper, DVM, Las Lunas, NM; Carol Holden, Sporting Life Farm, Middleburg, VA; Heather and George Humphries, Leesburg, VA; Robert Jack, DVM, President, American Association of Equine Practitioners; Ruth B. James, DVM, Mills, WY; William E. Jones, DVM, PhD; Mary Ann and David Kent, Kent Arabian Farm, Grand Rapids, MN; Lennart Krook, DVM, PhD, Cornell University; Mary Lebrato, Rio Linda, CA; Michael Martin, President, Thoroughbred Horseman's Association, Inc.; C. Wayne McIlwraith, BVSc, PhD, Colorado State University; Mary D. Midkiff, Equestrian Resources; Robert M. Miller, DVM, Thousand Oaks, CA; Larry Moriarity, Master Equine Dentist; Ed Noble, DVM., Ocala, FL; Roy Poole, Jr., DVM, PhD, University of California at Davis; James Rooney, DVM, Professor, Veterinary Science, University of Kentucky; Scott Savin, President, Florida Horsemen's Benevolent & Protective Association; Sue Stover, DVM, University of California at Davis; Bill H. Walmsley, National President, Horsemen's Benevolent & Protective Association; Alistair Webb, BVSc, PhD, FRCVS, University of Florida, Gainesville, FL; Gerald Wessner, DVM, Tampa, FL; Greg Wisner, Thoroughbred Pedigree Consultant, Dallas, TX; Holly Wright, J & J Tack, Lakeland, FL.

Sharing information is vital to our industry.

THANK YOU!   THANK YOU!   THANK YOU!

Sometimes I think I'm all alone and shouting against the wind. That is not so. I have a wonderful support system of family and friends who have encouraged me in my endeavors. To them I say, "Thank you." It is important that someone somewhere believes that what you are doing has value. These people, at various times of my highs and lows, have been there to give me the courage to carry on.

Mom and Jim - have always been ready to pitch in when the going gets rough.

My children - Alex, Nando and Victoria - have certainly shared in the overall adventure . . . helping me acquire the knowledge and experience I have put in this manual. We are all better people, in spite of the struggle and hardship we have endured. Adversity builds character . . . isn't that so?

Barbara, Jacki, Lucille, Marlene, Ubie and Walda - all have helped in their very special and unique ways. Special thanks to Matthew Mackay-Smith, DVM, Medical Consultant for *Equus Magazine*, for his comments and suggestions. My appreciation of the endless patience and guidance of the Tampa Bay Downs Stewards, Dick Kinsey, Charles Miranda, and Dennis Lima, must also be mentioned.

A special thanks to Lois, my type "A" pain in the neck editor, who tries to keep me on the straight and narrow. Due to her efforts, this edition is more logical and readable.

While speaking of editing, I must thank Taryl Elliot for the final fine combing of the text.

Charlie Camac and his son, Andy, deserve much recognition for their kindness and help over the years at Tampa Bay Downs.

Many, many others . . . owners and trainers who put up with my unusual methods, track personnel, entry clerks, stewards, stall men, grooms . . . I've learned from all of them. Exchanging experiences and sharing ideas helps us all become better educated about horses and training.

I hope my manual is the beginning of an open forum to share hands-on knowledge and improve the welfare of the horse and the future of HORSERACING!

FOREWORD

Many factors went into the decision to write this manual. The first was the need for more communication with those outside the racehorse industry who were considering becoming a part of it. My intent is to have a friendly dialogue with people who share my love of horses. The first few chapters are very basic and maybe repitious to thoses of you who are at home around horses. They are to help newcomers get a grasp on things. I hope to encourage all of you, especially the COMPETENT HORSEPERSON to consider racehorses. If you have competed in Rodeos, Hunter-Jumper Events, Horse Shows or other equine competitions, and trained your horse yourself, you may be experienced enough to train for racing.

I hope this manual will teach you to adapt your own circumstances to train a useful racehorse. You may have your own property or keep your horse at a boarding stable. Either option can work.

I recall those days of innocence when we naively said, ''Let's own racehorses!'' The learning process was slow, painful and filled with disappointment. We with mares and foals, it took a long time to get to the reality of the racetrack. Along the way, my family and I learned about fencing, animal feed, mare and foal care, and breaking and training.

The responsibility of raising and caring for animals was a good discipline for us all. The animals always had to be taken care of first. Our plans had to fit around their schedule. The children were able to earn a little towards their college, while being a part of our side business. Taxwise, this helped offset income from other sources.

We read trade magazines and discovered that stakes horses won the big purses. We could always trace the blood lines of our backyard horses to some famous racehorse. They all are related, if you go back far enough.

The real trials and tribulations came when the horses had to go to the track and a trainer. There were so many hurdles to overcome before getting a horse in a race let alone the winner's circle. There was another complete language to learn at the track. Terms like, ''break his maiden'', or ''fire the legs'' or ''blister the knees.'' What did it all mean? When I queried, I was assured I didn't need to worry my pretty little head about such things and was told, "Just send the check.''

I was the liaison between the person who paid the bill (my husband) and the person who wanted the bills paid (the trainer). Explaining to my husband why the horse wasn't running or describing to him some new wonder they were performing to enable the horse to run was not easy. My husband was a very high-strung, volatile doctor who didn't want excuses. Today, 20 years later, I remember him closing the encyclopedia after reading that Thoroughbred horse racing is the Sport of the Kings and saying, ''Well, we have breeding that goes back to Kentucky Derby winners on both sides. I want my horse trained for the Kentucky Derby. With good breeding and good blood there is no reason he can't win.'' He called the trainer and told him to train the horse for nothing less than the Triple Crown. After a few months, the trainer finally said, in exasperation, ''Doctor, this horse can't even beat my pony horse. He's not fast enough to work yet.'' At that point, my husband decided the trainer hadn't enough faith in our horse. We found someone else who was willing to tell him what he wanted to hear.

Everything suggested in this manual worked for me!
What can <u>you</u> do that works for you?

Another thing I remember about our first trainer was his billing creativity. In the 1970's he was charging $35 per day in base costs. He then itemized and charged extra for bandages, safety pins, electrolytes, as well as for legitimate items such as shoes and vet costs. In his own way, he got even for having to put up with a temperamental, difficult owner.

So we went to the races. The hardest part for us was having to face reality. After we invested $18,000 in the horse, he was going to have to run for a $3,500 claiming price. How could that be? The concept of someone claiming our horse, after all our sweat and money, was beyond comprehension. If you have been raised around the track you understand . . . outsiders and newcomers don't. We had to learn to "Put the horse where it can win." Unwillingly after a few humiliating races, we allowed the horse to be dropped to a level where he became a useful claimer . . . not the Triple Crown . . . but once in a while he helped to pay his board bill.

The illusion of racing and the reality of racing were so different that soon my husband refused to accept the collect calls from the trainer. He no longer wanted to hear the word "horse" spoken in his presence. Surreptitiously I had the horses shipped back to the farm to do what I could. About that time, my husband and I parted ways, for reasons that had nothing to do with horses, and I decided to give myself two years to see if I could train well enough to support the small farm myself.

At that point, I started looking for books on how to train racehorses. There were books that interviewed famous trainers, books about famous horses, one that had the routine of a known trainer, but nothing that worked in my situation. So, by luck, observation, and hard work, my own style of training evolved. I've done my homework, and in the following pages will share my knowledge and observations with you. I will continually stress that my way is not the only way. In fact this is one of the most important lessons for you to learn. There are many ways to "skin a cat." Open your mind. See how my suggestions relate to your circumstances. Don't be afraid to try your own ideas. But first and foremost, keep the welfare of the horse in mind.

Since Lois read the book and got hooked on racehorses, she has scattered some comments of her own through the book. She thinks that just because she has a hunter-jumper-dressage-cowhorse background, raises our foals to about twenty-four months and spends hours at the computer working on the book, she has the right to an opinion. She says, "I don't ride anymore - pushing 60 is exercise enough. Beyond that all I need is a geriatric pony horse, a chair in front of the computer, and the right to kibitz."

Whether you are training Appaloosas, Arabians, Paints, Quarter Horses or Thoroughbreds, a horse is a horse is a horse. Basic horse sense and training development are the same. The personalities of the various breeds differ. Thoroughbreds and Arabians are more hot blooded.

We all have been intimidated into believing the only place to train a horse is at the racetrack. Expensive for us . . . and unnatural for the horse. The joy of doing it yourself, in your own environment can be a major part of training. Your sense of accomplishment when the horse you trained wins will never be matched or forgotten. With this in mind, come with me and . . .

Let the games begin!

LET The GAMES BEGIN !

THE IMPOSSIBLE DREAM

TO BEGIN THE GREAT ADVENTURE . . .

THE IMPOSSIBLE DREAM
by Alex Del Castillo

I shouldered my sea bag and waved one last time at my ride as it disappeared over the hill. Home at last! I drank it all in with a thirst that was born from a long absence and made more acute by the rigors of Navy life. My steps carried me through the white pillars marking the entrance to our drive. Home was Rancho Del Castillo, all white board fence and lush green pasture and, of course, the horses. They were in large open paddocks along either side of the drive, trotting about with their ears perked up, placidly munching grass or fussing with a friend over the fence. Just doing horse things and being horses.

What looked to be an older two-year-old took notice of my presence, stuck his head through the top two boards and gazed at me expectantly. That earned him a pat on the neck and a rub behind the ears as I murmured in the low, soft tones that I had always used with our animals. As he nuzzled me in return, I found myself savoring the not unpleasant smell of a healthy horse. That may sound silly to someone who has never spent much time around the animals, or is so familiar with them that one stops noticing it. However, being on leave from the Navy, where cold metal, gray paint, hydraulic fluid and PineSol are the order of the day, a soft nuzzle and the scent of a horse's breath had the same effect as a home cooked meal. You have to understand, I feel pangs of sentiment whenever I catch a whiff of horse manure, even at a parade.

When I got to the house nobody was around. This was not unexpected as both my sister and brother had long since moved out and on to lives of their own. I had hoped to catch my mother between trips to the track, but instead only got a glimpse of her in the sharp white and red diesel pickup with a matching trailer as she pulled away from the barn and started on the oft traveled trek to Tampa or Calder, Hialeah, or Gulfstream in Miami. It was still relatively early and both sides of the two-horse trailer were occupied.

I considered what this meant with regards to when my mother might return. It was March, so her most likely destination was Tampa Bay Downs, then in season and an easy hour or so away. The early hour meant Mom probably intended to work at least one of her charges through the gates or get a timed work before the racing started at 1:00 PM. If neither horse were in a race that day, she could arrive at the track, work the horses, take care of any business on the backside and probably be home early in the afternoon. If she had a race, her return would be delayed.

Things had not always been so predictable. As a teenager I had spent my school weekends and summers, as had my siblings, helping Mom campaign our then meager retinue of cheap claimers. In those days that "crazy lady from Winter Haven" would show up at the receiving barn in a tired old Wagoneer and equally battle scarred red trailer. Old track hands would snicker as the harried red headed mother of three would direct her kids in the unloading of the horses from the trailer and then see to the transfer to stalls in the receiving barn. "You see", they would say, "she's got it all wrong. Race horses belong at the track, where they race; you can't ship in the day of the race and win". They would continue on about her other silly notions, but were tolerant, albeit condescending to this outsider. I noticed that many of these sage old experts had holes in their shoes.

In spite of the common wisdom, we did begin to win; nothing spectacular mind you, just enough to keep the bill collectors at bay. My mother's convictions, which fundamentally were based in the tenent that horses should be allowed to be horses, pure and simple, had begun to pay off. Early in the game she noticed that many horses kept at the track developed vices and personality problems. She always said a good racehorse need not be psychotic.

Training at home consisted of gallops through the adjacent orange groves, swimming in the lake and, perhaps, most importantly, spending most of the day in open paddocks as opposed to being cooped up in a stall all day and asked to go all out for one of the twenty-four hours. It was no wonder to me that horses kept at the track tended to be more high strung. A trip-wire psycho horse is not necessarily any faster than a sane one. I suspect many such horses expend themselves in antics before the race.

As time went on, my mother carved a respectable niche for herself and her methods. She was not alone in her philosophy of training, and people were starting to pay her to train horses for them. Her reputation was that of an honest trainer with somewhat of an unorthodox method. She shunned gimmicks and drugs, preferring to get many honest runs out of a healthy horse rather than race an unfit, injured horse maintained by painkillers or questionable surgeries. The key to her method was that of a sound foundation - her horses didn't start racing until they were fully developed and fit, somewhere around three years of age.

While it is true that three-year-olds race in the Kentucky Derby, many people don't realize how many youngsters are broken down and rendered unfit to race before their first win. It is only the exceptional and precocious that can be so successful at such an early age. Poor folks can't afford to pick the stars out of hundreds of horses. We have to do the best with what we've got. I shudder to think how many viable (not Derby winners, but horses that might have had respectable and profitable careers) horses have been squandered by having been pushed too hard, too soon. The fact that Mom is still in business without ever having to pay big bucks for "Blacktype" horses or stables of yearlings, proves the validity of her philosophy. It should also be noted that not one of the horses she instills with the aforementioned sound foundation has ever broken down at the track. This is no small feat.

As I write this, I gaze out to the back pasture. Down near the lake a small, unassuming gray mare munches on grass, now and then swishing her tail at the occasional fly. It occurs to me her story will help illustrate my remarks thus far, as well as bring me to the point of these ramblings. Paul Marriott (right, the hotel guy) donated what seemed to be an unpromising member of his extensive stable to the Florida Boys Ranch, where Mom was a volunteer, for use as they saw fit. The director of the facility realized that he could not afford to keep this animal and another filly, and offered them to us for $5000 "on the cuff". Although at the time against the ropes financially, my mother took them on credit.

Both fillies were entered into Mom's regimen, but it soon became apparent that one of them, although fit, didn't have what it takes to win races. The other, a little gray named First Prediction, after months of jaunts through the grove and swims through the lake, seemed ready to prove her worthiness at the racetrack. After a second and a third place showing at Tampa Bay, a trainer offered us $25,000.00 for the filly. Although the ten-fold return was tempting, the resounding consensus of my sister, brother, and me was "Oh, Mom, don't sell the filly"! Though based on sentiment, that decision proved to be wise financially.

First Prediction, with her unremarkable size and tremendous stretch run, came to be a leading Stakes filly in Florida. She was dubbed "The Iron Maiden" for her ability to run and consistently win as often as every eight to ten days or so. Of course, with every win the Boy's Ranch received a donation.

Now retired after some one hundred plus races and winnings of over $300,000, First Prediction is the embodiment of Mom's racing philosophy. Were it not for the unlikely chain of events and gut feeling, this horse would have been doomed to obscurity, profiting no one. How many other First Predictions are out there, needing only the individual training and sound foundation that big money owners and trainers don't give them?

You say, "Gee, well, that's a nice story, but I'm not a trainer and don't know much about racing, etc.". If you have bothered to read this far, I expect it is safe to assume you have some interest in horses. No doubt many of you compete in shows or the like. I did, but eventually lost interest in merely winning ribbons and trophies. I don't mean to disparage showing in any way; it builds horsemanship and allows one to be rewarded and recognized for his or her labors and efforts.

My point (I know, finally!) is that training Thoroughbred racehorses and campaigning them offers all of that and more. Nothing can compare to the thrill of the home stretch run. The horses giving it their all in the finish - necks outstretched, ears pinned back and hooves thundering. Jockeys clad in brightly colored silks, perched high and forward on their mounts cajole them for that last bit of speed as they vie for position. The noise of the crowd crescendos to a roar as people cheer their picks. Then on the outside of the pack you see it, your colors (there is no mistaking as no two designs are the same) on your jock, on your horse. The leaders are beginning to tire and your horse is inching past the pack, fourth, third, second, and now neck and neck with the leader. "GO, GO, GO!" you scream, flailing your arms, pounding on the person next to you who doesn't notice, caught up in the moment himself. Fifty feet to go, jockey and horse are one, and yes, did you see, they nose ahead and then finish! I can't do justice to that feeling. Your heart is in your mouth, there is just nothing like it, you have to experience it.

I don't mean to give anyone the idea that racing is all sweetness and light. There are tough breaks and lots of hard work to get through before you step in the winner's circle for the picture. Thing is, the effort that goes into training a racehorse at home is comparable to that of preparing a serious show horse. The rewards from racing, however, far exceed those of showing. I mean besides the emotional high, there is, of course, the money. Few horses conventionally trained ever win, much less show a profit. Most of our horses are of lack-luster backgrounds, but have won at least once.

If you show or just keep a horse, why not give it a shot. The horse eats everyday whether you race it or show it or just ride it. Don't think you can race to pay the rent; but if you are lucky and work hard, anything you get is pure gravy. Just because you train your Thoroughbred to race doesn't preclude it from other endeavors if it just doesn't win. Many of my mother's horses have gone on to become very competent and fit hunter-jumpers after their racing days are over.

You may never win much, but that just sweetens it when you finally do step into that winner's circle. Besides, you never know, you might find your own First Prediction. We're still looking for another one.

Alex Del Castillo
U. S. Naval Academy
Annapolis Maryland   June, 1993

TO BEGIN
THE GREAT
ADVENTURE. . .

Owning a racehorse should be a pleasure. Saturday afternoon television flashes ecstatic owners winning thousands of dollars for a minute and half of work on the part of their horses. Some of the winners cost millions in a sale . . . others as little as $2,500. It looks easy. Go to a sale, buy a horse with your spare change, and win the Derby. Why not! These are not unreasonable goals. People on television do it all the time. However, when you get involved, you will learn that centuries of effort and experience are involved.

Keep in mind that the BEST expert advice and millions of dollars DO NOT GUARANTEE that the horse will make it to the races . . . let alone win a race. Perhaps this is why we all have a chance. The most obscure breeding may relate to great bloodlines and throw a winner. Around 40,000 foals are registered with the Jockey Club every year. Only a small percentage ever win a race.

This is not intended to discourage you, it is to prepare you for the reality of racing. An educated owner is a great asset to the racing industry.

Another goal of this manual is to help you avoid suffering the many humiliations I have endured over the years. A prime example is the day my mother came along on one of my first trips to the track. She was not a horseperson, but I was stuck, short of help and needed an extra set of hands.

I had two horses to work that morning. While I was cooling the first one, the other came back from the track. "Mom, finish walking this horse. I have to take care of the other one." The horse my mother took was on a very long lunge line, because I was also short of proper equipment. A few minutes later when I checked to see how my mother was doing, to my horror, I saw she had tied one end of the lunge line to the bumper of my truck and 20 feet away the other end was connected to the horse . . . who at that moment was starting to graze. "Mom, quick, go to the horse's head!" Too late! As we watched, the horse took a few turns in a circle effectively wrapping the lunge line around his legs . . . more and more with each turn. Finding his legs restrained, he did what any Thoroughbred would do . . . he had a fit. He fought and struggled against the restraint of the lead line until finally his own violent struggling threw him to the ground with a thump!

Owning a racehorse should be a pleasure.

This whole, embarrassing, scenario did not go unnoticed by anyone within a thousand feet of the receiving barn . . . surely half the population of the backside. I stuck the horse I had into the nearest open stall and ran over to the struggling animal, who was flailing his legs to release them from the line which by now, was wrapped in a tight tangle around all four legs. With the whole world watching, I cautiously freed the horse . . . trying to keep an impassive look on my face. "Ho hum, horses try to hang themselves on my bumper all the time."

"Mom", I said, "What possessed you to tie the horse that way? You never, ever tie a Thoroughbred . . . especially not with a long line!" "Goodness", Mom said, "I see cowboys tie their horses like that all the time on TV. I didn't know I shouldn't. Besides . . . my back was bothering me!" It took years to live down that terrible display of poor horse management. To this day, I blush when recalling the "Show" mother and I put on for the backside. Fortunately, the horse only suffered nylon rope burns and swollen legs . . . no broken bones, torn ligaments or other serious injuries.

There is a lesson or two to be learned here. One is never tie up a horse with enough rope to hang himself. The other might be to never take your mother to the backside. "Well", Mom says, "She doesn't ask me to help her anymore!"

In the following pages, I want to share with you the joys and anguishes of racehorse ownership. Whether you start out as a breeder watching your own foals develop, or as an owner buying a prospect, a racehorse will be one of the most challenging endeavors of your life. It comes with no promises and plenty of pitfalls.

The primary lesson is always have competent people with horse sense working around your animals.

The Horse... Where to Get Him... What to Look For!

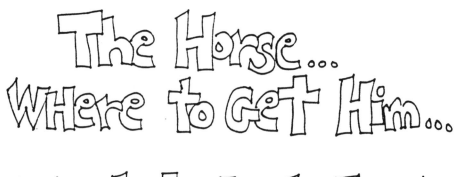

SALES AND BLOODLINES
CONFORMATION

SPECIFIC CONFORMATION TO BE AWARE OF
   Front legs with tied in tendons
   Over at the knee, Back at the knee
   Long pasterns, Short pasterns
   Straight or shallow in the hind end, Cow hocked

   ! INEFFICIENT FLIGHT PATTERN

   TRAITS TO BEWARE OF
      Brown Bag . . . Double Dexter . . .

         . . . Epidemic

SALES AND BLOODLINES

Even when buying a horse for someone else, I am a bargain hunter. This doesn't mean I want the cheapest horse around, which can turn out to be very costly. It does mean I want the most horse for the money, whether the price is $5 or $50,000 dollars.

Before going to a sale, study the catalog. Generally there are anywhere from 100 to 1,000 horses listed in the catalog, depending on the size of the sale. The catalog tells you a great deal about each animal's history and family connections. It is not mystical.

Much more weight is given to the dam's (mother's) side of the family than to the sire's (father's). It is generally believed that the dam influences the talent of the offspring more than the sire, except when the sire is very dominant and all his offspring look like him, act like him, and have his build.

Many people put a lot of weight in black type. The animal whose name is written in black type is a winner of a stakes race (a race in which entry money was paid). This is considered the most difficult and prestigious type of race.

Any horse with black type on his page in the sale is considered more valuable. You must observe where the black type occurs; the closer the blood relation to the animal, the better.

When a horse has black type in the first paragraph, it generally means that the dam, a brother, or a sister has some running ability. If the black type appears in the second dam, you are into grandmothers, great aunts, and cousins.

The catalog sales page tells all about the sire and how successful his offspring have been. It will also give the sire's racing history.

Look for a dam who has run, and has had offspring who are runners. Such a horse can be very useful even if there is no black type.

So, first look for horses who have dams and sires who have run successfully, and then dams who have useful offspring who "last" and have run. Look for soundness and talent in a bloodline. If various offspring have made $20,000 or $30,000 dollars within a few years, they are useful horses. If they make that much in a year and have run for four or five years, better yet!

Go through the catalog and fold over the pages of horses that you like. Sometimes I'll like a particular sire because of characteristics I have seen in his offspring. For instance, "On to Glorys" have heart and are extremely strong boned and resilient. Certain bloodlines run well on a particular track. We all want success, so performance counts. Look for a horse suited to your situation.

Once you have identified the horses you like in the catalog, go to the barns and look at each one. Ask the handler to take the horse out and watch him walk, check his legs, and note your observations on his page in the catalog. If you are a novice, be sure to have a competent advisor you trust guide you

If you see a horse with a flaw you can't live with, put "no" by his name and don't consider him . . . even though he may appear to be a bargain in the heat of the bidding. Examine every horse ahead of time so you don't buy an unknown horse foolishly in the heat of bidding. At that point it is too late to examine him properly. It could be that he is worth

Keep your cool in the heat of bidding!

the money, but unless you have examined him thoroughly ahead of time, resist the urge to buy. They all look good under the lights in the auction ring. It is very deceiving.

Establish ahead of time your limit for each animal, taking into account bloodline, conformation, and your gut response to the animal. Now, with the catalog pages folded and notes on the horses, you sit down for the action. Wait until the bidding settles on a horse you like; and if it's in your budget, go for it.

If you buy a horse, go immediately to the barn and have a vet check him out. For about $300 the vet can take X-rays of joints, scope the horse, and look for any problems that would keep him from being a useful racehorse. If the horse has a **paralyzed flap** or other listed problems, you may be able to return him to the seller. This examination must take place within a very short period of time, so do it at once. Depending on the sale rules, you may still have time to buy another horse. Read the front pages of the catalog for the sale rules and regulations.

When you buy privately, you still should have the horse vet examined and scoped before closing the deal. It is money well spent, to avoid loosing your time and money on a horse with built-in problems. A legitimate seller will allow such examinations. If you know nothing about conformation and how it relates to racing, find an astute person to help you.

 **Do not buy a horse until you know what to look for or have a competent trustworthy advisor!**

Typical Sales Page

Relatives —

The horse —

Father →

Mother →

Half brothers and sisters

Grandmother on Mother's side

Hip No.		Barn
40	**Chestnut Colt**	**4**

Half-brother to 8 winners, including Key Policy ($82,875). Out of sister to OUT THE WINDOW ($408,353, Laurance Armour H., etc.), Let Me In (dam of GUARDS UP, $150,825; CUT THE MUSIC, $131,377; HOW TO KNOW, $126,615), half-sister to Excluding (dam of TAIPO, $60,498).

Chestnut Colt
April 26, 1989

- Qui Native
  - Exclusive Native
    - Raise a Native
    - Exclusive
  - Qui Blink
    - Francis S.
    - Winking Star
- Clem's Ex
  (1967)
  - Clem
    - *Shannon II
    - Impulsive
  - Exclusion
    - Shut Out
    - Bee Ann Mac

By **QUI NATIVE** (1974). Stakes winner. Sire of 9 crops of racing age, 135 foals, 102 starters, 72 winners of 313 races and earning $3,324,011 in N.A., including Native Mommy ($491,430, Mutual Savings Life Ladies H. [L] (FG, $60,000), etc.), Sheena Native ($393,782, Majorette H. [L] (LAD, $53,100), etc.), Exclusive Greer ($241,138, Pioneer H. [O], etc.), Native Drummer ($110,257, Forego S. (LAT, $12,058), etc.), stakes-placed Link [L] (3 wins to 3, 1991, $148,693), Qui Square [O] (8 wins, $107,205), etc.

1st dam
CLEM'S EX, by Clem. Sister to **OUT THE WINDOW**. This is her 13th foal. Dam of 11 foals to race, 8 winners--
Key Policy (c. by Diplomat Way). 6 wins, 4 to 7, $82,875.
His Ex (f. by True Colors). 8 wins, 2 to 8, placed at 9, 1990, $76,005.
Mischievous Saint (f. by Explodent). 5 wins, 2 to 5, $73,933. Producer.
Colorex (c. by True Colors). 5 wins, 2 to 6, 1991, $73,638.
Batchelorette (f. by On to Glory). 7 wins, 4 to 7, $56,230.
R. T. Saxon (c. by Royal Saxon). 6 wins, 4 to 6, $49,425.
Babblejack (c. by Sezyou). 9 wins, 3 to 5, 1991, $46,571.
Johnny Two Dance (c. by Pollux). 16 wins, 2 to 8, $45,637.

good!

2nd dam
EXCLUSION, by Shut Out. Placed at 3. Dam of 10 foals, 7 winners, incl.--
OUT THE WINDOW (c. by Clem). 22 wins, 2 to 7, $408,353, Laurance Armour H., Stars and Stripes H., Better Bee H. twice-once in ntr, etc. Sire.
Excluding. 2 wins at 3, $9,925. Dam **TAIPO** (c. by *Ballydonnell, $60,498).
Oui Madame. 18 wins, $53,448. Dam of **Oui Henry** (c. by Flag Raiser, $94,-330, 3rd Hawthorne Juvenile S.-**G3**, etc.). Granddam of **WHITE MOMENT** (f. by Balance of Power, $51,440), **OUTOFAJOB** (c. by Marshua's Dancer, $30,880), **Whodatorsay** (f. by *Star Ice, $223,936), etc.
Let Me In. Dam of 10 winners, including--
GUARDS UP (c. by Cornish Prince). 7 wins, 2 to 5, $150,825, Jerome H.-**G2**, Keystone H., 2nd San Pasqual H.-**G2**, Leland Stanford H. Sire.
CUT THE MUSIC (c. by Stop the Music). 5 wins, $131,377, [Q], 3rd [Q].
HOW TO KNOW (c. by Green Ticket). 25 wins, 2 to 8, $126,615, Lakefront H., 3rd Thomas Edison H., Midwest Championship H.
Back Out. Dam of **Closed Corp** (c. by Affiliate, 5 wins, $88,002, 3rd [Q]).
RACE RECORD: Has not started.
Engagements: OBS Championship S., Florida Stallion S.
Registered Florida-bred.

←Fees have been paid for these Engagements!

CONFORMATION

Many books discuss the conformation of horses. Some go into great detail about angles and relationships of degrees of slope of shoulder to length of leg, etc. Generally, form and function do go hand in hand, but I have seen some poorly conformed horses beat well built ones time and time again.

My uncle, a breeder of Quarter Horses, once said that good conformation doesn't get in the way of being a good runner. Indeed, good conformation has little to do with the innate gift of speed a horse may have. Poor conformation will perhaps hinder a horse from lasting long term, but he could have a world of speed.

Many trainers are frustrated by horses with high speed and crooked legs. Why? If you have a car with one bald tire and three good ones, you can probably go many miles with the bald tire as long as you don't go fast. Zoom to ninety miles an hour and you may have a blow out. Racehorses are somewhat the same. As long as you don't redline the system, the horse will last. When you start racing and asking for high speed at a sustained distance, your weak "tires" may become a critical factor. When I started training, I used to gallop my horses six miles at an open gallop, and they flourished. Then, when pushed to high speed, the stresses on imperfect joints began to take a toll.

As a trainer, you must consider conformation carefully. Some flaws are easier to live with than others. There are horses so talented that they run faster than the average horse without redlining their systems. As your horse becomes progressively more competitive he will, by the nature of the sport, find himself in tougher races. As you win on one level and progress to another, you will find where your horse should be running; in claiming races, allowance races, or stakes.

Wise trainers with less than perfect horses try to keep them where they don't have to run too hard to win. Some horses are so honest and game that they will try no matter what. The trainer who is attentive and monitors the horse's legs can tell when a race has caused damage.

Now, let's talk more specifically about structure. We must judge those conformational faults we can live with and those we can't. **My judgments are based purely on personal experience and are by no means the only accepted opinions.**

My first choice among horses would be a **well balanced horse with very correct legs.** If both the sire and dam were stakes winners, their well built offspring should have an edge. Yet, we need to remember that if both parents were great, they could be a hard act to follow.

If our first choice is not affordable, what do we settle for?

A horse must fit together well. This sounds very unscientific, but as long as his parts seem to blend together, he can be useful. For example, I've seen many Quarter Horses bred and fed to have huge muscle mass. They look great at first glance. They have a burly chest and big hind quarters, but from the knees down the horse will have light cannon bones and small feet. This kind of horse will not stand up to racing, and I doubt that he will be able to do much performance work since his body mass and bone structure are so out of balance.

Look for a horse that fits together well.

At the other extreme, a light boned horse is useful only if legs and frame are in proportion. I had a mare so light framed she probably didn't weigh over 900 pounds. Her bones were like titanium. She was very correct and very tough. She never had any kind of leg problems. As a unit she worked great. She was a useful claimer who ran every ten days comfortably.

Northern Dancer was actually a small horse. Photos show he was a well balanced package on sturdy legs, though he did toe out. Such a horse is a joy to ride. They are even and solid in movement.

Some horses have unusually long backs and short legs. This type of horse is prone to sore backs since the span between the front and rear legs is long and less efficiently supported.

When you come across a huge two-year-old, remember **a big boned horse generally needs more time to develop.** The pressure on his joints is greater and he may gallop "heavier" and be harder on himself than a lighter horse. Just as with a gangly teenager, he must work harder to get his act together and to coordinate himself. He may take longer to find his stride. **Size does not guarantee speed or length of stride.**

If you see a Thoroughbred with large muscle mass like a Quarter Horse, he may genetically have more of a tendency to "fast twitch" muscles. He may be more efficient in sprints than in long races. There are many theories about fast twitch and slow twitch muscles, and whether training tends to encourage one type of muscle over the other. It is said that long gallops develop slow twitch, long distance muscle bunches: speed work develops fast twitch, quick responding muscle bunches. Since more than just muscle goes into developing a racehorse, by training the horse with my methods you let the horse tell you whether he wants to run long or short, although genetics may be a more dominant factor than method of training. (See Section on Phase II Training.)

The other type of Thoroughbred commonly seen is lanky, with smooth slab-type muscles and a svelte look. His muscle, even developed, will not be bulky. A trainer might suspect that he will develop into a distance horse. Of course, the bulky look can sometimes be created with steroids. (See Section on Medications.) All sorts of varieties come in between these types. I had a filly with a tremendous chest and no rear end. She has the lungs but no rear power. **Remember, all parts of the horse must fit together smoothly for the exceptional horse.** But, imperfect animals may find their own competitive level . . . and, in the right hands, do very nicely for a long time.

You should look for a horse with an intelligent eye, large nostrils and a good attitude. Usually a "kind eye" is an indication of a sound temperament and a manageable horse. See if you recognize "The Look of the Eagles". I know that sounds romantic, but . . .

Anyone in horseracing is going for "The Impossible Dream"!

SPECIFIC CONFORMATION TO BE AWARE OF

Front legs with tied-in tendons

The horse may be light boned or heavy boned. However, if the tendon is tied-in behind the knee, it could be a point of weakness, when redlined. Of course, a good training foundation always helps. Look for solid short cannons with parallel lines when the horse is viewed from the side.

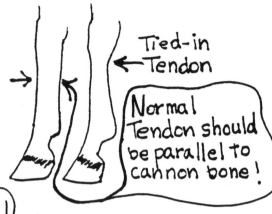

Tied-in ←Tendon

Normal Tendon should be parallel to cannon bone!

I'm not so bad! But my friend won't hold up To RACING!

Over at the knee

I don't hold this against a horse, as it may improve with exercise. The horse can always improve with a good foundation. Many good runners have been over at the knee.

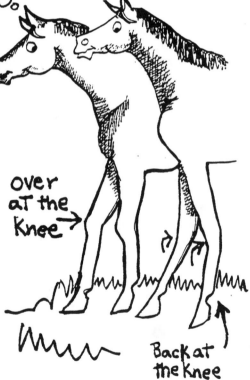

OVer aT the Knee →

Back at the knee

This is a problem to avoid. It will cause pressure on knees and ankles. Even though exercise and fitness help, it is easy for this type of horse to tire and chip joints when redlined. Depending on the severity, he could be a very poor racing prospect. If you see this in a stallion who has not raced, don't breed to him. He probably couldn't hold up to racing himself. Why look for trouble?

Back at the Knee

12

Long pasterns

Long pasterns become stronger with training. The horse will be comfortable to ride. The longer pasterns are like better shock absorbers. In racing you must make sure such a horse is very fit. When he starts to tire, his fetlocks will drop and he will have a tendency to run down on them when he is redlined. This means the fetlock hits the track surface, and the horse can get burns or open wounds. I have seen this type of horse being cooled out after a race, often having tremendous tissue damage in the fetlock area. You can prevent injury by putting on bandages with pads to protect his fetlocks. After a workout or two at the track, you'll be able to see if your horse has this tendency. If he does, always protect him. (See Section on Legs Bandages.)

Long Pasterns.

Short upright pasterns

Horses with these come with their own set of problems. If the horse is upright, he will tend to pound and be choppy on his front end. As well as providing a more uncomfortable ride, this conformation puts a great deal of **stress on the joints.** The shoulder could become sore easily, especially if the horse is running on a hard track. He might have an edge on acceleration out of the gates. He just **doesn't have good shock absorbers** and may run better on a heavy track or on a turf course. These surfaces are kinder to his joints.

Short upright Pasterns

←Short→

Straight or shallow at the hind end

These horses seem weak in the rear. They tend to have stifle or hock problems.

Cow Hocked

Cow hocked

Unless it is severe, horses with this problem seem to be very agile and athletic and run just fine even though they wouldn't win any Conformation Classes. →

13

INEFFICIENT FLIGHT PATTERN

If you look at some horses from the rear, it appears that their flight pattern is very inefficient when they walk and trot. It looks as if they make a circle with their hoof, before they put it down for the next stride. A **toed-in** horse circles the foot to the outside, which is called **paddling**. A **toed-out** horse circles the foot to the inside, which is called **winging**. I tended to eliminate these kinds of horses, because I thought the trait showed inefficiency of movement and weakness in conformation. Having been forced to train horses like this, I learned that **many horses look inefficient at a walk and trot, but at a gallop or run, the pattern was completely different.** The legs could be two solid pistons, straight in their flight pattern at high speed and very efficient at covering ground. So, don't lose hope even if your horse looks like he will trip over his own feet. When he grows and develops, he may be great. On the other hand, horses with slight deviations at a walk or trot may be very inefficient at a gallop.

Toe in   Toe Out

Remember that horses have been bred for speed over the years. **Many crooked legged horses have tremendous speed. We must not eliminate horses just because of less than perfect angles. When we know they have weaknesses in their structure, we must give them time for the bone to mature and more preparation with long, slow gallops during their early training.**

Some horses seem to withstand and tolerate their conformational flaws. Others **show warning signs right from the beginning.** If you have a horse with a crooked knee that carries persistent heat in the knee after each work, you are being warned. **The horse is telling you he can't tolerate that level of stress.** If you continue to redline a horse in this situation, **he will break down before he runs.** Unfortunately, some trainers will drill to the point of breakdown, rather than tell the owner the horse won't stand up to training. Others will recommend surgery, injections, etc.

My own feeling is that if a late two-or three-year-old **shows these problems in training,** especially my kind of training, **he is not a good racing candidate.** I advise owners to **get out now,** rather than spend another year of training and medical problems. They may **ruin the horse** anyway. Many horses can't stand up to the rigors of training and racing. If this is the case, find them a home where they can be useful as pets or riding horses.

Telling owners not to put money into a certain horse has been one of my biggest problems. They don't want to hear this, and probably will find another trainer willing to try.

Many crooked legged horses have tremendous speed.

TRAITS TO BEWARE OF

Horses are a lot like people. They have different personality traits, and just as **some people are hard headed, so are some animals.** If you perceive certain undesirable tendencies in your horse, don't continue training the animal. There are macho type people in this world, who believe they can straighten out a bad horse. However, some traits cannot be changed. They are in the animal and appear when you least expect them.

If you are new to training horses, it is not good to start out with high strung animals. I started with Quarter Horses. They are more tolerant of beginners. The mistakes you make during your learning process generally are not as crucial to an Appaloosa, Paint or Quarter Horse. Thoroughbreds can react so violently, when mishandled, that they may injure you or themselves.

For handling normal, non-quirky problems, Mark Rashid has written a wonderful book, *Considering the Horse*. It is a series of narratives about horses with behavioral problems. He may not deal with any of the specific problems you encounter, but his philosophy may help you find solutions to your problem horse. He opens the horse's mind to his readers and emphasizes the importance of horse sense

Leave complex horses with difficult personalities to the professionals.

Brown Bag

He was raised here at the farm, out of my first wonderful mare. The horse was never mistreated and seemed quite normal. He was broken uneventfully, started the trail rides properly, and was no more difficult than any of the other animals I trained that year. When we started to do long, steady gallops, he would swerve left or right in a 90 degree turn. It didn't matter if there was a tree, a fence or any other obstacle, and there usually was.

Sometimes he would go days without doing this, and then suddenly do it again. We couldn't anticipate his behavior. It didn't seem to have any relationship with external stimuli, location on the route, or whether it was early or late in the gallop.

When he misbehaved, I would yank, shank and spank doing everything to let the horse know this was bad behavior. He seemed oblivious to the punishment.

One day, when the horse was about 30 months old and nearing track time, I was riding him. (I am large and heavy and hoped this would make it hard for him to pull his tricks.) He bolted, and much to my disbelief, ran smack into a 12 foot high irrigation pipe. I had pulled to the right and to the left, but to no avail. The horse ignored me and crashed into the pipe.

Lying on the ground with my left foot on his belly, to keep him from stepping on me, I thought. "That's it! Its too dangerous to train an unpredictable horse alone in the fields. This idiot needs the controlled environment of the track"

A trainer at the track wanted him. I agreed to sell, but forewarned the trainer about the horse's bad habit. I explained in detail how the horse veered to the right or left without warning. The trainer said, "No problem."

Later, I asked the trainer how the horse was doing. "Galloping fine," said he. "Has he tried his sharp turns yet?", I asked. "Nope," said he. " Do you warn the rider before you put him on," I asked. "Do you tell him about the horse?" He said. "Hell, no, he'd be afraid to ride him. I don't say anything." A point well taken.

This information made me very uncomfortable. I am incapable putting a rider on a horse that has a hang-up, without warning him. I constantly hear trainers saying, "That's the rider's problem. I don't want to give him ideas about the horse."

To make a long story short, the horse was put in his first race. Unfortunately, he got the number one hole. He broke out of the gates, hung a left into a rail and lost the race. The trainer sent him back to the gates, got him blinker-approved, and he won his second race. He's back at the track again this year and is still as erratic as ever. He has won some races, but he still hangs a left or right when you least expect it. You never know if he will run or bolt.

Interestingly enough, Brown Bag's sire has thrown various runners with the same tendency. It seems to be a genetic trait. Good luck if you try to change something like that! **Leave a horse like this to the professionals.**

Double Dexter

Who could forget Double Dexter? While in the receiving barn she dug four-foot holes in the floor. I'll never forget walking up to her stall door and only seeing the tips of her ears, because she was standing in a pit. This filly was so erratic and nervous that no one believed she could possibly run after expending so much energy waiting for her race.

Many felt Double Dexter would be better off living at the track. Little did they know that she already had. For the month she spent there, she would gallop, fret and dig in her stall until she was exhausted. Then the ding-bat would fall asleep, rest, awaken, and start all over again. It was hard to keep weight on her.

Double Dexter was simply nervous and high strung. Interestingly enough, she was basically happy at the farm. She had her friends and held her weight.

She was a small but extremely plucky little filly with bones of titanium. Never sore out of a race, she had tremendous resiliency; but she could lose a race at the gate because she was so nervous.

Each year Double Dexter got progressively better. At five, she was almost manageable. If you drove in half an hour before the race and unloaded her to run, she didn't fret and went right to racing.

The stewards at Tampa Bay were good to me. They would let me arrive close to race time, for which I was very appreciative. This helped Double Dexter tremendously. She won two or three races each year at Tampa and did pay her way.

Double Dexter almost killed her owner in a trailer while being loaded. The horse lost control and overreacted hysterically to the tight quarters. She went into a frenzy and flung herself every way until she was cut loose. The owner was trapped inside the trailer with her and was almost crushed to death. Dexter "scooched" under the butt bar of the trailer to escape. Luckily, both owner and horse survived, but that episode gave me half of my gray hair.

Get a horse with a reasonable personality.

17

One day someone offered $2,000 dollars for her and the owner said, "Sell." As far as I know, she is running in Puerto Rico. She was sound enough to run for many years when she was sold.

This kind of horse is very tricky to handle, and only good help should work around such a hyper animal. The horse is not being mean, just over-reactionary, but still can be dangerous. If you are not extremely competent, don't put yourself in a threatening situation by trying to handle an ''impaired'' animal. **Take heed . . . don't look for trouble . . . get a horse with a reasonable personality.**

Epidemic

There are probably people in Mountaineer Park who still remember Epidemic. He was a huge brute of a horse I bought as a maiden in October of his fourth year. In Florida, a horse must win a race before he is five or he can't run, so I knew I would have to work fast.

Epidemic was a powerful, broad-boned hunk of a horse. He looked like he lifted weights in his stall, he was so muscular. When galloping him in the grove, a ring bit meant nothing to him. Nor did the silly person on his back. It was like being on a runaway train when he took off. Realizing the danger, I told my son Alex (the 6'4", 240 pound son) that the horse needed some attitude adjustment.

Alex is basically gentle natured. He felt his sheer strength could handle anything this horse could try. Being 18, Alex knew bullets couldn't pierce his skin; so he condescendingly agreed to give Epidemic a spin in the grove.

Ten minutes later, the horse came galloping back, riderless. Five minutes after that, with pieces of tree protruding from his clothes, Alex came limping home. He mumbled about how the horse had no mouth, no feelings, and no response to anything.

So . . . I decided this horse would do better at the track.

Since he had run before, I took him to Miami and put him in a race. We threw the jock up on the horse's back in the beautiful paddock area of Hialeah. The horse started to trudge off, and to our amazement, he literally knocked over the groom, who fell with arms and legs flailing. Epidemic stumbled over him, walked through the flowers and into the fence of the paddock.

I scurried through the flowers, after the horse. The jock was still sitting on Epidemic's back in amazement. As he jumped off, he said, ''I'm not riding this ox!'' I was left to drag the horse back to the parade area.

I managed to find another jock, and the horse ran uneventfully, arriving 8th out of 10 horses. He did, at least, stay on the track when aimed in the right direction. Apparently, the only way to handle him was to run him.

When Tampa opened he had one month to break his maiden. Six days after the Miami race, he ran fifth. Five days later, he ran fourth. Four days later he was third. I reentered immediately and three days before the end of the year, on his last chance to win, he ran second.

A man from Mountaineer Park bought him for eight or nine hundred dollars and hauled him home. He won the first time out.

**Learn from the past and dream of the future.
Things will eventually work out.**

Later. I heard that the horse had some kind of screw missing, though he could run. The owners got rid of him, because he would walk over people and things. He simply wasn't controllable. None of this surprised me. He was another good horse to get rid of, even at a loss.

The older we get and the more experience we have, the wiser we become. There are many challenges I have undertaken out of sheer ignorance. Since I survived the ordeals, they were learning experiences - not to be repeated.

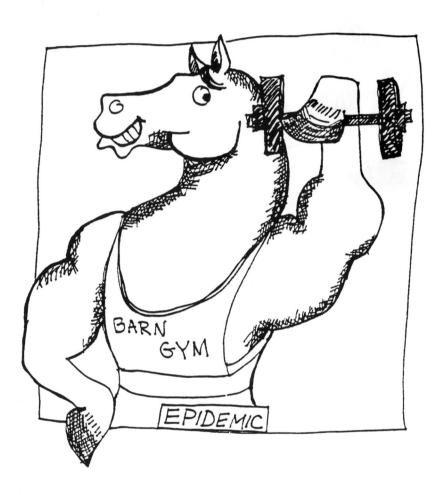

The message is this: observe and learn from everything you do. Remember what works and forget what doesn't. Don't berate yourself if you made a wrong decision.

Ignore the "Monday Morning Quarterbacks". Just carry on.

Farm Layout and Friends

Farm Layout

Barn or Stall Area
Paddocks
Fences
Starting Gates
Wash Rack Area
Bathing Horses

Farm Friends

Chickens . . . Goats
Dogs
A Visit from the Vet
Two of the Most common Equine Ailments
Less Common Equine Ailments
Equine Dental Care

FARM LAYOUT

Barn or Stall Areas

The ideal situation would be nice large paddocks, each with its own large stall. You could turn the horse out for a portion of the day or confine him. This arrangement would work for anyone with one or two horses. For those of you with several horses, a row of stalls with common walls utilizes materials more efficiently.

My farm is small - only 13 acres. The logistics of having many horses of both sexes is challenging. I solve the problem by having two barns. One is for the females - the girls dorm. The other is for the boys. I do this to avoid crucial mistakes at turn out time. Sometimes you will have help that doesn't quite understand who you said to turn out. **A filly in heat next to a racing colt can cause damage to both. Avoid accidents.** Always try to keep paddocks and stalls for colts and fillies completely separate. Young horses remind me of teenagers, **constantly thinking of having a good time and procreating.**

Learn to read body language when working around animals. **Be aware of what they are saying to each other with their switching tails and squeals. You could be hurt if you're not paying attention.**

I prefer a large, airy pole barn with a very high roof. Florida has such mild winters that our stalls can be very open. My barn has four **stalls, each with its own small paddock.** The stalls are 14' x 14', nice and roomy. **The paddocks are 14' x 20', enough space for a horse to doze in the sun if he wants, or sleep out under the stars, which they seem to enjoy at certain times of year.** Best of all, usually they choose to drop their manure in the far corner of the outside paddock rather than dirty the sawdust in the stall. This not only helps save sawdust, but if your schedule gets hectic and you don't clean the stall-paddock area for a few days, it is not crucial, because the horses are not standing in manure. **All the horses that have been raised on my farm drop manure outside.** However, horses from the track tend to drop it in the stall. They had no choice.

Lois made the following comment about stalls: "As a child I thought we were doing horses such a favor to stall them, give them a home, and protection from inclement weather. Later, I realized that what seemed nice to me might not be so nice for a horse. Maybe they actually preferred being outdoors where they could roam freely. Perhaps the comforts of home did not offset being incarcerated. All too often, we tend to judge what an animal wants or needs from our own prospective. Try to think about the animal's natural life-style and how he will react physically and mentally to your ideas, before making decisions about his well being."

Even when the farm is full, every horse must have a stall during the heat of the day. I also put the horse in the stall to reinforce rest a day or two before a race, always allowing him turnout time. The stall-paddocks are completely lined with conveyer belting. These are active racing horses; they like to roll on their backs and could get their legs caught in the rails. Hot tape is secured to the top board so they don't lunge at each other too much. This arrangement is riskier than enclosing them in the box type stalls that most racehorses live in. Horses are herd animals. They like to nuzzle and talk to each other. Socializing keeps them mentally healthy and allows them more

**Allow their formative years to be more natural.
They will be more sensible and adaptable as they mature.**

tranquility long term. It helps avoid the vices so prevalent at the track. As horses mature, they are more adaptable to the racetrack environment.

The aisle in front of the four stalls was originally just hard packed dirt. It occurred to me to store the bedding sawdust there until it was needed in the stalls. Now **whole loads of sawdust are dumped in the aisle.** This provides about two feet of sawdust that settles into a nice base. The sawdust lasts two to four weeks. When cleaning stalls, **sawdust is easily raked from the aisle into the stalls.** This short cut is very convenient, keeps the sawdust dry and protected from the elements, and **has cut my stall cleaning time down to almost nothing.** When I see dirt under the sawdust, its time to order another load. **This simple adaptation has saved me energy, time, and money.**

All my feed buckets clip into a screw eye. They can be removed and scrubbed when necessary. Hay is put under the feed buckets so that any spilled grain falls on it. **I am completely opposed to hay nets.** Hay nets cause back problems. Horses are grazers, not browsers (though they can nibble leaves from trees). **Horses are built to eat off the ground. When they twist their heads to eat at shoulder level, they do not employ normal physical movements.** Ideally, both feed tub and hay should be on the ground. If your horse paws at the bucket on the ground, raise it and make the necessary adjustments. When a horse has a back problem, he is fed on the ground or with the bucket in a hole. As he eats, he is flexing and exercising his back without even realizing it. A rubber mat is placed on the ground under the tub. The hay ration is put on the mat. When the horse drops grain as he eats, it falls on the hay. Hopefully, the hay and mat will reduce the amount of dirt he ingests.

My partner, Lois, who keeps our broodmares in pastures, feeds on rough cement patio blocks in order to reduce sand intake. It also keeps the horses from standing in the mud during rainy season. Later she noticed that it helped wear the horse's feet to a natural angle. Always be aware of the side effects of your innovations.

All paddocks and stalls should have automatic watering devices. They can be easily installed with PVC and are real time savers.

Your own stable and paddock areas may vary considerably. Different geographic areas need different types of stalls. Ask your land university or extension office for stall and barn recommendations. Then study your needs and make your barn as convenient and labor saving as possible!

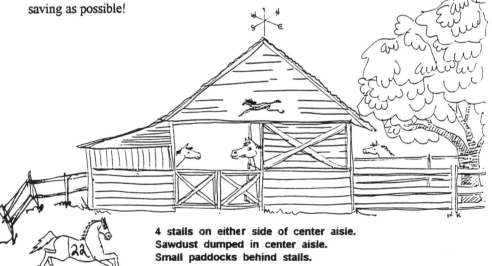

4 stalls on either side of center aisle.
Sawdust dumped in center aisle.
Small paddocks behind stalls.

Paddocks

Some of my horses live in small paddocks which are not attached to their stalls. These paddocks are approximately 50' x 100'. During the day, each horse gets to spend at least an hour in a large grassy pasture. The farm has four grassy pastures.

Rolls of old conveyer belt are useful for lining any small paddock. It discourages the biting of knees and lunging through the fence. The horses can run freely, frolic and rear. Horseplay is necessary and helpful. However, we don't want them hurt. Horses love to roll in close quarters - invariably next to the fence, because it's sandy and soft from their hooves tearing up the soil. They tend to roll into the fence and get their legs caught between the fence boards no matter how close or far apart the boards are spaced. This can cause scraping of tissue and lacerations on their legs. Using conveyer belt between boards has proven to be good protection for horses who are allowed out. Those of us in racing are aware that **horses can inflict a great deal of damage on themselves just being horses.**

Every paddock must have water and a **red mineral block.** This is mandatory here in Florida due to the intense heat. The horse must be able to regulate his own salt intake as necessary. Each paddock has its own feed tub out of reach of neighboring horses. It is important that each horse eat his food at his own pace without harassment from his neighbors.

Salt Block

recycled conveyer Belt

Hot wire "ribbon"

Wood Board

Safe Paddocks

For safe paddocks, be sure that all nails or dangerous items are far from the inquisitive lips and bodies of your horses. Bored horses can get into trouble with anything in reach.

Fences

Good easily visible board fences are my first choice. Their main drawback is maintenance and the fact that they become brittle with age. When a horse, while frolicking or by accident, crashes into a board fence, there is a danger of him being impaled. In major Thoroughbred farms, miles of double fencing are utilized to keep horses from playing across the fences. It is an extra safety factor when fences are broken. Needless to say, it is expensive for most of us to put up board fences, let alone double fencing. There are new types of vinyl fencing. I have had no experience with them. They should be worth investigating.

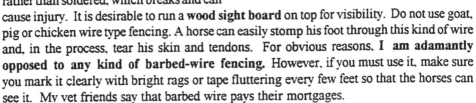

Many types of wiring are being sold as fencing for horses. If you decide on **horse** wire fencing, use the woven type rather than soldered, which breaks and can cause injury. It is desirable to run a **wood sight board** on top for visibility. Do not use goat, pig or chicken wire type fencing. A horse can easily stomp his foot through this kind of wire and, in the process, tear his skin and tendons. For obvious reasons, **I am adamantly opposed to any kind of barbed-wire fencing.** However, if you must use it, make sure you mark it clearly with bright rags or tape fluttering every few feet so that the horses can see it. My vet friends say that barbed wire pays their mortgages.

I use electric tape across the top of all my paddocks. It helps separate animals that want to horseplay across the fence. They may clunk their heads together, but they respect the hot tape. I tried hot wire but found that it was a terrible danger when the electricity went off. The horses would fight and break the wire off the holders. The loose wire could easily tangle around a leg and sever a tendon. I solved this problem by wrapping the wire around each holder several times so that, if the wire did break, it would be less than eight feet long and less apt to tangle around delicate legs. Ribbon or tape is easily seen and will break rather than strangle or tighten. Hot tape can always be used temporarily until proper fencing is installed.

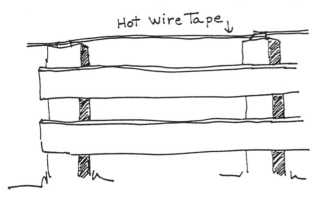

Hot Wire Tape ↓

Safe fences for safe turnout.

Starting Gates

Everyone feels that it's necessary to have a starting gate at the farm. Frankly, I think **gate work is one of the last things you worry about in training**. However, it is always a good idea to **encourage your horse to walk into small areas** and to learn that he doesn't have to fear such experiences.

Have the foresight to build the gates at the beginning of your training program. I have a two-stall pretend gate built of wood. (Use any materials you have around.) The sides are padded with rug, and **a guide board extends outward from between the two stalls to encourage the horses not to veer when breaking.** At one time I had a barricade board across the front. Supposedly we could yank it open and hustle the horses out. Experience has taught me this isn't necessary. **You need stalls, open as shown to walk horses in, to stop them and back them out or to walk them through.** Eventually you can gallop them out. **Finishing touches of breaking out of the gate should be left for track training.** Gate crews are the experts and need to have the horse work out with them. This is discussed more thoroughly in the Training Section.

My gates are positioned at the base of a hill. When the horse eventually learns to gallop out, he is going up hill, which will help strengthen his hind end. Some trainers believe that starting on a hill is very difficult on a young horse. Others believe training on hills is good for conditioning. Be judicious and make your own decisions based on how your animals handle the work.

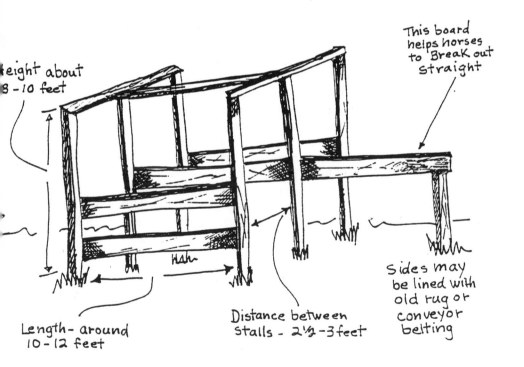

This board helps horses to Break out straight

Height about 8 - 10 feet

Length- around 10 - 12 feet

Distance between stalls - 2½ -3 feet

Sides may be lined with old rug or conveyor belting

Pretend starting gates may be made out of PVC or leftover lumber.

Bathing Horses

Before you start bathing any horse, be sure to have everything you need at the head of the wash rack - shampoo, hoof pick, and a grooming box. Never leave a horse unattended while you run to look for something. **Always bathe the horse at your wash rack area.** In Florida, we bathe our horses very frequently. If they are not bathed every three or four days during the hot, rainy season, many horses develop rain rot or some other kind of skin itch. Being outside a great deal, they get caught in the rain. When the rain is over, they roll in the sand to dry off. The soil nurtures many bacteria. **By scrubbing our horses every three or four days, we kill the bacteria and cleanse the skin.** (Often Azium, a steroid, is given to horses to relieve skin itch. Isn't a little bleach and soap preferable?)

My shampoo recipe is quarter cup of bleach to a gallon of water with a squirt of Palmolive liquid or some other common household soap. (Buy it on sale.) If you prefer, you can use Betadine or any of the liniments with disinfectant qualities. I find that bleach disinfects the skin, and inhibits the cycle of itch, and have had good results over the years. When I am lax during the rainy season, the itch begins.

To bathe the horse prepare the soap, water and bleach in a two gallon container. Hose the horse very aggressively with a nozzle sprayer. **The skin should be drenched and stimulated by the hard hosing.** Dip a scrub brush in the solution and scrub the entire body with the mixture. Take the horse's tail and dip it completely in the bucket. The bleach is great for getting grime off the tail. If you rinse in a reasonable amount of time, it doesn't bleach the tail. Then, having first picked out the feet, dip the whole foot in the sudsy bleach solution. Scrub all the feet with the brush. Using the nozzle at medium pressure, spray all over the body and rinse out the soap and bleach. The dirt pours off and the skin is stimulated by the water massage. Be sure to remove **all** the soap and bleach. You do not want your horse's coat to dry out or become irritated.

After the bath, release the horse from the was rack and while holding him on a loose shank try to hose water directly on his face. Be careful of his eyes and ears. You want him to become accustomed to the sensation of water or dirt hitting him head on. It prepares the him for the sloppy water or mud that can be flying at him during the rigors of racing.

While bathing your horse, you can learn a great deal about the him. **If he is sensitive to being scrubbed or rubbed in a particular area, try to determine if it is because he hurts or if he is just ticklish.** The clues he gives help you guage his overall state of health. As you handle your horse, **you learn his idiosyncrasies. Learn to be tuned into how he reacts during baths and grooming.** The first thing most horses do when turned out after a bath is roll and get dirty again . . . a nice layer of dirt probably discourages flies. That's all right . . . at least you know he was clean!

You can handle a young horse alone with the proper layout.

Wash Rack Area

The wash rack area is one of the most important areas on your farm. At the track two people are usually needed to handle young horses who can't be tied and are very nervous. Most of us must work alone. so it is essential that we design our layout efficiently. As you can see by the drawing, my wash rack consists of a large concrete slab approximately 14' x 14' covered with rubber matting. I have a sturdy round hitching pole supported by two sturdy posts. These can be wooden or steel pipe. Drawings of my wash rack are included. You can adapt your facilities according to your needs and availability of materials. Remember, **these are suggestions.** Certain points are essential. **The hitching pole must be round** so that the lead line slides easily when looped around it. This allows you to pull the lead line, forcing the horse to stand closer to the hitching pole. **You are also able to release him quickly if it becomes necessary. My principal wash rack is completely enclosed by fencing.** I use this rack with new and/or more fractious horses. **It is imperative that they be confined and learn good behavior during baths or treatments.**

After a few lessons the horse will learn that the hitching pole is not to be feared, and you will find yourself more comfortable bathing him. If he throws a fit at being confined, all he can do is fight and pull himself loose if you allow it. **He will still be confined by the perimeter fence** and the lead line will still be on him. making it easy to catch him again and loop the lead line around the hitching pole. Always close gates and be sure an area is safe before you handle a fractious horse. Before my wash rack was confined, if the horse got loose. he could gallop all over the place getting into trouble or harm.

Even alone. you can control his head while working on his back legs by looping a longer lead line or lunge line around the hitching pole. You hold it in one hand while you are at the rear of the horse using the other had to wash his legs or whatever. If your shank is 20 feet long, you can teach the horse to move forward by looping the lead line around the hitching pole and tapping the horse from behind with a buggy whip. This way he learns that a tug on the head and a tap on the rear mean that he is to go forward.

If your horse has not been handled much, especially around his legs, loop the lead line around the hitching pole to control him while you rub his legs and body with the buggy whip. If he kicks to the touch of the whip, yank, shank and sharply say, "No!" After a few lessons. he learns that the whip is an aid not to be feared and stops kicking at it. Another way to accustom him to having his legs and body touched. is to hose him all over until he accepts and enjoys it.

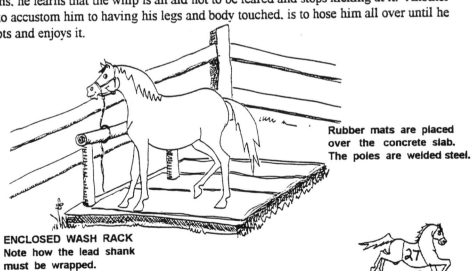

Rubber mats are placed over the concrete slab. The poles are welded steel.

ENCLOSED WASH RACK
Note how the lead shank must be wrapped.

27

FARM FRIENDS

Chickens

Anyone who has come to my farm knows I can't discuss its layout without telling about my chickens.

This all began when my children joined the Four H Club. One of their many projects was proper chicken raising. When the project was completed, it was easier to turn the chickens loose, than worry about their feed and water. The chickens reverted to their clever, cagey ways in no time and soon took up residence in the hay barn at night. During the day they did "manure patrol duty". People even asked if I had trained them to seek out every pile of manure and very efficiently peck and scratch to break it down! Their work effectively broke up the piles in the pastures, thus helping control the fly problem.

The incessant raking on the part of the feathered stable help breaks up the fly cycle. **If a fly egg laid on manure is left undisturbed for 24 hours, another fly is added to the population.** If the egg is disturbed by rain or by a little crew of chickens pecking to get undigested grain, the egg does not hatch. **Breaking up manure also helps the process of pasture fertilization.**

There can be a danger of salmonella from chicken manure. Investigate the situation in your area to decide if the effect is worth the risk. Never allow the chickens to contaminate feed and water areas. Use your horse sense. Sometimes we can become overly cautious about the dangers in our environment. A healthy horse should be able to co-exist with a certain amount of bacteria.

Horses learn to tolerate the chickens and even enjoy their flapping and noisy conversation. Actually, some become great friends.

Goats

Goats are a good, if some-what odorous, companion for inse-cure horses. They are easy to keep, are allowed on the backside, and offer entertainment to both horse and barn help. If your horse is more tractable with such a companion, be sure to have the companion goat dehorned and neutered.

Even horses enjoy good company.

Dogs

Since we have discussed chickens, we should mention dogs. I have owned many dogs over the years and have found some to be dangerous around horses while others are non-threatening.

Shepherds have an uncanny herding instinct. One shepherd we hand raised from four weeks knew from the beginning that he shouldn't bother the horses. As he matured, he seemed to look and see if there were any humans around. If he thought he was alone, he would slink toward a horse grazing in the field. The horse would immediately sense the dog, react nervously, and trot away. The dog was then in his glory! Once the horse started to run, the dog would joyously chase him, snapping at his rear legs. There was no way to break the dog of this habit. It was almost as if he said, "The devil makes me do it!" This became such a problem we had to get rid of him.

Rottweilers instinctively want to bite the rear end of the horse. This is very dangerous, especially if you happen to be riding a fractious two-year-old. It is even upsetting to an old steady animal. I won't have the breed, because you can't fight instinct!

The older I get, the more I try to eliminate trouble. Some dogs are jealous when you start handling your horses. They must be tied up before you begin your work. I no longer have that kind of patience. Too many horses have stomped on me, when they sensed a threatening animal sneaking up behind them. One of my horses ended up in the swimming pool because a dog chased him into a frenzy.

Its good to have dogs around horses. Its good for them to learn to get along. Start with puppies whose parents you have met. I have had more luck with large dogs that have no herding instincts.

Through trial and error you will find what you can live with.

A Visit From the Vet

The State Veterinarian for the winter meet at Tampa Bay Downs, Jerry Wessner, was kind enough to give me this information on vaccinations. Jerry graduated from the University of Pennsylvania Veterinary School in 1965. He was a practicing racetrack vet for many years. His help with this section is appreciated.

Coggins Test

Every horse should have a Coggins Test. This test is named after Dr. Coggins who developed the test for detection of Swamp Fever or Equine Infectious Anemia (EIA). EIA is a viral disease transmitted from an infected horse through blood transfer. This transfer may occur by blood contaminated needles or syringes, mosquitoes, flies or any vector or means that allows EIA contaminated blood to come in contact with circulating blood in a healthy horse. Horses that contract EIA have the virus in the white blood cells for life.

Usually an infected horse will show intermittent fever, depression, progressive weakness, weight loss, edema, and either progressive or transitory anemia. The disease may incapacitate or kill horses with the anemia, or it may go quiescent and never cause anemia again. The quiescent stage is the most dangerous.

Before the Coggins Test, many horses were infected through insect vectors or multiple use of needles and syringes. The Coggins Test detects both the carrier and the infectious state. Most racing jurisdictions will not allow horses to race if they have a positive Coggins Test. The majority of states allow the infected horses to live if suitable quarantine facilities are built and quarantine measures adhered to. Most states prohibit the interstate shipment of positive Coggins horses. Although this disease will probably never be eliminated, economic losses of horses have decreased dramatically since the advent of testing was coupled with strict control measures. Some states require testing every six months, while others only require annual tests. Whatever your state requires, be thankful you will probably never see this disease.

Vaccinations

Vaccinations or immunizations are injections made up of either killed or modified live viruses or bacteria that do not cause disease in an animal, but offer the protection or immunity, as if the horse has succumbed and recovered from the disease. Vaccinate your horse. It is cost effective.

Tetanus Toxoid

All horses should be vaccinated annually with Tetanus Toxoid. All the unvaccinated horse needs is a small non-draining wound or abscess in the foot or other part of the body and, if infected by the tetanus organism, the animal will have a very painful and expensive illness. Symptoms of tetanus are a stiff sawhorse appearance, rigid tail and flickering of eyelid over eyes when startled. Tetanus causes spasms and a great deal of pain. Inoculate during the first year and repeat in four weeks. Boosters must be given annually.

Botulism

Botulism is caused by the same family of bacteria that causes Tetanus. It is characterized by muscular weakness that leads to paralysis. Death ensues from paralysis of

The cost of a vaccination is far less than the cost or treatment of a disease.

respiratory muscles. A minute amount of toxin can kill a horse, so beware and vaccinate. Inoculate during the first year and repeat in four weeks. Boosters must be given annually.

Potomac Horse Fever (PHF)

This is a disease that originated in Virginia and is caused by pleura pneumonia-like organisms (PPLO) which are very similar to organisms that cause Rocky Mountain Spotted Fever. PHF is characterized by severe diarrhea and sometimes laminitis (founder). Horses that have both diarrhea and laminitis are hard to save. An immunization is now available.

Encephalitis

Encephalitis means inflammation of the brain and coverings, or meningitis. This virus causes horses to be very ill. Since the brain is involved, CNS signs will be evident: blindness, blind staggers, convulsions, circling, head pressing and abnormal behavior. There is a trivalent vaccine currently available... Eastern, Western, and Venezuelan. It is almost 100% effective when given early enough.

Strangles

Strangles is a respiratory disease caused by a bacteria called Streptococcus Equi. This disease is somewhat spotty now, but if it does appear, your land and area will be contaminated for seven years. The disease is manifested by high fever and swelling and sometimes bursting of the sub-mandibular lymph nodes. Symptoms are fever and large swollen glands under the jaw. Three vaccinations given seven to ten days apart the first year and then repeated annually are recommended.

Flu and Rhino

There are 35 viruses that can cause respiratory disease in the horse. These viruses offer no cross immunity. Theoretically, it is possible for a horse to be continually infected with 35 distinct respiratory viruses. Recovery from one would not offer any protection from the other diseases. The two main viruses are Flu and Rhino. Many two-year-olds at the racetrack seem to have chronic cough and respiratory disease. Discuss with your vet ways to prevent or control the Respiratory Disease Complex in young horses.

Equine Protozola Melitis

EPM is a neurologic disease of horses, caused by a protozoan parasite called Sarcocystis nuerona. Exposure has been reported to be as high as 90% in the racehorse population. Exposure means that the horse has ingested the parasite, that it is in the horse's body. It does not mean that the parasite has invaded the nervous tissue yet. Many factors enter into a horse getting an active infection. The immune status of the horse probably is the most important. Stress is another important factor. Active infection can follow exposure anywhere from two weeks to two years and is probably related to stress to the animal. Keep in mind that steroids lower the immune system and could leave your horse less able to resist active infection.

Establish a vaccination schedule.

Deworming

Your vet will suggest the best worming program for your area. Keep in mind that your goal is to control parasites in your pasture as well as your horse. (Be sure to read about my Chickens.) Part of an article by Rupert P. Herd, MVSc, PhD, Department of Veterinary Preventive Medicine, College of Veterinary Medicine, Ohio State University is quoted below. See how up to date you are in equine parasite control.

12 Common Deworming Myths

"MYTH - Repeated deworming is the only effective method of worm control.
TRUTH - Seasonal (spring/summer) strategic treatments are just as effective for adult horses as are year-round treatments. Twice-weekly removal of dung is even more effective that repeated deworming and greatly reduces reliance on chemical control.

MYTH - Tube deworming is more effective than paste deworming.
TRUTH - Paste deworming has proved to be highly effective in millions of horses worldwide, and it is easier, faster, and safer than tube deworming. Tube deworming is best replaced by crucial services such as monitoring parasite control with egg counts.

MYTH - Qualitative fecal egg counts are just as good as quantitative fecal egg counts.
TRUTH -This is true in small-animal practice, in which you only need to know whether the animal is infected. In equine practice, you need to quantitatively measure the degree of pasture contamination, the presence of drug resistance, and the best interval between treatments.

MYTH -Fecal egg counts provide a measure of the severity of worm infection and the size of the worm load.
TRUTH - There is no correlation between the number of eggs passed in feces and the number of worms in the horse. Horses with severe larval cyathostomiasis commonly have low or nonexistent fecal egg counts because the larvae responsible have not reached the adult egg-laying state.

MYTH - The large strongyles are the most important worm pathogens in horses.
TRUTH - This is no longer true because there has been a dramatic drop in their prevalence in most horse-breeding regions since the advent of modern anthelmintics in the early 1960's. The modern drugs have been and still are effective against the large strongyles, with no indication of drug resistance occurring.

MYTH - Modern drugs are effective against all worm states, including hypobiotic and encysted cyathostomes.
TRUTH - No anthelmintics approved in the United States are effective against the encysted cyathostomes of horses. Even repeated high doses of modern anthelmintics have failed in the treatment of larval cyathostomiasis.

Your goal is to control parasites in your pastures as well as your horse.

MYTH - Rapid rotation of drugs every few months will prevent the development of drug resistance.

TRUTH - The common practice of rotating dewormers at every treatment or several times a year has been associated with the rapid spread of resistance in the United States. By contrast, there are no reports of resistance developing on farm that practice an annual rotation of drugs using only one dewormer each year.

MYTH - Horses can be treated every 30 to 60 days, year after year, without anthelmintic resistance developing.

TRUTH - The more frequently a dewormer is used, the faster resistance will develop. Overprotective treatment programs (e.g. 12 treatments per year) are not only unnecessary, but are counterproductive because they raise the risk of drug resistance and other drug-related problems.

MYTH - Treatments given according to set calendar months without regard for epidemiologic principles provide good parasite control.

TRUTH - Many of these treatments are given at the wrong time of year to prevent serious pasture contamination and do not prevent horses from ingesting large numbers of pasture larvae.

MYTH - Risk of reinfection decreases after a "killing frost."

TRUTH - Subzero temperatures and heavy snowfalls have little adverse effect on third-stage infective larvae on pasture, unless there has been alternate freezing and thawing. Infective larvae will generally survive on pastures of winter, but die off when temperatures rise in late spring.

MYTH - Harrowing pastures at any time of year provides good parasite control

TRUTH - Harrowing is beneficial during hot, dry periods when pasture larvae are exposed to sunlight and desiccation. Harrowing in damp, overcast conditions simply spreads viable larvae from roughs to lawns and heightens the risk for grazing horses.

MYTH - Pasture rotation is an effective method of parasite control.

TRUTH - This approach cannot be relied upon for good parasite control because of the prolonged survival of infective larvae for up to one year on pastures. I may even increase the risk of parasitism if weather conditions favor larval development at the time when horses are rotated to a fresh but contaminated pasture."

Deworm with your climate not your calendar.

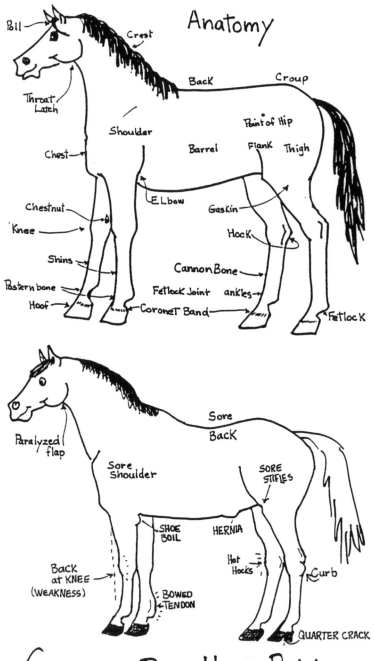

Anatomy

Poll

Crest

Back

Croup

Throat Latch

Shoulder

Point of Hip

Chest

Barrel

Flank

Thigh

Elbow

Chestnut

Gaskin

Knee

Hock

Shins

Cannon Bone

Pastern bone

Fetlock Joint

ankles

Hoof

Coronet Band

Fetlock

Paralyzed flap

Sore Back

Sore Shoulder

SORE STIFLES

SHOE BOIL

HERNIA

Back at KNEE (WEAKNESS)

Hot Hocks

Curb

BOWED TENDON

QUARTER CRACK

Common Race Horse Problems

Two of the Most Common Equine Ailments

I will be brief here. Time and experience will teach you what you can handle. There are many basic horse health books. Try to have good reference books. I strongly recommend *The Merck Veterinary Manual*, Published by Merck & Co., Inc., Rahway, N.J. and *How To Be Your Own Veterinarian (sometimes)*, by Ruth B. James, DVM, published by Alpine Press, Mills, WY. "Merck's" gives very technical information, whereas Dr. James gives wonderful hands-on advice.

Colic

This is the most common ailment you will encounter. It may be a slight tummy ache or a death threatening blocked intestine. The horse may not want to eat (a very important sign) and will turn his head and look at his stomach. As the pain increases, he may paw and stomp, roll gently or violently, or just appear off. Call the vet and follow his instructions.

Cuts and Lacerations

These are frequent and can be caused by barbed wire, splintered boards, tree branches, etc.. If the wound is open and bleeding profusely, confine the animal and put pressure on the wound with a clean rag or cotton, holding the bandage in place with vet wrap if possible. Horse blood tends to coagulate quickly, so try and stop the bleeding and then call the vet. Don't panic.

If your horse has small nicks and scratches, remember aggressive hosing is the best treatment. Where there are many flies and heat, hose the scratches a few times a day. This will inhibit irritation to the skin caused by the drainage of serum from the wound.

When the legs are scraped or cut below the knee, the swelling or edema can be frightening. Light exercise (hand walking, free roundpenning at a jog, or turnout) will help alleviate the edema, as will aggressive hosing.

Less Common Equine Ailments

Refer to the Glossary for definitions of specific ailments and terms such as Anhidrosis (Non-sweater), Azoturia (Tie-up), Bean, Bleeder, Blister, Bog Spavin, Bone Spavin, Bowed Tendon, Bucked Shin, Capped Hock, Contracted Feet, Cord-up, Cracked Heels, Epiphysitis, EIA (Swamp Fever), Founder (Laminitis), Joint Capsule, Navicular Disease, Neurectomy, Nerved, Osselets, Osteochondrosis, Popped-A-Splint, Quarter Crack, Quittor, Rhinopneumonitis, Ring Bone, Roarer, Sesamoiditis, Shoe Boil, Speedy Cut, Splints, Superficial Flexor Tendon, Suspensory Ligaments, Thoroughpin, Thrush, and Wolf Teeth.

Consult a vet for any symptoms you are unfamiliar with. 35

Equine Dental Care

A horse's mouth can be the source of a great deal of trouble if the trainer is not on his toes. Many problems in controlling a horse may be related to his teeth and mouth. When a horse tries to bolt, swing his head or fight the bit, it may be simply because his teeth are bothering him. For a while, one of my horses would bolt and run all over the track uncontrollably. I interpreted this behavior as fear and nervousness at the track and used a pony and various other devices were trying to control him. The problem occurred when the jockey "took a hold" of him. It hurt his mouth. Had I thought about teeth, much time and effort could have been avoided solving his problem, because once his teeth were filed he was a different horse.

Many thanks to Larry Moriarity, Master Equine Dentist, for some of this information. Horses have two kinds of teeth. The incisors in front are commonly called nippers. The molars in back are commonly called grinders. The nippers were designed to enable the horse to obtain food when grazing. The grinders masticate food for digestion. Keep in mind that these teeth were designed for grazing, not eating out of a feed bucket. Many dental problems arise from eating feed.

The upper jaw is wider than the lower, causing the upper molars to grow downward and outward. The lower molars grow upward and inward, hence the molars do their work on a bevel. Due to the grinding of food, the enamel on the free sides of the molars receives no pressure, allowing the outside of the upper molars and the inner side of the lower molars to grow to sharp extended points. Filing the molars to make them even is called floating.

Floating can be performed either by your vet or by a farrier trained to do this. For more serious problems your vet should be able to recommend a good dentist. Most racetracks have resident dentists. Ask in the office for information about the track equine dentist.

Signs of teeth problems include lugging, slobbering, cribbing, bolting of grain, indigestion, colic, scouring, nervousness, cutting of the cheeks and tongue, a change in chewing habits, dribbling of feed, washing feed in the water bucket, and holding the head to one side when eating. If you notice weight loss, it could be caused by a dental problem. Your horse may not be grinding his food enough to digest it. You may also notice halitosis, swelling of the face, and refusal to eat hard grain.

According to our equine dentist, incisor deformity can result in malocclusion. Severe dental problems can lead to TMJ (Tempular Mandibular Joint - Migraine headaches). In such cases the atlas bone can become misaligned which can affect the entire skeleton. Another worst case scenario would be pockets of bacteria in the gums and cheeks caused by dental decay.

Open Wide!

Avoid dental problems. Have your horse's teeth checked.

Teeth-Determining Age

1 YEAR

All deciduous incisors (baby teeth) are visible. Centrals and intermediates are in contact. Chewing surface of the centrals show wear. Upper and lower corner incisors are not in contact. The dental star in the centrals and intermediates is a dark line on labial (lip) side of cup.

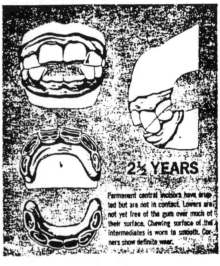

2½ YEARS

Permanent central incisors have erupted but are not in contact. Lowers are not yet free of the gum over much of their surface. Chewing surface of the intermediates is worn to smooth. Corners show definite wear.

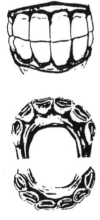

5 YEARS

Permanent dentition is complete. All teeth are in wear. Canine teeth have erupted completely. The centrals and intermediates show wear on the chewing surface, but cups are still visible and are completely encircled by enamel. Corners are beginning to wear.

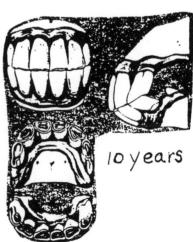

10 years

37

EQUIPMENT

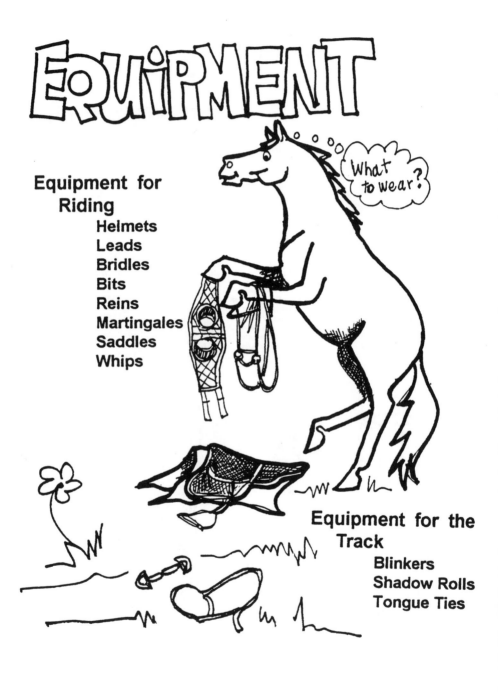

What to wear?

Equipment for Riding
- Helmets
- Leads
- Bridles
- Bits
- Reins
- Martingales
- Saddles
- Whips

Equipment for the Track
- Blinkers
- Shadow Rolls
- Tongue Ties

EQUIPMENT FOR TRAINING

This section will briefly cover basic equipment you will need in training an average racehorse with no known quirks or problems.

Helmets

Before you get on a horse, it is mandatory that you automatically put on your riding helmet. There are many varieties available. You may purchase them at tack shops and racetracks. I have a special fondness for the Jofa hockey helmet, because one saved my life. Lois was saved by a hard hat (and head). Any of the approved safety helmets you choose will be acceptable.

Leads

Whenever you handle a horse, use a chain shank over the nose. Never hurt the horse or yank on him unless his actions demand it. When his behavior is unacceptable, punish him immediately to swiftly teach him you won't put up with dangerous comportment.

Bridles

For the training stages, any style leather or nylon head stall with a nose band and chin strap will be suitable. When your horse is ready for the track, you may want to purchase some fancy racing tack.

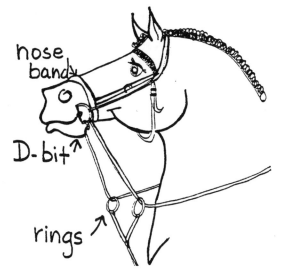

Bits

Start training with a simple D snaffle. It is not too severe and allows decent control of the horse. A nose band will help teach the horse to keep his mouth shut and to keep his tongue under the bit.

In the second stage of training, as the horse grows stronger and into more speed or shows a harder mouth, you may find you need more control. Get professional advice on more effective, stronger bits. Generally, it isn't necessary to go to severe bits. Sense how the horse likes to be ridden and decide what is most suitable for your horse. Be aware that each horse acts differently. Some like to lean against the bit . . . others like it barely in contact. Each horse will evolve his own way of going.

Introduce new equipment at home.

Reins

Use reins that do not slip through your fingers. When the horse is in a lather, slippery reins can be a real problem. Braided leather or rubber padded reins are good choices to help you keep steady contact with your horse's mouth, especially when you get into the Speed Phase of training. Leather or suede gloves also may be helpful.

Martingales

Use a set of "rings" or a running martingale in the early stages of training. It discourages a horse when he tosses his head or rears. It also teaches him to "give at the poll" when you rein in, rather than allowing him to stick out his nose and try to fight. Martingales should not be used at the track for speed works or races.

Saddles

When you are breaking your horse, you will have to decide what to put on his back. Either a western or english saddle is suitable. When you free roundpen, a western saddle is good to accustom the horse to something flopping around on his back. When I start riding, I go to an english exercise saddle, because it has nothing more than a "tree" type structure covered by leather with stirrups attached to it. It allows me to feel how the horse is moving. Since I recommend long stirrups at this stage, the early riding style is almost like being bareback with stirrups.

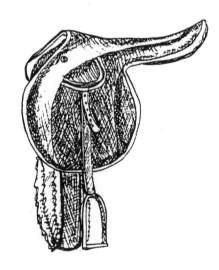

Use any saddle you possess for Phase I training. When you begin Phase II training, a western saddle may be too structured for you, the horse, and the style of riding you will be doing. I recommend you buy an exercise saddle at this point, so the horse will not be inhibited and can move easily.

Washable nylon girths covered with fleece are easy to clean and don't rot if you wash them frequently or live in a very humid area. Leather girths mold or rot quickly unless they are oiled frequently. Frequent oiling is a lot of work for the do-it-yourselfer.

My preference in stirrup leathers is also nylon. Nylon has never broken on me without substantial fraying as a warning, something I can't say about leather.

Avoid excessive equipment.

Always use a good thick pad between the saddle and the horse. If you are riding a number of horses, use a clean saddle cloth of washable cotton under the saddle pad of each horse to avoid the sweat and bacteria being carried from one horse to another. Although training saddles are lightweight and will not be on the horse for hours and hours at a time, remember that many back problems are caused by poorly fitting saddles. Be sure the saddle fits your horse and is properly placed on his back.

Whips

You or your rider should always take a riding crop or whip when riding young horses. This is to accustom them to it as a **training aid**. The jockey is **expected to carry a whip and use it as needed** in the race. If the horse has not been accustomed to it at home, valuable time may be lost while teaching him about it at the racetrack.

Always Wear Your Helmet when you Ride!

Keep equipment clean and in good repair.

EQUIPMENT FOR THE TRACK

Specific problems tend to show up when you begin training at the track. Then depending on how your horse behaves, you will have to decide whether to use blinkers, more complex bits, tongue ties, etc. **Your trainer and rider will be able to tell you what equipment will help solve specific problems.** Always analyze whether the horse needs a change in equipment, or whether something you are doing is causing problems in his behavior.

Some trainers use all sorts of equipment "just in case", right from the beginning. Much of the equipment may hinder the horse rather than help him. This can be confusing to the animal. Add one item at a time, and observe his behavior after each addition. Always introduce new equipment at the farm in a familiar environment. Then try it at the track.

If your horse is racing, be aware that any change of equipment, such as blinkers, must be declared when entering the horse in a race. The less equipment necessary to do the job, the less chance for confusion or mistakes.

Blinkers

Blinkers are used to make the horse concentrate on his business. They keep him from veering or bolting. They are also used on timid horses who don't want to pass others or on horses who are distracted by the crowd.

A colt who is more interested in the horse next to him than the race may need blinkers. The jockey might say the colt is "hanging". It means he doesn't want to pass the horse next to him. Blinkers may stop that behavior. Sometimes blinkers will cover one eye leaving the other open. Sometimes half blinkers are used. There are endless blinker configurations. Trainers will try anything to get a good run out of the horse! Remember Gate Dancer? He had blinkers with ear muffs attached so he wouldn't hear the crowd. Don't laugh, he won a lot of races that way!

Shadow Rolls

Shadow rolls may be used to encourage a horse to drop his head. He must lower it to see over the lambswool covering on the nose band. The lambswool band also blocks the horse from seeing his shadow and shying at it.

Tongue Ties

If you notice your horse continuously fussing with his tongue over the bit, under the bit, and around the bit, and you know his teeth are not bothering him, he may need a tongue tie. We use tongue ties for a variety of reasons. Primarily to maintain the tongue in its proper position. Some very nervous horses will curl the tongue behind the bit during a race hampering their ability to take in sufficient air. Other horses will have a tongue that is too long for their mouth, making it necessary to accommodate it for them. If the horse has a loose palate tying the tongue may help keep the soft palate in its proper position. At times

Keep it simple.

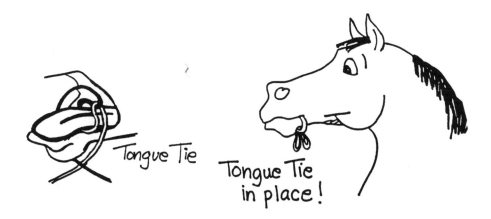

Tongue Tie

Tongue Tie
in place!

the rider feels the horse is not breathing properly and will recommend trying a tongue tie. You may even hear the trainer say, "I don't know what his problems is. Let's try a tongue tie."

Tongue ties can be made of a variety of materials. You can purchase a ready made tongue tie at the tack shop, or you can make one out of soft cotton flannel pieces an inch and a half or two inches wide by about 18" long. The leg of a nylon pantie hose also makes a good tongue tie. One trainer I knew used the wide rubber bands.

A word of caution. When I see a horse with his tongue tied and hanging out turning blue, I wonder how that can help him run a race. Be careful to tie the tongue tight enough to keep it in position and loose enough to allow circulation. Have a seasoned trainer teach you how to tie the tongue.

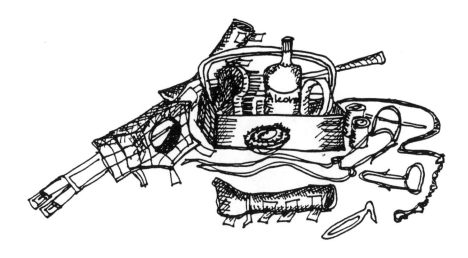

Try to have 2 complete sets of tack so that your truck is RACETRACK Ready!

FEEDS and SUPPLEMENTS

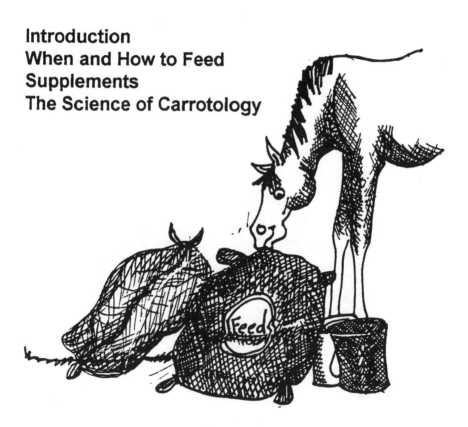

FEEDS AND SUPPLEMENTS - Introduction

In various parts of the world, you see people eating different basic foods as their mainstay. Whether it is potatoes, rice, wheat, or corn, supplemented with meat, fish, or combined proteins, there is a tremendous diversity of diets.

When it comes to feeding horses, you will find a multitude of opinions. Owners have come to me with charts, scales and very intricate instructions on how their dear little horse must be fed. They assure me that they have calculated exactly how much he needs because he burns X amount of calories per work. I marvel at their precision . . . how do they know so precisely ?

It is extremely impractical to have different feeding menus on large farms. (The exception being a horse with a specific problem.) The more complicated the feeding program, the more opportunity for mistakes and accidents. Too many steps may confuse your help.

All of my animals receive the same basic feed mixture. Everyone on the farm is fed a 12 percent sweet feed mixed locally that has more corn than oats. Pound for pound, corn is much higher in energy than oats. University studies have shown that corn converts most efficiently into glycogen, which fuels cells during anaerobic stress. The amount of feed given to each horse varies depending on his size and level of training. Don't miss the articles in the back of the book on Osteochondrosis and its relationship to overfeeding.

Every animal gets free choice hay, usually fertilized coastal, which is also about 10 percent protein, and is locally grown. My basic feed measurement for Thoroughbreds - yearlings, two-year-olds and up - is about four quarts of the mix twice a day. Yearlings and two-year-olds need food to build and grow. The more mature horses are easing into racing and need to replace fuel that is burned. Quarter Horses are easy keepers. They seem to need less than half as much feed as the Thoroughbreds. When a new horse arrives, until he adjusts to the feed, he is given a third of the usual amount, gradually increasing it to the four quarts, twice a day.

Corn converts most efficiently into glycogen, which fuels cells during anaerobic stress.

Observe who finishes and who leaves feed. Once your horses are stabilized within your feeding program, **augment the feed if an animal looks too thin. Cut it back or increase exercise if he's too heavy.** Some large racing horses need as much as eight quarts twice a day.

Since each metabolism is unique, it is imperative that you understand what kind of "keeper" your horse is. Personality can be a major factor in feed consumption, sending the charts right out the window. Is the horse high strung or laid back? What's his genetic background? Some bloodlines are historically easy to maintain and others are more difficult. There may be other influences too subtle for us perceive.

Sometimes, horses appear high strung because they are given high protein feed which is not burned off with a reasonable training program. Fifteen minutes out of the stall doesn't burn many calories.

My training program requires horses to be turned out every day for a few hours. If they are being over-fed, they can run and frolic to burn off their excess energy. The point is, although charts may say a horse needs so many pounds for so much work, it is really a very subjective figure. **Look at your horse . . . is he carrying enough weight or does he look drawn?**

Horses in the interval training program, where they are worked every four days and galloped miles in between, develop muscles with a "hard" look. When I was following the interval training program, my horses looked drawn and over-trained. **The program was drilling out their speed and brilliance.** When a horse's muscle gets too hard a look in the interval training method, it is not usually because of lack of feed. Mine were eating huge and frightening amounts! **The look stems from overtraining.** It is important that you learn to **tell the difference between overtraining and underfeeding.** If your horse is eating huge amounts of feed, is on a good worming schedule and still looks ribby, it may be that you are **overworking** the animal. The problem can be frequent high speed works without time off for the animal to rebuild in between these stresses. This is especially hard on young animals.

Two, three, and four-year-olds are really very much like teenagers. A tremendous amount of food energy goes into building bone, muscle and tissue. Just as teenagers get big hands and feet and skinny bodies before they fill out, horses go through adolescent growth spurts.

Good feed, good training and lots of turnout during this growing period are imperative. At five, a horse is considered mature in bone and body. If we race judiciously as they grow and develop, and allow time for rebuilding between races, we are forming a useful, strong animal that can last many years!

Some trainers, thinking that their horse needs more feed (when really he may be over-trained), will add pure corn oil or other kinds of fats to the feed. There are horses that may be unable to metabolize excessive fat and may develop pockets or globules of fat which constrict major vessels. This in turn may cause impairment of blood flow.

An excess of anything can be dangerous!
Learn to know your animal and feed accordingly.

WHEN AND HOW TO FEED

Did you notice that I mentioned giving grain twice a day? In the old days, while innocently imitating track procedures, I got up in the dark and woke up the horses to feed them. When they galloped two hours later, I worried that it might be too close to a heavy meal. Eventually, it occurred to me that I had breakfast when my work was done, so the horses could do the same.

Now, I get up at dawn, (the actual time varies greatly from summer to winter) give all the horses hay, and turn out those who go from stalls to paddocks. **The animals loosen up in the paddocks, frolic, and socialize while I pick out the stalls.** After their ride, roundpenning, or swim, they go back to their turnout paddocks until feed time. They can still nibble on the hay that was given at dawn. At ten AM in the winter or nine AM in the summer, they are given their grain and supplements along with enough hay to last all day. Depending on their schedule, they are stalled during the day and turned out at night in the summer - vice versa in the winter. They are fed hay and grain again at dusk.

During the hot summer days, they are fed in the cool of the evening. In the winter, they are fed while there is enough light to visually observe how they look, before they are tucked in for the night.

This schedule makes sense, because animals are sensitive to earth rhythms, whereas we tend to be more tied to the clock. If you work and must arrange your horses around your schedule, that is fine. Animals are adaptable and can live with many different situations. **The most useful animals are those that aren't ruffled by unpredictable circumstances.** Races and traveling schedules will break up their routine soon enough.

The racetrack routine is very restricting. The track is only open until ten o'clock for works and training. All the horses must be finished by then. Doing most of the training at the farm, you are able to adapt the training program to suit your life-style and schedule. You can have horses and another life, too.

Once a week, all of my horses are given four quarts of bran well saturated with water and perhaps a squirt of corn oil. To avoid confusion, bran is always fed Sunday morning. No supplements or other products are added. Some horses are like children when confronted with healthy food. They say, "Yuk . . . bran again." Others devour the bran. Still others try to hold out, only finally choking it down when there is no hope of real feed. Those who refuse to finish get it stirred into their night grain.

Bran mash again? It must be Sunday!

We live in an area where horses can ingest a great deal of sand when grazing on short grass. The bran seems to control the problem of sand colic. Keeping fresh, properly cured hay in front of them also helps with this problem.

Speaking of hay. . . a few comments. People rave about alfalfa for horses. Alfalfa is very high in protein, about 18 percent. For me,

Animals are sensitive to earth rhythms.

47

this is too rich to combine with the high protein grain the animals are being fed. A lower percentage of protein in their roughage is preferable. If needed, I might give a one-inch flake of alfalfa once a day as a treat! In our effort to provide the most nutritious feed, we forget that the animal might find it comforting to eat a lower quality hay all day long, instead of a small amount of high protein hay for a short period. Munching on hay or grazing is very soothing for horses. Why not let them fulfill their desire to chew? After quickly consuming high protein pellets that fill their nutritional needs, they may start chewing on boards, doors and other surfaces out of boredom. Work with the animals' intrinsic needs. Remember, they are grazers.

If you are feeding your horse too much protein, his manure will be more like cow manure - soggy and wet possibly with a heavy pungent odor. To remedy this, give more hay and less high protein grain. You'll see the difference!

Here are some general comments about feed. A 12 percent sweet feed mix should be available from a reputable local feed mill or company that mixes feed for your area. Read the guaranteed analysis. It should tell the crude protein, fat, fiber, etc. Trace minerals and vitamins should be mentioned. Ingredients such as folic acid, selenite, etc., either occur naturally in the feed or are added to the mix. This is mentioned so that you don't go overboard with supplements. When the horse is racing and you feel he needs help, you may want to add a little more of this and that, but too much supplement is dangerous.

Doctors Krook and Maylin have stressed in their book, *Race Horses at Risk*, that **many breakdowns are attributed to abusive overfeeding and supplementing to push early growth.** This has resulted in animals with improperly developed bone. Cysts of cartilage form in the bone, which weaken its overall strength. The bone caves in when put under the stress of racing. This type of breakdown happens time and time again.

It is disheartening to think that a healthy looking animal can have serious internal faults. If you want to know more about this subject, read the book. It is an eye opener. *The Merck Veterinary Manual, Seventh Edition"* has the following comment on treatment of Osteochondrosis "...In addition to surgical considerations, nutritional imbalances must be corrected, and toxic elements eliminated. **Overfeeding of high-energy feeds is a common error.** Exercise must be regulated . . ." Be very careful not to overfeed. High protein and low exercise can lead to Osteochondrosis.

For questions about feed and problems to be aware of in your area, call your local extension office or nearest agricultural university.

My whole philosophy is this: Remember the natural life-style of the animal and try to keep him in a way that allows him to be a horse.

Don't try to fool Mother Nature.

SUPPLEMENTS

This subject could be debated forever. There are testimonials for all kinds of products. It is easy to fall into the vitamin and health food syndrome. True health food fanatics live restricted lives that revolve around strange diets. Some of us think "Death is better than eating that stuff!"

Go back to Mother Nature. Horses are grazers. They meander constantly to get a bite of grass here, a few seed heads there, a lovely salad over yonder all courtesy of their environment. I am instinctively frightened by the amount of grain we give these horses. They would have grazed for many, many hours, burning many, many calories to encounter that much protein in the wild. We stress our animals in ways that are not natural (sustained high speed, with weight on their back), so we assume that we must compensate.

Overall we have improved their life-style in relation to the dangers of the wild. However, we stress their metabolism, especially if they are honest. I tell my horses that nothing in life is free and that they must perform for me in exchange for the comforts they are given.

The amount of weight a horse loses in a race is amazing. **The one minute and twelve seconds of racing can take so much out of the animal that he needs days to recuperate.** This is where supplements may be necessary. After being over stressed, the horse needs help to rebuild. A horse may be dehydrated for a few days after a hard race. In Florida, during the severe summer heat, this is especially true. I give a handful of electrolytes for a few days after the race, always checking his skin to see how he is doing. To judge how the horse is re-hydrating, pinch the skin on his neck and see how long it takes to snap back to normal from the pinch. The longer it takes the more dehydrated he is. **Remember that electrolytes are also assimilated from a good diet and a salt mineral block.**

The time a horse needs to rebuild himself is the best

Horses are grazers.

barometer of his overall ability to withstand the rigors of racing. I am opposed to jugging a horse after a race to speed his recovery. Jugging means having the veterinarian give the horse a solution of electrolytes and IV fluids intravenously. The whole structure of the horse is stressed in a hard race. . . the bone, muscle, and soft tissue. By jugging the horse you make him feel better than he really is. It is better to allow the horse to mope around for a few days - self imposed rest. **His body tells him he needs rest, and that in itself will make him rest. When he is recharged, he'll tell you by frolicking when you turn him out.** Most horses I've trained show a definite pattern. If they have tried hard and raced honestly, they are a tad off their feed that night. They might be slightly off for another day or so. By the fourth or fifth day it seems that their own endorphins make them feel high off the race. They are on their way to rebuilding. When turned out they frolic and cavort. Light free roundpenning and maybe one flying open gallop and they are ready to race again on the tenth day.

After a few races or hard works, you begin to discern between a robust horse that needs and wants to race frequently and a horse that is hard on himself in a race. Unlike many humans who can push themselves and come back stronger, when a horse is pushed too much, he is capable of doing himself real damage. When he has an adrenaline rush, he is capable of running on a fractured leg or doing other equally harmful things to himself. The rider on the horse urging him to go faster and faster may make the horse overexert.

The cost of training a horse at the track is so high that owners put too much emphasis on the horse's daily behavior. If he has one bad day or is slightly off his feed, there is a tendency to over react. "Call the vet . . . we're losing time." At home you can be more relaxed about allowing him rebuild-days and giving him time off. **We all have bad days. Horses are no exception.** They are not machines! Blood tests and X-rays for every minor bump get to be very expensive. At home you have another great advantage over the track; you can constantly observe and monitor your animal.

Although horses should get all of their nutrition from well balanced feed, I do use a vitamin supplement. There are a great many out there. I will share my recipe with you, as an example. You can develop your own program and preferences.

Pour a 25 pound bag of Clovite into a large, clean container. Add 5 pounds of brewers yeast, which is high in vitamin B and amino acids. Add a 3-to-5 pound container of vitamin E and selenium. (Check your soil or talk to your vet; your area or feed may already be high in selenium. If so, don't use it. Too much or too little can be harmful.) Add a 3 to 5 pound container of biotin (believed to be good for hooves). Stir this concoction thoroughly and give about 2 ounces (a handful) to each animal in his morning grain feed. I may give actively racing horses a squirt of Red Cell (a liquid vitamin supplement) or the equivalent for good measure. You may think my attitude is a little cavalier. Basically the metabolism gets its nutrition from well balanced feed. These are really just extra backups.

If your horse's gums aren't pink and healthy, check with your veterinarian. See if your horse is wormy. Have a blood chemistry run, if there is a problem. In a well fit and conditioned horse, the gums will flush up pink very quickly during exercise, indicating an efficient cardiovascular system. When horses swim, they curl their upper lip making it

Your role as a trainer is to know when enough is enough.

easy to assess how long it takes them to go from light pink gums to rich strong pink, as they exercise. It's a good gauge of their cardiovascular efficiency.

Time has been taken here to discuss the above because there is a **tendency to oversupplement and overdose the horse.** A huge amount of money is spent on feed supplements. Observe what works. Read the literature and judge whether it makes sense. If a talented horse is kept happy and healthy, he will run. If it makes you feel good, give your horse a pinch of this and a squirt of that. Try not to overdo. The kidneys will have to work overtime to filter the excess additives out of his system. One simple all around vitamin once a day should be adequate for his needs. Anything above and beyond that should be studied for real value and cost.

A local Feed Mill should have the proper mix for your area! It should be fresher than feed shipped in from far away. Check with the nearest Agricultural University for Specific Nutritional needs in your area!

No magic powders will help a horse without talent.

Del Castillo's Feeding Schedule

Dawn Turn out horses to individual paddocks (after feeling and checking Legs!) Give Hay ✱ note whether or not all grain was eaten!

9 or 10 AM Grain and Hay and Vitamins — Tuck back in stall - all morning work done! (all feed supplements are added at this feeding)

Afternoon - Turn out for an hour or so... depending
Sometimes I gallop, round pen or swim in the afternoon — depending on schedule

½ hour before Dark Hay and Grain - Tuck Horses in for night ✱ ✱ ✱

Hay 3 Times a day
Grain 2 Times a day
Bran - Sunday A.M.

THE SCIENCE OF CARROTOLOGY

You are probably wondering, "What the heck is carrotology?" Early in my endeavors with horses and racing, a friend came to visit. She loved horses. She knew nothing about training . but was an expert in nurturing. For years. Claire has returned and taught the horses how to eat carrots. Yes, they sometimes need to learn this important skill. Claire's husband. George. is a sharp handicapper from way back. He also comes to see what the horses have to say. Sometimes Claire will come in and tell me. "You know, Aly says his shin is bothering him!", or share some other observation. I dutifully go out and check the animal to find that she is instinctively right.

Over the years. she has befriended all of the horses on the farm. She does have her favorites - she brings gourmet carrots to First Prediction. She shares her carrots. kindness, and advice with all the horses. They all know Claire and George by sight. and nicker to them when they arrive.

It is very special for the animals to have someone who does nothing but love and care for them. When I had quite a few horses. I assigned girl riders to specific horses so that they would take a personal interest in them.

You will be warned time and time again not to fall in love with your horses. This is business - be pragmatic! You must realistically appraise the ability of the animals you are training, but **that does not preclude caring and loving them**. Some animals are so honest and noble that one can't help but admire them. **There is nothing wrong with having feelings. It might help the racing industry tremendously to have more feeling and caring individuals involved.** All horses should have a support group like George and Claire. Find some "Grandparents" for your horses.

George and Claire

**Give your horse a kiss on the nose.
Let him know you care!**

**Bandaging
and
Leg Support**

**Solutions for
Special Problems**

Shoeing

The Duck Foot

LEGS, BANDAGES, AND SHOEING - Introduction

Walking down the backside shedrow is like walking along a horse hospital ward. Nearly every horse has some kind of bandage, poultice, plastic wrap or scabby paint on his legs.

Years ago, I was bewildered by terms like blistering, firing, poulticing. They were a foreign language to me, but all the trainers and grooms seemed to know what they were talking about. With time and experience, I learned that was not necessarily so.

My opinion of firing and blistering is mentioned in other chapters. Briefly, the theory is to insult the area with a chemical or physical burn, causing the body to supply blood to the injured area and to create scar tissue. Doesn't the actual problem do that? Don't fractures, bucked shins, and other injuries cause swelling, heat, and therefore increased blood supply to the injured area while the body is trying to heal?

In any case, I'm told a good blister (i.e., huge swelling and scabbing of skin caused by a caustic agent) will straighten things right up. Some trainers recommend training during the healing process. Others may stall the horses. There are many theories, but not much concrete evidence that any of this voodoo is more valid than rest and massage. Doesn't massage also stimulate heat and blood flow? Think about the animal's problem from a competent horseman's point of view and see if the solution your trainer or track vet suggests makes sense. An experienced veterinarian who knows horses . . . not just racehorses . . . can give you an answer. Racetrack veterinarians are very good at keeping compromised horses going. Is that your goal? If you explain your philosophy to the racetrack veterinarian, he can advise you accordingly.

There are reasons for using bandages. They are good support for an animal trying to defend his injured leg. He puts so much weight on his good leg that it can stock up from the added stress. Under those conditions, both legs should be bandaged. A horse that has a cut or wound should be bandaged and medicated for a few days to get the healing started. Then begin gentle irrigation (hosing) to encourage blood flow to the area. This helps the body form new scabs, which enhance the healing process and allow the wound to heal from the inside. A wound that scabs over and heals on the outside may leave a pocket of infection inside. When the wound is set and no longer oozing or fragile, usually after three or four days, the area should be exposed to air.

Horses that are forced to stand in their stalls most of the day tend to stock up. Standing bandages are put on them to keep the filling down. Wouldn't **walking them twice a day or turning them out be preferable to having them bandaged all the time?**

There are a few things to remember about bandages:

> Never leave them on while the horse is turned out. As he moves, they can slip and bow a tendon from the constriction or come loose and tangle.
>
> Never leave a bandage on for twenty-four hours without rewrapping it.
>
> Never put a bandaged horse in a van and assume that he will be checked. Send the horse with a groom or don't wrap his legs.

Most importantly - don't fool yourself into thinking your horse has healed from an injury because his leg is tight after removing the bandages. Leave him unbandaged with free movement in order to properly assess his recovery.

TRAINERS GET A FALSE SENSE OF SECURITY WHEN BANDAGES SUPPRESS SWELLING. SUPPRESSED SWELLING DOES NOT MEAN HEALING HAS TAKEN PLACE OVERNIGHT!

**Bandages have their place...
be sensible when you use them.**

BANDAGING AND LEG SUPPORT FOR RACING

Vetwrap is a support wrap used all over the country. Some trainers I highly respect use Vetwrap on all four legs of every horse, in every race. This can be expensive, about ten dollars a throw, and dangerous if the groom is not completely competent. Many a horse has been injured by incorrectly applied bandages. Unless I know that a horse has a tendency to hurt himself or get into trouble, I don't wrap him.

Once in a while, a horse will get into a scuffle coming out of the gates or in the heat of the race. Vetwrap would protect tendons that might be cut or injured in such instances. Statistically, the chances of such injury are slim. If you are a super cautious person or your horse tends to hurt himself, be safe rather than sorry. Don't forget that damage may also be caused by incorrectly wrapped bandages. Always supervise the wrapping or do it yourself.

"Polos" are the soft cushioned bandages, in bright colors, seen on horses during their early morning workouts. They protect the animal from hitting himself during the workout, but are never used for races.

There are new bandages on the market every day. Like supplements, they promise miracle results. Some are supposed to keep a horse from bowing . . . hard to believe. There are many variations on the theme of support and strength. Some tests suggest a decrease in leg concussion with particular types of wraps. They could be very beneficial to a horse with tendencies toward leg problems. Wraps may also decrease the amount of damage done if a horse does break down in a race. At times you might want to wrap a horse for racing. Let your horse sense tell you when to do so. **If you have a horse that is compromised or has bad ankles, by all means give him the extra support if you choose to race him.** It might be helpful under racing conditions.

**Always use your own judgment and
horse sense.**

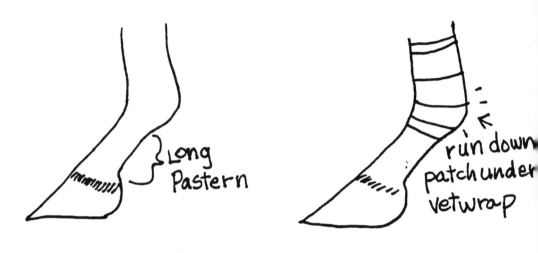

SOLUTIONS TO HELP SPECIFIC LEG PROBLEMS

Horses with long pasterns have a tendency to run down during a race, even with the best conditioning. As fatigue sets in, the fetlock drops lower and lower. Eventually, it can hit the track, causing a burn or worse injury. Trainers try to avoid this problem by using rundown patches. Rundown patches are pieces of material that are placed at the point of impact and wrapped with Vetwrap. Patches of plastic, rubber, or leather are available for the same purpose.

If your horse comes back from a work at the track with a burn on his fetlocks . . . on either the front or rear leg or legs . . . make sure he has protection the next time he goes to the track - after he has healed. **Don't allow the burn to become a chronic problem.** It could hamper the animal's desire to run.

A protector made from a motorcycle inner tube has worked on some of my animals. Motorcycle inner tubes being smaller than automobile inner tubes and larger than bicycle inner tubes are just right for protector material. I have created various types of leg, heel, and fetlock protectors using them. Someone showed me one of the styles, and the others have been devised as the need arose. They can be left on the horse all the time. After a few minutes of stomping their feet, the horse forgets them and accepts them as a second skin.

Illustrations on how to make them are included. They work very well for some horses and eliminate hitting problems in certain cases. Horses can be raced wearing these protectors.

Avoid initiating chronic problems.

Style 1   Style 2   Style 3

Style #1 - Protects the fetlock area from rundown . . . either front or back legs. You might wrap Vetwrap over it in a race, so it doesn't twist around. This style is useful to protect the hind hooves from hitting the front ankles if your horse has that tendency.

Style #2 - Protects the balls or heels of the front feet. You might have a horse that consistently catches himself while galloping and running. Make sure his feet are well balanced, the toes aren't too long, and try this.

Style #3 - Protects the front of the rear ankles and coronet band from being hit by the front feet. A horse that brings his rear legs up and under, interfering with his front action, will show hitting and cuts around the coronet band and ankles. One rear hoof may also hit the other in this area. If you see persistent random cuts around the rear ankles and coronet band, try this design.

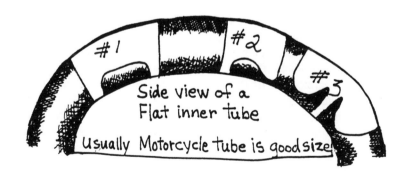

#1   #2   #3

Side view of a
Flat inner tube

Usually Motorcycle tube is good size!

SHOEING

To shoe or not to shoe. The question is easy for me. I never use shoes until the horse is nearly ready for track works. But, this is Florida, where, **if the horse is well trimmed, he has little use for shoes.** Initially, I thought shoeing was necessary. Then I wondered why? I tried not shoeing and found it was much better for the majority of horses. However, if his white line is splitting or he has a specific need, shoeing should be considered.

Keep horses in training on a good trimming schedule. Use a simple trim. The line of the pastern should continue straight through the hoof. You take each foot individually and trim or shoe to its own characteristics. Some very simple drawings are included that encourage you to consider the horse, not an abstract angle someone has deemed as the perfect angle. Horse's feet are as individual as our own. Horses may have skinny "muley" feet, very shallow and platter-like feet, a great hoof wall, or weak hoof wall. Some are white (the "lore" being a white foot is a soft foot) and some are dark.

Feed supplements may help strengthen the hoof wall. Biotin with methionine is deemed helpful. Making sure your horse has all his trace minerals is a must. A clean dry stall is also essential. Check the old shoe of your horse if he's living in a stall or at the track. If you see erosion on the shoe where its sits on the hoof (usually by the nail hole), it is caused by ammonia from urine. This means the stall is not being kept clean and dry.

Have your horse jog barefoot on the road to see the natural wear down pattern of his hooves. A little concussion is good for the bones. It seems to be tradition to put training plates on the front of the horses and sometimes all the way around. If your area is rocky or hard, or your horse is chipping, by all means protect the hoof. **If all is well, don't rush into it.**

If the horse is crooked legged, shoeing can help his performance dramatically. If he hits himself when he runs - his front foot cutting his ankle, etc. - various shoes must be tried until the right combination is found.

As a new owner, do you know that your horse's shoes might cost more than yours, and that he needs a new set every six weeks? This is generally an extra expense on your monthly training bill and may run from $40 to $80 dollars or more, depending on your location and the complexity of the job.

I have wanted to start some of my young horses racing barefoot. However, the stewards tend to be somewhat inflexible. They say a horse that starts barefoot will have to race the entire meet barefoot. With that option, it was better to use shoes than risk putting my animals at a disadvantage.

Decide when to put on shoes after a gallop or two at the racetrack. Our local track is heavy and sand covered. Therefore, I have the farrier file down the toe grabs or put a rim shoe on. **Toe grabs can cause problems, especially on hard, unforgiving surfaces.** If your track is very hard and you have toe grabs protruding, the way the horse breaks over is changed. This is not as much of a problem on a heavier track that has "give."

Aluminum racing plates are generally used for racing. They are light weight and easy for the farrier to shape. If you turn your horse out with plates on, he'll sometimes catch himself while frolicking . . . the toe of the hind foot "grabs" the heel of the front foot.

Many, many foot problems are started in the name of good training.

That's the price I'm willing to pay for his peace of mind. Make your farrier aware of this. Having him make sure that the shoe doesn't hang over the heel of the foot will help. Bell boots, on the front, might help too.

Trainers at some tracks change the shoes if the track turns sloppy, or use one kind of shoe for turf and another for dirt. Changing shoes too frequently is not good for the wall of the hoof. **At some racetracks, you must get permission from the stewards to change the style of the shoe.** This is because the shoe style can impair or improve the horse's performance. One trainer I knew used heavy, thick steel shoes on his horse for all training and working. When race time came, he changed the shoes to light weight aluminum and the horse felt much more agile. His performance improved with the change. At today's major tracks, the trainer probably couldn't get away with such tactics.

Horses with hoof problems may need more frequent sessions and special treatments. There are many new products and innovative styles of shoes. It is important that your trainer be experienced enough to separate a gimmick or fad style of shoeing from a therapeutic, innovative device. Usually there will be university studies on innovations and rational testing to show the usefulness. Ask the trainer what the shoe is doing and see if it makes sense to you. If it sounds like witchcraft . . . draw your own conclusions.

My horses rarely have foot problems. I believe a great many problems are started by the enforced inactivity of an animal. Walking, grazing, and moving are integral parts of being a horse. Being overfed and forced to stand in a tiny stall all day and then asked to run guts out is sure to set up the horse for problems. The dark moist environment of a stall allows thrush and fungus to thrive. The Section on Bathing explains about dipping the feet in diluted bleach water or scrubbing the frog with a mixture of soap and bleach. This practice is a tremendous help in controlling fungal problems as are stalls with an outside paddock where the horse may choose to drop manure.

The combination of poor shoeing, lack of legitimate exercise, standing all day and overeating puts great pressure on the feet. Combine this with infrequent shoeing, coercing a long toe and no heel, and you will probably make a complete mess of the horse's feet.

Toe grabs on a hard surface may change the break over action

Right   WRong   WRONG

If you have specific problems, speak with the experts and read, read, read.

Many horses that have lived at the track for years before coming to my farm have very deformed feet. A horse that had been on the track for three straight years was sent to me suffering from persistent abscesses in his feet. They apparently tried to cure the abscesses with shoeing. This was a huge, beautiful, seventeen hand horse. He arrived with bar shoes. His feet were falling out of them. The feet wanted to grow larger than the shoes permitted. He was the equivalent of a Chinese woman with bound feet.

It was obvious that his feet were bothering him. The heels were so contorted and contracted they couldn't breath. When a horse moves, it is necessary for the hoof to flex. There was no way the hooves on this horse could flex with bar shoes. They were nailed in position. His heels were malformed and "contracted." His frog and hoof shape were completely distorted. When I told the owner he had been improperly shod, he commented that he had paid over $2,000 for shoeing in the last year or two.

The most important thing I did for this horse was pull off his shoes and have him constantly turned out and moving in deep sand. The sand was kind to his feet, and the movement allowed blood supply to reach the feet. After about eight months, the heels had started to relax and we could clean them without too much trouble. The abscesses had formed in the folds of the heels, surely due to the filth trapped there. Aggressive hosing helped stimulate blood flow and clean the area.

The same adage used for physicians applies to trainers. "Above all, do no harm!". There are many good books about shoeing. Make it a point to read some.

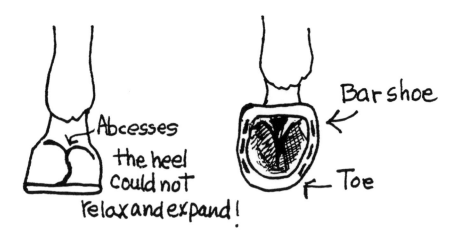

The basic principal of hoof repair is simple. Do whatever it takes to allow the foot to land flat and fly true. If one part of the hoof strikes the ground before the rest, trim away the "long" area or build up the short side with a degree pad.

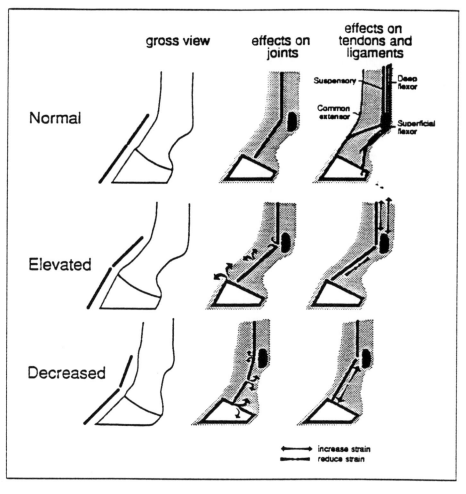

	gross view	effects on joints	effects on tendons and ligaments

Normal

Elevated

Decreased

increase strain
reduce strain

Effects of different hoof angles on the joints, tendons and ligaments of the lower forelimb. Increasing hoof angle flexes the two lower joints of the phalanges and slightly extends the third joint, while decreasing the hoof angle has the opposite effect on these joints. Lowering the heel increases tension on the deep digital flexor tendon, while elevating the heel decreases tension on this tendon and increases tension on the superficial digital flexor tendon and suspensory ligament.

This shows very clearly the effect hoof Angles have on the Joints!

Drawings appear in Legs, Bandages, and Shoeing. from Hoof Balance and Lameness: Improper Toe Length. Hoof Angle, and Mediolateral Balance, by Olin Balch, DVCM, PhD, Karl White, DVM, Doug Butler, PhD, CJF. FWCF and Sarah Metcalf, DVM, from the Compendium of Continuing Education, Practical Veterinarian 17 610: 1276-1283, 1995. Reproduced with permission.

The following debunking of some "Footlore" was published in **Equus Magazine** © 1995, Issue 219, (Reprinted with permission of Fleet Street Publishing Corporation) in **A Hoof-care Primer**, by Emily Kirby and Celia Strain. The article is well worth reading and keeping in your files.

Footlore and Truth

"Footlore - If horses' feet aren't cleaned out at least once daily, they will become diseased.
Truth - For horses confined to quarters with mucky footing, frequent cleaning may well be necessary, but horses living on clean earth probably enjoy some protection from the mudpack that remains undisturbed in their feet.

Footlore - Hoof length and angle can be manipulated to improve a horse's speed or performance.
Truth - Quite the contrary is true. Any shoeing manipulation that unbalances the foot or alters its natural flight pattern serves only to introduce awkwardness and undue stress into a performance. The shoeing changes that *do* improved speed and way of going are those that return balance and efficiency to the stride.

Footlore - White feet are weaker than dark feet.
Truth - The pigment granules injected into the horse as it grows from the coronet do make a dark hoof wall slightly more brittle and resistant to abrasion, but unpigmented horn is not inherently weaker. If this were the case, a striped hoof would alternate between strong and weak areas depending upon the color."

This shows how the hoof should fall when well balanced! ..

The essential goals of hoof management . . . are maximum efficiency of movement and minimum risk of unsoundness.

Drawings and text from *Land Flat, Fly True*, by Matthew P. Mackay-Smith, DMV, with Emily Kilby, *EQUUS Magazine*, 1995 Issue 197. (Reprinted with permission of Fleet Street Publishing Corporation).

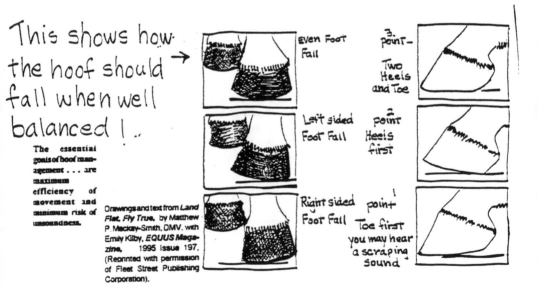

Even Foot Fall

Left sided Foot Fall

Right sided Foot Fall

3. point - Two Heels and Toe

2. point Heels first

1. point Toe first
you may hear a scraping sound

64

Shoe for balance and efficiency of stride.

THE DUCK FOOT

In Florida we sometimes use the term "duck foot" for the way many horses' feet start to look after years of shoeing with the mistaken belief that a longer toe will allow the horse to have a longer stride. The theory is that the long toe forces a horse to throw his foot out further, enhancing the length of his stride. (Obviously. If he doesn't fling the toe forward, he'll fall over it.) Making the toe longer puts more pressure on the tendons. Look at the mechanics. Isn't this is a perfect set up for bowing tendons?

With all the stress we put on the horse, let's not do more damage by fooling with the natural angle of the hoof. Long toes, high speed, and hard surfaces are a perfect combination for breakdown. Stand back and look at your horse while he is standing on a level surface. Have him trimmed to follow the healthy logical angle that keeps the hoof and pastern on the same line, as shown below. Thoroughbreds tend to have very little heel, so usually we are working on toes and maintaining whatever heel we have.

Equus Magazine©1991, Issue 170, contained a very clear article on hoof angles entitled *Balanced Hooves*, by Barbara Robbins. You can obtain this article by calling Fleet Street Publishing at 1 (301) 977-3900). The logic of good shoeing is discussed.

When in doubt . . . use your horse sense.

Hauling

Hauling and Shipping
  - Introduction

A Few Suggestions
  from an Experienced Hauler

A Few Suggestions on Loading

Equipment for Horses Being Hauled

HAULING AND SHIPPING - Introduction

When you are going to do your own hauling , you must be aware of the many pitfalls along the road. I have trucked over 400,000 miles and have learned a few things along the way.

First and foremost ... maintain your equipment.

Make sure your truck or hauling vehicle is large enough and strong enough for the load. Be sure your hitch is properly attached to the frame of the vehicle. **Make sure your hitch dealer is reputable and installs the recommended size hitch for the weight involved.** There are charts indicating the proper ratio of hauling vehicle wheel base to trailer length. **Never exceed the recommended limits.** In the old days, vehicles had real bumpers. Some hitches were attached to the bumper. Very bad, because the bumper was only attached to the car by bolts. For heavy duty hauling, a variety of hitches attached to the frame of the vehicle by bolts or welding are available.

When hauling a four-horse, bumper-hitch trailer with one or two horses, never put both horses in the rear of the trailer. **Always put more weight on the tongue to avoid fish-tailing.** If you have ever experienced the horror of fish-tailing, you know the sheer terror of having no control whatsoever over your vehicle. It is a hard way to learn about weight distribution. If you are hauling a two-horse trailer with one horse in it, put the horse on the left. No, not so you can look at him in your mirror, though that's an added benefit, but because on two lane roads it keeps the trailer more stable when there is no shoulder on the right. The horse's weight could cause the trailer to pull and slide off the right side. **Think stability!**

Always have rubber mats on the floor of the trailer. A little bedding on top not only gives the horses stability, it makes manure removal easier. You don't want your horse struggling to keep his balance because of poor footing. Horses seem to prefer having something to prop themselves against while traveling.

My horses seem to travel better when they have bars or walls to brace against. If you watch a lone horse rolling by you in a stock trailer, you'll notice that even though he has the whole trailer, he'll be braced against one side and corner to balance himself. If you are hauling one horse, put up the center bar to give him some support. Think about it. If you were standing in the middle of a trailer rolling down the highway, and had no use of your arms, how would you maintain your balance? Maybe by wedging yourself against something? **Any dividers between horses should have rug or rubber padding all the way down to the floor.** My very expensive trailer did not have this. Once a horse stepped on the coronet band of his neighbor. You cannot afford this kind of injury.. It is primarily a problem in trailers where horses travel side by side. In a slant load trailer the horses are staggered and do not seem to step on each other. Examine your trailer and install the necessary safeguards.

The black rubber bungee type straps used by truckers are excellent tie-downs in a trailer. They allow the horse movement but stretch and pull the horse's head back to where it should be. Put snaps on either end and clip one end to the halter and one to the trailer. A hay bin or a hay bag (the only place to use one) should be in front of the horse so that he can nibble during the trip. Be sure it is tied high enough so that a leg can't get tangled in it. Have extra lead ropes handy in case of emergencies.

**Keep your trailer clean and
in good repair**

Stress can predispose horses to disease, particularly respiratory disease when associated with shipping. The quality of air that the animal breaths during transport can affect the lungs. Gases, such as ammonia, carbon monoxide, and hydrocarbons, can impair the horse's ability to clear the lungs, hence setting the stage for illness.

If you are traveling in hot country, remember how much heat a horse's body creates. Always keep the windows open. Have you ever seen very closed-in trailers with no air circulation, rolling down the road in the summer? Did you wonder if the owners opened the trailer to find a horse with heat stroke? In hot weather keep the trailer open for breezes. If your windows are in the front of the trailer, make sure your horse is tied loosely enough to move his head out of the wind, if he wants. Never tie him so tightly that he can't drop his head, cough, sneeze and generally make himself comfortable. He can get a crick in his neck or back if he must carry his head in an awkward position.

The question of whether horses are better off facing front or back is often discussed. Sharon Cregier, PhD, in her book, *Alleviating Surface Transit Stress on Horses*, University Micro Films, Ann Arbor, MI, strongly recommends having horses face backward in transit. Although rear facing trailers are difficult to find, it is believed that horses travel better in them. You may want to investigate this option when buying new equipment.

My horses seem to like the equipment I have. Horses are pretty adaptable. They even stand sideways in some vans. The fashion in new vans and trailers seems to be at an angle, a slant load, which is okay, too. Don't worry unless you have a problem with a particular horse.

As long as the horse has good air circulation, and is not too hot or too cold, he should be all right.

A FEW SUGGESTIONS FROM AN
EXPERIENCED HAULER

When my teenaged sons were entrusted with the horses and equipment, they were told, "**Drive as if you have no brakes!**" Of course, this was a typical worried mother, forced to depend on the reliability of a seventeen year old. (My God, how could I?) But, actually, that is very good advice. **You must never think, even if you have super electric brakes, that you can haul a trailer with a horse in it driving the way you drive a car**. Zooming up to lights and having to stop quickly just won't do with a horse in the back. He'll be sitting beside you before you know it. Remember, his body mass is high. If you throw it around, it can be very unstablizing to the towing vehicle, and very hard on the horse.

If you drive as if you have no brakes, you'll shift cautiously up to speed, and try to coast down when coming to stop lights, downshifting if you have a manual transmission. This is better on your equipment and the horse. No sudden jerks to start and no hard braking to stop.

When you get into the vehicle to haul, take a moment to think. **Under no circumstances feel pressured or rushed.** If you are running late, accept that you will arrive late, and let it go. There is nothing more horrible than a trailer wreck with live animals.

Initially, I found hauling very perturbing. Driving my horses and children down the turnpike in torrential rainstorms, or trying to stay on a tiny two-lane road with giant semi-trailers breathing down my neck and having no place to pull over, was terrifying. I would imagine a horrible twisted wreck featuring my trailer in a mangled mess. It was necessary to make a conscious effort to block that image out of my mind and imagine myself arriving safely at the racetrack. When you get in your vehicle and are ready to start your trip, stop; close your eyes and image yourself arriving safely at your destination. Take a deep breath, remind yourself not to hurry and have a good trip! Over the years, I have had to force myself to concentrate on this kind of positive imagery. Don't disregard the dangers. Control them as best you can by driving safely and soberly with proper equipment.

It is impossible to avoid the summer thunderstorms in Florida. Go slowly and cautiously when you're caught in inclement weather. You can listen to good tapes for amusement. In the North, plan your racing and track training to coincide with the good weather. You probably don't want to be hauling on icy roads or in snow storms. Plan to train at home or lay up in the bad weather and run when the snow and ice is gone. **Work with the environment, not against it.**

CB radios are a big help when you are traveling in unfamiliar areas. Truckers give good advice on routes, traffic and conditions. The CB was essential, especially when I was broken down on the side of the road. Yes, this does happen, even with the best of care.

In my ten years of shipping into races, a race was never missed due to hauling problems. Being a female, and training from the farm, I was acutely aware of how bad it would be to miss a race because of an equipment breakdown. There have been close calls, such as a wheel falling off the four-horse trailer in the middle of the cane fields at ten o'clock at night. Luckily, a trailer repair-man made the mistake of answering his phone at eleven PM. He gave in to my pleas and worked on the axle, with the three horses in the van. We were back on the road by two am. The horses made the races in plenty of time. (We had to make the races. One

Drive as if you have no brakes!

of the horses was owned by a syndicate of five lawyers. All they needed was some kind of silly excuse such as a wheel falling off. . . Ha!)

Both of my trucks are capable of hauling either trailer at all times. You don't have to have back-up equipment if you are only training for yourself. **If you are a professional, you must have back-up . . . the worst possible things happen at the worst possible times.**

One of my trucks broke down three hours into the Miami trip. A call home and the other was on its way. Fortunately, I have great kids and wonderful neighbors willing to help me in a pinch. Another time, an engine, 5,000 miles beyond the 50,000 mile warranty, blew because of a faulty water pump. (On some diesels, this is a common occurrence every 50,000 miles.) Rather than arranging a tow home, I had the truck and horses towed to the racetrack 100 miles away. The time to worry about the truck was after the race . . . the horses came first.

Never, never, never unload a horse on the side of the road! If the horse is having a fit in the trailer, that's where he will have to have it. It would be worse to unload him and risk having him get away from you. He might run into the traffic and cause havoc. No matter what, keep the horse in the trailer until you are in a farm where you can unload safely.

Years ago, I kept Rompun, a tranquilizer, in my glove compartment for emergencies. There are very stringent rules about needles on the backside of the racetrack and I was afraid of entering the racetrack with anything like that. I have discussed this problem at length with the track vets, but found no solution. I just haul and pray. If you have problems with a hysterical horse, go to the nearest policeman, police station or fire station. They will help you find a vet in emergency circumstances.

Never feed a horse heavy grain before a trip. Give him hay along the way. If it is a long trip, give him a handful of grain every now and then so he doesn't think he is being starved to death. Always offer water when you stop. Generally, on a three-to-six hour trip, you'll only need to stop for gas and water. Feed your horse when he is settled at the track, the night before the race.

I go to Miami the night before the race, because the trip is five- to-six hours. The trip to Tampa is an hour and a half, so we go the day of the race. Birmingham is 12 hours away. On that trip, we stop for water, but never unload.

When shipping in to the track, it is handy to carry two water buckets and one feed bucket for each horse unless you are staying at or near the track. You only need one bucket of each if you are staying close enough to the track to check and water them frequently. In hot weather, they drink a lot of water and need two buckets of water in front of them. Take feed portions tied in plastic bags and already mixed with vitamins, etc., and a couple of bales of hay.

Have a complete set of equipment is on hand so that you are prepared at the track. A complete set of racing equipment (bridles, blinkers, etc.) is kept hanging on hooks in the back seat of my truck. An exercise saddle with extra girths and saddlecloths also lives permanently in my truck. Everything is ready to use. There is a complete grooming kit with brushes, tape, alcohol, and Vicks for the nose, tongue ties, and various little items. A separate set of equipment is kept at the farm. **If you don't own enough equipment for two full sets, make an equipment list. Check it twice before you leave to be sure you are prepared at the receiving barn.**

Will yourself to arrive alive.!

Have all the paperwork necessary to get through the stable gates: Coggins, health certificate, and registration papers. Try to be respectful and courteous to track personnel. This is not always an easy task, especially if you have been braving storms, bad traffic or crazy horses. When you get to the receiving barn, unload your horse as efficiently as possible. My routine is down to a science. It takes me fifteen minutes to unload, feed, tuck in four horses for the night, and hose out the trailer. Always clean the trailer. Ants are attracted to manure. They taught me the hard way to hose out the trailer immediately upon arrival.

Once at Calder, after a long day at the races, my four horses were loaded one by one in the big trailer. I was so eager to get on the road back home, that the swarm of red ants devouring manure went unnoticed. In the darkness the night before, I had failed to completely remove the manure. While pulling out of Calder, I heard a great deal of kicking and stomping in the trailer. I knew better than to ignore it, and pulled over. The horses were in a frenzy because ants were crawling up their legs and stinging them. I immediately returned to the receiving barn, unloaded all four horses, scrubbed and hosed them and the trailer. An hour later we departed again and arrived home very late that night.

When you embark on your travels, be calm, cool, and collected. Keep a few rousing tapes in your truck. *This Land Is Your Land, This Land Is My Land* is a great song to sing as you cruise across beautiful expanses of open countryside on your way to the track. Visitors accompanying me in the truck grumble about my off key singing and archaic music, but that's okay. It keeps me going. *Michael, Row Your Boat Ashore* always gets my blood pumping. It can keep me awake for an extra ten miles at the end of a long haul. Friends tell stories about trips from hell when referring to escapades where they were trapped for six hours in my truck enduring a gamut of music, from *If I Had A Hammer* to Tschaikowsky's *1812 Overture*. (Played loudly, the cannons sound like they are being shot from the back seat . . . guaranteed to wake you up if you are drowsy). These friends also complain about getting grease or a little dirt on their clothes when they help me load the horses. What are good friends for but to share exciting times; so what if they get a little sweaty or dirty along the way.

**Think of the fun you and your friends will
have when you all begin your
GREAT ADVENTURE!**

A FEW SUGGESTIONS ON LOADING

I have just come in from struggling with a horse that was not taught to load when she was young. Perhaps this is the best time to discuss loading techniques. **You must have obedient horses that load with no problem under all conditions in order to successfully train off the farm.** The ideal way to teach a horse to load is when he is very young and you can shove him around. Teach him eat in the trailer. Take a bucket of feed and have him follow you in or put mama horse in the trailer to eat. He will easily learn not to fear the DARK BOX.

Horses purchased at sales usually have not had much experience in loading. You may need ten strong men and a vet with a tranquilizer to get the animal into a small trailer. When you get him home, the first thing to do is teach him to load. If you have time, try leaving your trailer in the pasture. At feeding time, put the horse's food in the trailer. Begin with feed on the ramp. Move it further inside each day for a week or two until he is comfortable eating inside the trailer on his own. Then practice loading him at random times without enticement.

Unfortunately, I seem to receive horses that have been allowed to run free for two years, pulled in, run through the sale with the help of mood altering drugs, and then sent to me as the fuzzy haze from the drug wears off. By this time they are frightened of their new environment and react appropriately.

In such a situation where they must be loaded immediately, it is good to have two, or preferably three, strong men. **Begin with no prejudice about the horse.** I actually act as if I expect the animal to docilely enter the trailer with a slight tug on the shank. Have the trailer parked and attached to the truck in an enclosed field. If the animal gets loose, he will not be able to go far. The ramp should be easy to step onto and at a gentle angle. My first trailer did not have a ramp. The horse had to step up and into it. If your trailer doesn't have a ramp, don't worry. He can learn to step into it.

Horses apparently perceive the ramp as a bottomless pit. Their general reaction is, "Oh, boy, I'm not stepping on that!" They throw up their heads and pull back hard - horse body language for "No!" (Have a shank with a chain on the horse for these lessons. Put the chain is over the nose, never under the chin. That would encourage him to throw up his head further and rear on you.) At this point, yank hard on the shank and let him know you won't permit negative behavior (pulling back and refusing to do as you bid).

Teach loading early!

Use a twenty foot shank when loading. If a horse does pull it out of your hands, you can still grab it fast. Be very vocal with naughty horses. Say, "No!" sharply. If the horse continues to pull back, I'm of the school that says, "You want to pull back, then go back!" Yank, and if he continues to back up, continue to yank sharply on the chain. At this point it is probably better to put the chain over the gum, under the lip. (This seems to be an acupuncture point. Pressure on the gum may influence his behavior positively.) You don't want to do any damage, but you want this animal to respect you when you say, "No!"

The minute he stops pulling back, praise him and gently lead him forward. If he balks and pulls his head back again, yank hard. It is imperative not to allow the horse to get in the habit of pulling back and rearing to fight you. You must be firm about unacceptable behavior. **A horse that rears is a terrible danger.** When he stops pulling back, your helper can tap him on the rump to encourage the horse to go forward. When he does, he is praised and there is no pressure on his head. Never yank on the horse unfairly or in unfounded anger. It must always be clear that punishment is for negative behavior, not because you are having a temper tantrum.

It may take just five minutes or a couple of hours for the horse to realize that if he goes with you there is no pain, and when he fights you he is punished. When you get back to the ramp, and he still refuses to step on, go inside the trailer and pull and control his head while the two strong helpers lock hands behind his tail and literally shove the horse inside. Once he is in, close the doors quickly. Praise him and feed him. You can take him for a short ride. Then open the door and back him out, allowing him to turn his head to see where he is going. Walk him around for a minute and ask him to go back on the trailer. If he refuses, go back to step one and shank and yank until he is willing to obey. Usually, the fight is not as long or as difficult the second time.

This system usually works. Remember, **if you are going to start the loading process, plan to spend the whole day, if necessary, until you get the horse in the trailer.** If you give up before he is in, **you'll have double the trouble next time.** You may have the same situation getting him into water to swim, generally you will have a big fight the first time, then a few mini fights, then it gets easier, until the horse discovers that the trailer or the water isn't so bad after all.

Whenever it was time to work with a difficult horse, he was told, **it's the trailer or DIE.** Hopefully, he would get the message early, before we were both exhausted. The best time for loading lessons was when my sons, the six foot three cowboy type and the six foot four wrestler, were handy. One horse, Street Beat, knew how to load when he came to me. He was not afraid of the trailer. But he had a "Maybe I will, maybe I won't!" attitude. The horse pulled his trick one day in Miami, when it was time to load up and start the long trip home. Since I usually handled loading myself, I didn't expect a problem. He balked and became difficult. He acted like a horse's ass, backing into cars and doing all sorts of dangerous things. He seemed to know that I couldn't wale the tar out of him there. Finally, several strong men had to help me load him. I made up my mind he wouldn't pull that on me again.

The next afternoon, I called my son out and we began **THE GREAT STRUGGLE.** It was June in Florida. The humidity was easily equal to the temperature of 101 degrees. We started the loading process and the horse balked. We did my "if you want to back up, back

Never start a lesson you can't finish.

up" routine. He backed all the way to the fence before he would stop and come forward. My son, Nando, was driving him from behind. Every time the horse got near the ramp, he would balk. Again and again, we struggled. After an hour and a half, my son, the horse and I were standing there panting glowering at each other. The sweat was pouring off of us in buckets. Nando said, "Mom, do you think he could die in this heat?" I figured the horse was at least as sturdy as we were . . . and we weren't dead yet. I said, "Nando, I don't think so . . . but if he is going to die, he is going to die in the trailer!" Street Beat must have heard me, or decided that today we were not going to give up. He acquiesced, strolled into the trailer, and never balked again.

There is a mental game going on here. Horses are animals. If they can dominate you, they will. **You must dominate them mentally and convince them that you are physically dominant also.** You may need to use equipment to prove your point. Use what you must, but always be fair to the animal. **Many times they are legitimately frightened** . . . other times they remind me of my children between fourteen and twenty one . . . **stubborn and willing to test you every way they can!**

   **Horses respect those who command respect.**

SUGGESTIONS ON LOADING

Don't start unless you have the <u>time to finish</u> the job!

Assume the horse will cooperate!

<u>Praise</u> and <u>Reward</u> him when he obeys!

<u>Punish</u> him when he is bad.

"Yank and shank" if necessary!

Get him in the trailer, <u>feed</u> him, <u>pet</u> him, <u>praise</u> him.

Unload him.

Reload him.

Have a helper behind the horse to drive him forward.

Come on... you can do it!

EQUIPMENT FOR HORSES BEING HAULED

Various types of wrapping and bandaging exist for horses during travel. Personally, I prefer the neophrene boots that cover the leg from below the knee to over the hoof. They attach with velcro, fit nicely, and protect the coronet band as well as the lower leg. Using fleece and bandages is very time consuming if you ship frequently. You can put the shipping boots on in a few minutes and be ready to go. I use boots on the front legs only. Horses tend to fuss and kick, trying to get them off their hind legs. (That's my excuse . . . if you prefer, put them on all four legs.) The boots cost around $65 dollars a set, and are worth the investment. They can be washed and wear well. (A company called Tuffy Products Bighorn, Inc., makes them).

Beware, many horses have what are called "bandage bows". Bandages can slip or be put on too tightly and cause damage to the tendon. On a long trip, **someone must continuously check the wraps or the horse is better off without them**. One of the worst stories is about a trainer who wrapped his horses' tails so they wouldn't be rubbed raw on the trip. The van hauling the horses from Florida to the North broke down for several days. The horses were given food and water and were cared for, but no one thought about the tail wraps. When the horses arrived and the wraps were taken off their tails, it was too late. The blood supply had been inhibited. The horses lost their tails and the trainer lost his job. He surely never expected such a delay. Be very suspicious of wrapping for any period of time, unless there is a medical reason. Don't create problems. If the trip is long, some trainers pull the shoes and leave the horses barefoot. Be sure your horse has competent supervision when he travels. Shipping boots, bell boots and leg wraps all contribute to the safety and comfort of the animal if they are competently utilized.

Happy Trails!

PREPARE TO HAUL HORSES

Have the <u>correct equipment</u> for the job!

Have your <u>vehicles well maintained</u>!

Have the trailer <u>well padded and safe</u>!

Have <u>good air circulation</u> for the horses!

<u>Drive as if you have no brakes!</u>

NEVER DRIVE UNDER STRESS OR IN A RUSH!

Be prepared. Have <u>plenty of gas</u>!

Have your horses' <u>travelling papers in hand</u>!

Read the map!

Training Aids

Treadmills

Chart Keeping

Swimming

Heart Rate Monitor and Interval Training

TREADMILLS

My experience with treadmills is limited. According to what one reads, they are very useful for gathering data on heart function and general physical conditioning. Much information has been compiled about exercise physiology by having horses train on a treadmill. They have also been used to study horses with paralyzed flaps. It has been possible to film the actual flap movement during aerobic and anaerobic exercise. This information has enabled the veterinary community to understand how the flap actually works. Treadmills are also used to study blood chemistry while the animal is actually performing. In cold and snowy areas, when there are no other alternatives, they can be useful to keep horses exercised. A certain amount of muscle development can be maintained using a treadmill.

However, be leery of using a treadmill for fitness training a racehorse. When a horse is taken out and ridden, he develops various sets of muscles. He also learns skills for coping with the environment mentally and physically. **All the hours in the world on a treadmill will not help a horse walk out boldly in a field, or not be frightened by a covey of quail, a rabbit scampering, or a dog showing an interest in him. Nor will it develop the muscle and balance necessry to carry a rider while performing.** All elements must be dealt with in training. This means taking the young horse out and having him learn from experience.

Show people use the treadmill to develop certain muscles. Since our goal is to develop a useful, strong, resilient horse, real galloping is our best tool. Try to combine logic and common sense with scientific knowledge. A great deal of damage can be inflicted utilizing mechanical aids that are supposed to help. Think of a horse galloping on a treadmill. Can the breakover of the hoof be the same as on a natural surface? This alone could change his gait and put unnatural stress on the joints. Under certain conditions, the treadmill might be useful. A real gallop is preferable in my opinion.

**Use your common sense.
Choose what will work for you!**

DAILY TRAINING CHART — JUNE 1996

POSTER BOARD — Should be large enough to do whole month →

	1	2	3	4	5	6	7	8	9	10	11	12
Pregnant Mare		Trim		Bathe					Bathe ③	W	Bathe	
Mineola Gold	Raced- Calder	shoes Reset	quiet when Turned out	Better	Bouncing- HAPPY	R.P. good	Swim Feels good		Hard fast gallop here	W	Enter for Race?	Race? Miami!
2 yr old Colt	R. Pen	trim	Swim R.Pen	Ride① 3Miles	Legs OK	R.P. No saddle	Ride→ 7miles	No Filling Legs good	R.P. Legs good	W	Ride 3Miles Better / out	R.Pen Legs good ② Ride
2 yr old Filly	④ Runny Nose green mucus!	No Fever cough		mucus clearing-	No cough			R.P. No cough	Trail Ride 3miles Day	W	good Nough cough No shots / Bouncing	Trail ride 3miles good! Clean!

Very hot - horses in 10AM-4pm - Out at night! MANY Baths!

① He is silly - Looks at everything over reacts - very skitterish!

② acting better- goofy 1st mile but then settles in - some galloping and trotting!

③ watch out- itch starting on Back - Bathe after each Rain!

W = wormed with ivermectin on June 10th

④ Filly Has Bad cold + cough- green mucus- put vics- cleaned nose- Turned out in small pen- not near any other Horses- a little off feed!

Put any notes or special Treatments here- identify what was done- why

Your charts will show Trends!

USE to! Color Ink! HIGHLIGHT

CHART KEEPING

Charts are vital. You must write down all your observations. When you return from handling your horse, write down whether he was lethargic, pissy, or extremely bright, etc. A pattern will emerge indicating how your horse reacts to his training. **Your observations tell you how durable he will be** and how frequently he can race.

Since you are galloping or working every third or fourth day, your comments will tell a great deal about how he is responding physiologically to the insult and stress. Your comments will provide a base line reference as to the level of filling the horse has after work . . . slight amount on front and back . . . just a little in one joint only (beware). **Note any and every change.**

Write down Everything!

Your horse might have needed five days to rebuild from the first few three mile gallops. As you monitor, you might find he starts recuperating after three or four days. As his body becomes more efficient and competent with the training, he may soon recover the next day. Some light fillies are tuckered out for five or six days after a race. They only need to be turned out with a kiss on the nose and some nurturing between races. These are examples of the type of information you should put on the chart.

A sample of one of my charts is included. I use a large size poster board and line up the days of the month across it. Any comments that don't fit into the squares are put down below. Write down any work done on the horses; teeth, shoes, worming, etc. Different treatments may be highlighted with different colors.

Although these charts get pretty messy, they enable you to review past years and see how the horse evolved. You can see if there were signs early on that were missed. The chart shows this because notes about filling and heat are carefully kept. Your notes will show that some horses are consistently off their feed for a day or two after a work or race. You will note that others bolt out of the stall, leaping and carrying on the day after the race. Put it all down, and train accordingly. Be very, very specific in your observations about eating, attitude, soreness, edema, or heat. Knowledge about your animals is the key to keeping them sound and happy.

Good trainers are observant trainers!

SWIMMING

Swimming is excellent. It takes all the weight off the horse's joints and makes him feel good. Just mulching in the water is therapeutic. However, swimming should not be used instead of galloping to train a healthy horse. Galloping prepares a horse to be a runner.

Swimming is good for an injured horse, under certain circumstances. When a horse is recovering from bone trauma and the injury is still too compromised to allow him to be turned out to frolic and feel good, **swimming will help him get his blood circulating without the bone concussion** that would cause more injury. Having an injured horse jog in the water is good, too. The water deflects the concussion of the hoof striking the ground and the horse begins using his muscles sooner than he would in complete confinement. It's excellent also if the horse has had a temporary strain.

However, if your horse has open, festering wounds, it may be better to allow some degree of healing before you have him swim. These wounds should be hosed on a daily basis. Use your own judgement, as to the severity of the wound, in relationship to water. Salt water might be helpful. Avoid swimming "bleeders". It stresses their lungs so intensely, they may start bleeding immediately.

Horses that have foundered will get great relief walking, floating and moving around in the water. If the founder is severe, this might be the only relief they get from the pain. When First Prediction foundered, we put her on a 20 foot shank and let her float, while we sat on the dock reading or contemplating life. Doubtless, this water therapy helped her recover from the severe founder.

Use swimming the same way you use free roundpenning. It keeps a horse supple and allows cardiovascular exercise between gallops. It is especially useful in the summer, when it is a convenient way to cool the horses.

Between races, when a horse is "dead fit" and competing, he could swim every other day and be free roundpenned on alternate days. This keeps the horse fresh for races and relieves any soreness from the last race. If you have an old class horse with lots of aches and pains, swimming is probably good for him between races. This kind of horse needs to be kept healthy and comfortable. The races keep him fit. **He only needs recovery time after the races to rebuild from the trauma.** Used this way, swimming is a good maintenance tool.

Never use swimming as the only form of exercise.

The horse must always be turned out and allowed to move. Some farms religiously swim horses. They take them from the stalls, walk them to the pool or lake, swim them and put them back in the stall. This is not good. The horses' bodies are only developing swim movement patterns. Their bodies must also develop regular running patterns. They also need concussion to the bone to maintain its strength, integrity, and development. Therefore, **galloping, interspersed with free roundpenning and swimming is the recommended exercise program.**

If you don't have access to water, don't worry. Fortunately, my farm is on a lake. Our wooden dock was lined with conveyer belting in areas that might be dangerous. A floating dock was attached at the end of the stationary dock. To swim a horse, a shank is put on, and he is forced to swim around me while I stand on the floating dock. Some people swim horses out of small boats. I have no experience with this. If you have easy access to a body of water, enjoy it.

Swimming can be used as a treat for the horses, as a therapy for injuries, as a part of the training program, but never as their only source of exercise.

Go to farms that offer swimming and learn how to do it properly and safely

You can swim your horse in a lake by using a dock and teaching the horse to swim around it-

Rubber padding so horse can't go under dock

Swimming is refreshing and good exercise for a sore horse.

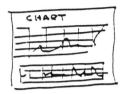

HEART RATE MONITOR AND INTERVAL TRAINING

Early in my training endeavors, I read everything possible and attended seminars. One seminar, held in Philadelphia, was on sports medicine. Tom Ivers was the main speaker. He was teaching "Interval Training". At that time, his program touted workouts every fourth day and miles of galloping on the other days. The horse was never given time off to rebuild. As a beginner, I thought it sounded like a good program. I used the heart rate monitor, but allowed for track "variations". My horses were galloping in heavy sand and hills. His were galloping on a flat predictable surface.

The interval training method encourages long slow miles, up to a point, and then many speed works within the galloping program. It contains very specific instructions on how to build up speed. The program emphasizes high tech monitoring and is quite structured. It depends on equipment which separates the trainer from his animal. **The trainer may focus on interpreting the numbers and ignore the physical signs the animal is showing.** The program is very aggressive, physically, for young animals. It requires many miles of galloping on a daily basis at the track. It is also very demanding for the trainers and exercise people. **Too grueling for man and beast.**

I was able to do the speed intervals with the proper distance, follow the spiking of the heart rate in full speed, observe how long it took to recover, etc. The most important information the heart rate monitor told me was that my training route certainly did "fit" the horses. Their recovery from sustained high heart rate was well within the recommendations. They were working harder and going slightly slower than they would on the racetrack, because they were carrying more weight and galloping in heavy sand. That was fine with me. Pure speed could be honed at the track. The monitor taught me they were cardiovascularly fit.

However, we must keep in mind that we are training a complete body, not just the heart and lungs. My horses lost tremendous amounts of weight, even though they consumed huge quantities of feed. They also developed swelling in the fetlocks if they did the recommended speed works and gallops. If they rested a day or two, they came back with a better attitude and were much fresher. During the third stage of Ivers' program, they seemed to be over drilled and would go off their feed. **The problem with the program stems from demanding too much speed too frequently.** This holds for racing, also.

In the third stage of interval training, you are asked to give tremendous amounts of feed and gallop many, many miles. I believe my methods are kinder to the horse and trainer. At that time, Tom said that a horse in his program will be doing five-eighths of a mile with faster and faster works, honing into five furlongs in a minute two, a minute one, a minute, fifty nine seconds, etc. There are horses that, on their best day, with the best training in the

Never over train.

world, can't deliver five eighths of a mile in a minute flat, or a minute one or two, etc. If his training were that consistent, every horse Tom put through the program would become a champion. There are many basically untalented horses that show good conformation, heart rate, etc. Unfortunately or fortunately, talent and other undefined qualities come into the picture .

Before trying Tom's methods, my horses were galloping about ten miles a day, and I'm not light. I have never been under 160 lbs. (God, what an admission!) I had been a recreation director, and felt drilling and pushing, etc., would work on horses as well as it did on humans. This was a mistake. **Horses and humans do not develop equivalently.** One of the most important differences is that **the horse has a built-in overdrive system.**

According to *A Marvel of Design* by Karen Kopp Du Teil, *EQUUS Magazine,*©1992, Issue 180, (Reprinted with permission of Fleet Street Publishing Corporation) the equine spleen stores an emergency supply of red blood cells, amounting to a third or more of the body's total supply. When the horse gets excited, his adrenal glands release adrenaline , the "fight or flight" hormone, which tells the spleen to contract and release its reinforcement troops into the blood stream. The horse is unique in that his innate built-in "fight or flight" ability has been honed through the centuries. When he needs a surge of power, his spleen kicks in and he is given an extra shot of red blood cells. This in turn can increase his oxygen intake nearly 35 times from rest to run. By comparison, human athletes are highly trained to develop their oxygen delivery capacity. At the height of their training, they can only increase their oxygen intake about 10 times. **Therefore, the horse is a natural runner and his training is to enable him to sustain his gift of speed.**

Based on my observations from galloping my own horses for about 18 years, I do not believe that works or races every four days, with miles of galloping in between, make the horse faster. It may make him stronger or more fit, but it wears down his brilliance of speed in the process. **He doesn't have time to rebuild from the trauma of an honest work or race to replenish red blood cells and release fatigue toxins.**

When I had sets of four or six horses, they were "insulted" (stressed), and then rested and allowed two to four rebuild-days to rest and recuperate, depending on the phase of training. As explained in the training chapters, **the rest days are vital for the rebuilding process.** Turnout and free roundpenning are my way of allowing them free but loosening up time.

Tom Ivers' interval training is highly intense; and remember, we're working with animals that have brains, personalities, various likes, dislikes, and tendencies. None fit into the heavy training schedule completely. **Controlling to the second every work on a given day is asking a lot from horse and rider.**

I hate to tell you some of my predicaments, while trying to read the heart rate monitor strapped to my thigh, control the horse and keep the electronic leads underneath the girth, where they would give an accurate reading. It must have looked hilarious. We barely missed the trees many times when I was concentrating on the numbers instead of the horse.

Tom says each horse is slightly different and that his training should be adjusted accordingly. I agree. There are many ways to train. **The monitoring did help me assess and understand the horse's cardiovascular system.** Usually the horse's physical signs provide the same information, if you know how to interpret them. **The horse's attitude and body will indicate to you his readiness to do another round**. Horses brought up with a solid incremental foundation ease very nicely into speed logically and naturally. Let them tell you what they are physically able to do.

The horse's "fight or flight" ability has been honed through the centuries.

The heart rate monitor is a good device to measure an individual's recovery time. It teaches you about cardiovascular function. You can train quite well without it. There are subtle changes going on in the horse that don't register on the monitor until it is too late, such as fractures, etc.

Another thing I learned with the heart rate monitor was that on extremely hot days, after the exercise, the horses would continue panting although the monitor showed the heart rate was back to normal. Why? The horses were trying to cool off. The panting was lowering their body heat.

A group of horses that I had trained following Tom's methods were sent to Chicago. They were two and a half years old and were honed, not an ounce of fat on them from miles of galloping. When they arrived in Chicago, the track trainer was upset. He felt they looked gaunt. (The stress of the trip probably made them a little dehydrated.) I told him to allow them a few days to recover from the trip and to gallop them. He followed the instructions, then called and said, "They certainly are the most fit horses I've ever received." I learned that having a horse that honed was not appreciated. I had done three times as much work as any other trainer, and the track trainers weren't really happy. The trainer told the owner the horses needed more weight (fat) before he would continue training.

All the galloping in the world does not make a horse run faster than he is able to run. Therefore, it is imperative that as a trainer, **we seek the way to allow the horse to develop his own natural speed without breaking him down**. Our main job is to do no harm along the way.

My overall view of interval training as taught by Tom Ivers in *The Fit Race Horse* is that it is entirely too much work, too much stress on the limbs, and too much feed being passed through the horse. Over all, it is **too intense a program for a young horse.**

Although I don't agree with all of Tom's methods, there is a great deal of extremely valuable information for both owners and trainers in his books. They are fun to read and were invaluable to me. My program evolved from a combination of training programs and experiences. It is incremental and track training interspersed with rest, common sense, and hands-on monitoring.

Let the horse tell you what he is physically able to do.

A chain
shank is a
useful aid in
controlling fractious horses!

BASIC TRAINING

WEANLINGS TO EIGHTEEN MONTHS - GROUNDWORK

YEARLINGS - EIGHTEEN TO TWENTY-FOUR MONTHS

TWO-YEAR-OLDS - AT TWENTY-FOUR MONTHS

MR. BLUEJEANS

WEANLINGS
TO EIGHTEEN MONTHS -
GROUNDWORK

If you are raising your own foals, a good book to read about handling them from birth is Dr. Miller's *IMPRINT TRAINING OF THE NEWBORN FOAL* If you have bred your own horses and have some youngsters out in the field, here are a few tips that might help them develop into better racehorses. If you have a big field, chase the youngsters or throw dirt at them to encourage them to run the perimeter of the field in a group. You can observe a lot about their personalities, learn which are dominant and which are not. By encouraging them to run, you have also already started the process of disciplined galloping.

When handling weanlings, make a special effort to teach them to lead like young ladies and gentlemen. Have them walk in and out of places like trailers and accept being tied. The drawing in the Wash Rack Section shows you how horses should be tied in order to allow you to control them . . . or let them loose if they are in a panic.

Our foals are raised on a cattle ranch. At birth they are in a paddock next to a landing strip. They soon become accustomed to the noise of airplanes. The landing strip is also used for culling, cutting, and working cattle. Although this is a lot of commotion for the foals, they adapt very well. As weanlings, Lois begins taking them for walks. She starts by taking them a few steps from their paddock and slowly encourages them to walk around the barns and machinery. We feel that this gentle exposure to the world enables them to accept the bustle of the track. A word of warning: Be extremely careful if you decide to walk your weanlings. Their size makes them easy to control, but you do not want to hurt them or teach them to be afraid of strange places and sounds. Also beware of permitting cute antics which could be dangerous later on. You must teach confidence and discipline.

It's good to teach weanlings to stand at attention and be confined while still very young. You can save a lot of tough training time by teaching them that it's natural for you to lean on them, rub your hands up and down their legs, lift their feet, and generally hang all over them. All of this ground work accustoms them to being handled, which eventually becomes second nature to them. If you have a trailer, this is a good time to feed them in it once in a while and take them for a ride.

Even as weanlings horses can learn voice commands, such as "NO!" for negative behavior. Don't expect too much more from them . . . they're just babies. Horses are animals God designed to be grazing or constantly moving. Try to keep them as close to their natural behavior and environment as possible.

Providing a natural environment is the foundation of my training. Horses are natural herd animals. They like to be together, to jostle each other, to scratch each other on the back, and to horseplay. Eventually, it will become necessary to isolate them in their stalls. We want to put that off as long as possible.

Let them learn as many social interaction skills as they can.

YEARLINGS - EIGHTEEN TO TWENTY-FOUR MONTHS

Before we start, I want to remind you that your goal is to develop a strong horse that will be able to run for years. You are not preparing your horse to run as a two-year-old. You will begin his career later. If he has talent he can run for many years.

Start yearlings with what I call free roundpenning. Free roundpenning is done in a rather large corral or small paddock without putting a lunge line on the horse. With a long whip, encourage the animal to gallop around the perimiter. Ask him to gallop steadily two to five minutes at a time, alternating directions. By doing this once a day, or once every couple of days, you **encourage their bodies to learn the discipline of galloping at a sustained speed for an extended period of time**. Even as yearlings, we want them **to start developing their racing muscles**. By nature, horses like to frolic. They stop and start, run in spurts, and whirl around. By imposing just a little bit of discipline on that natural activity, you encourage development of the galloping muscles. In addition, you can begin to establish a few halter training points. After their gallop, they should be taught manners; how to walk, stop and back up on a lead. Always be sure to handle and rub their entire body.

Only free roundpen. Lunging young horses in tight circles puts excess torque on green bone and can cause sore muscles and bone problems. People spend thousands of dollars breeding the best horses for potential speed, then inhibit their natural ability with counterproductive training.

To free roundpen, use an area at least 100' x 100'. Smaller circles are too tight. Use as large an area as you want. At the ranch, we use a paddock about 100' x 160' (Lois needs the exercise). If the paddock is too large, the horse will outsmart you and stand in a corner, unless you chase him. Makes me wonder, "Who is roundpenning whom?" But maybe you need the exercise too.

Initially, your yearlings can be free roundpenned in a group of the same sex. When they get older, they should be worked separately, because they frolic wildly and will kick each other. **There is a danger in galloping horses together at any age**. By the same token, **it teaches them to handle other bodies in close proximity**. Even if they get bumped or bruised, they have a good six to ten months to heal. It is important for them to learn to gallop and carry themselves together in a group. Many people will disagree on this point, but I believe in the school of hard knocks. **In my experience the more interaction the horse is exposed to when young, especially socially, the better adjusted he will be when he goes to the racetrack.**

When Thoroughbreds are what we term ''hothoused'' and prepped for sale, they are separated from their friends and not allowed to play with anyone or be turned out. I remember buying a yearling at a sale. I brought him home and put him in a medium size paddock that had a four-board fence. A horse was on the other side of the fence. When the new horse arrived, he was turned loose. He looked around in amazement. As the neighboring horse came over to say, "Hello", the yearling took one look at him, turned around, crashed through the four-board fence and galloped down the road. He was terrified of seeing another animal coming toward him.

Don't rush! You want your horse to last many years.

Fields are a safe place for your horses if the fences are good and strong. The animals will get to know their environment. The general consensus seems to be that, when a horse is up for sale, nicks and scratches will detract from his overall value. Therefore, the poor yearling is kept in isolation to keep him pretty. In addition, yearlings are given all the food they want to fatten them up. This is where many future problems commence. A diet too rich in protein and calcium can start bone problems that appear later! Presented groomed and polished, these yearlings certainly look very beautiful for the sale.

About November or December in the yearling year, it's time to tack. Begin with the headstall and bit - no reins. Leave it on for several hours at time for a couple of days until he eats and drinks normally with the bit in his mouth. Make sure there is nothing in his stall-paddock area that he can hang himself on. Wearing the bit for a few days teaches the horse to accommodate the bit in his mouth. Eventually it will become second nature to him.

Now he graduates to a surcingle. Begin in a small paddock. Let him wear the surcingle for a couple of days, when he is turned out in the paddock. You can use a pad with the surcingle for more comfort. After he is accustomed to the surcingle, add reins to the headstall. Pass them through the rings on the surcingle, buckle them on top, and free roundpen. Avoid restraining the head with the reins. Leave them very loose.

When our student accepts this equipment, he graduates to a saddle. Put the saddle on for a few hours at a time and let the horse loose in a paddock. When he is fully accustomed to the tack, he can be free roundpenned.

My preference is to start with a western saddle, without any stirrups but with the floppy fenders. This rig weighs a good 30 to 40 pounds. When the fenders flop, the horse probably will buck initially, but he will get used to it.

Next put on the snaffle bridle again. This time run the reins through the hole in the pommel and over the saddle horn and free roundpen.

Some trainers like to "bit-up" a horse using the lunge line. They make the horse gallop in either direction with the surcingle and bridle "setting his head". My feelings are that a horse should not be forced to carry his head any tighter than is comfortable for him. Therefore, I do not lunge in this fashion. Racehorses should not have their natural movements restricted this early in the training process, especially their head movement. They should learn to carry their heads naturally.

Observe your horse's natural way of going.

In some areas, shoes aren't necessary for young horses. Keep hooves well trimmed at a natural angle. Remember that the natural angle is the angle where the hoof continues on a straight line through the angle of the pastern. (See Section on Shoeing.) A competent farrier can help you. If the horse has a particular problem with his feet, or has splitting hooves, use protective front plates. If you have a rocky soil or hard surfaces and must use shoes, by all means do so. I personally try to avoid shoes until the last possible minute.

Late in the yearling year, you should not be doing enough work to strain your horse. You are free roundpenning him only 15 to 30 minutes every third day at most and giving him time to rebuild. "No pain, no gain," is a saying that is true to a certain degree with young horses, but it is better to wait an extra day than to rush them. If you follow the every third or fourth day training schedule and turnout, you provide two or three rebuild-days to evaluate the effect of the training on his body.

You must be very thorough in your evaluation. Feel his tendons, sesamoid bones, suspensory ligaments, knees and ankle joints. The day after you free roundpen him, it is very important that you observe whether your horse has a tendency to be congested in his lower leg near the ankle and whether he is carrying fluid in the tendon sheaths. If he does, it is the reaction to the stress you have given him. Don't worry. After a day or two of rest, it should go away and his legs should be tight. When his legs no longer show filling and his skin is nice and firm around the tendons, usually by the third day, you can resume training.

A late yearling with no weight on his back should not show any kind of physiological change in the front legs. Swelling may commence later, as you start more aggressive training with weight on his back.

Many trainers tend to be too aggressive and demand too much, too soon. Remember, the horse does not need to be fully developed for racing until his third year. You want to develop him to bring out his full potential. Day by day you demand a little more and allow him to come back stronger. This is a very logical and easy process, if you have patience and do not force him physically or mentally. Don't ask him to gallop or behave too long. At this point he has a short attention span and you do not want to push beyond it.

Young horses have a short attention span!

Always praise and leave your training on a positive note.

Free Roundpen
with Saddle and Bridle

Until your horse is about 24 months old, he only needs to be free roundpenned every third or fourth day with rest and turnout time for rebuilding in between. Have him gallop a good steady, level gallop five to ten minutes in either direction. After the training he received as a weanling, he should be used to having his feet cleaned, being bathed, groomed and loaded into a trailer. Now your horse has learned to respect the bridle. He has gotten bucks and kicks out of his system and accepts a certain amount of restriction with the bridle and saddle. Be sure you always use good equipment. It would be a bad lesson for him to learn that he could buck off a saddle and potentially the person on it.

As your horse approaches 24 months, you will have to consider whether or not to geld him. To be or not to be is the question. We all nuture the dream of finding the super horse who will win races, stand at stud, and be a famous sire. In reality these horses are few and far between, and the market is full of good sires. So you must be realistic and decide if you want the hassle of handling and keeping a stallion.

If you do decide to geld, you might be interested in an article Lois ran across about castrating cattle. The article mentioned that testosterone is the inhibiting agent in the body's production of growth hormones. Consequently, animals that are castrated very young never close or solidify the growth areas on the long bones. They continue growing, which is why they may be taller. Therefore, their muscles also become longer and more svelte, and the animal may look slightly feminine when compared to the non-castrated animal. This article raised several questions in our minds. We wonder if horses respond similarly to castration. If they do, would having an open growth area be a source of weakness in the legs of a racehorse? We are seeking answers to these questions and encourage you to do the same. We will share our findings with you via the Newsletter, as soon as possible. One conclusion we reached was to allow our colts to be at least 24 months before gelding.

Another interesting consideration regarding gelding is mentioned by Ruth B. James, DVM, in her book *How To Be Your Own Veterinarian (sometimes)*. She suggests that a good time to begin riding your horse is immediately after he is gelded. He will need 30 to 60 minutes of exercise daily to avoid inflammation and aid the healing process. Rather than free roundpen him, start riding. His discomfort may keep him from trying to send you into orbit.

Free roundpen and turnout!

TWO-YEAR-OLDS - AT TWENTY-FOUR MONTHS

As your horse is nearing 24 months, there is a certain escalation in his training. It is a natural progressive evolution that allows the horse to graduate to carrying weight on his back. If you just got your horse, and he has had no training, give yourself a month or two for teaching him the ground work discussed in the Yearling Section.

Remember there are many wonderful systems of training. If you have one that works for you, use it. My suggestions are for those who really don't know how to begin. **You must have strong riding and training experience if you plan to train your own horse. Do not attempt to train if you are not an extremely competent horseperson.**

A two-year-old can carry a pretty large person. I was intimidated by an article that said no one over 90 lbs should ride racehorses in training. I weighed substantially more. I have found, through experience, that a young horse can carry a lot of weight . . . if it isn't for too prolonged a period of time . . . or too fast. If you weigh 150 to 160 lbs, you can start riding your horse when he is between 24 and 28 months.

Before you mount your horse it is **imperative that you put on your safety helmet.** This cannot be overemphasized. There are many different helmet styles. Any reputable tack shop sells them for sale.

When you mount your horse, remember to make all movements very clear. Be very patient with him. Try to think like the horse. Never punish him for something he fears. If he is disobedient on purpose, say, "No!" and punish him firmly.

With young colts in particular, I look them in the eye, say, "No!", and shake my finger. I observe whether or not they tend to be respectful. If not, I brandish a whip. You must be very careful not to accept negative behavior in a two-year-old. They are like teenagers. They will try anything and everything until you draw the line. **It is much easier to draw lines before they get bigger, stronger, and smarter**. Their respect for you has to start now!

Since you are starting to ride, everything you do with the horse is crucial. Every movement you make must be very clear. He must not take advantage of you in any way, shape or form. Start to ride your horse for 15 minutes every other day, for the first month. Riding every day, or even every third day, is acceptable. The frequency is not crucial, at this point.

Do not allow bad habits to commence.

During the first month, ride him in a large pasture. Teach him to stop, turn around and back up. You might try some figure eights, at a trot. Use any solid basic training method. Jim Lyons, Pat Parnelli and others have excellent methods for breaking horses. Basically, get him to understand all of your commands and to respect you. After a month or two, when you feel he is cooperating, you can walk, trot, canter, and do figure eights. Then you can begin Trail Riding. (Phase I)

Teach Respect!

Positive imaging is very handy, when riding a two-year-old. Horses are somewhat psychic. If you are riding a two-year-old , and you see a piece of paper blowing in the wind or a cloth flopping in the wind, your natural instinct is to think, "Oh, my God, he is going to shy." What you do instead, is think very positively and "image" your horse obeying you and going by that blowing cloth or paper. Put an image in your mind, and **mentally will the horse** to go right by whatever it is that frightens him. **You give him the courage to do it.** If you tense up and expect him to shy, he will fulfill your expectation, because that is the message you have transmitted. It is a real challenge and exercise of mind over matter for you to override your natural fear of the horse acting up, when logically he might. You must will him, with a tremendous mental power and body language, to go on and through whatever is frightening him. He must obey your commands and do what you command.

My daughter had a horse named Mullikin Stu. She wanted to jump with him, but he had her over a barrel, because she was afraid he would balk at the jump. She would get on the horse thinking," He's going to balk, he's going to refuse to jump." Mullikin sensed her anxiety. He'd come up to the jump and refuse it, because it was the message he received. It took a lot of work to encourage my daughter to believe that this horse was going to jump over the fence. When she reached a fence, she learned to whack him on the behind while thinking, "YOU WILL GO OVER THIS FENCE." Mullikin obeyed the command and they had no further problems. You must achieve this attitude with your horse.

The importance of being mentally positive and powerful, when you are teaching horses, cannot be overemphasized. It has nothing to do with body size. The smallest jockey can handle the largest horse. It has to do with a knack and finesse in handling the animal.

Be aware that your mental attitude is quickly transmitted to and adopted by your horse. If you are angry, sad, annoyed, or upset, the horse will sense and reflect or react to your mood. This can commence a vicious circle. It sets the stage for negative behavior, an unproductive training session, or worse yet a setback in your training.

Teach respect gently, but firmly.

There is a great deal of equipment out there to help you. I must admit to always using a lead rope with a chain over the nose on my horses. Before you jump to any conclusions, you are welcome to come and see that none of my horses have a ridge of scar tissue from chain abuse. It is seldom necessary to shank a horse hard, but when it is necessary, I can if the chain is there. Most of the time, my horses are docile and completely willing to cooperate. Very early in their training, they learned the ground rules. They must obey me, they must go where I tell them to go, and they must follow where I lead.

One of the most important things for you to learn at this point in training is regular **daily monitoring of legs**. You will be asked to make this a nearly religious habit throughout all phases of training. My daily monitoring pattern for two-year-olds, when they begin to be ridden, is as follows:

The first day, before you ride him familiarize yourself with his legs by running your hands around the knees, down the front of the cannon bone and around the ankle. Then go to the back of the knee and run your hand down the back of his leg. Learn how your horse feels. His tendons and the skin over them should feel very tight. You should not feel any edema, pockets of fluid, or sponginess. You should be able to cup your hand under the fetlock and feel very firm bone and tissue. This is a two-year-old, who should have no infirmities, swelling, or problems. When you ride him, which is only for about 15 or 20 minutes, your goal is to get him to obey you at a walk, trot, stop, etc.

The next day, in the morning, particularly if he is stalled up during the night, you must monitor his legs again. Run your hands over the knees, the cannon, the shins, down the back of the tendon and cup around the fetlock. On the day after you start riding your horse, or sometime within the first month, you may notice a little edema where you cup your hand under the fetlock or around the ankle joint. **It is normal to have some filling the day after you exercise your horse.** All you do is feel it and say, "Okay, he has some edema." and note it on his chart. Don't ride him, just turn him out. He needs rebuild-time. The next day bring him in and monitor his legs again. The edema should be down, or almost down. It should certainly be less than the previous day. **You are learning how to monitor your horse's response to the training stress you are giving him.** Usually, by the third day the edema is gone and his legs are nice and tight. **This tells you his body is adapting to the "insult"**

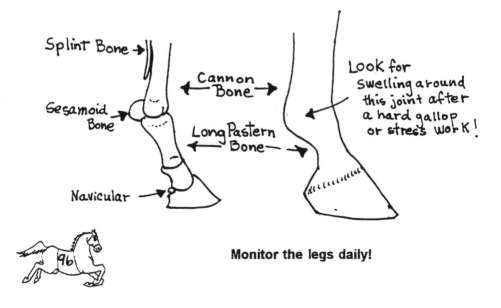

Monitor the legs daily!

you are giving to his system. "No pain, no gain." This animal will become strong and gradually adjust to carrying weight without damaging himself physiologically.

Often when people find edema the day after a horse has been ridden, they want to put on leg bandages. **Do not put bandages on two-year-olds when they have edema that is related to new work.** Monitor the situation. Within three days the edema should be gone and you can ride him again. Stress him again, by riding him 15 or 20 minutes. Don't worry if he has edema again the next day. **You will find that the horse will slowly and surely adapt to the work he is doing.** As he becomes accustomed to the work, increase the time you are riding him - just don't overdo it.

A certain amount of fluid retention around the sesamoid bones, where you cup the fetlock is perfectly normal, in front and rear legs. The filling should be equal in the two front leg joints, but not necessarily equal to the filling in the two rear legs. It is only mild congestion in either set of legs and is nothing to fear. **Frequently, you will find more congestion in the front legs.**

The horse's legs should not be congested in the first month. As you progressively increase training, you will increase tissue insult. **As long as you do not ride the horse until after the**

Long before a horse is obviously lame he may have filling and heat in the joint! Learn to read EARLY SIGNS

Feel the Knees, Ankles and Tendons every day Observe them before Training and after Training

edema is down, you will not harm your horse. The physiological change that you see and feel in the legs is a perfectly normal adaptation to the incremental stress of race training. If the horse only gets acute edema in one leg, or shows acute lameness or soreness, you are dealing with a different problem and should address it.

For this preliminary Basic Training, work on having your horse obey commands while you ride him. He must be controlled. You must be able to stop him and to turn him. Don't leave your confined area until you both understand the basics.

Now you graduate to the Trail Riding Phase.

GOALS BASIC TRAINING

Have horse comfortable being
handled, bathed, led, and saddled.

Feed in the trailer at times.
Hopefully, he will enter
the trailer quietly.

After he is 18 to 24 months,
<u>free roundpen</u> in a large area
every <u>third</u> or <u>fourth</u> day.
Do about five minutes in each
direction at a gallop - or until
he gets into a good sweat.

FEEL AND MONITOR JOINTS!

Establish what is
"<u>Normal</u>"
for your horse!

Keep young animals <u>outside</u> and
running <u>free</u> as much as possible.

MR. BLUEJEANS

Mister Blue Jeans

This Section is for the "over the hill" trainers who can no longer ride their own two-year-olds. At 50-something, I must find ways to get the job done without injuring my body. I no longer ride two-year-olds. Since my children are grown and gone, good help is sometimes hard to find. It has been necessary to evolve a way of preparing the 22-month-old yearlings for riding without getting hurt. Saddling them with a 60 pound western saddle and free roundpenning them every third day is a good beginning. From the ground I can teach them to go forward, stop and turn. As they progress, it is possible to find riders willing to work on weekends. For the midweek training session, Mr. Bluejeans rides the western saddle. Mr. Bluejeans is easy to come by and to work with.

You take an old pair of sturdy bluejeans, tie or sew each leg at the bottom and fill them with sand. When they are full, tie the waist and bingo - a midweek rider. Be careful. Don't develop a hernia trying to lift this 80 pound load of sand onto the saddle. You'll find a way.

Once Mr. Bluejeans is mounted, you tie his legs to the stirrup flaps and his waist to the horn. Then off he goes. The horse is now free roundpenned with at least 140 lbs of weight on his back. Twenty minutes of galloping with Mr. Bluejeans' weight flopping around, gives the horse's structure the weight-bearing stimulation it needs. The horse also learns to accept weight without fighting a live rider.

Be innovative. Seek solutions. A friend of mine had saddle pads made to carry lead weights. He put weight on his horses that way. Always bear in mind the goals you want to achieve. Then find a way to achieve those goals within your budget, in spite of less than ideal circumstances.

You do what you have to do! Mr. Blue jeans can help!

Innovation can solve many problems.

99

THE THREE PHASES

OF

INCREMENTAL

TRAINING

Introduction

Phase I - Trail Riding

Phase II - Aerobic Fitness

Phase III - Speed Development

THE THREE PHASES OF INCREMENTAL TRAINING - Introduction

You have a green-broke two-year-old, at this point. He has been worked in a relatively enclosed area. For a month or two he's been taught manners. He's learned to stop, back up, do circles at a walk, trot, canter, and do figure-eights at a trot. **Now you're ready to embark on an eight-to-ten month journey to make a racehorse out of him.**

It is imperative that you understand your Training Program. **You only saddle and ride your horse every third or fourth day. The other days are "rebuild-days". These are days that the horse is not saddled. He is primarily turned out.** However, you may want to swim, roundpen, teach loading, or any other lessons your horse needs. **These "rebuild-days" are vital, even when he is racing. This is his rest time, the time he needs to recover and rebuild.**

To better understand the concept of incremental foundation training, think about blisters on your own hands. If you are not accustomed to hard work (maybe you spend your days at the office) and then decide to do some gardening one day, using the shovel usually creates blisters on your palms. You can only do so much before the pain of the blisters tells you the tissue can't take any more trauma. You call it a day. A few days later you notice that calluses have started to form where there were blisters. Your hands are tougher and you can return to your task. If you gradually increase the time you work with the shovel, always allowing your hands to heal between sessions, you soon have tough hands with hard calluses that are able to handle heavy labor.

This training program uses the same process. **A young healthy horse is given incremental stresses to judiciously "challenge" his body.** It is the equivalent of callusing or toughening the joints and sinews of his structure. If you don't stop shoveling when your blisters start to form, you begin to destroy the tissue and ruin your hands.

With horses, if you continue training and pounding a horse that is showing a reaction to the stresses on his body (slight filling in the joints), you begin to destroy the tissue and joints. **Never overstress the body in the process of toughening**. That is why monitoring the joints is so important. You observe how the body is adapting to the increase of stresses on it. Horses that never show a reaction to the stresses can continue with training. Horses that develop inflammation need time for their "blisters" to heal before the training continues.

Under no conditions should you medicate or wrap a horse that shows this normal response to the stresses on his body. He only needs to be turned out and allowed movement until he is ready to go again.

Think of the calluses on your hands. They were blisters until they became the tough hard skin that could tolerate heavy work. **No physical reaction ... no adaptation to more work!**

To achieve this incremental foundation building, the training is divided into three Phases. Each Phase has it's own logical goals, but is flexible, in terms of time, to allow for individualization.

In Phases I and II, from 24 to about 30 months, you are going to deal with going three miles at a walk and trot with some galloping. **You will progressively increase the galloping every third or fourth day, until your horse can do a solid three miles in a relaxed gallop.**

NO PAIN - NO GAIN!

This will take about six months and is the goal in Phase II. You will have ridden over various terrains, up and down hills, and included many left and right turns. **Your horse will have learned natural lead-changing, and will have developed superb balance and surefootedness.** His mental attitude will be excellent and keen because he has been turned out and is "horse-happy." **At no time during this period, have we asked your horse for speed.** At no point during these four to six months does he need to see the racetrack.

In Phase III, between approximately 30 to 34 months, (sooner if your horse has handled Phases I and II with no physical or mental problems) you develop speed in your athlete. **Speed is where redlining and danger begin.** It is the last thing you request.

Start this training process riding with full weight in the middle of the back. As the horse becomes more fit, begin to ask for more speed within the distance. Finally, at the track, take off the weight. **Your horse has learned to carry heavy weight a long distance. Now, he hones into high speed, short distance, and light weight.** My goal is to develop a very tough resilient animal. When you get to the track, the horse thinks, "Gee, this rider only weighs 100 lbs, I have been carrying about 175 lbs over hill and dale and through sand. Here the track is flat and smooth. This is a piece of cake." He should be able to continue training and running soundly at whatever achievement level his conformation and genetic gifts allow. This is the most you can ask of any horse.

Never pull back or Stop a horse That is shying or Propping!

Always push young Horse FORWARD - Even when Frightened!

Give your horse the courage to go forward.

The Program

Day 1 ride the horse -

2 Turnout
3 Turnout
4 Ride Horse
5 Turnout
6 Turnout
7 Turnout

sample weekly exercise program

Day 8 Ride horse
follow day 2 - 8 again

The horse is fresh
and sound on each
exercise day!

He <u>recovers</u> and <u>rests</u>
on rebuild-days !

He <u>progressively</u>
builds <u>stamina</u>
with each ride!

Turnout is
a kind of cross
Training for a horse!

Work hard, Rest and Recover

Work hard again

As a horse becomes fitter
in second and third Phases,
he may need 4 or 5 rebuild-days
between Breezes.

I can do That!

He must <u>recover</u>
and <u>rebuild</u> from
the <u>stress</u>.

His legs and attitude
tell you when he is
ready to stress again.

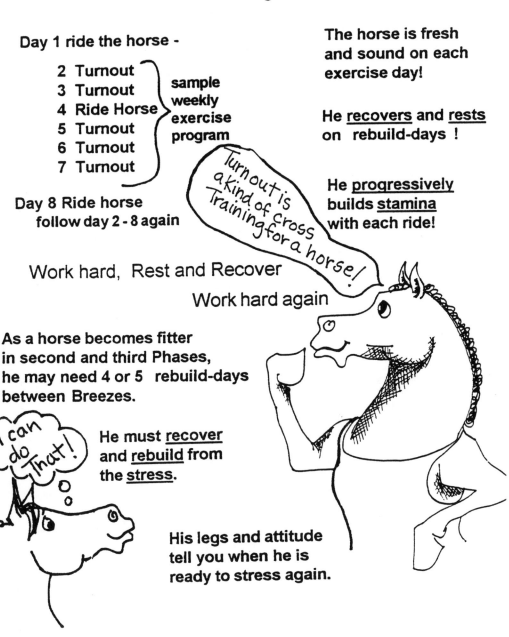

PHASE I - TRAIL RIDING

You are ready for Phase I when Basic Training has been completed. Basic usually takes a month or two. Your horse will go forward easily, walk, trot, canter, stop, backup, and do figure eights. Now, at about 24 months, (his age may vary depending on the horse and circumstances) you start trail rides and establish your route. Find a route that will cover a minimum of three miles. I prefer five miles to allow for warm-up and cool-down.

Only ride every third day, the other days are rebuild-days. When you do put a saddle on your horse's back, he should go at least three miles. Over the next two to four months, speed is gradually increased from walking, to trotting to a light gallop.

Your first goal is to get through three miles on your horse. At first, this may take an hour or two, depending on you, your horse, and his attitude. As he goes out on the trail, he will shy, look around, react to every little distraction and generally be silly. Remember, he is young. Everything is new and frightening until he learns more about the big world out there. **Ask a friend with an older, steady horse to ride with you. The older horse will help calm the younger one.** If necessary, you can put a lead shank on your future racehorse, and let your friend lead or "pony" him down the trail.

The first few times you traverse your route, it will seem to take forever. Carry a riding crop and tap him on the rear to make him go forward (the same way you would if you were on the ground). Do not over react and get angry with the horse at this point. His wariness is natural. Don't start fighting a horse who is not being mean. He's just cautious and insecure. **You must give him the courage and confidence to go forward.**

At the beginning, wear your stirrups long. **Your legs help control the horse and help you defend yourself when he shies and acts like the two-year-old he is.**

Sit flat on the horse's back **with your body straight and your weight in the center of his back.** You can use either an english or a western saddle. Let him learn to carry your full weight.

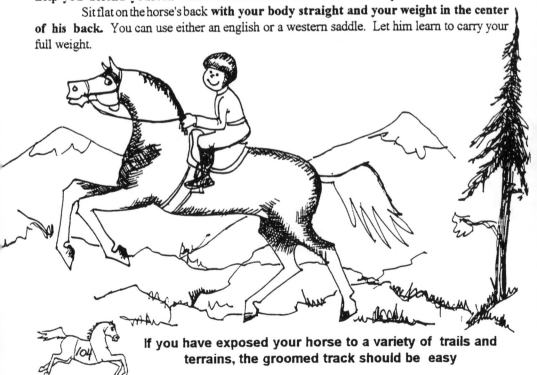

If you have exposed your horse to a variety of trails and terrains, the groomed track should be easy

At this early stage, do not make an issue of elements that frighten him. For example, if he encounters a water puddle and refuses to cross it, let him go around it . Then approach it from the other direction and encourage him to step into it. However, if the situation threatens to become a knock down, drag out fight, it's much wiser to gracefully avoid the conflict for the day. **Get him to like going three miles, without major problems or major fights.**

After you feel he

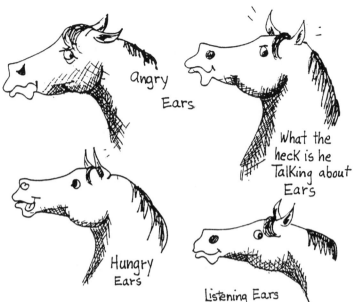

is more or less confident with the surroundings, start being more firm with him. **Start helping him overcome unreasonable fears.** Try to see how he perceives the environment. Have a comfortable, relaxed, trail ride (nearly an oxymoron on a two-year-old). Usually, after four or five rides on the same route, the horse will begin to relax.

The horse's ears are his Barometer . When you first started riding him, were his ears so tense that they looked like they could snap off? The ears warn you about his fear; they let you know what looks strange and should alert you to the propping and wheeling that young horses are prone to do.

When the horse is relaxed on the route, start asking him to gallop. Don't force things, just "cluck" or "kiss" and encourage him to go forward willingly. At first he will gallop in spurts, then he'll drop back to a walk as he tires. That's fine. When you think he has caught his breath or has rested a little, encourage a trot or gallop again.   Just kiss to **urge forward motion.** Then drop back to a trot or walk. Then kiss to gallop again.

Your first goal is to get through three miles. Your second is to get through three miles with as much trotting and gentle galloping, as your mount can tolerate comfortably. Never push for speed. A nice, light, relaxed gallop will do. At some point, usually after a month or so, you'll find you cover your three miles mostly trotting and galloping. Now you must try to bridge the trotting to all galloping. Again, always allow the horse to drop back to a trot when he wants. **He will willingly gallop further as he adjusts and becomes fitter and stronger.**

You'll find that when you start galloping, some horses will dip their heads... be ready for a buck. When this happens, sit very far back in your saddle, yank up his head and urge him forward with your heels. He must have his head down to buck. Make him to lift it and gallop out instead.

Never stress him or ask too much.

Remember you only saddle and ride your horse every third day. The other days are rebuild-days when he is turned out. You may free roundpen him on the rebuild-days, but its not necessary. Your horse's bone is very green and young at this point. Don't push him. He will over stress himself easily if you're not tuned in and sensitive to what is good for him.

If your horse doesn't eat the night after you've done the three miles, you have over stressed him. Wait until his appetite returns, before you stress him again. Monitor his body frequently, as discussed in the previous Section. Be especially religious about the leg monitoring and make sure any ankle or knee congestion is down before you stress him again. The day after you ride, early in the morning before he has moved enough to reduce inflammation, is the best time to see how his body is tolerating the stress. It is normal to find edema or congestion around the ankles, both front and rear. If the horse has been turned out loose in his stall paddock overnight, any filling caused by the previous day's stress should spontaneously be down by morning.

Make a habit of monitoring his legs daily to see how long it takes him to rebound from stress and note it in his chart. You will see a pattern. Remember, ankle congestion after rides is a sign that you have stressed tissue and tendon, and that they are reacting and rebuilding to tolerate the stress. If your horse becomes lame or has heat or more swelling on one leg than the other, you must address the problem. This could indicate a muscle strain or pulled tendon, which requires therapeutic rest. Always remember to observe your horse as he moves freely in the paddock. Notice if he seems sore, lame, or stiff. He should walk out of the soreness from his work within a day or two, and be ready to ride again. If he doesn't seem quite right after three days, give him another day off. You have plenty of time. **The horse needs time to grow and time to just be a horse. If you rush him, you will regret it.**

Another aspect of training deals with starting gates. Diagrams of pretend starting gates are included in the Section on Farm Layout. Ride him up to the gate and stop him. Let him look. Ride him through the gate. Do nothing more. Every time you go out, which is every third or fourth day, if he is calm and you have his attention, ride up to the gate, stop, walk in, stop, and walk him out. Don't ask for any speed. One of your goals for the 28th month is to get your horse comfortable with the gates. Have him walk into the gate, stop, back out, stop, walk in, stop, and walk out of the gate. No speed. No jumping. You only want the horse to be familiar and completely relaxed around the gates.

If you have gates for two or three horses, it is better. You can walk them all in, stand them all together and walk them out. They may get a little nervous. Do not let them get frightened or upset when they walk into the gates. This is a very important and crucial time. It will become part of their routine. In Phase II, when the horse has more sense and miles under him, you may try the "stand in gate, gallop out routine". Right now, don't worry. The trainer at the track will teach him to break out of real gates with other horses.

In this first phase, you're teaching your horse to go forward for a sustained period, to obey, to learn about the big world, to go over various terrains, to go on uneven footing, and to carry weight for a sustained period in the middle of his back. By the end of Phase I, your horse should be able to go three miles at a slow, perhaps slightly erratic, gallop and recover a normal breathing rate, after a period of cool-down, before reaching the barn.

 **You are now ready for the Aerobic Phase.**

GOALS - PHASE I

Trail Riding

By the end of Phase I, your horse should be able to be ridden a <u>minimum</u> of <u>three miles</u>.

3 MiLes!

He should be able to gallop more or less - three full miles - <u>even if erratically</u>.

He should be <u>recovered</u> and <u>breathing normally</u> when he returns to the barn.

He should be ridden <u>only</u> every <u>third</u> or <u>forth</u> day the other days are <u>rebuild days</u> for turnout and rest.

Ideally he should be 25 - 27 months of age.
(if broken at 24 months)

Continually check legs - charting congestion - if any.

Do not ride him until his legs are <u>normal</u> and <u>recovered</u> from his previous ride.

Encourage
<u>Confidence</u>
<u>Steadiness</u>
and <u>Sense!</u>

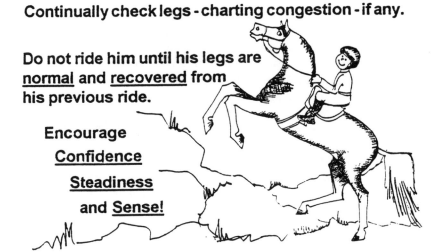

PHASE II - AEROBIC FITNESS

As you enter Phase II training, your horse should be able to get through three miles at a gallop. Perhaps he gallops erratically, but he does it. Now, you will work toward **Aerobic Efficiency**. You will begin to gallop three miles at a steady open pace, only slowing down for sharp turns or steep inclines. You are teaching him to gallop and turn at the same time, trying to help him get his legs under himself.

Remember, as a rider you are trying to go with the animal. While sitting flat on his back, not up high in stirrups, look for a comfortable settling in on the horse's part. He should recognize that he has a three mile trip in front of him. You want to help him get through this in a workmanlike fashion. The horse may be a little aggressive the first mile or so. Relax and steady him. You have lots of time.

His ears should start to relax as you progress in aerobic work. He should be familiar with the route and, as he becomes more comfortable, there should be a steady rhythm to his gallops. His head and neck should flow and rock without tension. His ears should flop forward and back as his head goes up and down.

Get the horse to do three miles aerobically. This means he is breathing "within" himself. Hopefully, you will start hearing a relaxed fluttering sound in his nostrils as he gallops. This shows good relaxation, and implies the horse understands he is going to gallop for awhile. The noise is similar to that made by gently closing your mouth and expelling air in a "Burrrrr" or "Purrrrr" sound. Your lips will tickle a little if you're doing it right. I make this noise, when I am galloping the horses. Remarkably, it encourages them to do the same. They mimic the sound.

Horses that fight and are not relaxed will breathe differently. They make a firmer and more determined noise. You must work making this type horse relax. Often, the horse will fret and fuss in the first mile, begin to relax and settle in during the second, and finally even out and concentrate to finish the third.

Developing a fit, aerobic horse takes about three months. You should still ride no more frequently than every third day. He needs his rebuild-days. **If he seems dull, has persistent congestion in his joints, or has any other problem, wait until the fourth or fifth day.** Always turn him out every day. Free roundpen him on the third or fourth day until you feel he can do three miles again. There should be steady improvement in strength, ability, and agility as he progresses. However, **there will be a ride or two that make you think you've gone backwards, instead of forward. Don't get upset! It's only natural.**

Keep your exercise chart current. When you get off the horse, record all your impressions. The horse is dull today, bright, sore, cantankerous, he did not eat, etc. Make notes about your horse's personality, attitude, and physical response. Later on, these notes will help you evolve a training program that suits your horse.

Fillies tend to overdo. They try to give too much and have a tendency to be off their feed after a gallop. Some will need more time off between exercises.

If you stable your horse at night, you will notice in the morning when you turn him out that the day after his exercise he is more sedate than other days. Usually by the third or fourth day he will bound out. Some horses are so stout they can use another mile beyond the

Don't rush. You have plenty of time.

basic three. If they're holding up structurally and they want to keep galloping, let them go another mile. It's good for them to come home tired, **not over-tired, or anxious, but relaxed.**

During this more or less three month period, **you are looking for long, steady, relaxed gallops and a good mental attitude.** There should be an evolution to a strong three miles, with an eventual mile warm-up in front, and a mile cool-down after. The horse should not be breathing hard when he gets back to the barn. As he becomes more efficient, he will go the three miles in less time. You can **encourage the horse to pick up the rate of his gallop**

as he progresses. Encourage more efficiency of movement in the gallop by collecting his head and urging him steadily forward. He should not be shying or hesitating, but galloping forward smoothly and steadily . **AT THIS POINT, NEVER LOOK FOR HIGH SPEED.**

Try to gallop in company. If you have a pleasure horse, a friend or spouse can ride him beside you. This will steady your horse. Soon, your horse will leave them behind, as he learns to gallop relaxed and with a ground-eating stride. (Lois says, "If your horse can't beat the pony horse, retire him now") If you and a friend are doing the same program, it is a great experience for the two of you to gallop side by side. Take turns going in front and behind each other . . . bumping each other. Learning to pass horses and learning to listen to the rider are important lessons for youngsters. Teaching your horse maneuverability will help him be agile when he goes to the track. This is a good time to experience dirt in the face, and some of the other indignities of a race.

Continue going to the pretend gates. Stand inside, back out, go forward, and gallop out from a flatfooted stance. If there are two riders and two horses, all the better. Remember, no speed . . . just gallop out side by side. It may be better to do this after your long gallops when the horses are settled. Hustling them out of the gates will make them **too high, too soon. Gallop them out quietly encouraging them to go straight.**

By now you have both become more confident in your route and in the horse's ability to handle it. You will now find that you have more contact with your horse's mouth. As you increase your speed you want to increase control, or "steering". You'll lean with him around curves and pick him up if he starts carrying his head too low. You'll start guiding more with the reins. At the end of Phase II you will want to start pushing him into the bit more.

Racehorses are helped and held together by the jockey's control of the head via bit contact. Horses evolve their own way of going. Some like to pull and have you hold them. Others gallop kindly with a loose rein. **When you "pick up the bit" and take a tight hold, they know it's time to start going faster.** You and your horse learn how to get along together to achieve your goals. The horse must obey and respond to your guidance. In turn, you learn what he likes. You develop together.

You must always have control.

GOALS PHASE II

Aerobic Fitness

By the end of this Phase, your horse should <u>gallop</u> a <u>steady, strong three miles</u> with one mile <u>warm-up</u> and at least one mile <u>cool-down.</u>

Gallops should get <u>progressively stronger</u> and <u>faster</u> as he grows more <u>mature</u> (but <u>not redline full speed</u>).

He should be <u>relaxed</u> and <u>breathing rhythmically.</u>
He should <u>cool out</u> by the times he is <u>back</u> to the barn.
He should have been <u>ridden</u> at least <u>half and hour,</u>
even though the real gallop doesn't take that long.

<u>Trail ride</u> and enjoy the scenery while <u>he cools with a rider on his back.</u> <u>Carrying weight</u> in the <u>middle</u> of <u>his back strengthens his whole structure!</u>

<u>Ride only</u> every <u>third</u> or <u>fourth day.</u>
The others are <u>"rebuild-days"</u>.

Constantly <u>monitor legs</u> and <u>joints</u> for <u>filling</u> and <u>heat!</u>

Hopefully he is still <u>turned out</u> for at <u>least</u> a <u>few hours.</u>

No riding with   (or all day or all night)
a rider until his
<u>structure</u> is <u>normal</u>
from last <u>gallop!</u>

He should be <u>stalled</u> for a portion of the day
or night to <u>accustom</u> him to <u>partial stall life!</u>

Keep your eye on his ears. Remember they are a barometer of how he is handling the training you have given him. When he was younger and less experienced, his ears were straight up and forward, looking with trepidation at all the new sights. The ears were his radar. Now his ears should be relaxed, showing a more confident animal.

In the 28-to-30-something month period of training, you **start to stall your horse for a least part of the day** in order to help him adjust to being in the stall, and to protect him from burning up too much energy. **You want him to direct and concentrate his energy into his gallops.** Find a routine you are comfortable with and stall him either all night or all day. He will learn to be in a stall and act like a good boy. Remember, at the end of his training period, when he is 30 to 36 months old, he will have to go to the track. If he stays there, he will probably be confined in a stall for 23 hours a day. This is a very hard adjustment for horses who have never been asked to be in a stall at all. If you want a horse to be a racehorse, he must spend time at the racetrack, unless you are able to race off the farm!

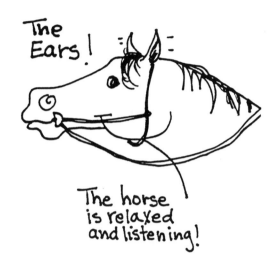

The Ears!

The horse is relaxed and listening!

You may need more equipment now. Your horse probably began with a D snaffle bit and nose band. You can graduate up to all levels of control with your equipment. Equipment should be added as individual horses present individual problems.

Continue to reinforce trailer loading and unloading. We discussed loading and taking him for little rides when he was a weanling. This is important for the horse. When he actually starts being hauled, it shouldn't be traumatic. He should enjoy it. My horses have been good haulers. They didn't necessarily start out that way, but they became seasoned, happy, travelers.

At the end of Phase II you should have achieved the following goals: The horse has developed an ability to go longer distances more efficiently, with a gradual stacking of stress to the system. There has been a slow progressive building of strong bone, tendon and aerobic air. There has been good healthy mental growth and a desire to run without fear or pain. He is galloping a strong steady three mile gallop with a mile warm up and a mile jog cool down.

If you are an extremely competent rider, you and your horse are ready for SPEED!

PHASE III - SPEED DEVELOPMENT - BREEZING

Early in my training days, I wondered, "What's the best way to train a racehorse? How do you make the transition from a fairly fit useful horse to a racehorse? What are the methods?" I searched for answers in training manuals and trainer's notes, but no one seemed to explain the **transition from gallops to speed in a safe, logical manner**.

First of all, you must remember, SPEED KILLS. A horse can gallop six miles over hill and dale, jump 20 fences and come out feeling fine. But if he hasn't been properly prepared, ask him to go full speed for six furlongs to a mile and you will encounter many problems.

As I mentioned before, compare speed stress in a horse to a car with everything mechanically perfect, except a bald tire. You might be able to go forever at 50 mph but try to go 90 and the tire will blow! The horse's weakest point (legs, heart, or lungs) is equivalent to the bald tire when you go to sheer speed.

Phase III explains the transition to speed. In Phase II, you have developed a sound, fit horse able to do reasonable work for a sustained distance. Now we want to hone his speed.

If you are not an extremely skillful, strong and confident rider, or your terrain is dangerous (due to cars, roads, steep inclines, sharp turns, dogs, etc.) and you don't have a few straightaways on your route, now is the time to send your horse to the track with a trainer or start shipping-in for morning works.

Speed in a horse is the equivalent of all out sprinting in the human athlete. Anaerobic muscular fitness is required. This involves developing and conditioning the "fast twitch" muscles. These muscles operate under conditions of high lactic acid production, for very short periods, producing an oxygen debt. This muscular conditioning is best done gradually, by asking the horse to extend into bursts of full speed, followed by aerobic recoveries.

Fast twitch muscles are activated, developed and physiologically primed by speed bursts. In a relatively short time, the horse can be honed to a fine-tuned, powerful sprinting machine. **The previous months of slower gallops provide the necessary structural and cardiovascular basis for this transition.** After building bone, joint, and lung fitness, you turn to speed gallops, called "breezes", to achieve peak muscle fitness.

Once you start breezes and are kissing or clucking to the horse and letting him extend out, you can get in trouble. When a horse tastes speed, you open Pandora's box. If at any point along the way, you cannot control the horse, STOP RIGHT THERE! Send him to the track. It is very dangerous not to be in control of a horse that is starting to run full speed, particularly on uneven terrain. Speed makes horses both stronger and stronger willed. This is good for the racehorse, but is dangerous when tearing through trees.

 **The horse tells you when he is ready to go to the track. When he is, let him go.**

To transition into the actual development of Speed, you take your Phase II horse who gallops steadily for three to five miles, and **allow him to breeze along the safest portions of the route.**

My galloping route runs through an orange grove. (See Route I drawings.) It is a circular route, approximately one mile long, with very sharp curves on two sides and a long, straight stretch that provides a four-furlong (one half mile) breeze area. Your route could be through wooded trails, be more hilly, involve flat desert, or be a 100 acre pasture. Adapt your route to provide safe breezing for your horse.

My route consists of multiple laps around a circular route. There is about a mile ride to get to and return from the route. The first mile of the route is done at an open full gallop. The second mile, I **kiss to the horse and let him extend or breeze in the safe part of the mile, if he wants to.** The third mile, I let him do what he wants, not pushing him or asking him for more. If you are fortunate enough to have safe three-to-four furlong sections in your training route, and you feel competent in what you are doing, you can kiss to him and have him breeze in these sections, if he is willing. Remember, you always go three to five miles, but kiss to him only in the second mile of the route. Allow him to ease into full speed. Never, never whip or push the horse to run. **Let him breeze in a natural manner.** Let the horse ''come back to you'' after the breeze. Never pull him up sharply. Let him develop without having his natural desire to stretch out impaired. Make sure you have room to do this. Only ride him every fourth or fifth day. On his rebuild-days between breezes, turn him out in the pasture or free roundpen him. During the first month or two of Phase III, allow him to breeze slightly every time you ride him.

As you progress with speed work, the secret is to **let the horse extend out to his own capabilities.** You don't want to push him to the edge too soon. **Remember, fillies may try to run too hard, too soon.** You must be cautious about how much you allow the animal to do. This is where the art of training enters. If you are at all insecure about how much to allow your horse to do, or if you are not tuned in to how much your horse can handle, it's time to turn the horse over to a racetrack trainer.

The art of training is sensing how much your horse can do without harming himself.

Route I

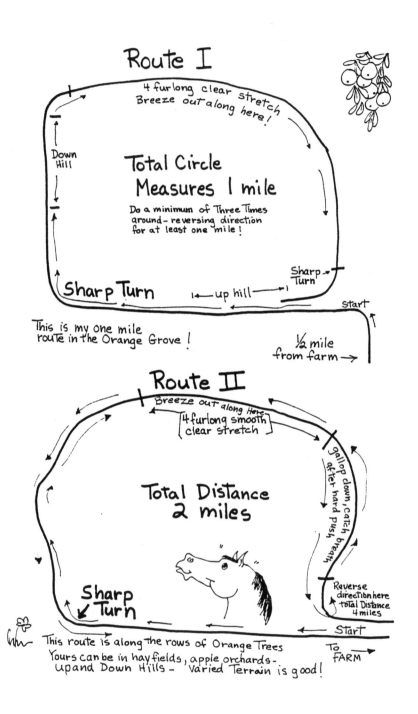

4 furlong clear stretch
Breeze out along here!

Total Circle
Measures 1 mile

Do a minimum of Three Times
around - reversing direction
for at least one mile!

Down Hill

Sharp Turn

up hill

Sharp Turn

Start

This is my one mile
route in the Orange Grove!

½ mile
from farm →

Route II

Breeze out along Here
4 furlong smooth
clear stretch

Total Distance
2 miles

gallop down, catch breath
after hard push

Reverse
direction here
total Distance
4 miles

Sharp
Turn

Start

This route is along the rows of Orange Trees
Yours can be in hay fields, apple orchards-
up and Down Hills - Varied Terrain is good!

To
FARM →

At this point in training, **the horse expects to gallop at least three miles, no matter what.** Horses adapt differently to speed stress. Some will be finished by the third mile and return to the barn at a walk or trot. Let them slow down when they want. Never push them. Others, even when tired, will maintain a gallop and try to extend out more on the breezing stretches in their route. It depends on the personality and ability of the horse.

If you find that your horse wants to go fast for the first mile, but slows down the second mile, even though you kiss to him, do not force him to do the third mile. The horse is probably trying to tell you that, by nature, he is going to be a sprinter. He is going to run early and then get pooped out. Hone into building his speed in two miles. Two miles at your best route speed should give him enough foundation to finish a 6 or 7 furlong race at top speed when he goes to the track.

On the other hand, if your horse cruises the first mile, hits the second mile fast when you kiss to him, then slows down some before running a very strong third mile, you probably have a distance horse. He will need a certain amount of time to gear-up to full speed. This type of horse will need ample warm up time before a race.

As you go into this last phase of fitness, **you should be using an english saddle, because it is lighter.** You will notice, as you start to gallop or breeze out, that you naturally tend to lean a little bit forward, stand up in your stirrups, and put your weight over the horse's withers. **When the horse levels into high speed galloping, it helps him if you are slightly up off the saddle and not sitting on his back.** At this point, it is better to shorten your stirrups a little. Shortening the stirrups, does not mean shorten them to jockey length, just to a length that makes you comfortable, so you can lift your weight and rock on top of the horse, rather than remain sitting flat on his back when he goes into his breezes. In other words, you **evolve from sitting flat on the back to a more forward seat, with the concept of trying to hinder the horse as little as possible with your weight.**

If you can imagine walking along carrying a loosely tied knapsack which bounces and flops every time you start to run, you can understand what a horse feels with a loose rider going thump, thump, thump on his back. You want to be in as tight a position and in as tight a package as possible. **Leaning forward and standing slightly, in the stirrups, as you allow him to rock under you and extend out, is a very natural, wonderful feeling.** You should grow and ease into this . . . just as the horse is growing and easing into his breezes. Between the breezes, you still sit flat on his back. You have already developed his muscles to carry your full weight. When he goes to the track he will be ridden by a jockey who is substantially lighter than most of the people doing this training. **When the horse graduates to a light-weight person, for a shorter distance, on a faster surface, he will have great power and endurance.** At this point, the logic behind the program comes together beautifully.

As you progress in the speed work, you will notice that your horse is no longer carrying his head in a relaxed manner. He is now leaning more against the bit. You will have to take a tighter hold on him. You want the horse to respond to your signals and believe me, you want his mouth to get somewhat harder and firmer at this point. Always use two hands. Grab a handful of mane, hold the horse very firmly with **mane and rein in each hand**.

During these last few months of training, you have to key in to what your horse wants and is capable of doing.

The more you extend into speed, the firmer the contact you need with his mouth. I equate it to a tighter and well connected steering wheel. When you are driving a car slowly you can have a rather relaxed hold, with a certain amount of play in the wheel. **When you are going at a high speed in a car or on a horse, you must have complete control.**

Encourage the horse to lean against the bit. Have very firm contact with him as he is breezing out. This will help him when he goes to the racetrack. Contact with a racehorse's mouth is very different than what you may be accustomed to in dressage or jumping. The jockey maintains the horse's balance by encouraging him to lean against the bit. Jockeys often "take a cross" on the horse's neck. (The right rein goes over the neck to the left hand and the left rein goes over the neck to the right hand. This way the jockey can keep a firm contact on the bit and yet brace himself against the neck.)

Watch the ears as your horse rolls into breezes. When he tries to run harder, he will concentrate more. Instead of having his ears "scoping" and looking at things on the trail, he will now have them cocked back listening to his rider and eventually straining with all of his body to run his hardest. His ears will be flattened, not as in anger, but showing the concentration necessary to run hard, carry his rider over the terrain and obey him! Observe horses in the stretch during a race. Most are concentrating and have their ears back. When a trainer says his winning horse galloped across the finish line with his ears perked up, he means that his horse didn't have to work hard to win the race.

Any time your horse misbehaves give him a sharp whack. Use the whip to guide and discipline him. You don't beat him, unless he deserves to be beaten. **The horse should experience the whip as an aid to discipline . . . not as punishment.** Always have your whip handy. If he goes into his gallop and wants to buck rather than gallop like a gentleman, crack him and say "No" in a very firm voice. Also, yank his head up and urge him forward with your heels. Let him know that negative behavior is not acceptable.

Mane and
Rein in
each hand!

Pretend gates - preferably
angled up a hill !

As long as there is a good turnout pasture for the horse on his rebuild-days when he isn't working, he can exercise on his own. If you want to ride your horse on the rebuild-days, or if you don't have a proper place to turn him out, very specifically ride him on a different route and direction where you never, ever gallop. Take him for a nice trail ride of some kind. The point is, that when you do a particular route, a horse learns exactly where he is allowed into speed. **You must change the pattern on rebuild-days or you will fight him the whole way.** If you insist on riding him on these rebuild-days, you don't want to fight him or confuse him.

Do not over train. This cannot be over emphasized. Be very careful to never over work the horse. If you ride the horse any more frequently than every fourth or fifth day, or push him too hard, he will start loosing weight. **The minute you hit the higher speeds, excess fat will start melting off him.** If you work him too much, he will come back trembling and highly agitated. He might have loose, watery manure. You must use your skills as a trainer now. Look at your horse very carefully. He might seem dehydrated the day after a speed work. Always monitor his legs and write your comments in his chart. Remember, if there is any kind of swelling, edema or heat, you must turn the horse out, swim him, free roundpen him, or walk him. **Do not ride the horse until all swelling has completely disappeared. By not wrapping his legs and by observing him carefully every day, you will perceive how much recovery time your horse needs.** Each day his structure will toughen as he adapts to the work.

Do not over train!

If you feel that the horse has strained something, twisted a leg, has different kinds of swelling, or has a pull and is not evenly stocked up, check with your vet. You might have to do some bandaging.

As you progressively hone into more speed, you start to stress every fiber of the horse's body. It is believed that it takes at least four days for a horse to recuperate from a hard anaerobic push. **He will need more rest, free movement, and time to recuperate and rebuild between breezes** as he bridges to high speed. You will eventually back off his breezes to every fifth day, then every sixth day, with turnout and free roundpenning in between on his rebuild-days. As **he gets fitter, he will start thinking speed.** If he begins to get speed-crazy, look for a trainer. Make your target date for the racetrack.

Remember, no more long slow gallops. **You are now flying through three miles.** Your horse is anticipating the run. You are probably doing the equivalent of a two minute mile, with speed spurts on your three mile route. You are only slowing enough to turn safely and maintain control of the animal. My mare needed two full miles to gallop down, after she did her hardest push in the third mile. Never inhibit the horse if he wants to continue to gallop down, even if it takes three miles.

Let the horse come back to you! He is working out the lactic acid build up from the oxygen debt created by a hard gallop! SLOW GALLOPS IN BETWEEN ARE NOW CONTRAINDICATED. From here on out, we are **honing for speed with open gallops easing into breezes.**

All racehorses are considered three-year-olds in January, regardless of the month of their birth. Since I do not race the horse until he is nearly three, I try to hone the horse into race condition by the time the track opens near me. You should be doing the same thing.

The horse tells you how much he can do
But you must learn how to <u>Listen</u>!

How he eats — how he acts —
How he responds To increments of <u>Stress</u> in Training —

This is how the horse <u>tells</u> You!

GOALS - PHASE III

Speed Development - Breezing

Start speed spurts within Three mile route.

> Always ask for speed in second mile.
> Repeat in third mile if horse wants.

Horse may eventually want to run hard at the same spot in first mile - that's okay -
But always ask for speed in second mile.
Soon you have three stretches with speed spurts within three miles.
You slow for turns and uneven areas -
Now your horse tells you how he wants to run.
Early speed - Late speed - Steady speed.

Discuss with a Trainer when your horse should go to the track.

> Your horse should only be ridden every fourth or fifth day.
> The other days are rebuild-days.

He is now starting to go full speed for the spurts in the three mile route. He needs REBUILDING - RECOVERY time.

Always have free choice hay - good grain and augment feed if he looks "sucked-up". On rebuild-days - TURN OUT and OBSERVE MOVEMENT. He may be quiet the day following a gallop - He may be bounding and full of energy by third or fourth day. FREE ROUNDPEN horse if he feels great and its not time for gallop!

AIM for TRACK!

Start BREEZES at track about every seven days with free roundpenning in between!

MONITOR LEGS

Adjust this schedule to what you perceive as appropriate for your horse and terrain!

A WORD ABOUT QUARTER HORSE AND OTHER SPRINT RACES

Those of you who are training Quarter Horses often ask how this program fits your needs. You must understand that the *Backyard Racehorse* incremental foundation training prepares any horse for his future performance. When you monitor the legs, you can see when the horse has been stressed too hard and how much he can tolerate. The younger he is, the longer it takes for congestion to go down after he has been stressed too hard. Don't be surprised if it takes four or five days for his legs to get tight again. It takes as long as it takes. A horse can start racing at two if his body has shown you that it can tolerate the work. If he can't, give him time.

Flat Racing

Follow the program in the Trail Riding and Aerobic Phases as stated. The main difference appears in the Speed Phase. The Thoroughbred program is aimed at developing speed for several furlongs. A Quarter Horse race will be about as long as the short speed spurts in the Thoroughbred gallops. Since you do not have to develop distance speed, you may not want to do more than one or two speed spurts. You can graduate to the track as soon as your horse is galloping aerobically with little or no effort.

When you transition to the track, have the rider warm up your horse with at least a mile gallop and breeze him out of the gates. If he breaks well, don't keep returning to the gates. **Always be sure your horse "comes back to the rider" and fully gallops down after a breeze or race** to eliminate the lactic acid from his system and avoid tie-up.

Once he breezes out straight and knows to run hard - put him in a race. **Instruct the jockey to warm him up well before the race** - at least a mile - and to allow him to gallop down as far as necessary afterwards. Almost any horse can breeze or work two or three furlongs.

Your goal is to enable him to tolerate the wear and tear on his body from the stress of weekly races (no works between races). To achieve that goal **you give him a solid foundation and turn him out for a few hours every day between races to rebuild.** Of course, if he has wrenched something in a race, he will probably need more time.

Quarter horse races are pure speed.

Barrel Racing

Those of you who are into Barrel Racing are probably saying, "How does any of this apply to me?" The incremental foundation training is essential for your racing too. You want a sound horse that will last.

Most of you will be training at home and shipping-in for your event. That in itself will help you have a sound horse. If you are not conscientious about your training and only ride your horse to race him, please read the Section on Bleeding. Are you pushing your horse in the same manner? Barrel racing horses are also know to bleed. Think about their training and ask yourself if the horse had enough foundation.

Those of you who must keep your horse at a training center should try to ride at least twice a week. Be sure your horse gets plenty of turnout time on the days you don't ride.

Barrel racing horses usually start a little older and race for many years. That is fine. Take as much time as you need. They need plenty of time to develop bone that will withstand the torque on their legs when they race. Because of that torque and the stress to the legs and lungs, you must give your horse a very solid incremental foundation if you want him to be sound and to last.

I cannot overemphasize the importance of monitoring legs and allowing the horse to have rebuild-days. Since you are not redlining your horse, he will not need as much rebuild time as the Thoroughbred program suggests. You will must evaluate just how much he needs.

My suggestion is that you follow the Basic Training elaborating on it to achieve your goals of bending and flexing the horse. Use what ever training method you prefer. You will probably continue that training through your Trail Riding and Aerobic Phases, since it is more complex than the Basic Training needed by a Thoroughbred.

Although you spend much time working circles etc. in an arena, by taking your horse out and exposing him to a trail gallop route with plenty of bends and turns, you will teach him natural lead changing, balance, to keep his feet under himself, and to gallop freely. It will provide a pleasant break to the training for both horse and rider adding a needed dimension to your training.

Continue with the Aerobic Phase until you get a steady two-to-three mile gallop with good aerobic efficiency. This will give plenty of stamina for the short runs around barrels, should help avoid any future bleeding problems, and will develop good strong legs. The concussion provided by galloping is vital for building bone and strong legs.

You can virtually skip the Speed Phase. It would only make the horse hot, teach him to lean into the bit, and make him difficult to handle. Your only real speed spurt is the dash after last barrel. Any fit horse can handle that. Speed training for it would be counterproductive.

Be sure to use your horse sense as you adapt this program to your needs.

Many thanks to Holly Wright at J & J Tack in Lakeland, FL, for her help with this topic.

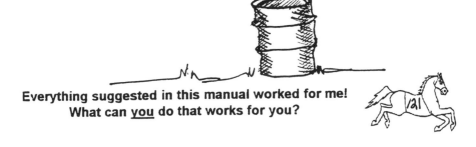

Everything suggested in this manual worked for me!
What can <u>you</u> do that works for you?

THE TRANSITION - FARM TO RACETRACK -
Introduction

First, congratulations! If you have gotten this far, you have achieved a great deal. You have a horse that you have been nurturing and developing into a running machine. He should like to run and should be chomping at the bit at the threshold of pure speed for a prolonged distance. **How do you bridge from the speed spurts you have been doing within your three to five mile route to a speed machine?**

I am going to discuss two ways of handling the transition from farm to racetrack. Although the basic training theory is the same, the life-style of the horse is different. Therefore, I will repeat each step of training, for each option, so that there will be no misunderstanding as to how the horse is handled.

The first option is presented to those of you who live close enough to the track to haul your horse in and have found an astute trainer willing to work with you.

The second option is for those of you who must keep your horse at the track. You want the trainer to understand what your horse is ready for and how to cope with him on the rebuild-days when he should not be tracked.

A Cooperative Track Trainer is worth His Weight in Gold!!

Ideally, the first option is preferable. It is the best for you and the horse. I realize that it is not always possible for you to keep the horse at home and ship-in. There are many *Backyard Racehorse* advocates. Contact each other when you are working with the logistics of track training and need some help. Cooperation between people with the same mind set works . . . even though we frequently feel we can do things better by ourselves.

I am continuously increasing the list of trainers and farms that work with my program. This list can be obtained through the *Backyard Racehorse Newsletter*. **As the Newsletter grows, we will network our information and have a solid base of Backyard Trainers.**

Backyard Racehorse Newsletter is a network for
Backyard Owners and Trainers.

FIRST OPTION - WEEKEND HAULERS

If you live in the North, you should plan to start your horse on the track in the spring. It's no fun to be hauling or aggressively riding in cold, dangerous weather. Always accommodate your training schedule to the weather. Training in snowy country will be more erratic than in warmer climates. Those of you who live where weather is not a factor, can aim to breeze your horse at the track in November or December of the two-year-old year. If you are in the last phase of training and ride every fifth or sixth day and free roundpen in between, the horse will be ready to go to the track.

Here in Florida, I have my horses ready when the track opens in December. Northern horses will be a little older when they first visit the racetrack, as they will be in their three-year-old year. This is fine. You want your horse to last, so you give him growing time. You are not in a rush. You want your horse to run as a three, four and five-year-old. **You forego the early two-year-old money and the early two-year-old breakdown.**

When your horse is doing three aggressive breezes within the three mile route, he can go to the track. It is time to begin the official breezes and works. **To work and to breeze are specific track terms** which are almost interchangeable . . . but a breeze is slightly less aggressive than a work. A work should be challenging but not as hard as the ultimate test, the race. **To breeze the horse means to let him run as fast as he can,** kissing to him and encouraging him, **but not hitting him.** He should be a tad under his absolute top speed. **To work the horse means to ask and "drive" or hit him.** A trainer will have his horse work with another horse in a pretend race. Many horses are redlined in their works and are tuckered out for the race. If it looks like the rider is asking for everything the horse has, that is a hard work. An honest willing horse will give you everything he has even in a breeze. He is eager to please unless he has had a bad experience while running. Then he may hold back and refuse to try at all. That is why **I like the animal to grow into his or her speed.**

Works are done at the track. At **such high speed it is dangerous to try a work at home. You may be breezing your horse at home as long as you have safe, clear stretches on your route.** Works are generally picked up by the official track clocker. He can tell when a rider is "setting" a horse down and will "pick him up at the poles" and time the speed of the horse for each furlong. Some trainers don't want the clocker to pick up the time. They try to sneak a horse in very early when it is dark or the track is very busy. It doesn't usually work. The clockers in Florida are astute. They can recognize a horse by the way it goes and they don't miss many works. The clocker then asks the rider the name of the horse as he heads back to the barn. If the rider or trainer purposely gives the wrong name, he can be fined. The clocker turns in the sheet of timed works to the office. The times are then printed in the *Daily Racing Form* so the public has access to the information. **You need at least two official works in order to start your horse the first time.** This requirement may vary from state to state. Check the regulations in your area.

The track trainer will tell you the ground rules at his track. You need guidance with the logistics . . . what time you can arrive to work out in the morning . . . how long you can stay in the receiving barn . . . whether he has an open stall that you can use over night and so on.

**When your horse is ready for the track
let him go!**

You must establish your relationship with the track trainer. Most of them are used to having complete control of the horse and charging you day money. A track trainer willing to work with you as a ship-in is invaluable. As a ship-in, you interrupt the trainer's schedule. But, if you are willing to pay, the trainer will find the time to work with you. You can offer him a flat fee for the mornings he works with you. He will co-ordinate getting a rider and will help you with any logistical problems that arise. If he is interested and willing to run your horse, negotiate his piece of the purse. **A good trainer's co-operation will help you greatly.** Listen to him, learn all you can from him. Hopefully, he will establish a good working relationship with you. You can't even get into the backside of the racetrack without the trainer signing in you and your horse. He carries insurance and is responsible for your horse while he is at the track. **The trainer's overhead is high.** Take this into consideration when negotiating the relationship.

You now have a trainer who has agreed to work with you and your horse is ready to go. **The first time your horse visits the track, it should be a getting acquainted trip.** Your trainer should arrange for a rider who can spend plenty of time with your horse. Pay the rider double the going rate and he will take the extra time necessary to familiarize your horse with all the new experiences at the track.

As the rider takes a few turns around the shedrow, your horse will see the everyday hustle and bustle. **With his stirrups long, the rider should then take the horse to the track and jog him the wrong direction on the outer rail for the circumference of the track.** During the ride your horse will see horses galloping by. All he is expected to do is look around at everything. If the horse becomes agitated or nervous during this first mile, have him do another one. He needs to become comfortable with his new surroundings.

Fractious horses may need a pony for the first trip or two on the track. Your trainer can make whatever arrangements you need. When your horse has completed the jog in an acceptable manner without being ponied, the rider should turn the horse

How much water does your horse drink after a WORK?

around to the right direction, and do a collected gallop the full mile of the track. If the horse gallops well, and the rider finds him capable, the rider will kiss to him and allow him to "breeze down the lane" (Home Stretch) during this full-mile gallop.

Stress to the rider that he must not pull up the horse sharply after the finish line. He must let the horse gallop out as far as he wants to go. If the horse wants to gallop out another full mile, so be it. **The horse will slow down on his own when he is tired and "come back to the rider"** (*Backyard Racehorse* term for allowing the horse to slow down when he is ready . . . we should have been doing this all along in our build-up gallops.)

The way your horse handles this first trip tells you if he is fit if he is not too green about the new environment. Some horses are so busy looking around they don't apply themselves to the run at all. Your horse should want to run since you have been galloping him a strong three miles. This first session should have allowed the horse to expend enough energy to slightly stress his system. When he returns to the barn, watch how long it takes for him to get his breath back, and observe how he drinks water while he is cooling down. If he only takes a few sips, you probably didn't stress him much. If he sticks his head in the bucket and tries to guzzle the water, you know he wasn't fit enough for the work he did and might be over stressed.

It is common for the horse to **cord-up** with his first works. Actually, anytime he tries too hard and is not fit enough, this can happen. **Cording-up** means that his back muscles are over strained. As you cool him out after the breeze or work, you will see a tightness along his back. Ask your trainer or groom to show you what to look for so that you understand. Make sure you note in the chart that he **corded-up. Do not increase** the distance of his breeze until he returns with a normal back. As far as treatment goes . . . I cannot overemphasize rebuild-days with turnout and movement until he is bright and bounding again. I have never had to give medications for cording-up. I allow rest and then try again!

Listen to the rider. He may say the horse tired fast or was very strong and didn't seem tired at all by the experience. Remember what the rider says, and when you get home dutifully note the information on the horse's chart.

Monitor his legs the next morning, as you have done throughout this program. It should not surprise you if you find some congestion around the ankles. It is a very typical reaction the first time the horse is on a hard surface. Observe everything about your horse . . . how he eats . . . what his attitude is . . . how his limbs look. Turn him out as you usually do and record everything. On each successive rebuild-day, observe, check, and note. By the fourth rebuild-day, he should be eating normally and his legs should be fine. If they are not, let him rest until they are. By this time, he should be feeling good and want to frolic. The stress of this work should have triggered his endorphins and he should be rebounding and feeling high.

During this time, free roundpenning for 15 or 20 minutes to get him in a good sweat should be enough on the rebuild-days.

Continue to turn out and monitor.

Six or seven days later, go back to the track. Have the rider jog the horse or walk him the wrong direction around the track again... the full mile so he can again see everything. **Then have him turn the horse around at the finish line and let him gallop strongly and openly a full mile, breezing him down the lane. He must allow the horse to continue past the finish line until he slows down and "comes back to the rider."** We are trying to bridge the speed spurts from Phase III into solid five and six furlong works.

Horses should never be pulled up hard after the finish line when they are really rolling. Pulling up hard is very dangerous. It causes a great deal of tying-up, because the body doesn't have time to eliminate the lactic acid in a normal fashion. Always permit the horse to keep moving until he settles down.

Think about an Olympic Sprinter. When he crosses the finish line, he doesn't just stop. He jogs beyond the finish line and continues to move to avoid severe leg cramps. A similar phenomenon happens to your horse when he does a hard push. Lactic acid builds up in his muscles due to oxygen debt.

This introduction to the track is very logical. **It teaches your horse that he will always be asked to run down the lane.** He learns **that the finish line never changes but that the starting gates do.** (The gates are moved around the track so that no matter where the race starts, **it always finishes in the same place ... in front of the grandstand.) You learn how fit your horse is by how far beyond the finish line he carries out the work.** You see whether he really needs a lot of warm-up before a race by observing whether he is running faster in his work or breeze down the lane or whether he runs early and is tired by the time he hits the home stretch. The pattern of an early run or a late run will begin to emerge.

The rider will tell you if your horse is stronger after the finish line and wants to run long, or whether he wants to run early and not be rated. The track trainer's observations are very important to you.

**The rider can give you his candid opinion
of your horse's behavior.**

After this second trip to the race track, you repeat the same routine as after the first trip. If all goes well, consider sending your horse to the gates on the third trip. You can begin to get him used to the process. The first time send him to the gates after he has done his breezes. He should be tired and easier to handle. He can also be cooling down as he walks from the track to the gates. The crew will have the rider stand the horse in the gates and then gallop or walk him out. It will depend on what the horse is capable of doing. After a few lessons, the horse should be ready to break from the gates. When the Starter (head of the gate crew) thinks the horse breaks well, he will give you a gate card. Put your confidence in the gate crew and heed their advice. They have had tremendous experience and will know how to handle your horse.

One thing to watch for at the gate! Some jockeys just hold the reins. When the horse leaps out, the jockey may try to maintain his balance with the reins. The bit **jerks the horse's mouth** just when we are trying to teach him to break efficiently. If the poorly trained jockey does this a few times, the horse will learn to connect leaping out of the gate with a hard yank on his mouth. Soon, even if the jockey doesn't yank, the horse will throw his head up in anticipation of the yank. This will distract him and he will not break efficiently. Tell the jockey to **hang on to mane and rein** when breaking. A pull on the mane in no way inhibits the horse's head keeping him from breaking properly. Watch your exercise boy or jockey at the gates. **Don't allow bad habits!**

As you progress you will see a change in the horse. He will start anticipating the track and the breezing. **Have him learn to put his energy into the gallop at the track if he gets over-anxious.** By the third or fourth trip, when the horse knows what the racetrack is all about, it is probably not necessary to do the mile jog the wrong way. **Tell the rider to back up to the wire (go the wrong direction around the track to the finish line), turn around and immediately go into a strong gallop and breeze four furlongs down the lane.** Have him permit the horse to gallop out as previously explained. If the horse comes out of the four furlong breeze well and recovers well, on the next trip ask for five furlongs. If he does this well, have him breeze out of the gates the next trip. If he handles each challenge well, continue to increase the distance and/or speed until you get a good five or six furlong in a time acceptable to race. The trainer will tell you about times and conditions on the track. He will tell you about your horse's work as compared to others at the track.

To get an idea of whether your horse is breezing or working viably, look at the clocker's sheet or racing form on the date you last worked your horse. Compare your horse's time and distance to the other horses on the list. If your horse is two seconds slower than average, he needs to be tighter. Work the same distance next week and see if he can go faster. If he improves, step up his distance.

At this point, you have shipped-in to the track once a week for approximately six to eight weeks, and free roundpenned for 15 to 20 minutes every third or fourth day at home. **Do not turn out your horse the day before a race or a work.** Stall him that day and night. It will give him an edge.

Do you have your gate card? A gate card is the official permission from the Starter, stating that your horse has been schooled and has broken from the gate in an acceptable manner.

You should now have a gate card and be doing fairly tight works.

If your horse's shins are going to be sore, they may start now. Don't get upset if they do. Look at the Section on Bucked Shins and proceed from there. Remember, bucked shins are a common set back, not the end of the world. This is why the farm is so much better than the track. You have time to allow the judicious healing of Bucked Shins. **Treat them cautiously. When they improve, continue training.**

Once you have a strong five furlong work, with a strong gallop after the finish line, look for a race. Many trainers like to work a horse until he's perfect before they enter him in a race. Not me. **I use the first four races as part of the training process. I consider them the last four works.** Accept that it may take about four races for the horse to learn to break well, run straight and begin the concentration necessary to become a useful racehorse.

After four races, the horse should be well, fit and running as honestly as he can. You will have to judge whether he got a good break and had a good position before you can determine what kind of horse he is. There is some fine tuning that goes on at this point. Your trainer will help you with these things. He might feel that the horse needs blinkers. Many trainers put them on automatically. I personally wait to see if they are needed. Let the horse go with as little equipment as possible. **Aids like blinkers, stronger bits, and tongue ties should be used only when necessary.** Rely on the advice of your track trainer - if the advice makes sense to you. If it doesn't make sense, question it. Ask why he recommends things and try to think from the horse's point of view. Always try to help your horse. Read the Section on Setbacks.

Remember to **continue monitoring your horse**. See how he is the day after works and races. Monitor his legs, see how he's eating, observe his attitude and write it all down in his chart.

TRACK BREEZES

The first time or two, go the wrong direction a full mile to give the horse time to see all activity before galloping. Have the rider use long stirrups!

Beginning at <u>finish line</u> (after wrong direction mile), gallop horse in right direction.

At top of <u>Stretch</u>, kiss to horse and <u>Breeze</u> to <u>finish line!</u> Let horse continue Breeze and <u>Come Back</u> to rider.
> (This way you don't inhibit a fit horse
> from getting the exercise he needs!)

He may <u>Breeze</u> a <u>furlong</u> or <u>two beyond finish line</u> keep timing and see where the horse slows down.

OBSERVE:

**Where horse tires -
How long it takes to cool -
How much water he drinks
-**

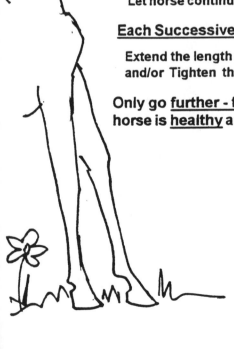

Next Trip to Track

Begin the same - Then Breeze 3 furlongs from finish line.
Let horse continue Breeze beyond finish line (if he can).

Each Successive Work or Breeze

Extend the length of Breeze
and/or Tighten the Speed.

Only go <u>further - faster</u> if
horse is <u>healthy</u> and <u>sound!</u>

A Little more...
a little faster!

a little fitter!

Typical Chart Notes

Trip #1 Breezed 2 furlongs in 24
Trip #2 Breezed 3 furlongs in 39
Trip #3 Breezed 3 furlongs in 37
Trip #4 Breezed 4 furlongs in 52
Trip #5 Breezed 4 furlongs in 50
(Continue until you have 6 furlongs
in 1:18 or so.)

SECOND OPTION - TO THE TRACK TO STAY

Not everyone should consider training their own racehorse when it is time to go to the track. The racetrack is another world, **a whole new set of rules.** Trainers at the track are very adept at entering horses and appraising chances for a particular horse in a particular field. An honest trainer will tell you if he agrees with your methods and ideas or not. You must find a trainer who shares your philosophy. Then allow him or her to call the shots.

When a horse that has been trained by the methods in this manual is sent to the track to stay, the transition can be hard. The horse is feeling good and has been allowed to run and frolic for a few hours every day. **In the racetrack routine, his every movement is restricted.** The amount of time he is ridden and exercised is decreased, and he has no turnout.

When I first started training, my horses went to the track after having undergone a more aggressive training schedule. They had been galloped five to ten miles everyday. When I turned them over to the trainer, the first thing he said was, "What's wrong with these horses? They just stand there. They're so quiet." I, of course, was offended. My "children" were just being good. I had turned them out every day and galloped them hard. When they went into a stall they were tired and well mannered.

A week later I came back to the track. As I walked by my sweet horses in their stalls, they lunged at me or anyone else who happened by. They were like all the other unhappy, bored horses who are not allowed to frolic. They were full of pent up energy they couldn't release.

Bad habits can develop in horses who live at the track. These habits evolve over a period of time because the animal can't cope. He is not allowed normal living and is bored, nervous, frustrated, in pain, or all of the above.

When you go down a typical shedrow at the track you'll see animals bite at you, lunge at you and weave back and forth. Others are cribbers. They bite the stall door or feed bucket, and suck air in through their mouths. **These traits are manifestations of the frustration of being in an unnatural environment.** They help to alleviate the horse's boredom. **Most of these vices disappear when the horse is living at home and turned out.** However, some horses are high strung and are always nervous.

My horses soon became cranky like all stalled horses. Then they began having a great deal of trouble with tie-ups. I asked the trainer what the horses were doing. He told me they were being sent to the track to gallop one mile. As they came back, they all seemed to have tie-up problems. **Tie-up is manifested by a shortness of stride, generally in the rear, and in severe cases the inability to walk. The horse may paw the ground with his front feet and have spasms in his rump muscles. Trembling, sweating and obvious stress accompany these symptoms.**

After galloping one mile my horses were being pulled up, turned around and brought back to the barn. The problem was obvious to me. They were used to galloping five to ten miles. A one mile gallop was like a warm-up to them. No wonder they were tied-up. They were full of energy, had a one mile warm-up . . . and were told, "That's it." They surely headed back to the barn bouncing and full of desire to run, with fuel pumped into their system that had not been burned.

If you find a trainer willing to listen to how you want your horse started at the track, he is worth his weight in gold.

Tie-up is a phenomenon that was seen a great deal in the last century. At that time horses were worked everyday but Sunday. On Sunday they didn't move. Their metabolism had to adjust to the different Sunday routine. When they went to work on Monday, their muscles had "locked". To avoid this problem feed was adjusted and the horses had some kind of exercise on Sunday.

When my horses had the problem at the track, it was because they had been over trained. **They were too fit and had too much of the wrong kind of work. I was galloping them too long and making it more difficult for them to adjust to the confinement of the track.** So, I took them all home and developed the program that I am teaching you.

No matter how it is approached, **it is difficult for horses to adjust to being stalled 23 hours a day. The younger they are the more difficult it is.** They want to bound out of the stall in the morning. This intimidates the groom and he will over shank the horse unless he is really tuned in and realizes the horse just feels great. You don't want your horse to be punished because he feels good. You can only hope your trainer has good help. These are things for you to be aware of that should be discussed with your trainer.

When the trainer takes your horse on the track for the first time, he must allow the rider to ride with longer stirrups than usual. He should have the rider take the horse in the wrong direction, completing the circumference of the track while allowing the horse to walk, jog, and look at everything. If the horse is nervous and over-reacting, have him ponied. Do a second mile while trying to relax and accustom him to the activity around him. Since the horse has had a lot of under-saddle experience and mental growth with you, he should not be too over-reactive.

Young Horses can find Confinement Difficult!

Don't fool yourself into thinking your horse is fine if you have been <u>Masking Symptom</u> <u>With Medications</u>

When the horse has settled down, have the rider turn him around and gallop the full mile in a relaxed manner, allowing the horse to breeze down the lane and gallop out as far as he wants after the finish line. If this means going a whole extra mile, assure the rider and trainer that it is all right.

Always allow the horse to "come back" to the rider. It is very important for the horse to be allowed to gallop and slow down when he wants. If he doesn't get comfortably tired, you'll have an animal that builds up energy. He will start fighting the rider. Your horse will be fit. He just needs speed honing. He does not need miles of drilling, slow gallops or hobby horsing. He does need to become accustomed to the track routine. Assure your trainer that the horse must return tired or he will escalate his energy level.

For the next three days, the rebuild-days, your horse should not go to the track. **Continual trips to the track on a daily basis and the stacking of stress to the bone, common in conventional training, tend to break down young horses.** Ask the trainer to have someone hack the horse around the backside of the track for half an hour instead of going to the track.. **If there is no other choice on the rebuild-days, have him ponied for a least a mile or have him walked to the gates to stand in them.** At some tracks, a paddock may be rented and you can turn the horse out to frolic for a least an hour a day. **Again, I stress that daily pounding on unnatural surfaces eventually breaks down a young horse. In allowing your horse time to rebuild in between the track gallops or works, you keep him from many track breakdowns.** Many horses in conventional training do not survive the training process.

If a horse can't survive the training process, there must be something wrong with the process.

Why is training causing breakdown during a young horse's development? **Standing for 23 hours, which inhibits blood circulation, followed by running hard is the scenario which makes horses more prone to breakdown.** Your trainer may not like to hear your methods. They interfere with established routine and demand more from his help. But you want a healthy situation for your horse. **It is your goal, as an owner, to have the trainer get the best for and from your horse. You and your track trainer can reach compromises that suit you and the horse.**

You are into your fifth day at the track. On the first day, the horse breezed out after a mile or two jogging in the wrong direction to see everything. Then, hopefully, he had two or three rebuild-days without track pounding after his session on the track. If all was well, he could have been walked to the gates to stand and gallop out on those off days. If he did, he will only need a few more visits to the gates before you start incorporating every fourth day breezes with breezing out of the gates.

Now you must give the trainer some leeway with your horse. He may do every fourth or fifth day breezes. As the horse tightens and becomes more efficient and honest, he may need more time in between breezes and works to recover and rebuild.

Rebuild-day recovery time should be equivalent to an hour or more of turnout, or some kind of off track trail riding or ponying, no pounding, but lots of movement. Have him taken a couple of times around the track the wrong way, if you have no other alternative. The idea is movement without hard pounding. After four to six weeks of training at the track, you should get a handle on the horse. **He'll be trying harder down the lane and be more willing to quit after the finish line, as the works lengthen to racing distance.**

At this point, **if there is swelling, sore shins or lameness, do not give Bute and continue training. Allow the horse to rest and recuperate from soreness. Tell**

Don't get into the habit of ignoring pain on young unruined horses by masking it.

the trainer you don't want jugs. **You don't want Bute every night and you don't want pain-masking medication. If there is pain, it is for a reason. A young three-year-old should not have pain.** If he does, he should be allowed to walk out of his soreness.

I am not opposed to helping an older horse, who has soreness and stiffness, and needs Bute to run.

If pain killers are used the trainer cannot observe what is brewing in the young horse. In traditional training, if the pounding on the track surface causes soreness and filling, the trainer may give Bute, poultice, and wrap. This inhibits swelling. The next day it is impossible to determine the true status of the legs. The horse is sent out again and the process is repeated. **The horse's problems are masked by wrapping, poulticing, and medication.** When the horse goes bad, everyone is so sorry and no one can imagine why this happened with such up to date care. This is where overuse of systemic corticosteroids may begin.

You can now understand why I prefer shipping in. **It is life at the track that wears horses down - too little work - too much speed - at too young an age.** The horse stacks the stress of trauma from the track surface and over a period of time problems appear. **Turn-outs and free galloping are very important parts of training - especially for young adolescent animals.**

IF YOU CAN KEEP HIS TIME ON THE TRACK DOWN TO LEGITIMATE GALLOPS, BREEZES OR WORKS, YOU WILL DEFEND YOUR HORSE FROM MANY OF THE TRACK BREAKDOWNS. EXTRA TIME FOR GROWTH AND REBUILDING IS IMPORTANT.

Remember, these are the equivalent of the horse's teen years. **You want him to survive training and grow into a useful mature horse.** Beware of trainers who want to use a lot of medications on your horse. The horse should be sound, healthy and young enough to handle the work without chemical support.

At this point in training, you should read and follow the instructions given to week-end haulers. Let the trainer work or breeze the horse every five or six days depending on how the horse holds up. **When the horse is fit enough to go a strong five furlong work and gallops out strongly, put him in a race.** This is a difficult request for the trainer who values his starts-versus-wins track statistics. There is nothing like a race to find out whether or not the horse wants to be a runner. After four races, you should be able to tell if he is a cost-effective race horse. These are my suggestions. Your trainer may have a different approach. Respect and listen to him. He may want the horse tighter and ready to win the first time out.

If your horse appears to be trying hard in the races and has no legitimate excuse for losing, his best is probably not enough to justify the expense of the racetrack. Try not to be pulled into putting more and more into a horse that doesn't have the talent. It is not cost-effective. If he doesn't have racing talent, you still have a sound horse for another endeavor where he may have talent. If you are training at home, the expenses are not as great and you can afford to be more patient.

Remember you can't give a horse talent he doesn't possess.

A MESSAGE TO FARM OWNERS AND MANAGERS

Today, horse farms are struggling to survive. They face major problems with labor and Workman's Compensation. If you understand the concept of the training presented in this manual, you will realize there are many ways to continue training at the farm and cut down the costs of riders by two thirds. **If a twice-a-week riding program is initiated, the labor and stress of getting out, galloping, bathing, and leg wrapping young animals every day is eliminated.** At the same time you will find that your horse develops progressively, at the rate that his structure can tolerate. You are training horses while listening to their individual responses to the stress put to them. Many tune up more quickly than anticipated . . . they show no filling with each progressive gallop, and therefore can continue right on to the races.

Since you are turning them out on the rebuild-days, there is no need to wrap and paint legs; they will adjust to the work load. **Be sure you or your employee monitors and charts any filling and waits until it is down before galloping the horse again.**

It costs you less to handle horses this way, and they are in real training. They are growing, developing and thinking. You will be pleasantly surprised at how little expense there will be to treat and medicate these animals. You're not over-stressing them so they have strength to resist major infections. Again, the free movement and being outside a good portion of the day, in itself, will improve the animals' life style.

Whether or not you race off the farm will be a decision that you and your owner make. Obviously, I prefer it. Keep in mind, once your horses learn the track rules and routine, they really don't have to be cooped up at the track between races. Some may need a gallop or speed work between races (every horse is different). Depending on your location, you should be able to handle the logistics. **Horses living at the track only get about fifteen minutes actually on the track on any given morning.** You could arrange for riders at the farm to do more and develop them better with the twice-a-week schedule and rebuild time in between. Most track personnel cooperate with ship-ins. You may schedule your trips to the track so that you, too, only go once a week to work horses or combine a work in the morning with a race in the afternoon.

Turn out is a very important part of TRACK TRAINING - It allows rebuilding from the Track pounding between Works and Races !

136

Standing in a stall for 23 hours out of every day, does not develop a resillient athlete

A MESSAGE TO TRACK TRAINERS

We have chosen a difficult but rewarding business. I hope that as you read my program you will keep and open mind and try to find ways to adapt some of the ideas into your routine. Many times as you train, you find you are having to treat problems that are created by track circumstances.

A problem my horses have had only at the track, for example, is cracked heels. At some tracks, the dirt has stones or bits of shell in it. When the horse gallops on this surface every day, he can develop chronic cuts and bruising. Some tracks put chemicals on the surface for winter racing. These chemicals cause burns and chronic problems when horses must train on the surface every day. Washing fetlocks, pasterns, and heels with castile soap and rubbing them with bag balm or other lotions to help the injured tissue is very time consuming and work-intensive. These problems slow down training.

One track was famous for making horses sore in the shoulders and stifles. Trainers had no choice but to use the track and contend with muscle soreness. On the other hand, my horses would run or work and go home. They were usually sore the day after the work and fine by the second or third day. They walked and grazed while healing on their rebuild-days. They went into races feeling good and could take it easy until the next race or work. It was not necessary to give any kind of medication, because the horses were always bucking, kicking, and feeling good by the third or fourth day. By noting their activity on a chart, patterns would emerge indicating how much time each horse needed before he was ready to run again.

If you ship-in and gallop or work them on the track and then take them home, they can be turned out to heal between visits to the track. **The routine I suggest allows them to recover from the experience and be healed in time for the next race or work.**

Please be open to working with owners who want to be somewhat involved and ship-in horses for training. This can be a source of more horses to actively race in your stable and opens the door of our sport to more people who will help fill races.

Everyone gains from a compromise.

PARTNERSHIPS, SYNDICATES, AND DEALS

The Agony and the Ecstasy

Some friends formed a syndicate, went to the sales, bought a fairly expensive horse and started the process of racing their GREAT HOPE. First I got weekly reports about how the filly was doing everything right, how she loved to gallop and was doing very impressive works. Then she had some predictable setbacks. After sore shins, coughs, inconsistent works, and problems in the gate, the trainer picked a date and said the horse would start. How exciting! What anticipation! The friends called me. They had already planned the next race, a little stake, that she could go in after her first out and, of course, first win. They told me they had the leading rider and he was very high on the filly. She went off favorite, the owners convinced she would smoke the field. She did run a very viable race but finished second. This is not bad for a first race. The jockey, however, was now a bum that did not pressure the filly in the stretch . . . "If he had, she would have won . . . he fell asleep in the stretch!" I suggested they buy the tape and watch the re-runs. They did and saw the jockey really rode as well as could be expected. The horse simply tired. She would probably be fine and tighter for the next race.

When a horse loses, owners seek excuses . . . some reason why he didn't win. The main reason most of the time is that the horse was outrun. Good horses will win in spite of difficulties, bad breaks, being boxed in, too wide, etc. They win in adversity. Cheap horses barely win, even when everything goes just right. They are the claimers that fill the bottom races. As an owner, be judicious. See what really happens in the race and learn about your horse.

As a trainer, I get the horse to the first race to see what he does and how he comes out of it. Then I eliminate the excuses that might have caused him to lose. If he broke poorly, more gate work. If he hits himself, farrier work and leg wraps. If he shied or seemed to hang, blinkers. If he was uncontrollable, different equipment. Each new piece of information gleaned from the jockey after the race and observed by me must be interpreted in terms of the performance of the horse. When we finally get a fair race from a fit horse with no interference or problems, we know what we have. If he was running high, you can always drop him. If he was at the bottom, maybe he can win through his conditions.

Deals

In an ideal world, all owners have plenty of money and trainers don't have to make deals. Not so in the real world. The economic situation is such that we have had to become creative in our endeavors. Trainers may make a 60-40 or 50-50 split or whatever you both agree on. Half interest in the horse may be given to the trainer or a percentage of earnings, etc. It is important to define what expenses are paid by whom before splitting the earnings.

A friend suffered a perfect example of this problem. The deal was 40-60. My friend retained ownership of the horse and 40 percent of his earnings. She was paying 100 percent of all extra expenses such as ponies, vets and shoeing. She was surprised to find the trainer deducted his 10 percent earnings fee off the top before factoring the 40-60 figure. She also

Good rapport between owner and trainer is essential.

found that he had given highly questionable and unauthorized treatments and medications to the horse. He told the track bookkeeper that he had access to her account and obtained the earnings checks. Much after the fact, my friend found that from the $47,000 her horse earned, she was given a total of $7,000. It was a hard lesson to learn.

When you make a deal, spell out everything: Who pays for shoes, ponies, treatments, feed, hauling, and vet bills. I recommend to all trainers that with any deal, the actual cost of feed, bedding, etc. must be paid or the trainer can loose money as well as his time and effort! The percentages of ownership may be written on the horse's papers. All contingencies should be spelled out.

I have lost money on the majority of my deals. This is usually because I get untried horses and must spend time in developing them, only to find they don't have talent. Chances of having a winner are slim, but we all pursue the dream of the horse who can bail us out.

If you own a useful, performing animal, trainers will be more willing to make a deal. A formed, talented horse is a joy to train.

A trainer came to our area looking for horses. He called the owners of solid allowance horses and offered to train them free of charge. The current trainer of one of these horses heard about the call and gleefully told me how he had "punched the daylights out" of the pushy newcomer.

Owners, Trainers, and Deals

Always clarify the monetary arrangement with your trainer. It is imperative that costs be set on the training of your horse and that you understand the best and worst possible scenarios. An excellent sample of an Owner/Trainer Agreement was published by *The Thoroughbred Owner*, the official publication of The National Association of Thoroughbred Owners (NATO) in their Fall Edition of 1995, and is included on the following pages. I suggest two small additions. Under the heading "Compensation" it should be understood that often the trainer only receives 10 percent of the win purse. Some ask and get 10 percent of all earnings

A Trainer's role is to develop the Personal Best of each horse
WITHOUT
breaking him down in the process!

Owner/Trainer Agreement

A clear agreement of understanding between an owner and trainer can be the key to a healthy relationship between them. NATO receives many calls from owners regarding transactions with trainers. In most cases, a relatively new owner has recently hired a trainer, and the trainer assumed the owner knew all of racing's "standard" practices. Owners have been surprised to be billed by the trainer for 10 percent of their horse's winnings. Owners have been surprised when their trainer took a commission, sometimes hidden, from the sale of their horse. Owners have been surprised to learn about serious injuries months after their occurrence. Sometimes when an owner fires a trainer (or vice versa), a confusing, unpleasant experience can ensue. Many of these basic problems can be avoided, while greatly benefiting the owner/trainer relationship, with some version of the following owner/trainer agreement.

The owner/trainer agreement printed here, as a service to NATO's members and readers, is just an example of subjects which can be addressed in such an agreement. Such an agreement can be modified to ensure that your unique concerns are addressed. It is suggested that you contact your personal attorney in the state where you are racing if you desire to enter into such an agreement with your trainer.

OWNER/TRAINER AGREEMENT

THIS IS AN AGREEMENT entered into by and between _____ ("Owner"), and _____ ("Trainer"), on this day of _____ , 199___.
It is hereby agreed and understood that _____ , a licensed owner in the state(s) of _____does hereby wish to retain _____ , a licensed Thoroughbred trainer in the state(s) of _____ .

The terms and conditions of this agreement are as follows:

1. **GENERAL:** Owner retains Trainer and Trainer accepts the responsibility to Owner for training Owner's Thoroughbred horse(s), as listed in Schedule A (see attachment). These horses shall be incorporated by reference including any additional horses that Owner may choose to send to Trainer, as acknowledged by Owner and Trainer by written notice or telephonic means.
2. **TERM:** The term of this agreement shall be for a term of one year and shall begin on the date stated above unless Owner terminates this agreement sooner (see "Termination" in paragraph 8). This contract shall be automatically renewed for an additional one year under the same terms and conditions unless Owner provides written notice to Trainer at least two weeks prior to the termination of this agreement.
3. **CONDITIONS:**
   A) Trainer shall render to Owner to the best of his/her professional ability the training of Owner's Thoroughbreds. Trainer must render to Owner the best of care in the training, maintenance, care and control of Owner's Thoroughbreds. These duties include, but are not limited to, the care and conditioning of such Thoroughbreds. Owner shall at all times be included in the determination of what races shall be best to achieve the goals of Owner and Trainer relative to Owner's Thoroughbreds.
   B) In the event that any of Owner's Thoroughbreds shall need the services of a licensed veterinarian, Owner or Owner's representative shall be notified immediately. Trainer shall discuss with Owner all major decisions affecting the health or well-being of any of Owner's Thoroughbreds.
   C) Trainer shall confer with Owner regarding all major decisions regarding Owner's Thoroughbreds. Owner shall have the ultimate decision regarding claiming races, stakes nominations and other entries of Owner's Thoroughbreds. Trainer shall be responsible to discuss all decisions regarding the health, well-being or success or probability of success of each of Owner's Thoroughbreds.
   D) Trainer shall discuss all business decisions with Owner prior to acting upon such things as: Jockey selections, training location and all major decisions of a general management policy. Owner will consider all recommendations made by Trainer, but Owner shall have the right to make the final decision unless Owner elects to defer to Trainer's decisions or judgement.
4. **COMPENSATION:**
   A) Owner agrees to pay the prevailing per-diem rate charged by Trainer for training a Thoroughbred racehorse, which is $_____ per day per horse. Any increase in the day rate charged by Trainer will not be charged to Owner without notification and acquiescence of Owner.
   B) Owner hereby agrees to pay Trainer 10 percent (10%) of all purses earned by Thoroughbreds included in this agreement, and which officially finish in first, second, third or fourth place within a race. Trainer will not receive a percentage of purse bonuses paid to Owner in the form of owners' and/or breeders' awards unless such terms are agreed to in writing as an addendum to this contract.

READ the Contract !

A GOOD CONTRACT IS FAIR to ALL!

C) Any breeding rights to successful horses that are to be sold for stud purposes or to stand as a stallion of Owner will be subject to an addendum to this contract and shall be negotiated by Owner and Trainer. The parameters of what must be accomplished by Trainer shall appear within the addendum.

5. **SALE OF OWNER'S HORSES:** It is hereby agreed and understood between Owner and Trainer that there shall be no commissions paid to or received by Trainer from the purchaser without the express consent in writing by Owner. Owner shall not pay any commission to Trainer unless Trainer procured the buyer for Owner's Thoroughbred. If Trainer procures a buyer, Trainer shall then be entitled to a sales commission of five percent (5%) on the net proceeds of such sale. If the sale is procured by Trainer and one or more individuals disclosed to Owner, then the commission shall be divided between them. All funds from any sale as contemplated in this agreement shall be made directly to Owner from the purchaser. Trainer's interest, if any, shall be paid directly to Trainer by Owner. Owner shall have the prerogative to approve or disapprove of any sale of Owner's horses at all times and shall not be obligated to pay any commissions unless sale actually occurs.

6. **AGENT:** If Trainer is asked and agrees to represent Owner at any public sale of Thoroughbreds, Trainer hereby agrees to act as agent for Owner and agrees subject to this agency agreement not to accept any commissions or remuneration from consignors or their agents.

7. **BILLING:** All fees due and owing to Trainer shall be paid monthly. Trainer shall bill Owner at _____. Owner shall then be responsible for the payment of such bills in a timely manner. It is agreed by and between Owner and Trainer that such actual bills will be paid promptly. Credits for other expenses or income shall not be deducted from such bills, but shall be reflected in separate statements of account. It is hereby stipulated between Owner and Trainer that under no circumstances shall Trainer take The Jockey Club Certificate (indicia of ownership) of any of Owner's horse(s) out of the racing secretary's office. Any disputes shall be settled by arbitration with the stewards or their designee at the racetrack where Owner's Thoroughbreds are racing. However, nothing in this agreement prohibits Trainer and/or Owner from seeking redress from a court of competent jurisdiction.

8. **TERMINATION:**

   A) Owner has the right to terminate this agreement at will as to each horse covered under this agreement. Owner and Trainer each agree that if Owner desires to terminate this agreement, then Owner shall not remove horses unless Owner gives Trainer not less than seven (7) days notice of Owner's desire to remove said horse(s). Owner hereby agrees that Owner shall pay the per-diem rate as agreed to by Owner and Trainer through such seven-day period for each horse removed, whether Owner removes the horse(s) earlier or not. It is agreed to by the parties to this agreement that if Owner is apprehensive for the safety and well-being of Owner's horses, both parties agree that the official stewards or state veterinarians can be the sole arbitrator as to any actual threat to the well-being of the Thoroughbreds in the custody of Trainer. Owner hereby agrees that all monies due and payable to Trainer shall be paid to Trainer at the time of removal.

   B) Trainer shall have the right to terminate this agreement at will, upon seven (7) days' notice to Owner, but will lose any benefits agreed to between Owner and Trainer (i.e., paragraph 4 C) that have accrued regarding horses in Trainer's charge at the date of notice.

9. **ASSIGNMENT:** This agreement shall inure to the benefit of each party and shall be binding upon the successor, assigns, heirs and personal representatives of Owner and/or Trainer. It has been agreed to by the parties that this agreement shall not be assigned.

10. **MISCELLANEOUS:**

    A) This agreement shall be construed under the laws of the state of _____, and any action shall be brought in the state of _____ re: construction, interpretation or enforcement of the provisions herein.

    B) This agreement constitutes the entire agreement of the parties hereto. Any modification, addenda or additions shall be in writing and signed by the parties herein.

    C) It is further understood by and between the parties to this agreement if any part of this agreement is held to be illegal, invalid or unenforceable, the legality and validity of the enforceability of all remaining parts, or provisions shall be deemed to be valid and enforceable and shall not be affected. The rights and obligations of each party shall be construed and enforced as if the agreement had not contained the particular part or provisions deemed to be invalid.

    D) The parties to this agreement have affixed their signatures to this instrument to evidence their agreement and understanding.

_____ _____ (S) _____ _____
Witness to Owner's Signature   Date   Owner's Signature   Date

_____ _____ (S) _____ _____
Witness to Trainer's Signature   Date   Trainer's Signature   Date

. . . second, third and fourth place. Clarify what your trainer expects to get from the earnings of the horse. Nothing is automatic unless defined as such. Modify the terms as you and your Trainer see fit. Write down the details and sign the document.

I would also suggest clarifying exactly what the Day Money covers in your Agreement. A common practice is for the owner to pay day money, for example, a base price of $30 a day. This should cover feed, usual supplements, bedding, and daily maintenance of the horse. Vet bills, shoeing and special feeds or equipment will cost extra. One of my first trainers charged me for safety pins and cotton used to wrap the horses legs. He also charged extra for electrolytes and salt. Since I was already paying $35 a day in the early '80s, this kind of bookkeeping was abusive.

At most tracks, the trainer doesn't pay for the stalls or the upkeep of track. If he is at a training center or at his own farm, he will have that extra overhead. Depending on your arrangement with him, he may or may not charge for hauling from farm to track or from track to track. I knew one trainer who had no trailer and no place to train his horses where they were stabled. Four or five days a week he charged his owner $30 to haul the horse to gallop at the track. Needless to say, this doubled the training bill and that owner, quite upset, changed trainers upon receipt of the first bill. Clarification can avoid misunderstandings.

A trainer should have the tools of his trade. He should have saddles, a variety of bridles and other necessary equipment to conduct his business. If your trainer wants you to pay for buckets, stall guards, and other items that should be general expense items, be cautious. Owners should pay for special equipment pertinent to their horse such as a set of blinkers with a particular cut to them or an unusual bit.

Costs above the day rate may be charged for extra services. Pony horses, used a couple of times a week to take your horse to the track, might be listed as an added charge. Having your horse's hair clipped when coming from a cold climate to a hot climate could cost $30 or $40 dollars. If a trainer has his own pony and his own set of clippers, he may provide those and other services at no extra charge.

Above the initial day rate, your bill will include the vet charges. Some trainers go overboard with vets. They pull blood continually, have ultrasound treatments, laser treatments, Jugs (fluids put in IV), and a plethora of other medications. X-rays are taken frequently. (Remember . . . if it shows on the X-ray, the damage has already been done). Some owners love this technology and are willing to pay for it. Make your philosophy clear. Be sure your trainer understands how you want your horse treated. Communication and mutual trust is important for both parties. Vet charges have been known to cost as much as or more than training fees. A horse needing that degree of medical support perhaps should not be at the track. (See Drugs and Medications Section.)

It is not unusual to have extra costs on race day. Disposable leg wraps, such as Vetwrap, cost about $2 a leg. There are all kinds of "natural" herbs, sold in one-dose tubes, that your trainer might use. An oral paste composed of natural ingredients is preferable to an injection if it is used to help the horse. It depends on whether or not the trainer gets the results he wants. In any case, these little tubes cost from $4 to $10 each. There may also be a hauling fee on race day from one track to another or from the farm to the track. Most trainers are trying to do a competent job and are aware of the costs. If you have good rapport with your trainer, he will keep you up to date, and you should have no major surprises.

Clarify monetary arrangements.
Write down the details and sign the document.

SYNDICATES, PARTNERSHIPS AND VARIATIONS!

by Scott Wells
Ruidoso,NM

One of the most positive trends in horse racing in recent years has been the increase in the number of racing partnerships. For a number of reasons, these partnerships (and they can be extremely varied in their makeup) lend themselves to enjoyment of the sport at its very best.

Most notably, from a business standpoint, it is far better to own part of a good horse than it is to own all of a mediocre one. Basically, good horses cost about the same to maintain as "cheap" horses. The differences are that they: (1) usually cost a good deal more to acquire, and (2) have the potential of earning substantial income. Many owners who in the past attempted to operate on a middle-class budget while searching for a rags-to-riches horse have realized that there are usually more rags than riches in that approach. However, armed with their hard-earned lessons, and hopefully having experienced at least a taste of the thrills of winning, they now take a more intelligent approach to the sport by joining forces with friends.

That leads to another of the benefits of group ownership: fun with friends. I have trained for some very diverse groups who, though they may have had little in common otherwise, did share one thing. They had a terrific time racing their horses. Some were high-dollar players who wanted to be participants in every major decision. Other partnerships were compromised mainly of fun-loving race fans who chipped in, bought a couple of horses, and merely wanted to know in advance when the horses would race. Most groups fall somewhere between those two extremes. With proper preparation and proper guidance, along with the patience and perseverance which is obligatory, nearly any group can experience joyous, unforgettable days (or nights) at the races.

However, the best thing about racing partnerships is that the participants, by combining their resources, are able to purchase a better racing prospect. Recent racing lore is replete with stories of successful partnerships whose relatively modest investments have bought them ownership of stakes winning horses. Almost without exception, these successful partnerships are typified by: (1) a capable, honest, highly-communicative trainer, and (2) a written agreement which names one partner as the main liaison between the trainer and the group.

In the past, many owners approached racing with the attitude that racing is the Sport of Kings and they intended to be kingly. These days, they realize that the phrases "strength in numbers" and "the more the merrier" have their place in today's racing climate.

A good partnership can provide fun and benefits for all.

THE RELATIONSHIP BETWEEN
VETS, OWNERS AND TRAINERS

As you read this manual, do not misinterpret my feelings about veterinarians, owners, and trainers. In my desire to educate you, **the worst possible scenario is used when presenting cases.** My goal is for you to make your own informed decision as to how you want your horse treated. Your expectations about how your horse will perform must be tempered by the reality of his talent and soundness.

The trainer's role is to develop the horse to his personal best. Most trainers have the horse's welfare at heart. Their work is very challenging. Many trainers must move from track to track, depending on the season. They must pack their belongings and find a new place to live every three to six months unless they are lucky enough to have their own farm near tracks that are open year round. Their logistics and financial problems are great.

Compound that with the challenges of training young horses every year . . . horses that will have their own normal setbacks as they grow into useful animals. Every time there is a problem or slow down with the horse (which is to be expected), the trainer must call the owner with the Bad News. Most trainers, myself included, find this to be one of the most difficult aspects of training. **We don't like to deliver bad news.** We don't like the fact that the horse is showing problems or weaknesses and we don't want to stop him. Yet we must do what we perceive is best for the owner and the animal. How I dreaded the silence on the other end of the line when I said, "His shins are sore.", "He has a cough.", or "He needs time." I am aware that the owner is thinking of the per diem costs while the horse rests.

IT IS VERY IMPORTANT THAT THE OWNER AND TRAINER HAVE A MUTUAL RESPECT AND TRUST. Each must understand the philosophy of the other. The owner must believe that the trainer is doing an adequate job, and the trainer must understand the owner's intent in owning a racehorse. For example, many owners tie the hands of the trainer when they won't allow him to run the horse in a particular race. The owner generally thinks his horse is worth much more than the claiming price. It simply doesn't matter how much the horse cost or how much you have invested in him. He must run where he can win, where he can justify the training bills. Statistically, it is going to be a lot less than his cost. So trainers have the unpleasant task of having to tell the owner that his $20,000 dollar investment should start running at $5,000 if any money is to be made. It is possible that the horse will work his way up the ladder, but the start must be realistic. This is one of the many problems between owners and trainers. **We all want the Big Horse, and when the horse is mediocre or less there is disappointment on all sides.** The reality is that few horses will justify their cost. However, a good one can pay for many if we can only find him!

The other really unpleasant task trainers have is reporting to the owner that the horse didn't win. An excuse is expected. Many times the horse has run a good race, but just wasn't fast enough to win. What can a trainer say? The horse was outrun. If the owner is at the track, he can see for himself. That can make it easier . . . or more difficult . . . depending on the sportsmanship of the owner.

Trainers want to win . Each time they run a horse, they hope it will win, even if the form clearly shows there are more talented horses in the race. It does happen, and when it does

**Your expectations must be tempered by the reality
of the horse's talent and soundness.**

A Trainer can't make an
Untalented horse have Talent!
BUT! He can help a
Talented Horse run for
MANY YEARS!

the bettors mumble about how the trainer must have set that one up. They don't realize we're just as surprised as they are. The bettor is convinced that the trainer had a large bet on the horse and "made a score". It does happen, but not as often as you think.

My racing career began as an owner. I knew nothing about racing or the track. I loved my horses and wanted them to win, just like in the movies. An owner expects the trainers to know everything about the horse. That may eventually be true, but at first, the trainer is learning. Each horse is different. His idiosyncrasies must be observed through trial and error. The trainer must decide on the distance of the race, the equipment, and the style of riding that suits the horse. He learns this as the horse progresses. As frustrating as it is, owners must be patient and understand that the horse tells his trainer things with each race. Some of his perceptions about a horse may be incorrect and he will have to go back to the drawing board. **Eventually, the horse, trainer, and owner should evolve an understanding that will be beneficial to all.**

A major problem is an owner who pushes the trainer and demands action when the trainer feels the horse isn't ready. This can be disastrous. Mutual respect and communication will alleviate this problem. An educated owner is much easier to deal with. Since owners are paying the bills, they should be kept as informed as they want to be. Some owners don't want or need frequent updates. Others want to be very involved. Matching the trainer's style to the owner's expectations is an important part of good rapport.

Owners are paying the bills. It is their right to know how their horse is handled. They may be in racing because they love to go to the backside and walk their own horse or bring him carrots. They may only want to be in the winner's circle. **Seek out your own kind of trainer. Look for mutual benefit.**

Owners, please remember a trainer can do everything right and your horse can still have problems or not be a runner. If this happens, don't blame the trainer. The possibility

Trainer, Owner, and Veterinarian —

GOOD
COMMUNICATIC
A MUST

Mutual respect and cooperation are the key to any endeavor.

of winning is slim. Be fair and understanding. Something may happen to the animal after much hard work on the part of the trainer . If so, don't bad mouth him. Be fair, **there is a great deal of luck involved in training**. High strung, honed animals can be difficult to handle. The horse can be his own worst enemy. Just rolling in his stall, he can injure himself for life. These things happen even with the best of care!

Trainers have expenses like everyone else. Don`t get a horse unless you understand what the projected costs will be. Don't expect your winnings to pay for training. **Figure out how far you can go with no economic compensation and discuss that with the trainer. He can tell you how realistic your goals are.** Always be prepared for the worst case scenario . . . then you'll be pleasantly surprised when things turn out better. Hopefully with my methods, your horse will not suffer as much breakdown as is typical. Also it should not take as long to establish his ability and usefulness at the track.

The veterinarian who practices at the racetrack has special challenges. He knows and generally keeps up to date on the best therapy for the horses. He is aware that sometimes rest and turning the horse out are easy, rational solutions to many problems. But the vet can only recommend such solutions. When a vet tells an owner, "Just give him some time and turnout.", the owner almost feels cheated. His reply may be , "Don't you have some kind of miracle drug that will cure him? Off time costs money." Then the vet must admit that there are medications, and will often explain the side effects. After that, if the trainer and/or owner insist, the vet must try the next best treatment, usually some sort of medication. Next time you have a problem, ask the vet if rest and turnout would do the trick. If your horse has talent, you may be money ahead in the long run. Dr. Green (the pasture) is one of the greatest cures of all.

The fact is that racing is a business in which horses are expected to produce. Financial pressures cannot be ignored. Veterinarians can advise various treatments to help a horse run better and without pain. Much of the therapy is very good. A great deal of the medication is therapeutic and helpful. Tell your trainer and vet what you are willing to pay for, what kind of treatment you want for your horse, and whether or not you are open to allowing time and rest to be a part of the game plan. Veterinary medicine has made great contributions to the racing industry. Many horses have had successful surgeries allowing them to be useful and capable of earning on the racetrack. **Trust and a clarification of the owner's philosophy is necessary to avoid misunderstandings.**

Whether to operate or not, weighing the economic impact in relation to the horse's earning power, can only be decided when all the facts are presented. Removal of spurs and chips may return a horse to a very competitive level with little trauma and expense in relation to overall cost and time lost. My suggestion is to get various opinions and information on any problem in order to make informed decisions. Veterinarians work with trainers but are generally happy to discuss and explain cases and options with owners. As an owner, be clear about your decisions and what kind of vet bills you are willing to pay. If you don't want your horse to run on painkillers and steroids, make it clear! It may save your horse's soundness if you chose competent training over medications that mask problems!

If you are reading this manual, I hope it is because you want to be an informed owner and/or trainer. Communication and knowledge are the key to successful relationships between the owners, trainers, and veterinarians. Each person has a very important role to play with the horse and the racing industry.

By working together we can strengthen our positive impact on the sport of horse racing.

Medications

AT THE RACETRACK

MEDICATIONS AT THE RACETRACK - Introduction

My opinions here may cause me some trouble. Perhaps this section should be called "Ethics in Racing: Medications, when to use, when not to use." I must share a little background information with you here. My father worked for the Federal Government, the Bureau of Narcotics, while I was growing up in San Francisco. The "evil" of drugs was indoctrinated in me at a very young age. Perhaps this early training has made me more reactionary than most when certain options are offered to get a few more races out of a horse.

I am constantly interested in the cause and effect of whatever is being done to the animals. I was married to a physician for 18 years and have great respect for the tremendous benefits science and medicine have provided for us.

The problem in racing is the attempt to "fool Mother Nature", when often rest and time off from the pounding and speed will alleviate a problem before it becomes chronic or irreversible. At the track, the trainer is reluctant to stop a horse for a slight problem close to racing time. So he asks the vet for something to "help" the horse get through the race. "You know Doc, he's been training so good. Our race is next Tuesday and now he has this heat in his tendon." Red Alert! Now is not the time to stress that tendon by running the horse.

Many trainers don't or can't stop at this point. There is tremendous pressure from the owner who doesn't want another darn excuse. The owner may even insinuate he will look for another trainer. The trainer, in desperation, looks for a quick fix which unfortunately may "fix" the horse for the rest of his career. The horse runs with chemical help and strong bandages, and bows his tendon. Now he is compromised for life. The trainer shakes his head and tells the owner, "What a shame. He was doing just fine until that misstep on the track. Just bad luck . . . but, hey, there's another sale coming up and we'll throw this horse out for a year and see how he does next year." This scenario is simplistic, but such skits are being played all too frequently at the track.

In similar situations, I have felt pushed into a corner. What to do? Use chemical help for a few more races to indulge an owner, or lose the owner and watch the horse run well for a few more races with another trainer. Afterwards, the horse is never seen again since you can only "go to the well" so many times.

The following story is typical of the problems trainers have. At the end of a meet at Tampa, my friend told me he had a three-year-old filly he was sending to the killers unless he could find someone who wanted her. She had won a few races and was very game. "She's got a knee," he said, without elaboration. I knew better than to ask if cortisone had been injected in her knee, or how often she was injected until he couldn't get anything more out of her. I looked at her . . . she had powerful hind quarters and was a muscular horse. Her

Be aware of cause and effect.

knee looked "rough" but not puffy and full of fluid, though it was hot to touch. (Cortisone can eliminate heat and swelling, leaving the horse to think his joint is healthy even when it isn't.) I agreed to pay $250 for her and decided to throw her out to pasture for the summer and see how she was in the fall.

Since she was running at $3,500 claiming races when she was right, she was certainly not worth spending any money on, even for X-rays. Surgery wasn't feasible, because she probably had joint deterioration at this point.

It wouldn't cost too much to carry her. If she wasn't lame next season, I'd try galloping her. I loaded her and took her home.

A friend from the track heard about my purchase and asked to buy half of her for $125 and agreed to help pay her upkeep. This was fine with me. Trainers become horse poor very quickly. It was great to have someone to help pay for feed.

In the fall, she started training (my third and fourth day ride) and she tuned right up. She showed nervousness in the gates and had to be hauled back many times since she was left at the gate a few times.

She would become slightly lame out of the race, walk out of it, and be ready eight or ten days later. She was given Bute before the race but that was the extent of her medication. She had been on the Bleeders List, but I took her off as no signs of bleeding appeared and the Lasix seemed to do more harm than help. After an injection of Lasix, she would break into a sweat, have runny diarrhea and start urinating. She was running with a hard knocking gang of fillies and mares and did run viably in most of her races, once we solved the gate problem. To our great joy and astonishment she won a very game race where she was left last out of 12 horses. She did a tremendous stretch run and won by a nose. What joy!

Her next race was a lackluster performance. The jockey got off, and said, "You know she's not pushing off her left leg the way she used to. I think her knee is starting to bother her again". In view of that, I turned to my partner and said, "It's time to give her away." "Wait a minute," he said, " You know there are ways to keep her going." Enter the horns of dilemma. The money would be useful. By injecting the knee with cortisone, the mare would feel no pain and could continue running with the illusion of a sound joint. I knew we could get a few more races out of her before the ultimate breakdown. Just thinking about this, my own knees and ankles started to hurt. As close as I have been to financial ruin, I have not been able to condemn a horse to this kind of finish. I realized, in this case, the decision was not mine alone to make. My partner accused me of being naive. Ridiculous, since I knew as well as anyone various ways to keep the horse running. Unfortunately, I was

**Will your horse run on reality or camouflage?
Its your choice.**

also aware of the consequences of those methods. I said, "Listen, if you want, I'll give you my half of the horse. Take her to another trainer, camouflage the pain and have her run full speed with a compromised knee."

"Are you willing to be responsible for the injury that might result to a jockey, or the damage to the horse?" I asked. "If that's what you want, my half is yours. I can't even sell her the way she is. My choice would be to give her to a good home."

He looked at me. This was heresy. Something not too many smart trainers would admit is that **what you do today can cause breakdown tomorrow.** This is never presented as a cause and effect situation to owners. It is difficult for trainers to inform an owner that the horse could be incapacitated by trying to get a few more races. But, that is exactly what happens. Some trainers cleverly wash their hands of the responsibility. They just say they will "help" the horse feel better. The vet does his part by indulging the trainer and doing what the trainer wants. The vet might caution the trainer that when certain drugs are given, the horse should rest. The reality could be if the medication can't be traced and the horse can move, he will run. This is a great way for everyone involved to avoid responsibility when the inevitable happens. They can all commiserate about the bad luck - the "misstep".

Back to the filly and my predicament. My partner got my message and agreed to give the horse away. She is now herding cattle in Central Florida.

I will not train a horse that I know is in pain. Nor will I train a horse that is unaware of the pain he has. If the owner feels otherwise, the horse goes to another trainer. But I prefer losing an owner to the fear of someone being harmed or the horse breaking down. Obviously, I have lost owners and am not considered a sharp trainer when I refuse to use the "best" medical science has to offer. I'm in this business for the long run. I spend the time necessary to properly prepare the horse to run. That extra three to six months in the training program is costly, but worth it if the horse has talent.

This is why we need **new people in the business who can do much of the early work themselves.** Their horses will hold up better, and if they don't have talent, they will have another life as a hunter or riding horse. **Horses are not disposable items.** I will not turn them over quickly in search of the good one. Now I train one or two a year hoping they will pay off, but recognizing the odds against it. I am happy and I can live with myself.

Back to medications. **Anytime you give a horse a painkiller so he can run, you are in trouble. Pain is a warning sign.** Being over forty, I have a lot of aches and pains. I know that aspirin helps when my bones ache. Bute is probably the same for horses, helpful for slight problems. This doesn't mean mega doses. Some trainers say, "I love running that track; there are no limits on Bute." Too much of anything can be dangerous. **Vets see many horses with perforated stomachs caused by Bute abuse.**

One filly suddenly died on me two weeks after arriving from the track. The necropsy disclosed purple discolorations on the wall of the stomach . . . ulcers . . . where large amounts of Bute had eaten away the lining. Other horses on long-term Bute develop anemia or other blood disorders.

Many people don't worry about this, because the horses go to the killers when they're finished at the track anyway. Again, I can't, knowingly, set up animals for a short life. But in the racing business, where the owners pay a lot of money and want quick results, some

Should a horse that is unaware of his pain be forced to run?

trainers push horses until they produce or break down. There are always more horses coming along. Wouldn't it be more cost effective to rest the horse a few days and race many years?

Beware any time a trainer says to you , "He had a little filling in his left ankle, but he isn't lame." Next comes, "I don't understand. He never took a lame step." Could be true, but if you are astute, the horse generally tells you that problems are coming. He gets filling or heat in a leg, favors it, paws and digs holes in his stall, or he stands and holds his feet in a particular way to alleviate pain. The way he walks out after he has been stationary tells you something. Observe the signs. Figure out the reason for his actions. Don't simply mask the signs with drugs and carry on. **When the horse is off, turn him out every day and observe. When he starts frolicking and feeling sound, go back to galloping. No vet bills and, if you are observant, you should not have catastrophic breakdowns.** This is the basis of my methods.

Race day, for most owners, is very expensive. The vet gives most horses a "cocktail" the day of the race. Usually it consists of a combination of vitamins (B-12 or multi-vitamins), and possibly various kinds of corticosteroids such as Azium or Vetalog that are supposed to help with inflammation. If allowed, nervous horses may be given SoluDeltaCortef. This is supposed to help a hyper horse. It is also a steroid. Many trainers swear by these injections. I now avoid their use and only capitulated in the past under duress from an owner. At the time, I didn't realize they were corticosteroids. I have never seen them produce dramatic results on my horses. But then, my horses were always sound. One hyper filly dropped her head when given SoluDeltaCortef and almost snoozed in the gate. She didn't run well half asleep. On the other hand, Lois had a brood mare down from undetermined causes, probably acute shock and colic triggered by an abscess. When given a shot of SoluDeltaCortef, she literally arose from the dead like Lazarus. The vet still calls her the "Miracle Mare". Every medication affects every horse differently. Do your homework and make your own informed decisions.

Certain medications definitely make a dramatic difference on sore horses. Banamine is sometimes used a few days before a race. One owner claimed a horse from a very aggressive leading trainer . . . famous for how hard he was on a horse. Indeed, the horse won the race the day we claimed him, and I went to the spit box to pick him up. As he cooled out after the race he got progressively more lame. By the time I took him to my barn, he could scarcely walk, he was in such pain. When the owner came back to admire his horse, I said, "Watch," and led him out. The horse was very sore. The owner agreed for me to take the horse home, turn him out and observe how well he walked out of his stiffness.

At home he was turned out in a grassy paddock. It should have been heaven to a horse just off the track. Most animals frolic and trot around from the sheer joy of being able to roll and have free movement after the confinement of track life. This horse just stood in the middle of the pasture and didn't move. When he did walk, it was very painfully. I watched him for days, waiting to see any desire on his part to move without being prodded. He never had any. I called a friend who worked in the barn where the horse had been claimed and

**Observe the symptoms and figure them out.
Don't simply mask them and carry on.**

asked if there was anything they did with this horse to get him to train. He said that the horse never went to the track without Bute every night. I tried it and he at least moved, but did not appear to be free of pain. He still seemed quite sore when he galloped.

Another phone call revealed that if I wanted a good gallop, he would need to have 10ccs of Banamine . . . a non-steroidal anti-inflammatory drug. It acts like a super Bute and is a potent pain killer. The vet who treated the horse at the track advised me to give this medication two days before running or working him. This horse could only move with Bute. He could not move at all without help. I was so uncomfortable with the situation that I tried swimming him, but there was no way he could perform without the medications. He would go into races walking sound but come out lame. We had the vet try to pin point the problem but were never successful. The owner tried acupuncture and massage without much luck. He wanted to see his horse run.

It became more and more frustrating. I hated using medications, but knew he couldn't move without them. I was acutely aware that the owner figured since he claimed the horse when he won, why couldn't he win with me? The vet tried injecting stifles which seemed to make matters worse. At the same time, the owner decided to send the horse to Maryland. He became very sore on the trip as standing in a van right after getting his stifles injected is contraindicated. The owner and trainer both complained about his condition when he arrived. We had no way of knowing the horse was going through substance withdrawal. I vowed never to accommodate an owner against my own principles. Trying for results because the owner spent money and wanted action with the horse, not lay up, was not my game. After the trip, this horse was laid up for six months and then started to run without much success. Horses trained my way don't have these problems. They run frequently, and I don't ache because I'm asking a sore horse to run.

I can't leave this subject without mentioning anabolic steroids. A friend of mine, an orthopedic surgeon, has seen the results of using these kinds of steroids on human athletes. He sees a lot of tearing of the muscle insertion on the bone, because a muscle that develops beyond the size it is meant to be is too powerful for the connective framework. It is like putting a huge engine on a small chassis. Nature has devised a beautiful balance with form and function. If larger muscle were needed, stronger insertion ligaments and tendons would develop, along with the framework.

We come along and hyper develop one component (the muscle) while disregarding the rest of the system. This is very dangerous. **Many horses are on anabolic steroids.** These drugs are not illegal. They tend to create very "pissy" personalities. Fillies appear to be in a permanent "PMS" syndrome. Anabolic steroids can make some horses dangerously aggressive! It is questionable if anabolic steroids do enable a horse to run faster. There is no proof that larger muscle mass enhances intrinsic speed. Many gifted runners are not heavily muscled. Imagine the stress on a system when anabolic steroids which increase muscle are coupled with corticosteroids which weaken tendons and ligaments. Heart, lungs, conformation and every other component must blend together to have a great horse.

Try to run and win the right way.

My lovely mare ran four years without any kind of chemical enhancement. She ran on solid training against some super stars. She came back again and again and was clean legged. If you have a talented horse, you can run without all the junk. If the horse isn't talented, nothing will help. Since most of you are doing proper training with good foundation, remember my mare. She was born with a little more speed than average and she ran and won. No cheap shot, no gimmicks.

Try to run and win the right way. You will feel good about what you are doing with your animals. I've had many other horses not nearly as talented as First Prediction, but they ran persistently for years because they had time to grow and develop.

A TALENTED Horse can run with no medications and Last for YEARS!

Why do we have more <u>BREAKDOWN</u> and <u>BLEEDING</u> in racing today? Could it be because of the <u>Potent Medications</u> that give the Horse, the Trainer and the Owner the <u>ILLUSION</u> of <u>SOUNDNESS?</u>

You decide!

THE INFORMED OWNER

These opinions are very personal and are approached cautiously. Experience has taught me that most owners have no idea of exactly how their horse is being trained. They are often intimidated by the backside environment and terminology, a very dangerous and costly position.

This Section describes the purchase of a horse and the typical training routine at the racetrack. When your horse goes to the track, what I describe may or may not happen to your horse.

If your horse was purchased at a two-year-old-in-training sale, he was "cautiously" trained to breeze two furlongs. Many farms break their horses at 18 months and teach them to walk, trot, slow gallop and do figure eights. Depending on the date of the sale, the horse will be turned back out or begin his training, galloping every day or so. If his training begins, he will usually gallop no more than a mile and will be kept in a stall.

Think of what it might do physiologically to a young animal, with green unformed bone, when he is confined in a 12' x 12' stall for as much as twenty-three and a half hours a day. Is this a natural way to raise an athlete?

If your horse came from a farm where he was turned out most of the time during early training, he has a big advantage over the typical racehorse. When you drive through farm country, you see rolling hills with mares and foals grazing in pastures. Unfortunately, once horses go into training or sales preparation, many are stalled. Sales people don't want the horse to get any scratches or injuries that might make him look less attractive in the sale ring. They believe there is risk of injury if the horse is allowed to frolic and zoom around the pasture. Farm managers feel an obligation to protect the animals from such "dangers".

Short-term the horse is coddled and protected. Long-term, he is not learning to be comfortable with other animals. He is missing the natural exercise and growth necessary to be a resilient racehorse.

On large farms, when breaking yearlings and two-year-olds, long-term tranquilizing drugs are sometimes used to make them docile. The breaking process is easier and less time consuming. Many believe this is the only way to break and train fractious Thoroughbreds. I am not comfortable with this idea. The well adjusted, well trained horse will cope better with the racing environment if he has been allowed to develop and learn normally.

A day or two before the sale when these horses are asked to breeze for the first time, usually at the sale site, they will be pushed to get a good timed work. This is when many buck their shins. If the horse you want has bucked shins, buy him, but allow him time to rebuild, grow, and develop. It is too early to ask him to run fast, especially with so little foundation. Don't let him go directly to the racetrack. (See the Sections on Two-year-olds, and Bucked Shins.)

Most horses bought at two-year-old in-training sales are sent directly to the track. They are confined in their stalls, only let out once a day to learn to gallop on the real track. Galloping on the real track allows speed that could never be attained on your farm, speed that is unnecessary, in fact harmful, so early. Since they are not allowed to move naturally, this kind of training starts making them sore. They are only getting a mile or two a day, but they

Should an athlete be confined to a stall
23 to 24 hours a day?

get it every day. Because they are running intensely on the track surface everyday, with virtually no real warm -up or cool-down, the soreness compounds. These sore horses are given medication to allow them to continue training. Usually it is Bute every night.

No two-year-old should be medicated for that kind of soreness. It is much better to rest him and observe the soreness. When it disappears, continue his training. If asked to run without the needed rebuild-time, rest, and gentle movement required to adjust to their work load, these undamaged horses will become damaged.

At the track as the animal becomes more muscularly fit, he is able to go faster. This may be when bone chips start to appear. Then you have green bone, with chips, running on a hard surface. Sometimes the trainer will X-ray and allow the horse to continue training, if he feels the chip won't interfere with the speed. In this case, the horse can only continue with the help of painkillers, corticosteroids and wraps. So, the trainer wraps, gives support therapy, and continues training until the horse is injured. Any two-year-old that needs supportive medication and leg wraps is being over-trained.

The usual training will continue to be one or two miles daily, interspersed with a day or so of walking around the shedrow or on the hotwalker. As a new owner, I vividly recall going to the racetrack for the first time. I saw this type of training and asked if this was all they did. I actually said, ''15 to 45 minutes out of the stall and you charge $35 a day. No afternoon exercise?''

Some trainers, sensitive to their animals, see the problems coming and allow turn-out time back at the farm. Others capitulate, pressured by the owner who wants his horse running until he wins or breaks down.

The breakdown inevitably comes when the vet tries to "help" the horse continue training. He has to tell the trainer that there are medications that will enable the horse to continue running short term, but that they will be damaging long term. Corticosteroids in the joints alleviate symptoms. In conventional training even when the horse is sore, training continues. The horse runs unaware of the damage he is doing to himself, because he feels no pain.

As owners, you should know how to read the vet bills you receive from the track. They may tell you more about how your horse is doing than your weekly talks with the trainer, If you see X-rays on the bill, Red alert! Immediately ask why they were taken . If your trainer says, "Well, he was a little lame'' or ''There is some heat in . . .'' a particular area, tell him to **stop the horse until physical signs are gone.**

Often the X-ray shows nothing, and the trainer continues training. He may not realize that some kinds of damage don't show up in an X-ray until it is too late. By continuing his training program, he compounds the damage.

Once a filly was sent to me from the track who supposedly had bucked shins. They had continued training her and she had won a race, but the trainer told the owner that she just didn't want to be a racehorse. When I looked at the horse, she had very rough looking shins. I had her X-rayed before we went home.

When we got home, I noticed that she didn't want to go into her left lead and that she was slightly lame. Later, the vet called with the results of her X-rays. She showed a very clear crack on her cannon in the vicinity of the rough shin. Previous X-rays had not shown

Allow rest and rebuild-time.
Observe soreness.

the crack, though the horse certainly had physical signs of problems more serious than bucked shins. The lesson here is never ignore your own observations. X-rays and tests only help with diagnosis.

This filly was in training, lame and even won a race. Because the X-rays didn't show a break, she was pushed until damage could be seen. Had she been stopped a few days, when the shin problem started and allowed to heal, she may not have needed six to nine months of rest to heal a fracture. The fact is that there must have been some physical sign in her leg to trigger this X-ray. Until a physical sign disappears, whether the X-ray shows a problem or not, the horse should be turned out and rested. If the horse needs pain relief while he recuperates, by all means keep him comfortable. Do not resume his training program until the medication has been suspended and the horse has no further physical signs. Please be observant with your animals. This program is designed to teach you how to recognize problems.

The background on what might happen at the track should help you to understand that keeping the horse out and loose most of the time in his formative growth period, will allow him to withstand the track pounding. Many breakdowns in young horses could be avoided with a variation in the training regime.

The series of events that lead to the breakdown can sometimes be charted by reading between the lines of vet bills. Some vet bills from a leading trainer are included. They were received by a friend, when her horse was under the trainer's care at a major racetrack. The filly ran in stakes and was a fairly decent allowance horse. She was sent to this trainer by another trainer who told the owner the mare was fine except for a windpuff on her left front.

We will walk through this bill and pretend we are "Columbo". Let's see if we can reconstruct the scenario of the final breakdown of this filly.

Learn to recognize problems early on.

VET BILLS FROM A LEADING TRAINER

THE FOLLOWING VET BILLS ARE FROM AN ACTUAL LEADING TRAINER AT A MAJOR TRACK

TRAINING THROUGHOUT THE EIGHT MONTHS IS $45 a day...
vet bills, shoes, and ponies are all extra.

The horse was at the track a total of eight months. I am going to walk you through those months. This filly had placed in a Stakes and was a solid Allowance horse. She definitely had ability.

Month One

Upon arriving at the track, the horse was seen by the vet.

1/4	Wormed
1/5	X-ray left ankle
1/6	Tube oil
1/8	CBC Blood Chemistry

TOTAL VET COSTS $155

We see the trainer observed something as he had the left ankle X-rayed. The oiling of the horse on day six suggests perhaps a colic. A CBC would not be unusual for a new horse coming into a trainer's barn. There are no further vet bills this month. Perhaps the horse is getting used to the track.

Month Two

2/13	Electrolyte Vitamin JUG
2/13	Banamine Injection
2/14	Adequan Injection
2/15	Pre-Race Treatment
2/15	Pre-Race Injection

HORSE RACED ON 2/15

2/15	Post-Race Endoscopic Exam
2/19	Liver and Vitamin Injection
2/20	Bronchial Injection
2/21	Bronchial Injection
2/21	Inject Right and Left Stifles
2/22	Bronchial Injection
2/23	Electolyte Vitamin JUG
2/23	Banamine Injection

2/24	Adequan Injection
2/25	Pre-Race Injection
2/25	Pre-Race Treatment

Oh no - Not my stifles!

HORSE RACED ON 2/25

Electrolyte jug - IV fluids mixed with electrolytes and vitamins and perhaps other additives. Expensive and unnecessary.

Banamine - A very POTENT PAINKILLER! Lame and sore horses under the influence of this medication appear sound. That definitely means pain was masked! Notice Banamine was given two days before every single race that this horse ran! If administered less than forty-eight hours before the race, it might show up in the drug test!

Adequan i.m., Luitpold Pharmaceuticals, Inc., Shirley, NY. - According to the product insert, "Adequan . . . diminishes or reverses the processes which result in loss of cartilaginous mucopolysaccharides . . . by stimulating synovial membrane activity . . . and increasing synovial fluid viscosity in traumatized equine carpal joints."

Pre-Race Treatment - Perhaps an inhalant of some type to open the lungs.

Pre-Race Injection - Probably a mixture of corticosteroids or pain killers, such as SoluDeltaCortef, ACTH, Adenosine, Medicorten, and Prednisone.

Liver and Iron Injections - Maybe the horse had a low blood count.

Bronchial Injections - Throughout the horse's time at the track, she is given this medication the three days preceding every race. No one can give me a clear answer as to what it is. It might be a medication from Canada called Clenbuteral (a steroidlike product) that has been used as a lung medication and is now illegal.

Injection of right and left stifles - This tells us that the horse is going sore in her stifles. (Horses indicate soreness in the stifles when they are short strided in the rear legs. They may also have trouble backing up or turning in small circles.) The problem may be in the front legs. We see the manifestation in the rear, because the horse compensates by shifting weight to the hind legs. Usually, the stifles are injected with a caustic substance, possibly an iodine type product that causes scar tissue to form in the area. This is called an "internal blister". The track this horse runs on is noted for causing soreness. Stopping this horse and allowing her soreness to heal would be preferable to medicating. The best cure for sore stifles is turnout, long trots and slow gallops on a kind surface.

The Post Race endoscopic exam suggests that the horse quit in the race and didn't run well. The trainer was looking to see if she bled.

THE VET BILLS THIS MONTH WERE $435.

TRAINING CONTINUES AT $45 PER DAY.

BEWARE WHEN YOU SEE INJECTIONS IN JOINTS ON YOUR VET BILL! YOUR HORSE WILL NOT LAST!

Month Three

3/1	Wormed
3/1	Flu rhino vaccine
3/8	Bronchial Injection
3/9	Bronchial Injection
3/10	Bronchial Injection
3/12	Electrolyte Vitamin Jug
3/12	Banamine Injection
3/13	Adequan Injection
3/14	Pre-Race Injection
3/14	Pre-Race Treatment

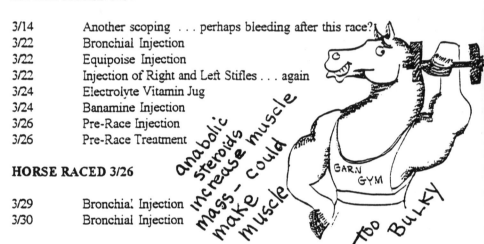

HORSE RACED 3/14

3/14	Another scoping . . . perhaps bleeding after this race?
3/22	Bronchial Injection
3/22	Equipoise Injection
3/22	Injection of Right and Left Stifles . . . again
3/24	Electrolyte Vitamin Jug
3/24	Banamine Injection
3/26	Pre-Race Injection
3/26	Pre-Race Treatment

HORSE RACED 3/26

3/29	Bronchial Injection
3/30	Bronchial Injection

The new injection this month is Equipoise, an anabolic steroid, which increases muscle mass. This is the same (banned) medication that caused such problems when used by the Olympic Athletes. Generally anabolic steroids are those that enhance muscle mass. You'll hear of weight lifters and runners using them. Corticosteroids are injected intra-articularly to alleviate symptoms of damaged joints. They are used systemically (injected intramuscularly) to alleviate swelling and pain. They are a short-term fix for sore horses.

Note that the horse has had her stifles injected again. They are bothering her, but she may not know it in a race, as all the medication she is given masks the problem. She'll be sore when the medications wear off!

She was scoped again. They must be expecting her to bleed. It is just a matter of time with all of these drugs.

TOTAL VET BILLS $400

Anabolic Steroids!

Month Four

4/1	Electrolyte Vitamin Jug
4/1	Banamine Injection
4/2	Adequan Injection
4/2	Injection-Right and Left Ankles
4/3	Pre-Race Injection
4/3	Pre-Race Treatment

HORSE RACED 4/3

4/8	Electrolyte Vitamin Jug
4/8	Banamine Injection
4/10	Pre-Race Injection
4/10	Pre-Race Treatment

HORSE RACED AND WON 4/10

4/21	Bronchial Injection
4/22	Bronchial Injection
4/24	Electrolyte Vitamin Jug
4/24	Banamine Injection
4/29	Bronchial Injection
4/30	Bronchial Injection
4/31	Electrolyte Vitamin Jug
4/31	Banamine Injection

Injection of Ankles !

The worst thing we see this month is the injection for the ankles. The price, $50, tells us it may have been cortisone, the first step toward the destruction of the ankles. Remember, cortisone is used for pain. When given to a human, they are instructed not use or stress the injury. Horses are injected and asked to run hard, starting the cycle of destruction described in Drs. Krook and Maylin's Book, *Race Horses at Risk.*

(The exception seems to be using hyaluronic acid, a substance that is similar to joint fluid. It seems to cushion rough joints and enhance healing. **Horses should always rest after these injections!**)

The rest of the medications are as previously explained. In spite of all the chemicals, the horse does win! Many of these medications are not necessary. However, some definitely "help" the horse run. Others, of course, are destroying the horse because she is able to run when she should really be resting and healing. Continuing with the animal in this manner is counterproductive long term. **As an owner, it is up to you to decide how you want your horse to be handled.** Look for a trainer who has time to work more closely with you and time to get to know your horse rather than load him with medication. Trainers who have small stables might have that kind of time. (This is not to condemn leading trainers. Trainers with large stables simply have less time to work with interested, involved owners.)

THE VET BILL FOR THE FOURTH MONTH IS $377

Month Five

5/2	Pre-Race Injection
5/2	Pre-Race Treatment

HORSE RACED 5/2

5/6	Encephalitis Vaccine
5/19	Bronchial Injection
5/20	Bronchial Injection
5/21	Banamine Injection
5/22	Adequan Injection
5/23	Lasix Injection
5/23	Pre-Race Injection
5/23	Pre-Race Treatment

HORSE RACED 5/23

5/25	Bronchial Injection
5/26	Bronchial Injection
5/27	Electrolyte Vitamin Jug
5/27	Banamine Injection
5/28	Adequan Injection
5/29	Lasix
5/29	Pre-Race Injection
5/29	Pre-Race Treatment

HORSE RACED 5/29

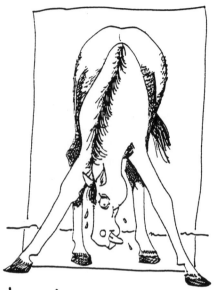

Lasix can dehydrate the HORSE!

This month the filly is put on Lasix. One more stress to an already stressed system. She did win another race this month. With all of the medications and then Lasix, it is admirable that the filly manages to finish races . . . let alone win one. This filly has been put in claiming races since her first start with this trainer. She has been progressively dropped in class with each subsequent race.

THE VET BILLS WERE $435 THIS MONTH

Be careful with LASIX in eXtreme heat!

Month Six

6/2	Bronchial Injection
6/3	Bronchial Injection
6/3	Inject right and left hocks
6/4	Bronchial Injection
6/9	Electrolyte Vitamin Jug
6/9	Banamine Injection
6/10	Adequan Injection
6/11	Lasix
6/11	Pre-Race Injection
6/11	Pre-Race Treatment

HORSE RACED 6/11

6/15	Bronchial Injection
6/16	Bronchial Injection
6/19	Electrolyte Vitamin Jug
6/19	Banamine Injection
6/20	Adequan Injection
6/21	Pre-Race Injection
6/21	Pre-Race Treatment
6/21	Lasix

HORSE RACED 6/21

6/28	Bronchial Treatment
6/29	Bronchial Treatment
6/30	Bronchial Treatment

In one of the races, the filly ran second. We see that this month the hocks have been injected, probably with cortisone or maybe an internal blister. Now she has been treated for sore stifles, sore ankles, and sore hocks. She still runs because she has "heart" and is not aware of her deterioration.

THE VET BILLS FOR THIS MONTH ARE $342

Injection of Hocks!

Month Seven

7/1	Electrolyte Vitamin Jug
7/1	Banamine Injection
7/2	Adequan Injection
7/3	Lasix Injection
7/3	Pre-Race Injection
7/3	Pre-Race Treatment

HORSE RACED AND WON! 7/3

7/12	Bronchial Injection
7/13	Bronchial Injection
7/14	Electrolyte Vitamin Jug
7/14	Banamine Injection
7/15	Adequan Injection
7/16	Pre-Race Injection
7/16	Pre-Race Treatment
7/16	Lasix

HORSE RACED AND WON! 7/16

7/17	Worming
7/25	Bronchial Injection
7/26	Bronchial Injection
7/27	Bronchial Injection
7/28	Bronchial Injection

Lasix! Bronchial Injections! Banamine! Adequan!

This month the horse has won two races. Incidentally, one purse in one of the races was taken back three months later. The DRUG TEST CAME BACK POSITIVE! Perhaps the buildup of so many medications finally showed through in spite of the fact that the horse was on Lasix, a drug that can mask test results. The trainer's comment when he found out, was, "I don't understand. I gave her the same stuff I give all my horses!"

I will agree with that. Sometimes the vet bills of other horses in his barn were on the same page as those of this filly. I could see that every horse got the same stuff. The filly had been progressively dropped in price with each race and that is how she was able to win.

TOTAL VET BILLS FOR THIS MONTH ARE $420

Drug Test Positive! Purse Taken Back 3 months Later!

Month Eight

8/1	Bronchial Injection
8/2	Bronchial Injection
8/3	Bronchial Injection
8/4	Bronchial Injection
8/5	Adequan Injection
8/6	Pre-Race Injection
8/6	Pre-Race Treatment
8/6	Estro IV (Premarin - used for bleeders)
8/6	Lasix

HORSE RACED HER LAST RACE 8/6

8/7	Eye Medication
8/13	Ultra Sound Tendon

Did you notice something different in this bill? The horse has been given Bronchial Injections for a more persistent period of time. I suspect she had a massive lung infection resulting from the bleeding. The medications may have suppressed this temporarily enabling her to run until the medication could no longer mask the damage to her lungs. These injections could be Clembuteral, a lung medication, or Prednisone, a steroid that is used a great deal in lung disease. It has many side effects, one of which is aggression. It is used very cautiously in humans, as the illusion of well-being can fool you into thinking that your lungs are well.

At this point, the horse has an accumulation of problems manifesting themselves. The bronchial injections may help get one more race. Since this trainer certainly knows the signs of distress, he took a final shot. The Estro IV (estrogen - a female hormone) also implies that there might be a problem with her breathing and/ or, her lungs.

I'm not sure the horse even finished the race. I saw her five months after that last race and her ankles were still swollen and misshapen. She had bowed the left front tendon down low and who knows what other damage had been done. It looked like the suspensory ligaments might also have been torn bilaterally. Unfortunately, there was so much disfigurement it was hard to tell. With time the ankles should start healing, but they will never be sound.

Had this horse been handled differently, she could have run for years. She did not have a bad step or bad luck at the track. **This is a text book case of abuse and poor management . . . all done in the name of Horse Training by a leading trainer.** This owner actually paid $45 a day to have a decent, talented horse ruined. He also paid enormous vet bills. Her bow may eventually heal, but she will never run again. She is only four years old. My recommendation to the owner was to breed her, if possible. (Steroids are known to cause fertility problems in horses. In the four years she has been retired, she has yet been able to conceive.)

As I reviewed this horse's history, I felt ill. Seeing the progressive use of medications, there is no doubt to the outcome. I hope you question what is being done to your horse . . . and then maybe he will have a chance for a lengthy career!

ANOTHER REAL VET BILL

This bill reflects a pattern of disintegration I have seen many times over the years in horses sent to me from the track because their performance seemed to be "tailing off". Observing them, I began to feel that I was running a "Betty Ford Clinic" for horses. This particular horse, NJ, arrived at my farm in December. The owner had called and asked if I would be willing to take it. The trainer had said there was nothing wrong with the horse. He had just tailed off. His form deteriorated with each race after he won his maiden race.

This horse, a colt, had been purchased in the March Two-Year-Old In-Training Sale and had gone directly from that sale to the racetrack. So, at the ripe old age of 24 months, NJ (the colt) found himself at the track. Keep in mind he was probably stalled and in training from the age of 18 to 20 months.

When he arrived, he really didn't look too bad. His joints weren't swollen or loggy appearing. It was obvious they had been fired, but he looked reasonably sound. He was very well balanced and proportioned. His legs didn't turn in or out. His conformation was correct. He was turned out in a small paddock. He didn't move when turned loose. He stood in the paddock and showed little interest in his surroundings. At the time this was attributed to the fact he might had been given a tranquillizer.

Upon my request, the owner sent me a copy of the vet bills so that I could try to reconstruct his experience and performance at the track. Let me share the bill with you.

Month One (March)

3/3	Fecal exam
3/14	Tying-up powder
3/24	Firing of shins
3/24	Kling bag
3/24	Tetanus toxoid vaccination
3/24	Firing paint
3/29	Kling bag

We may surmise from the treatment, that the horse was put into training, had a tying-up problem, and was given a powder for it. He then bucked his shins. The trainer wanted to keep him going, had him fired and kept him at the racetrack. It appears that he was probably walked and hosed until his shins were better as there are no bills for April. Remember, this is a 25 month old animal, confined to a twelve by twelve stall and walked once or twice a day for maybe half an hour.

Month Three (May)

5/ 9	Electrolytes and Vitamins
5/27	Fecal exam

Since there are no other bills for April and May, we may assume that NJ is training uneventfully, probably galloping a mile to a mile and a half with gradual increments of speed at the end of the gallops every few days. He may have gone to the gates on occasion. The actual time he spent on the track would have been about 15 minutes a day.

Month Four (June)
HORSE RACED 6/7

6/20	Electrolytes and vitamins
6/23	Bute
6/23	Medicorten
6/24	ACTH
6/24	Adenosine

HORSE RACED 6/24

These bills seemed tame compared to the bills we just examined. But why would a young healthy horse need painkillers and steroids every time he ran? Medicorten is a corticosteroid. **Medicorten and ACTH are very potent anti-inflammatory medications.** They are effective in treating chronic inflammation but have potential side effects that can leave horses seriously crippled. This combination of medications was the pattern throughout NJ's time at the track. It appeared that the trainer and vet were giving these medications just in case, since there were no X-rays or other signs of joint problems.

THE VET BILLS FOR JUNE WERE $130

Month Five (July)

7/11	Medicorten -
7/11	Bute
7/12	Adenosine
7/12	ACTH

HORSE RACED 7/12

7/16	Electrolytes and Vitamins
7/22	Bute
7/22	Medicorten
7/23	ACTH
7/23	Adenosine

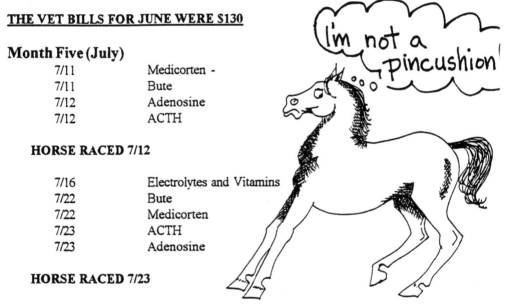

HORSE RACED 7/23

At least no Lasix or other breathing medication have been given.

THE VET BILLS FOR JULY WERE $136

Month Six

8/22	Electrolytes and Vitamins
8/22	Equipoise
8/27	Bute and Medicorten
8/28	ACTH
8/28	Adenosine

HORSE RACED 8/28

I didn't like seeing that he was given Equipoise (an anabolic steroid) usually contraindicated in colts. He might have been off his feed, depressed or unaggressive.

THE VET BILLS FOR AUGUST WERE $113

The vet bills were identical for August, September, October and November. He raced an average of twice a month in October and won his maiden race. He ran poorly after that. He arrived at my farm in December. I told the owner the horse was quite depressed and moving very slowly. He was probably body sore and needed time to heal. He had a little heat in his left knee, but showed no lameness at this time. The vet came out and checked the left cannon bone to rule out fracture from the bucked shins. The X-ray showed no fracture, and at the time the vet noted that he not was lame.

In the middle of January the vet had to return. The horse had begun to show lameness. He was only being turned out and fed. He moved very little but appeared to be in pain and manifested much more heat and swelling in all the joints. He looked very poor. I now wondered if he had chips in joints, as his overall movement had deteriorated. The vet again checked the horse, noting that he was lame in both front legs. The knees and ankles were X-rayed to check for chips. The X-rays showed no bony lesions and rest was recommended.

It was at this point that I started calling vets asking questions about the medications used on the horse. I was told that ACTH suppresses the normal function of the adrenal glands when used long term with corticosteroids, and that two to three treatments a month in the horse's formative growth period was excessive. I also learned these medications could explain why the horse was so depressed and why he showed no colt-like interest in any other animal. It could take months for his adrenal glands to start functioning again.

Please understand that I do not claim to be a PhD in Pharmacology or Veterinary Science. However, I felt the need to try to understand the basics of this very complex field. Some may accuse me of over simplification. The information I gleaned from veterinarians and pharmacologists is shared with you concisely and in laymans terms, because it is vital that we have a basic understanding of the contents of medications given to our horses.

During my inquiries, I saw the following article, *Good Steroids, Bad Steroids*, by Laura Hillenbrand in *EQUUS Magazine* ©1991, Issue 166 (Reprinted with permission of Fleet Street Publishing Corporation). I feel it is worthy of our attention and have included part of it for you. "Corticosteroids . . . synthetically replicate the basic structure of the hormone cortisol, which regulates many functions within the body, including reducing inflammation . . . Some forms have up to **700 times the suppressive power of natural cortisol**. Corticosteroids have proved to be the least expensive, fastest acting, and most effective anti-inflammatory medications ever used in veterinary practice."

Inflammation is a part of the healing process. When you inhibit inflammation, you are also inhibiting healing. Inflammation is also a sign that there is a problem. If ignored and suppressed, you enable the damage to continue. The article further states, "Along with the benefits, these substances carry potential side effects that can leave horses permanently, or even fatally, crippled... all forms of corticosteroid administration carry potentially harmful side effects. Repeated use of these drugs has been shown to handicap the adrenal gland, causing a drop in levels of several other key hormones as well as cortisol and creating hormonal imbalance... because they suppress the immune system and the inflammatory healing reaction, the drugs may also leave a horse vulnerable to undiscovered infection. **The greatest risk in corticosteroid therapy,** however, involves the possibility that the medication will so prevent the body's protective and restorative mechanisms that progressive structural damage occurs. This can happen in two basic ways. First, **corticosteroids can thwart or delay healing to such a degree that supporting capacity is never restored to injured tendons and ligaments, and essential structures such as the cartilage cushions between bones within joints are not regenerated.** Cartilage, which is naturally worn away with use, is slow to heal. **In horses repeatedly given corticosteroids** (especially when the drug is injected intra-articularly), **not only does the natural replacement of old cartilage stop, but the current wear greatly accelerates.** Eventually, **the cartilage is completely worn away and bone rubs against bone, leaving the joint crippled.** Secondly, the pain relief provided by corticosteroids, while doing nothing to cure injuries or inflammatory conditions, can **encourage a horse to use a damaged limb as if it were sound,** unknowingly risking catastrophe with each stride... all experts agree that high, frequent doses of the drug can inflict serious damage."

The article does suggest circumstances when the drug could be helpful. Usually short term, small doses, locally targeted. This information is shared with you because, at first glance, the medications NJ received are not alarming. They were only given when he raced. However, I soon realized that NJ was going through a "drying out" or withdrawal from the medications he had been given. He was now a mere 30 months old but moved and acted like a 30 year old.

Although he was fed and consumed enormous quantities of grain and hay, he lost weight and muscle tone and looked like the kind of horse the Humane Society would fine me for starving. He was self destructing in front of my eyes. By early March the horse was looking worse. I took him to the University of Florida Veterinary Teaching Hospital. They examined and X-rayed him and listened to his history. Their diagnosis was Degenerative Joint Disease. It was possible that the cartilage was completely worn down and could not regenerate, there was so much damage. They had no idea whether he could ever be useful racing again or even sound. At this point, the horse was 33 months of age and had been physically on the track only six months.

After much discussion with vets, he was given four injections of Adaquan* and then the oral equivalent Flexfree. (*GAG-Glycosaminoglycan - It helps cartilage growth, but only if the cartilage has not been totally destroyed).

In early May, NJ had acute swelling in his hind legs. I thought he might be going into renal shutdown or some other kind of metabolic problem. He was hauled back to the vet. The vet found the blood tests to be normal. After that, NJ seemed to recover somewhat. He

"Along with the benefits, corticosteroids carry potential side effects that can leave horses permanently or even fatally crippled."

started to develop a little muscle tone and began light exercise in July. He was subsequently sold to a person that understood he might never be sound.

The point is, this vet bill didn't appear to be excessive and the horse didn't appear to be in bad shape. **Only after he had withdrawal from the medications did his real state of health become apparent.** Why start this process? Train with common sense and leave medications for sick horses . . . not young healthy horses that only need time. Horses treated this way may never make it to a second season of racing. Many horses with similar histories and been unable to return to racing.

One day I ran into this horse's trainer at the track. He asked me about the horse. I told him how the horse had seemed okay when he arrived, but had gone bad in about two to three weeks. The trainer rolled his eyes heavenward, kissed his fingers and said, "Thank You, Jesus!! Can you believe it? While I have the horses, they're fine and then two to three weeks later with others . . . they go bad! And you know what? I know why they are so good with me! It's the medicine! I know what to use . . . thank you God for such good stuff!" This man truly didn't equate the medicine to the disintegration of the horses. He believed the medicine helped them. The fact that anyone can be so ignorant about the cause and effect frightens me. This is a horse trainer. He makes a living in the racing industry and he has not figured out why his horses only last one season.

So many of us are not aware of what is in medications we are giving our horses. I was not aware that SoluDeltaCortef*, Prednisone*, Vetalog*, Azium*, and Medicorten* are all corticosteroids. Since various medications are given persistently over long periods of time, it is not surprising that so many horses suffer the weakening of bone, suppression of normal hormonal function, and the lowering of the immune system. Minor colds and flues that normal horses should recover from in a week persist in these horses. Steroids suppress the symptoms and the horse keeps going. Then when lung problems do show up, they are more acute, because the horse has continued to perform when not well. Clenbuteral*, another steroid-like medication, again enables the horse to perform when he has lung problems and should be resting. Is there any wonder that there is more bleeding today? Horses are running with a false sense of health because of the potent qualities of the medications they are given.

Look at the list of brand names for medications and the explanation of what they are and what they do. Study your vet bills. Know what your horse is taking. "Something to make him feel good at the gate" is not an explanation.

Why is it that so many horses do not last more than one season?

Could there be something wrong with a training process that breaks down so many horses before they ever start one race?

 **Train with common sense. Leave medications for sick horses not young healthy horses that only need time.**

ONE MORE VET BILL ...
WOULD YOU WANT THIS DONE TO YOUR HORSE?

The horse in this story is a 24 month-old filly sold in a two-year-old in-training sale in April. The filly was beautifully conformed . . . she had no "weak tires". She breezed in her "sales work" two furlongs in 22 seconds. Obviously she was a filly with the gift of speed. She was shipped to her trainer and immediately went into training. Her owners told the trainer not to medicate her. The following bills tell the rest of the story.

Month One

5/19	Bute IV 2 GM
5/24	Bute IV 2 GM
5/25	Bute IV 2 GM
5/29	Bute IV 2 GM

Why were injections of Bute given directly into the vein? The trainer convinced the owners that it was so the horse wouldn't get an overdose . . . he had problems when tablets were given in the feed. My own thoughts . . . There is always a risk of infection when injecting . . . especially into the vein. The thought of giving a sound young filly bute just to do early training is offensive.

Month Two

BUTE !
BUTE !
BUTE

6/2	Bute IV 2 GM
6/7	Bute IV 2 GM
6/8	Bute IV 2 GM
6/11	Bute IV 2 GM
6/18	Bute IV 2 GM plus ACTH 40 MG
6/19	Bute IV 2 GM
6/20	Bute IV 2 GM
6/21	Bute IV 2 GM
6/30	Bute IV 2 GM

In the month of June, a period of early training, this filly has been persistently injected. I wonder about the pattern of the Bute. Is there a limit on the amount of Bute that may be used in that racing area? ACTH is a medication that stimulates the adrenal glands to secrete cortisol. When used with frequency, the horse's own adrenal glands will stop functioning.

Month Three

7/3	Bute IV 2 GM
7/4	Bute IV 2 GM plus a Flucort Injection
7/7	Bute IV 2 GM

HORSE RACED 7/8 - Showed promise.

7/12	Bute IV 2 GM
7/23	Bute IV 2 GM
7/26	Bute IV 2 GM
7/27	Flucort injection
7/28	Bute IV 2 GM

HORSE RACED AND WON MAIDEN RACE 7/29

7/31	Bute IV 2 GM

Now we have a horse on persistent Bute. Any pain or swelling will be masked with so much Bute in the system. Be aware that long term use of Bute is hard on all organs including the stomach. Horses may develop ulcers or perforated stomach at a very young age because of so much medication. Flucort is a potent corticosteroid that has lasting side effects.
This supposedly healthy young animal has had 12 injections this month . . . to run in two races.

Month Four

8/2	Bute IV 2 GM and ACTH 50 MG
8/5	Bute IV 2 GM
8/7	Bute IV 2 GM
8/8	Bute IV 2 GM
8/13	Bute IV 2 GM
8/14	Flucort injection

HORSE RACED AND WON 8/15

8/15	Bute injection 2 GM
8/16	Bute injection 2 GM
8/27	Bute injection 2 GM plus ACTH 40 MG and Vitamin E and Selenium injections
8/31	Bute injection 2 GM

The pattern continues . . . Bute, Steroids, and ACTH, twice this month. The vitamin E might be for possible tie-up.

Month Five

9/1	Bute injection 2 GM
9/2	Bute injection 2 GM
9/3	Flucort injection

HORSE RACED AND WON 9/4

9/4	Bute IV 2 GM post race
9/14	Bute IV 2 GM
9/15	Bute IV 2 GM
9/18	Bute IV 2 GM and a nerve block left front check ligament.
9/19	Bute IV 2 GM
9/22	Bute IV 2 GM
9/23	Flucort Injection

HORSE RACED - POORLY 9/23

9/24	Bute IV 2 GM
9/29	Bute IV 2 GM
9/30	CBC blood analysis

check ligament? Hard to diagnos!

We see the usual Bute used here, but there is also a danger sign. Why did they try to block the left front leg? Usually, when lameness has been diagnosed in a particular leg, but not the particular area, the vet will block different points and work his way up the leg. If the hoof is blocked and the lameness persists, the vet blocks the next joint higher until he reaches a point where the horse shows no sign of lameness. If a horse is not given systemic medications that reduce inflammation and heat, it is easier to determine that you are training too hard **BEFORE THE PROBLEM BEGINS**. In view of the Bute and steroids in this horse's system, it would be very difficult to find the cause of a problem. A diagnosis of check ligament usually means that they can't find out what the problem is. In this case, they blamed the lameness on check ligament. One thing sure, this horse has a real problem. Are you surprised?

Month Six

10/4	Endoscopic Exam, EIPH Negative - clean.
10/12	Bute injection 2 GM - CBC blood analysis serum.
10/14	Trimethoprim Sulfa 100- Treats pneumocystis carinii pneumonia and urinary tract infections, Endoscopic Exam EIPH Negative - clean.
10/15	Bute injection 2 GM
10/18	Bute injection 2 GM
10/19	Bute injection 2 GM
10/21	Bute injection 2 GM

| 10/22 | Flucort injection |
| 10/23 | Bute injection 2 GM - A non-steroidal anti-inflammatory |

HORSE RACED - POORLY 10/24

| 10/24 | Coggins test |

In this month it is quite clear that things are going wrong. They keep looking for bleeding. Probably to explain the poor performance. They have run blood tests and given other medications . . . trying to figure out the problem. Could it be the obvious? This animal was trained with no regard to how she was responding to the normal stresses of the gallops. The blatant use of Bute shows that. The persistent use of the corticosteroids which have a long-term cumulative effect could finally no longer keep her problems masked. It is very possible that the trainer felt he was "helping" this horse throughout the program. It is possible that he believes it is inevitable that all horses go bad and it is just a question of how many races we can get out of them before the ultimate crash.

This is the fallacy that must be changed. Horses can race for years! However, during the training process, the trainer must allow the horse to heal from the stress to his body as he grows more efficient. It has been said that the anaerobic fitness in a horse can be brought to optimum capacity in three months. I believe that is true. **But the fact is that the structure of the horse may not be mature enough, soon enough, to sustain his natural speed.** That is why we have "90 day wonders". They can run early but their structure will be pulled apart as pressure is put on green bone and improperly prepared tendons and ligaments. The whole picture must be taken into account. **If you push the horse too fast, he will not last in his career.** Look at the patterns of most modern day horses. They run brilliantly and consistently for a series of races, then they have breakdowns that sideline them for months, years or forever.

Owners must decide what they want. They must allow the trainers to train judiciously and not pressure them, or risk the consequences. By sharing these vet bills, it is hoped that owners will educate themselves as to what they are paying for in terms of real training and what is legitimate medical support.

The filly's last vet bill shows X-rays on November 3. At that point the owners, after seeing two lackluster races and the glint gone from the filly's eye, decided to give her rest and then aim her for a stake a few months later.

The vet exam at the farm reported a dull, depressed animal with little appetite, very quiet and unresponsive for a young Thoroughbred. Lame on the left front. Heat and puffiness in fetlocks. The animal was rested months until soreness appeared to be gone. She was put into light training and as she progressed, seemed to go sore when pressured with any speed. She was reviewed by a Vet University hospital and found to have a broken bone in the foot. This filly was retired as a three year old.

I wonder what kind of horse she might have been if she had been handled differently. She probably would not have won the early stakes that she did win because she would have started racing later. But she might have been around to race usefully for many seasons. She did have the gift of speed!

At 30 months of age, having spent six months at the racetrack, this horse was permanently ruined. Interestingly, endurance horses jumpers, three-day eventers, dressage, and even barrel racing horses are still competing up to 18 and 20 years of age. What is their secret?

COMMON MEDICATIONS:
THEIR USES AT THE RACETRACK

Pre-Race "Feel Good" Medications
ACTH - Adrenocorticotropic hormone
Adenosine
Azium (Dexamethasone) - a corticosteroid
Testosterone - an anabolic steroid
Triple A (a combination of Azium, ACTH
    and Adenosine)
Vitamin B-12

Muscle Soreness
Adenosine
Azium (Dexamethasone) - a corticosteroid
E-SE - Vitamin E and Selenium
Lactonase
Prednisone (Prednisolone) a corticosteroid
Robaxin (Methocarbamol) muscle relaxant

Pain Medication
Aspirin
Azium (Dexamethasone) - a corticosteroid
Banamine (Flunixon megulamine) a NSAID
Bute - Butazoladine (Phenyl Butazone) - a
    NSAID
Betamethasone - a corticosteroid
DepoMedrol - a corticosteroid
DMSO
Prednisone (Prednisolone) a corticosteroid

Circulation
Aspirin
DMSO

Anti-inflammatory
Azium (Dexamethasone) -
    a corticosteroid
Bute - Butazoladine (Phenyl
    Butazone) a NSAID
Banamine - (Flunixon megu-
    lamine) a NSAID
DMSO
Flucort - a corticosteroid
Medicorten - a corticosteroid
Prednisone (Prednisolone) a
    corticosteroid
Vetalog - a corticosteroid

Respiratory Problems
A-H Injections or granules
Azium (Dexamethasone) -
    a corticosteroid
Clenbuteral
DMSO
Glycopyrrolate
Prednisone (Prednisolone) a
    corticosteroid

Calm Down Medication
Calcium and Vitamin B-12
SoluDeltaCortef - a corticosteroid

Bleeder Medication
Amicar
Estro IV - estrogen
Lasix - a diuretic
Naquasone a diuretic
Intal (intra-tracheal)

Some of these medications are long-acting steroids. Others are simply vitamin mixtures. Others are mood-elevating drugs. Still others are potent pain killers. This is not a complete list. It is to familiarize you with names you will encounter frequently on the backside.

COMMON MEDICATIONS:
WHAT THEY ARE AND WHAT THEY DO

I strongly believe that we need to know what medications do for and to our horses. Given that belief and my lack of formal training in pharmacology, I have relied heavily on help and information provided by veterinarian friends and reference books for the next two Sections. *How to be Your Own Veterinarian (sometimes)*, by Ruth B. James has been widely quoted. She provides excellent information in layman's terms as to what each type of medication is and the potential side effects. Any bold type within the quoted material has been inserted at my discretion to highlight important information. Other heavily quoted sources are *The Merck Veterinary Manual, Seventh Edition, The Compendium of Veterinary Products, First Edition*, and *The Complete Guide to Prescription & Non-prescription DRUGS, 1995*.

I hope you will read these Sections with an open mind. A mind that is open to asking questions and seeking answers when things don't make common sense. In order to simplify reading, registered trademark names are provided for some of the medications referred to in the text. Those products without trademark names are generic names or do not appear in the *Compendium of Veterinary Products, First Edition*. All references to the medications are the compilation of information provided by professionals. My interpretation of the material is presented to you in layman's terminology. The cause and effect observations in this entire Section are based on my hands-on experience and are not to be construed as scientific evidence. These medications are extremely beneficial if used therapeutically. They must be used in accordance with the recommendations of the manufacturing company. If you have doubts about their use, refer to the product insert and your vet.

Anabolic Steroids

The following information is taken from *How to be Your Own Veterinarian, (sometimes)* by Ruth B. James, DVM.

"Anabolic steroids are drugs which are produced in the body to allow the young animal to grow normally. Synthetic versions of the same thing have been thought to make young horses grow larger and faster for show or racing purposes. They have also been thought to stimulate the animal's appetite and make him put on more muscle faster than he would otherwise--a lot like fattening a beef for slaughter . . .

The major problem with these wonder drugs is their side effects, most of which are reproductive in nature. Fillies may become masculinized. Abnormal sexual behavior is also seen. The animals may mount other mares and act aggressively toward them.. They rarely come into heat. If they do, the heat is brief and infertile.

Stud colts are also affected reproductively. They have low sperm counts, lowered sperm quality, and smaller the normal testicles. In some cases, they may become completely infertile. Sexual activity was not enhanced by these drugs in the controlled studies . . ."

The Merck Veterinary Manual, 7th Edition lists the following potential side effects: "Epiphyseal plate closure leading to stunted growth; decreased bone strength; and **reduced tensile strength of tendons**; . . ."

Trade names for some of these drugs: **Equipoise** - E.R. Squibb & Sons, Inc., Princeton, NJ; **Deca-Durabolin** - Organon Pharmaceuticals, West Orange, NJ.

Corticosteroids

The following pages are directly quoted from *How to be Your Own Veterinarian (sometimes)*, by Ruth B. James. Many thanks to her for presenting this information so well and for allowing it to be used here.

"'Corticosteroids' is the general name given to a group of hormones manufactured by the adrenal glands (which are found near the kidneys). These chemicals are produced by the body in response to stress. When normally produced, they help the animal to adapt to his surroundings. As manufactured chemicals administered by the veterinarian or owner, these drugs may help the animal to overcome insults to his body. Improperly used, they can render the animal helpless to defend himself against disease.

Horse owners and veterinarians often refer to this class of drugs as "steroids" or "cortisones". Both terms are shorter and simpler than saying "corticosteroids." Generic names include drugs such as dexamethasone, prednisolone, hydrocortisone, and flumethasone. **Azium** - Schering Corp., Kenilworth, NJ, and **Flucort** - Diamond Laboratories, Inc., Des Moines, IA, are perhaps the best know trade names. Other drugs such as **Depo-Medrol** - Upjohn Co., Kalamazoo, MI, and **Betavet Soluspan** - Schering Corp., Kenilworth, NJ, are injected into joints.

WHAT CORTICOSTEROIDS DO-AND DON'T

These drugs help to reduce inflammation and the body's responses to it. They often give considerable relief to acute problems. They may or may not help chronic problems by temporarily reducing inflammation and allowing the body to heal itself.

Steroids affect nearly every system of the body to a greater or lesser extent. They work on the brain, giving an increased tolerance to pain and often true pain relief. They give the animal a sense of well-being and help him to feel better. They also stimulate the appetite. Steroids increase acid production in the stomach; this may be harmful in horses who are not eating. They reduce mucus secretion in the intestinal lining causing decreased lubrication and digestion.

Steroids stimulate potassium loss from the circulatory system which may cause muscular weakness. They help maintain blood pressure and avoid fluid loss. This aids in shock by keeping fluid from leaking from the capillaries and helps keep the blood pressure normal. This fluid retention may allow the feet and legs to swell (a condition called edema).

Steroids increase blood flow to the kidneys and stimulate red blood cell production. On the other hand, they depress the lymph nodes which produce white blood cells; they also slow the movement of these cells. White blood cells act as garbage men in the body and literally "gobble up" bacteria in an infection, rendering

them harmless and disposing of them. **Thus, the fact that steroids slow down these cells may aid the spread of infections.**

Steroids lead to decreased antibody response. For this reason, they are used in human transplants to help keep the body from rejecting the transplanted organ. **This is definitely NOT a desired response in the face of an infection - we need to let the body have all the help it can.. Administration of steroids, especially without accompanying antibiotics, may leave the animal susceptible to disease or allow the spread of bacteria which are already present.**

Steroids affect muscles by increasing protein breakdown. If used for long periods of time, they **may decrease the animal's muscle mass and strength. They also decrease the growth of cells called fibroblasts. These cells form the major part of cartilage and scar tissue and help to heal wounds. By both these methods, steroids may significantly slow growth in young animals. Steroids also interfere with the formation of new bone. Recent studies at Cornell University have pointed to long-term steroid use as causing extensive skeletal damage in growing horses and ponies.**

Steroids reduce mucus secretion in the lining of the respiratory system. Mucus helps trap bacteria and viruses that are inhaled and helps keep them from getting to the lungs and causing infection. Less mucus can leave the animal more susceptible to respiratory disease.

Steroids do not actually cure any disease except adrenal insufficiency. Adrenal insufficiency is a lack of production of hormones by the adrenal glands; it is extremely rare in the horse. Steroids may also help specifically in "auto-immune diseases" where the body "becomes allergic" to itself.

In using steroids, we must balance the good effects against the bad. For example, we do not normally use these drugs with broken bones as they retard healing. If, however, the animal is in severe shock, it is better to use them on a short-term basis and save his life; he can't heal if he doesn't survive the initial shock. **Cortisones are also valuable with horses suffering from endotoxin shock, such as that occurring in salmonellosis.**

Steroids should be used at the site of the problem whenever possible, rather than put into the body as a whole. For instance, injection directly into a joint may cause less long-term damage than giving the whole horse enough to reduce the pain in that particular joint. An ointment may be a much better treatment than an injection of one of these drugs for a skin problem.. This usage gives much better results at the site of the problem while reducing the change of side effects.

Steroids help to relieve symptoms of arthritis and allergies, but do NOT cure these problems. The conditions usually reappear when administration is stopped. In addition, **long-term administration of cortisones may lead to destruction of joint cartilage and permanent damage to the joint surfaces, leading to incurable lameness.** Poor injection technique into a joint may lead to loss of the animal through infectious arthritis in that joint. If the steroids are accidentally injected into the tissues around the joint, they may induce bone formation in the soft tissues. This progresses over a period of several months and may lead to lameness. **To help avoid damage within the joint after a steroid injection, it is of the utmost importance to rest the animal for an adequate**

period of time after the injection is given. Because they slow down cellular growth, steroids may significantly retard the healing of damaged joints.

Cortisone administration is often accompanied by antibiotics to help prevent the spread of infection. These products are especially valuable when used together to treat pneumonia.

Steroids are used in ointments to help treat allergic and inflammatory skin problems. They may also be used in eye ointments. In this form, they are used on healed corneal ulcers to eliminate the blood vessels which grow out onto the cornea during the healing process. These blood vessels may eventually cause blindness if they are not removed.

IMPORTANT: Ointments containing steroids should NOT be used on eye problems without consulting your veterinarian. Using one of these products on a fresh ulcer, cut or scrape may result in rapid spread of the lesion and loss of that eye.

Where should you use corticosteroid drugs? They are valuable for animals who are in severe shock and may help to save the animal's life. They are helpful whether the shock is endotoxin shock due to salmonellosis or is shock from blood loss or severe pain because of an injury.

Full doses of corticosteroid drugs should not be given with phenylbutazone, but partial doses of both drugs together may be more beneficial than either given alone. Give an adequate amount of the drug to do the job., as recommended on the label of the product you are using or as directed by your veterinarian. Harmful effects are most frequently seen with smaller amounts given over long periods of time; this type of treatment should be avoided.

NOTE: Other than using this type drug to treat shock, steroids should only be given on the advice of your veterinarian.

NOTE: There are some conditions in which steroids should NOT be used. They should not be given to horses with kidney disease, rickets, or osteoporosis (weakening of the bone). They should not be given to animals with infections that are not controlled by antibiotics, nor to those with surgical or slow-healing wounds or broken bones. **They should not be given to horses under four years of age because they may severely retard bone growth.**

They should not be used with septic arthritis (arthritis with infection in the joint, such as joint ill in foals). They are of little or no value in chronic lameness with extensive bony changes, such as ringbone.

Administration of cortisones to horses in the last third of pregnancy may cause abortion or premature labor. This may be followed by foaling problems, death of the foal, retained placenta metritis, or all of these. Steroids should not be used in horses with viral diseases or tuberculosis. They should not be given to animals who are being shown or raced, as they are illegal and may show up in blood or urine tests.

Steroids are frequently sold in combination with penicillin/streptomycin products. The combined products should not be used where you DO need a steroid, as they are not generally in high enough concentration in these combinations to do any real good. Using both the penicillin/streptomycin and the steroid separately allows you

to use adequate, therapeutic dosages of each. Using one of these combination drugs where the steroid portion is NOT needed may lead to complications as listed above."

The following information is quoted from *The Merck Veterinary Encyclopedia, Seventh Edition:*

"Dexamethasone and betamethasone . . . are 30-35 times as potent as cortisol as anti-inflammatory agents . . . (With) cortisol and other glucocorticoids intestinal **absorption of calcium is decreased while renal excretion is increased** . . . These effects, in combination promote the mobilization of calcium from bone, and **bone strength is thereby reduced** . . . Side effects: Compounds with mineralocorticoid activity such as prednisolone and prednisone, tend to cause retention of sodium and water, hence, edema . . . Side effects relating to glucocorticoid actions include . . . muscle wasting and delayed wound healing. Altered calcium metabolism can, with prolonged treatment, lead to osteoporosis and bone fractures. Reduced GI motility, thinning of the gastric mucosa, and reduced mucus production may arise, but glucocorticoids are rarely ulcerogenic. Nevertheless, . . . steroids may potentiate the ulcerogenicity caused by some NSAID . . . **Repeated injections or long-acting preparations may induce degenerative changes in cartilage (steroid arthropathy)."**

Other commonly used corticosteroids or steroid-like medications are: Clenbuterol, Prednisone (Prednisolone), Betamethasone, SoluDeltaCortef, DepoMedrol, Medicorten, Flucort, and Vetalog.

DMSO

Another direct quote from Dr. James.

"This drug is really in a class by itself. The technical name for it is dimethyl sulfoxide. It is currently manufactured by Diamond Laboratories (Des Moines, IA 50317). This is a medical-grade product containing 90% DMSO. It comes either as a liquid or an ointment. Other DMSO is on the market, sold by feed stores and roadside stands. This is usually only 50 to 70% pure and may contain unknown contaminants. This less pure form is the one used as a paint thinner and solvent and should be avoided for animal or human use.

DMSO is recommended by the manufacturer and licensed by the Food and Drug Administration to reduce acute swelling due to trauma. At the present time, DMSO is the only product known which will carry other products through the skin. Cosmetic adds notwithstanding, the skin is a very efficient barrier against most substances. DMSO can be mixed with antibiotics, corticosteroids, and other drugs to allow them to be carried through the skin. For this reason it is very important to clip the hair off the area you are treating. Then wash the skin carefully (several times) with an antiseptic soap (such as pHisohex, Winthrop Laboratories, New York, NY 10016) and water. Dry the water off and rinse the area with alcohol. Allow it to dry. Then go ahead and apply your DMSO mixture.

Because DMSO tends to absorb water, it should be kept in a tightly closed container. Otherwise, the next time you use it, you may find that it has absorbed enough water from the air to be more water than DMSO. When adding other substances to it, a convenient way to mix them is in a clean glass fruit jar with a wide mouth. This allows you to use a paintbrush to apply the mixture to the animal's skin. Use only natural-bristle paintbrushes. Over a period of time, the DMSO may dissolve both plastic bottles and nylon paintbrushes. If you are applying DMSO with your hands, use rubber or disposable plastic gloves to keep it off your skin. If you get some on your skin, you may experience an unpleasant, garlic-like taste in your mouth. This means that the drug has penetrated your skin and is circulating in your bloodstream.

DMSO is often mixed with nitrofurazone solution and a corticosteroid to paint on bowed tendons, bog spavins, which have just occurred due to overusage, and similar problems. Some people tout the drug as a cure-all for whatever ails your horse. It's not THAT great, but does have some use in reducing acute swellings. It is used to help reduce hematomas, seromas, and other non-infectious problems where the skin is not broken. It is also useful when drugs, such as phenylbutazone (which must be given intravenously), have been deposited in the tissues outside the jugular vein. Used twice a day for several days, it may help to reduce the tissue irritation and reduce the chance that sloughing will occur from the phenylbutazone.

This drug should not be used on open wounds. DMSO should never be applied after blisters or similar drugs have been put on the skin, as it will carry them right into the tissues, causing a severe reaction."

Non-steroidal Anti-inflammatory Agents

Once again I turn to Dr. James.

"This is the name given to a class of anti-inflammatory drugs which are not related to cortisone. One of the best known of these drugs is aspirin. **Aspirin** - Mallinckrodt, Inc., Paris, KY, can be used in horses. As with the same drug in people, it is relatively safe, and has few side effects, especially when compared to other pain-killing drugs. Horse aspirin are huge pills, in keeping with the size of the beasts we're using them on.

Phenylbutazone is the generic name of the drug most commonly used to reduce pain in horses. Its best-known brand name is **Butazolidine**, otherwise know as "bute" - Wellcome Animal Health Division, Burroughs Wellcome Co., Kansas City. This drug reduces inflammation in a manner similar to aspirin and can help to lower fever. It is used to help reduce the pain in animals who have arthritis and helps to relieve pain due to colic.

The injectable form of phenylbutazone MUST be given intravenously and it can cause a severe reaction if some gets outside the vein. If enough is placed outside the vein, a large area of tissue may slough from the animal's neck, or an abscess may form. Tablets are available. The should be crushed and fed with grain. A paste form similar to paste wormer is available also from Wellcome Animal Health Division.

Full doses of "bute" should not be given with full doses of corticosteroids. These drugs have similar actions and may have adverse side effects when used together at full dosage; partial dosages of each, given together, are permissible.

Horses should usually not be treated more than five consecutive days with "bute" because of the possibility of side effects. The most severe of these is a blood disorder called aplastic anemia. This disorder lessens the number and quality of red

blood cells available to the animal. In the most severe cases, the body may not resume normal production of these cells and the animal may become severely ill. Other side effects include digestive upsets and liver problems. The latter may show up as icterus (a yellowing of the membranes of the eyes and mouth).

Drugs such as "bute" and other anti-inflammatory agents (new ones appear frequently) are valuable for keeping animals with chronic problems in use, when it is used sparingly and only as needed. Flunixin meglumine (**Banamine**, Schering Corp., Kenilworth, NJ 07033) is another of these.

Naproxin (**Equiproxen**, Diamond Laboratories, Inc., Des Moines, IA 50317) is a relatively new anti-inflammatory agent. It comes in packets of powder which are given to the horse with his grain and can be used in much the same manner as phenylbutazone.

One good example of use for these drugs is a rope horse with ringbone who was used in high-school rodeos. There is no treatment for the ringbone. The horse was 15 years old and it would be easy to tell the people to put him down. But why waste the animal's years of training and experience and the fine disposition which made him a champion? Better instead to have the owner give him "bute" paste before the weekend rodeos and rest and coddle the old fellow in between. In this manner, they may get several more years of usage without causing the animal excessive pain.

If a horse is being kept on a nonsteroidal anti-inflammatory agent for a long period of time, or is given the drug at intervals, as with the horse mentioned above, it is often worth trying more than one of these drugs. One may work much better than another for a given animal. Also, it may be helpful to alternate between them to keep the animal from building a tolerance to the medication and to keep side effects at a minimum.

IMPORTANT NOTE: Giving painkillers, such as phenylbutazone, or drugs such as corticosteroids to relieve an animal's pain is NOT a substitute for finding out what is actually wrong with the animal. Using these drugs in this manner is as smart as putting a band-aid on a broken leg and hoping that it will heal. If the animal does not respond to rest and the passage of a little time, consult your veterinarian for an accurate diagnosis."

The Merck Veterinary Manual, Seventh Edition had the following information on NSAIDs;

"Their low solubility . . . delays absorption. *In vitro* studies with phenylbutazone, meclofenamate, and flunixin have shown that these drugs bind to hay and this may explain why peak concentrations in plasma can be delayed for up to 18 hours in horses . . . Side Effects: The most common side effect is irritation and possibly ulceration of the GI mucosa. All NSAIDs exert this action to varying degrees . . . **With toxic doses of phenylbutazone (only moderately greater than therapeutic doses),** ulceration in horses has been sufficiently severe to cause hemoconcentration and death from hypovolemic shock."

Sulfa Drugs

The following information is again taken from Dr. James.

"Sulfas were the first class of drugs able to attack and retard the growth of bacteria. This effect allowed the body to overcome the bacteria and survive the infection. Sulfa drugs were developed around the turn of the century and came into widespread use shortly afterward, saving the lives of many people. Sulfas were extensively used on animals until antibiotics were discovered and put into common usage. Sulfa drugs are still occasionally used, either as injections (which must be given intravenously because the solution is irritating) or in eye and other ointments. They are also used in the form of a sulfa-urea solution which is very effective for removing debris from the surface of old, contaminated wounds (see Wound Medications)."

Calcium and Vitamin B

Calcium is an antihypocalcemic dietary replacement. Sometimes it is given with vitamin B on race day as calm down medication in horses. If used with diuretics such as Lasix, there is increased calcium ratio in the blood due to water reduction. If used with Bute, there is decreased pain relief.

Intal

An antiasthmatic, anti-inflammatory (non-steroidal). It is used for bleeding in horses and blocks histamine release from most cells. If used with cortisone drugs, there is a reduced cortisone effect.

Lasix

A diuretic (loop) antihypertensive. It is used for bleeding in horses. It decreases fluid retention by eliminating sodium and water from the body. If used with cortisones, there can be an increased potassium loss. The following is quoted from an article Dr. Sue Hengemuhle wrote for the *Backyard Racehorse Newsletter*, "Countless scientific studies have shown that furosemide (Lasix) effectively reduces pulmonary hemorrhage in horses with EIPH (bleeders). When phenylbutazone is given with Lasix, the pulmonary artery pressure rises back up to the values seen prior to giving the Lasix and bute; its as if you never gave Lasix if you give bute with it.

Glycopyrrolate

Is used for respiratory problems in horses. According to *The Complete Guide to Prescription and Non-prescription DRUGS, 1995*; "It blocks nerve impulses at parasympathetic nerve endings, preventing smoother (involuntary) muscle contractions."

Robaxin - Skelaxin - Paraflex.

Muscle relaxants and block the body's pain messages to the brain. In humans they are used as adjunctive treatment to rest, analgesics, and physical therapy for muscle spasms.

Hyaluronic Acid

The Merck Veterinary Manual, Seventh Edition continues:

"Hyaluronic acid is a normal constituent of connective tissue matrix and synovial fluid... Excellent clinical responses have been reported following the intra-articular injection of sodium hyaluronate in equine joint disease... although there are no serious side effects, local swelling has been described in some horses."

SETBACKS

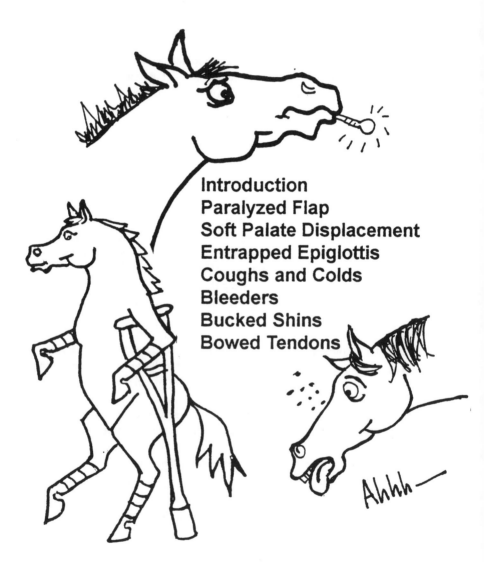

Ahhh—

SETBACKS - Introduction

Every owner enters into the joy of owning a racehorse with the illusion that the horse will start training, run faster and faster, and win lots of races. Unfortunately, it rarely ever happens this way.

Training a horse to be a sound racehorse is very much like raising children. You put in a lot of foundation, survive the childhood diseases, and the personality conflicts, before you arrive at a whole and complete person. Most of the time, with a horse, we don't know whether training is cost effective until we see how fast the horse can run. Sometimes we find we have spent too much money and effort on a slow horse.

No trainer can guarantee anything. In fact, it seems to challenge the fates if the trainer is foolish enough to say something like, "This horse is going to be a big winner." Disillusioned owners have told me many stories, even accusing their trainers of lying to them about horses. More than likely, the trainer was completely sincere. **He believed the horse he recommended for $20,000 would win back his cost, although statistically most horses will not pay their way, let alone their initial cost.**

If it were easy, trainers wouldn't have to work so hard and get up so early. A very clever trainer I knew told me my problem was not educating my owners properly. "Just tell them it's like owning a boat," he said. "The owner doesn't expect his boat to make him money. He has it for the pleasure it gives him." This might sound good, until you realize a boat doesn't humiliate an owner by running last in front of friends who have bet the boat very heavily.

Most of my owners are self-made men, the kind that can't relate to paying $20,000 for a horse, putting another $6,000 into training and being told the horse might be able to win in a field of $2,500 claimers. Who could relate to that, anyway? But, many times it is the scenario. It is possible **that the horse may be very useful at that level and steadily bring in enough money to justify his expenses.**

The joy of seeing your horse win at any level is a great experience. Of course, if the horse starts making money at a given level, he may be claimed. Other astute trainers or owners see that he is useful. They pick him up and make money from all your hard work. Nobody ever said life was fair.

I share this with you because many owners tell me they had bad luck . . . their horse got a cough . . . bucked his shins . . . popped a splint . . . Lord knows when he will run. This really isn't bad luck. It is very typical of a young horse going through normal experiences on his way to becoming a real racehorse. Just as our children experience coughs and ear aches in the process of growing up, **horses must encounter and overcome minor setbacks.**

Down time is expensive to owners paying $45 a day or more for training. Often the trainer, aware of the owner's attitude, feels pressured to continue training too soon when faced with a setback.

If the horse gets a cold at the track, he will probably be treated with antibiotics. Infections can bounce back and fourth in the shedrow . . . especially among young horses. This is another reason I encourage waiting to take horses to the track until they are more mature and have a higher resistance level. Coughs, colds and minor lameness are not as

Setbacks are part of developing a mature racehorse.

crucial at home as they are at the track. At home the horse has more space. Germs are less concentrated. It is easier to allow more time to recover when you're not paying expensive day money. Many times a few days or a week of turnout will allow the horse to fight the common cold or cough.

The following Sections describe common and predictable setbacks, and how to treat them. Remember, my way is not the only way. These are solutions that work for me.

Until you have more experience, many of you will want to confer with a vet about these problems. *Lameness in Horses*, by O. R. Adams and *Equine Medicine and Surgery*, by American Veterinary Publications were my "bibles" when faced with a setback. *How To Be Your Own Veterinarian (sometimes)*, by Ruth B. James is an excellent book on just what it says. An excellent book on anatomy is *Color Atlas of Veterinary Anatomy*, published by J .B. Lippincott Company, Gower Medical Publishing.

BE AN INFORMED OWNER!
Read and Learn!

Do your homework, constantly learn from experience. Never be afraid to ask questions if something doesn't make common sense to you.

PARALYZED FLAP

A paralyzed flap is a big setback for the horse. If you suspect this problem, your veterinarian will slip an endoscope into the horse's nose to see whether or not the horse has Laryngeal Hemiplegia (Paralyzed Flap).

Simply put, because of a malfunctioning opening, the horse is unable to take in the air he needs, especially when he is under stress. This is a very frustrating problem and is most dramatic for racehorses.

Many times you don't know your horse has this problem until you finally redline him. During a hard work, a young horse in training, may make a "roaring noise" or stop running hard for no apparent reason. A vet exam will confirm whether he has a lazy or paralyzed flap. Lazy flap is an early sign of paralyzed flap. A lazy flap is slow to open and close. Eventually it becomes paralyzed.

There is a surgical procedure to correct this condition. I have not had very positive results with it. In an informal survey of trainers, few felt it was worth the effort or cost. Unless your horse shows real talent, don't invest time and money in the procedure. Before making any decisions, go to a large veterinary center where many of these procedures are performed and talk with experts in the field. As in all medical procedures, methods are improved every day.

SOFT PALATE DISPLACEMENT

This breathing problem occurs when a horse is running and displaces his soft palate, therefore impeding his airflow. Sometimes tying his tongue will help. Sometimes surgery is recommended. As always discuss such a procedure with a reliable vet before making any decisions. (See Bag of Tricks and Equipment for Racing.)

ENTRAPPED EPIGLOTTIS

This is yet another variation on breathing-related problems which impede air flow. In this case the horse must be scoped for diagnosis. I understand that a very minor surgery can remedy this problem. Be sure to investigate all medical and surgical procedures thoroughly before making your decision as to treatment.

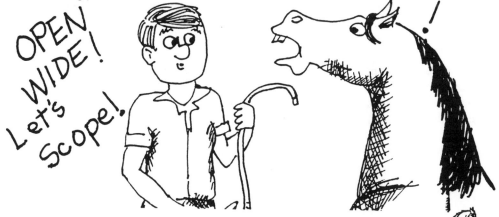

It's very frustrating when you find a horse with potential who suffers from any of these problems . . . it's all part of being in the business.

COUGHS AND COLDS

When you start working your horse and you notice he coughs deeply in an unusual way or is breathing funny, it may be a cough or a cold. There might be colored mucus, yellow or green, draining from his nose. Stop working him immediately! Turn him out unless the weather is cold and inclement, or he becomes nervous when he is out. If you must stall him, make sure he is walked or turned out briefly each day. He needs movement to help him cough and drain the mucus.

Never leave a horse in a stall 24 hours without some kind of exercise, even if he is ill. His legs can stock up and other problems can occur if you don't stir up his blood. Ten minutes of hand walking twice a day will help.

Three days . . . that is my magic number. If the horse doesn't show improvement in three days, call the vet. Of course, if he has a high fever, is in acute stress or looks severely ill, call the vet immediately. **Consult the vet before using any cough remedies or medications. Many have substances that must <u>not</u> be used within so many days of racing.**

Don't load a horse with antibiotics for minor illnesses. Use your common sense. Remember your first child. The pediatrician was called incessantly until you learned to relax and not over react. After you handle enough horses, you'll learn not to over react.

Allow your horse rest and turnout until he no longer coughs or breathes funny. Then try free roundpenning him. If he starts coughing persistently, he needs more rest. If he coughs a few minutes and then seems all right, continue the free roundpenning.

If your horse is stalled at the track in the winter, it is possible that the air he is breathing in his stall is more harmful than the cold air outside. Urine odors and germs get trapped in tightly closed barns. The horses toss all kinds of viruses back and forth among themselves. It is possible that chronic low-grade respiratory infections may be a cause of bleeding. Single stalls with a half door open to the outside are better for horses as fresh air can circulate through the stall.

Horses have ciliated epithelial cells in their nasal passages and upper airways. These cells are responsible for trapping dust, mold spores and other debris prior to their entry to the lungs. Drs. Jackson and Pagan of Kentucky Equine Research believe the ammonia from urine and manure in enclosed stalls damages these cells, leaving the horse more susceptible to molds and other pathogens.

Remember, if your horse has been given the various systemic steroids which are so popular now, his immune system will be very weak and he will be susceptible to any kind of virus. Medicorten, Vetalog, Prednisone, Prednisolone and Azium are all **steroids that will lower his immune system.** Don't use them as short cuts to racing young horses!

Horses seem to have fewer respiratory problems when kept outside under good shelter as opposed to poorly ventilated barns.

BLEEDING (EPISTAXIS)
EXERCISE-INDUCED PULMONARY HEMORRHAGE

Before I talk about bleeders, I want to share a story with you. Thirty years ago I lived in a small tropical village in Colombia, South America. Although I had always loved horses, I knew very little about them. On weekends, the local vaqueros and campesinos would come galloping into the village to have fun and raise cain. They rode their criollo horses . . . pretty little animals with fine Arab heads. The village was small. They would gallop back and forth along the main street, showing off and drinking, knowing that the young women in the town were peeking out of their huts to watch the antics. The cowboys would race up and down the street, spurring their horses to a wild gallop, yanking them to a halt, then whirling and racing off in the other direction. Often, a horse would collapse and sometimes die. Bright red blood would gush from his nostrils when he keeled over. At the time, although I had no understanding of equine exercise induced pulmonary hemorrhage, it was obvious to me that the horses were run to death.

You must understand that these horses were work animals. Their primary function was to provide transportation. The vaqueros constantly rode among the cattle looking for animals with wounds, cuts, or for a new calf with a fresh umbilical cord. Such an abrasion would provide access for the screw fly. In their saddle bags, the vaqueros always carried a bottle of "McDougal", a creosote based medication that eradicates and prevents screw fly. It would be immediately applied to any animal with an abrasion. The campesinos rode their horses up and down the narrow trails through the Andes mountains between their farms and town. These horses often doubled as pack animals carrying supplies up and produce, often coffee, down. They were not prepared for speed. Galloping was not a part of their daily lives.

Today there is endless discussion as to what causes bleeding. I can't help but think that one of the main reasons could be simply pushing a horse beyond his physical ability. Human athletes, when pushed beyond their limit, may show break-through bleeding in the lungs. Another reason could be the lack of preparation for the work asked of them.

Long before I saw these problems at the track, I saw horses overworked and bleeding. Could it be that obvious . . . more stress than the system can handle? Should we look for ways to teach a horse to run . . . but not run beyond what his structure can tolerate? Since horses can run themselves to death, are we setting them up to do more damage when we give them steroids and other medications that may enable them to run in spite of physical limitations and lack of conditioning?

There are many theories about bleeding and what causes it, but there are no proven answers. Typically, your horse is running, and in the middle of the race or in the stretch, he throws his head up and stops running well. His big moves and hard drives stop and he just gallops in. By the time he gets to the finish line, the horse might manifest bleeding by having blood pour out of his nostrils spattering all over his body. This is not a pleasant sight. The track vet and stewards make official notice of it and put him on the Bleeders List.

Bleeding might manifest itself with no visible problem . . . no blood . . . no throwing the head up. Your horse just fades and gallops in leaving you to scratch your head as you go back to the barn wondering what went wrong. Then after you walk him a few rounds and

**Until you have a bleeding problem,
you're not really even aware of what it means.**

let him drop his head to graze, you notice a trickle of blood coming from his nostrils. He too is a bleeder.

Some horses gush, others show a trickle and some bleed so little you don't know it until you've seen them race a few times fading in the drive. In desperation, you ask to have the horse scoped to eliminate the possibility of bleeding.

When you have your horse scoped, the vet will meet you at the barn after the race or work. The horse must have been stressed enough to trigger the bleeding. The vet will examine the horse with an endoscope to see if there is any bleeding that hasn't worked its way up and out yet. If the vet verifies that there is bleeding, he will send you to the State Vet, who will observe the horse and put him on the Bleeders List. (All of the rules mentioned apply to Florida tracks. Check the regulations in your racing jurisdiction!)

If your horse is put on the Bleeders List, it means that he must not run for two weeks and may be given Lasix four hours before his next race.

Once your horse is on the Lasix List, it is announced in the program and your horse must be on the grounds at least four hours before the race to have the Lasix administered by a vet. If your horse is observed bleeding through the Lasix, he will be ruled off for six months. If he continues to bleed, he will not be allowed to run. Some trainers, who fear the horse will bleed through the Lasix, instruct their grooms to keep the horse's head high after the race. The groom will lead the horse off the track with the horse's head resting on his shoulder so that blood does not drip in front of the officials.

Studies suggest that use of Lasix may improve any horse's performance, whether he's a bleeder or not. When Lasix is given, a horse tends to run better the first time back. The betting public likes knowing about Lasix administration. They think, "If the horse was

moving well before he started to bleed, he might move really well with Lasix." There is also a belief that if a horse is on Lasix, other drugs can be given and the test results will be clouded, making it possible to administer illegal or unproven substances under the cloud of confusion.

I personally am very uncomfortable with a bleeder. If you have to give Lasix, be acutely aware of the diuretic effect it has on the horse's metabolism. I believe it is very dangerous to use Lasix, especially in heat and humidity. One hot afternoon at Calder, two Lasix horses dropped dead in the same race.

Think about the effect of Lasix, a powerful diuretic, on the horse's system. Four hours before a race you take away his water bucket

Water is Taken away from Lasix Horses 4 hours BEFORE RACE !

and give him a shot of Lasix. Soon he starts urinating. Some horses react to the medication with trembling. Others pass a loose stool. They all lose fluid. The theory is that Lasix lessens the pressure against the capillary walls by lowering the volume of fluid. In effect, the same amount of red blood cells are being circulated through the system, but with less fluid. Maybe, because the blood volume is less, they don't bleed as easily?

What is really going on physiologically? When you are running a horse in severe heat with chemically induced fluid loss and he is redlining his system, how can he lower his temperature with sweat if his fluid volume is already low? Does this combination of stresses (heat, severe exercise, fatigue and lack of water volume) cause an imbalance in his electrolytes which can cause irregular heart beat, heart attack and death? An electrolyte imbalance can cause heart attacks.

I don't have any answers, but I do think Lasix must be used cautiously, and not too frequently. You must allow the horse time to recuperate from its effects. A Lasix horse needs supplemental help with electrolytes and plenty of time to recover.

The remarkable thing is that Lasix does improve some bleeders. Horses can run usefully with Lasix under certain conditions. However, if you race too frequently, your horse will start to show the effects and his performance will reflect them.

My horses, trained with the incremental stacking of stress (over the time period recommended), don't seem to bleed. I don't think this is coincidental. It is thought that bleeding does relate to speed work. We don't usually see it in horses doing long slow gallops. Bleeding has been observed in Quarter Horses who were flat racing and barrel racing. Early studies indicated a higher percentage of bleeders than among Thoroughbreds. Quarter Horses are not given much racing foundation since they are asked to run only short distances. Are they being asked to do too much without incremental preparation?

There are many theories to consider. Does it have something to do with the fragility of capillaries? Where does respiratory illness fit in? Could previous bouts of severe coughs or flu leave scar tissue that eventually tears and bleeds when the lungs are redlined? Is it the stress of the race, redlining the structure, that causes bleeding? Is it asking a horse, who has not been gradually brought up to the point of fitness necessary for the race, to run too hard, too soon? We must keep all of these possibilities in mind and train judiciously. Horses are very honest, and capable of giving much more than is physically safe for them. Fillies are always in danger of giving too much. If you work them too hard, too soon, you can ruin them for life. A horse should rise to the occasion and ease comfortably into running his best for a sustained distance. Some horses are overachievers and try too hard for their own good. They may bleed because the constantly give 110 percent and harm themselves in the process.

The effort of going into pure speed without incremental preparation could trigger a bleeding problem. To me, it is like flooring the engine of your car without a good, gradual warm-up. Sudden, pure speed is hard on a cold engine. It's even harder on an unfit horse's lungs and structure.

Be aware that there are also additives that can affect this problem. A situation that comes to mind is a filly that was sent to my farm to swim. She had undergone knee surgery. At that time MSM, a powder form of DMSO, was being touted as a great thing to speed up the healing of joints. The theory was that DMSO opened the blood flow to the capillaries;

Bleeding is a very complex subject.
If your horse has the problem, call the nearest university
or speak with a good vet and try to determine
what might help.

and the increased blood supply induced quicker healing (more good blood in, more damaged material out). I was told to give specified amounts of MSM to this filly, twice a day.

At the same time, a friend was suffering from chronically aching knees. The owner of the filly suggested that my friend take a spoonful of the same stuff two or three times a day. Everybody was talking about DMSO. My friend was in such chronic pain that he tried it. He jokingly commented that aside from an inexplicable desire to snort, whinny, and paw, he felt relief in his knees. Soon, he started having uncontrollable nose bleeds. They were so bad he had to be taken to the hospital to have his nose packed. Back home, he wondered if the nosebleeds were related to the DMSO. He stopped taking the powder and the nosebleeds stopped. He started taking the powder again and the nosebleeds resumed. Obviously this was not a medically controlled experiment, but I stored the information in the back of my mind.

Finally, the mare was sent to the track. I was told that upon her arrival, DMSO was administrated intravenously by a vet. Now the mare had been given powdered DMSO, DMSO IV, and knowing the racetrack, they were probably painting her knees with DMSO too. The horse started to run and she bled. She was put on Lasix. When she ran again, she bled through the Lasix, they had to take her home.

I told the owner about my friend's observations and asked him if he thought there could be any connection. He asked his vet and reported back to me that the vet said, ''No. No relationship whatsoever.''

I personally believe horses are given far too many substances that try to fool Mother Nature. Why not just keep your horse healthy, exercise him properly and give him time to rebuild from the extreme stress of a race?

Various vets have suggested that a horse might have a slight amount of bleeding when trying his hardest. They go on to say, if the horse is given time to heal from the intense race or work, there isn't a chronic problem. **They believe the problem starts when a horse has no time to rebuild.** Racetrack routine encourages works and or races every five days or so. What happens if the lungs are healing and the horse is dosed with steroids and mood enhancers, and then worked or raced five days after his last bleeding episode? More damage in the lungs, and retarded healing?

Hose the face when you bathe your Horse!

Then, because he's a bleeder, he's given Lasix, Bute and a plethora of steroids on the day of the next race. Now he's running with medications that may enhance his performance while tearing apart his lungs. Any emphysema sufferer will tell you how much Prednisone*, an adrenal corticosteroid, helps his breathing and mental attitude. He'll also tell you that his **symptoms** are relieved and he feels very aggressive. These are good qualities for a race horse, but **no healing** has taken place. The discomfort is gone, but the **damage** is still there!

After a horse runs several times with these medications, the damage catches up with him. It's not just using Lasix. It's Lasix plus all the steroids and pain-killers that cause such damage!

The two most important things a trainer should learn are how to develop natural talent and how to avoid breaking down the horse before discovering the lack of it.

There are many concoctions on the market to help control bleeding. Some have a basis in diet, some are homeopathic, some naturally lower blood pressure, some like rutin, help coagulation and some are complete feed programs.

It is far easier not to have to deal with bleeding at all. **The point is that most racetrack ailments are related to pushing a horse beyond his abilities.** If you begin with a sound horse and follow the incremental training program, maybe your horse won't bleed.

Before we leave the subject of bleeders, I want to tell you about two horses I had in my barn. One was a lovely, large, honest gelding. This horse showed ability and had speed and courage, but could not carry the speed far enough to win. He lacked the capacity to deliver enough oxygen to carry his speed for the distance. He tried hard every time he ran, but seemed to always fade in the lane. Since he was very fit and had come off of a good foundation program, I knew it wasn't lack of conditioning. He tried hard in the race, and was off his feed a day or so after the race, which told me he was giving what he could. He had been scoped and the vet declared him sound.

I informed the owners that he just didn't have what he needed to be a racehorse. However, he was so lovely, I felt he would have a good second career as a jumper or in the show ring.

The owners wanted to try "helping" him. He was sent to a leading trainer's barn in another state and put on the medication routine there, which included Lasix and all the legal chemical enhancements available. He bled through the Lasix and was ruled off the track. He never won a race. He didn't run any better than he had with me and without the medications. The owners spent thousands of dollars more and ended up with a compromised horse.

The other horse was an owner's "home bred" with very little racing blood in his pedigree. After a few works, I told the owners I didn't want to start this horse, because he showed no ability. They knew I didn't use medications or enhancements, so they gave the horse to another trainer who tried to "put speed" into him by beating him out of the gates every day. He tried so hard that within a week of this routine, after a two furlong work he was bleeding.

"Aha!" said the owners. "That's the problem! Let's put him on Lasix." They did. The horse started bleeding through the Lasix and developed a terrible lung infection. They tried to treat it for a while at the track, but finally he was so sick he had to be taken home. His lungs are probably ruined for life and he still doesn't have the natural ability to be a racehorse.

It is difficult for owners to accept and understand the concept of talent. They think maybe if you hit him harder or train him more aggressively, he will improve. Instead, such treatment may cause an honest horse to over exert and break down. The two most important things a trainer should learn are how to develop natural talent and how to avoid breaking down the horse before discovering the lack of it.

**As far as helping a bleeder goes, do your homework.
There is new knowledge available everyday.
Someday someone will have an answer.**

Bucked Shins

Sore Shins

Usually 2 or 3 days after a hard work!

The horse doesn't want you to touch them!

BUCKED SHINS

If the worst problem your horse has is Bucked Shins, consider yourself lucky. If handled properly, they are a minor setback along the way to a mature racehorse. They can occur at any age when the bone is challenged, although they are more common in young horses.

The general consensus of opinion is that Bucked Shins are a tearing of the periosteum sheath caused by concussion and speed, and are generally found in immature horses. They can be considered a series of micro fractures. They usually occur when speed on a firm surface "insults" the bone. They can easily become a saucer fracture if not handled properly.

When the horses on my farm ran on a kind surface, even putting on speed, they didn't have shin problems. When they started racetrack works, after about three works spaced seven days apart, the horses would get sore or bucked shins. Since by this time the horse is getting anaerobically fit, working five to six furlongs, **I believe the stress of high speed at a sustained distance on a firm surface can cause Bucked Shins or soreness.**

If your horse has sore shins, he will be touchy when you run your hand down the front of the cannon bone. If the shins are really bucked, after two or three days, you will see a little knot or swelling on the front of the leg. If it is severe, the horse may stop in the middle of the track work and walk back in obvious distress. Then if you even point at the shin, the horse will pick it up quickly and very clearly tell you that it hurts. Sometimes it is not apparent that a horse has bucked his shins until 2 or 3 days after the work. Frequently, I have felt a horse worked well and had come out of the work fine. Then two or three days later, during his daily monitoring when I think he's out of the woods, much to my surprise he manifests sore or bucked shins.

 Bucked shins are a minor setback if handled judiciously.

If the shins become extremely sore, have them X-rayed to rule out a true fracture. If there is no fracture, follow your vet's advice, which will probably be poultice and rest. He may suggest "cooling the shins out and firing" them. This is a thermal cautery. Heat is applied to a series of needles that are pressed onto the front of the cannon bone. It reminds me of putting gun powder on a wound to sterilize it.

Many trainers and vets swear by the method. I almost had it done to one of my horses, but at the last minute I declined because it made no common sense to me. They say, "Well, cooling the shins out and firing them forces you to rest the horse. He is so inflamed that you couldn't possibly train him until the swelling and reaction subside." This is a poor reason to administer the procedure. Must a horse be incapacitated in order to rest him? Some horses rebuck even with this treatment. So what is gained?

Chemical blistering is also a common remedy for sore shins. A very caustic solution is rubbed or painted on the horse's shins or completely around the front cannon bones. This causes a reaction like a terrible chemical burn. The legs swell up tremendously. The trainer then "works" on the legs until they come back to "normal", at which point he starts training again. Many trainers feel the blister and resulting scar tissue "toughen" the shins.

Over the years, I have found a solution that works for me. When your horse comes back from a work with sore or bucked shins, continue monitoring his legs every day and turn him out every day . . . all day if possible. To monitor him, gently and lightly run your hand down the front of the shin. His reaction to your touch tells you how sore he is. If the horse has been X-rayed and has no fractures, don't give him Bute. Observe how he walks and moves daily.

If he is really inflamed, by all means poultice him, but don't wrap the shin with more than two turns of cellophane. That's all - no standing bandages! Be careful with the cellophane. It can be put on so tightly in so many layers that it cooks the skin. After wrapping the horse's shins, turn him out. The next morning pull off the cellophane wrap and let the poultice dry and flake off. The following day hose until the poultice is entirely removed. Repeat the process if you feel it will help. Depending on the severity of the inflammation, your horse should not be as touchy on the shins after five days. At this point you should be able to tap the front of the shin with your finger. Learn how quickly he yanks his leg back in response your touch. He should gradually become more tolerant of the tapping. Always monitor his shins no matter how you think he is feeling, and write your observations on his chart.

When your horse seems better and is moving freely on his own in the paddock, gently free roundpen him at a light gallop. If the surface is hard, he may show a little soreness. Monitor his shins the day after the roundpenning by running your hand down the front of the cannon bone or tapping along it with your finger. You must do this every day and continue to note his reactions on the chart. If he is more sore, let him rest for two or three days before you free roundpen him again. If he is less sore, gently free roundpen him. When he is not sore, go back to training.

Work him again no sooner than 14 days from the first day of soreness. If he comes back sore, repeat the process from the beginning. He should heal more quickly this time because he is now starting to strengthen his bone and is laying more bone density on the front

Now you see why it only looks easy.

of the cannon bone. You are trying to encourage new tissue to be laid across the bone. While you don't want to push the horse to overdo and fracture the bone, you do want to ''judiciously insult'' the bone. You will get a feel for this as you go along. You must monitor your horse every day and refer to your notes on his chart to maintain a good point of reference.

Never work him at the track more frequently than every ten days when he has had sore shins, even if he is not sore after five days. It takes ten days to replace the calcium lost in a hard work at the track. By allowing a certain amount of healing and not confining or stopping the horse, his body can repair, rebuild and toughen the shins. It may take two to six months for your horse to come out of the works or races without being sore. If he shows no soreness when you run your hand down the cannon ten days after his last soreness, put him in a race or work him. If your horse is racing at this time, make sure he isn't sore going into the race. Don't give Bute and fool yourself into thinking he is not sore when he is.

None of my horses have rebucked after this treatment. Bucked shins must be ''worked through.'' When your horse has recovered, you will see that his shins have a thickness that makes them almost appear convex.

Your vet may have other ways of treating bucked shins. He may even turn the horse out for three months, which should not hurt him. I prefer my treatment. The horse loses little conditioning time and continues to race even as he heals.

Learn to read the Horses' Body Language!

Don't give Bute and fool yourself into thinking he is not sore when he is.

BUCKED SHINS

X-ray horse to determine
no fractures.

Sore shins usually appear after 3rd or 4th
speed breeze at the track - caused by
high speed at sustained distance on a
hard surface!

Horse will be <u>very touchy</u> when
you go <u>near shins!</u> <u>Check
severity of soreness everyday!</u>

<u>Give rebuild time.</u>
<u>Turn horse out!</u>
After 5 days or so, <u>he should
be able</u> to <u>free roundpen.</u>

Shin

a "bump"
might appear
2 days or so
after Speed
Work

<u>Don't give Bute!</u>
His soreness keeps him from hurting himself.

<u>Check Shins</u> on <u>6th day</u>.
If <u>more sore, leave alone</u> another 2 or 3 days.
If <u>less sore, free roundpen</u> again.

Each day that he is <u>less sore</u>
than the <u>previous</u> day, free
<u>roundpen again</u> until you go
back to a <u>strong fast gallop</u>
with rider.

<u>Work</u> horse at track no
sooner than <u>14 days</u>
from <u>1st day</u> of <u>soreness.</u>

He may be <u>sore again</u> after work -
turn out, free roundpen,
and gallop again when <u>not sore</u>.

You are working through "BUCKED SHINS"!

BOWED TENDONS

There is no such thing as a "Little Bit Bowed". As many trainers are fond of saying, "It's like being a little bit pregnant . . . you are or you aren't"

Bowed tendons are devastating for a racehorse. Whatever his ability, it is forever impaired by bowed tendons. It is good money thrown after bad to try and bring back a horse with a bow. Unless he is exceptional and can run somewhere cheaper, and still win, the trials and tribulations involved aren't worth the cost. Generally the horse will improve and give you hope. He will train well and then in the last work before the race (in traditional methods), or in the first race back he will rebow.

Believe it or not, most of this anguish can be avoided if you are tuned into your horse and follow my advice about monitoring his legs, turnout and rest between works. I have been training and/or breaking and prepping my own horses, since the late seventies. I recognize that a horse really can have a misstep or bad luck in a twist or fall and indeed bow a tendon. But that is the exception rather than the rule. There are many bowed tendons on the racetrack due to the lack of incremental training. Others are due to horses being wrapped and medicated so much that you can't tell if a tendon is "cooking" or beginning to go. I can't overemphasize the value of the solid incremental training and the extra time allowed in the process of development and how important progressive building is to the long term, overall structural integrity of a racehorse.

Some horses may be conformationally set up to have tendon problems. They may be very weak structurally with thin, weedy tendons, and/or tied in tendons, long cannon bones, or exceedingly long pasterns . . . all of which predispose such horses to breakdown when redlined. This kind of horse should be trained cautiously for racing. He is not a good candidate for the rigors of the track.

Even wonderfully built, strong tendoned, short cannoned horses can break down. Look in the stallion catalogs . . . time and again you see bowed tendons. Almost 90% of the time they are bowed on the left leg. These are horses with great breeding and wonderful bone. How did it happen? The training process on the track. It's almost a text book case study on how to break down a horse. Start with a strong, good feeling animal with green, unformed bone and tendon. Shoe him incorrectly, give him a long toe and no heel. Put him in a 12' x 12' stall. Overfeed him and give him too many vitamins. Don't let him out but once a day for 15 minutes to run like heck for a brief mile or so. Then walk him half and hour (even worse walk him on a hot walker) and put him back in the stall. (Did you ever notice how a horse walks head up with his back concave on the hot walker? Shouldn't he be able to lower his head and stretch his neck in order to flex and relax his back?)

Ask anyone who knows anything about exercise physiology if any but super unusual horses can tolerate this kind of treatment. Of course, we have tendon breakdown . . . the animal is willing to give more than he has been properly prepared for, and he is willing to run beyond his structure. Add in all of the chemical enhancements used in the name of good training and you'll see a complete program of breakdown. It is so predictable that I am appalled no one has truly tried to change this cycle of destruction. Believe me, I love racing. I want it to succeed, and I want us to act more responsibly on behalf of these magnificent animals.

Stop training!
Allow rest!

It is simple to avoid bowed tendons. Monitor your horse's legs every morning. **When you perceive any heat or swelling in the tendon area,** back off training. In this case ice and support wrap for a day or two may be indicated. Check with your vet. **Never give medications that mask the symptoms and fool you into thinking it has improved.** Give time and support. Read the warning signs. Interestingly, studies have shown that stopping the insult before real damage is done may lead to full recovery. Make sure the tendon is completely back to normal before continuing training. Healing takes as long as it takes. **You must wait on this problem or ruin the horse!** Unfortunately the tendon is usually bowed before most people catch it, then it is too late. They can only retire the horse and learn.

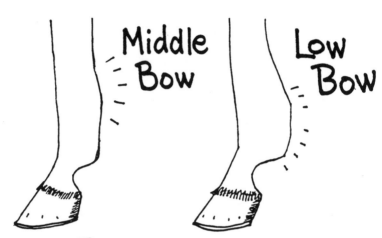

Middle Bow

Low Bow

Bowed Tendons turn thick
and Firm later - The first sign
of problems will be <u>heat</u> and
<u>swelling</u>! <u>Don't Keep Training</u>!
Allow Rest!

You have no control over a bow caused by poor
conformation or a bad move. You do have control
over a tendon that is starting to have slight heat or
filling - IF YOU WAIT!

Hmmm....

Bag of Tricks

Feed
Drawing Up
Pulling feed buckets
Bolting feed
Easy feeder
Feeding on the ground

Health
Girth gall
Loose palate
Ring on hoof
Sore stifles

Behavior
Introducing new horses
Little friends
Galloping in company
Vicks in the nose
Loading
Unloading
Handling hot and high horses
Cooling hot horses in hot weather
Kicking and striking in the stall
Rolling
Racing Company

Equipment
Introducing new equipment
Tongue ties

SOLUTIONS TO VARIOUS AND SUNDRY PROBLEMS WITH HORSES AND TRAINING

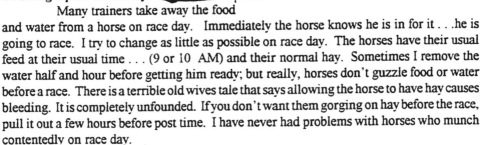

Feed

Drawing Up on Race Day

Many trainers take away the food and water from a horse on race day. Immediately the horse knows he is in for it . . .he is going to race. I try to change as little as possible on race day. The horses have their usual feed at their usual time . . . (9 or 10 AM) and their normal hay. Sometimes I remove the water half and hour before getting him ready; but really, horses don't guzzle food or water before a race. There is a terrible old wives tale that says allowing the horse to have hay causes bleeding. It is completely unfounded. If you don't want them gorging on hay before the race, pull it out a few hours before post time. I have never had problems with horses who munch contentedly on race day.

Pulling Feed Buckets an Hour After They Are Given

Horses are grazers who nibble all day in the wild. When I feed in the morning, the more aggressive horses gobble it all down fast. I prefer that they take their time and munch all day. They have been conditioned at the track to eat fast before their food is removed. Eating fast is not a good habit for the horses. It is much better to allow them eat slowly and throughout the day. My horses usually finish their morning ration by noon. Since they have free choice hay, they continue snacking throughout the afternoon.

Bolting Down Food

Horses who have lived on the track sometimes bolt down their food. It is nice to see a hungry horse attack his food with gusto, but eating too fast can be harmful and interfere with proper digestion. To slow him down, you can put LARGE smooth rocks in his feed bucket. He will have to work around them to get his feed. Be sure they are too large for him to bite into. You don't want broken teeth.

Easy Feeder

When feeding hay and grain in small paddocks, Ron Vlaming of Saugus, CA, recommends using a 50 gallon plastic drum. He lays it on its side and cuts an opening about 18" x 18" longways on the side. He then fastens it to the fence and bingo a feeder that eliminates hay from blowing away and keeps hay and grain off the ground.

Devise ways to ease your work.

Feeding on the ground

A wise vet once told Nancy Crone of Matinsville, IN, that feeding grain on the ground (in a container if possible) forces the horse to masticate in a way that helps clear the head and sinuses. The grinding of grain is more beneficial than hay, because it causes the most effective drainage. Thanks for sharing, Nancy.

Health
Girth Gall

When sores start to form where the girth is placed on the horse, plastic wrap or cellophane wrapped a few times around the girth may help. (Change girth covers if training several horses, in order to avoid passing on skin diseases and bacteria!) With every third or four day training, girth gall is less of a problem.

Bit with SealTex
wrapped on it To
hold down a Loose
or soft palate problem
A figure eight is used
To Keep mouth closed!

Loose Palate Problem

The horse makes a "funny noise" while running. Between the vet, the rider, and the trainer, a loose palate is diagnosed. This means that the palate displaces itself while the horse is running. Sometimes wrapping Sealtex (a rubbery bandage) around the bit will create a kind of mass that holds the horse's palate in place. Usually a figure eight or a "dropped" nose band is used to keep the horse's mouth closed. When this little trick works, surgery may not be necessary. It also eliminates the necessity of a tongue tie.

Ring on Hoof

When buying a horse, particularly a young one, always look at the wall of the hoof. It can tell much recent history of the horse. Good hooves have very firm and smooth sides. Various ring like indentations are not so good. The rings can represent a very high fever, sickness, stress, or an extreme change in feed. For example: in the yearling or two-year-old sales, you'll commonly see one ring about half an inch down from the coronet band. It probably occurred when the horse was pulled in off of the field to be fattened and coddled for the sale. An acute change in the horse's life-style took place. He was stalled and his feed was augmented without allowing him the normal movement and exercise he previously enjoyed.

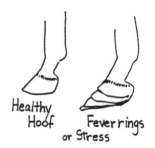

Healthy
Hoof   Fever rings
or Stress

This type of hoof is a very common at sales. Since the hoof grows about 1/4 to 1/2 inch a month, depending on the season, feed, environment, and genetic background, you can estimate when the horse was confined. Most sale horses need to be turned out for a month or two after you purchase them. Don't eliminate a horse for a few rings. Do be aware of probable cause. A horse with many, many rings has probably foundered and should be avoided as a race prospect.

Sore Stifles/Locked Stifles

Fit horses confined to a stall may have a temporary loss of control in the stifle. In his article *Unlocking Sticky Stifles*, *EQUUS Magazine* © 1992, Issue 180, (Reprinted with permission of Fleet Street Publishing Corporation) Matthew Mackay-Smith, DVM, Medical Editor, has the following to say about this problem:

"Stall confinement of fit horses, particularly heavily muscled ones, and especially those tending to overstraight hind legs, may lead to the temporary loss of control of the patella (knee cap) in the stifle so that it "locks up." Usually this is painless, but it looks alarming because the horse can't flex the affected leg(s), and hops about struggling to get a leg forward. Sometimes, the horse's reaction bruises the joint or strains it, causing lameness.

A recent review of stifle surgeries found that convalescence is often longer than anticipated, and the stifle(s) may become arthritic several years later. Thus, there is some reluctance among veterinarians to perform the surgery unless it is unavoidable.

If a horse starts locking his patella(s) after a rest, and was never known to do so before, then continuous turnout in a large paddock or pasture and progressive exercise to build muscle tone are usually sufficient to cure the problem. If there is recurrence in a horse who has done it before or who has had a lifelong tendency to "lock" one or both stifles, more strenuous calisthenics (working up hills, pulling a log) may be necessary to keep the stifles smoothly flexing."

Behavior

New Horses at the Farm

Allow any new horse time to adjust to a new home. Let him become secure in his environment. He will learn quickly where to get his food and water and meets his friends over the fence. Don't attempt to train until you feel he is comfortable in his new surroundings. This usually takes three or four days. After he becomes familiar with his area, he'll run back to his secure home . . . his stall or paddock . . . if he gets loose. That is another good reason to allow him to have his own particular stall or paddock. Don't move him to a different one every night.

Little Friends

Some horses are very insecure. They may do well with a little goat, miniature horse or some other animal. You'll see many such friends in the stalls with the animals at the track. In the receiving barn at one track, I saw two full grown horses in one stall. One was obviously a Thoroughbred and the other a huge grade horse. The owner, a woman, explained to me that the mare was a bundle of nerves. She could run but was so nervous before the race that she would fret her energy away. When they tried having her pasture mate come along, she was much better. A good trainer does what he can to get the best performance from the horse. Sometimes you find yourself looking pretty silly. But that's okay. How did the horse run?

Galloping in Company

Try to have friends ride with you on occasion, so they can gallop along side, in front, and behind you. This accustoms your horse to galloping with other animals. Have the other rider bump you and lean against you and your horse. Let your horse learn that this touching is no big deal. Always try to keep him relaxed.

Vicks in the Nose

Colts and fillies are very sensitive to odors . . . particularly of each other. To eliminate the danger of them thinking distracting thoughts, rub Vicks or any strong menthol based salve into the nostrils before racing and hauling your horses. It seems to kill their sense of smell for a while. Vicks is always used for works and race days to help clear the nasal passages. Horses eventually connect Vicks in the nose with a race. (Some states do not allow Vicks on race day. Be sure to check the regulations in your jurisdiction.)

Racing Company

There is a saying on the backside, "Keep yourself in the best company and your horses in the worst." It means put your horses in the easiest races you can find. The softer the competition, the better the chances of winning!

Loading Horses

When loading, once the horse is in, immediately close the back door or ramp so that he can't decide to back out while you are still fumbling with the butt bar. The butt bar and other things can be taken care of when the horse is well confined by the closed ramp or door.

Unloading Horses

Don't open the back trailer door or ramp until someone is holding the shank at the horse's head . . . ready to back him out. Often, the horse will see the door open behind him and start backing out while still tied up. Then he throws a fit when he finds he is still tied.

Handling Hot and High Horses

Never try to make a hot or an excited horse stand still. It is much easier and better for him to keep moving. It distracts him from his fear and works off the lactic acid buildup after a heavy work. It also works with the animal's natural instinct to move. Let's face it, we are not strong enough to hold a horse if he really wants to move. Let him think it was his idea. If you fight him, he will get even more excited fighting you.

Kicking or Striking at People in Stalls

Dog collars with small lengths of chains attached can be buckled above the horse's knees or hocks to discourage persistent striking or kicking while in the stalls. When the horse kicks or strikes, the chains slap against his legs, teaching him not to misbehave. (Idea from Donna Harper, DVM)

Cooling Hot Horses in Hot Weather

When cooling my horses after a work or a race in the terrible heat of the summer, I hose and hose them every turn around the barn to drop their temperature and cool them. It's so hot and humid some days in Florida that the horses never dry off. They maintain a constant sweat. By hosing all over the body each time you walk them around the shedrow, you help them lower their body temperature. They cool out much more efficiently. You can feel the body heat drop, as the cool water flows over the animal. We hose and put them in the stall wet with a fan blowing on them.

At home, after a hard gallop in the summer, their tack is pulled at the lakefront. They are taken into the lake to cool off. The lake water is so tepid, it does not shock them. It is important to keep them moving if they are still breathing hard. It took about 40 minutes to cool them, before I started using the "lake" method. Now it takes about 10 minutes, plus another 10 minutes for floating and fooling around. They come out of the water feeling refreshed and relaxed. Since swimming is impossible at the track, we walk and hose, walk and hose.

Rolling

Even if he's not in a paddock or pen, a horse loves to roll - especially after his bath. If you can find a sandy area or a pile of sawdust somewhere around the backside it would be great to let him roll there before putting him back in his stall. Rolling helps him straighten out and stretch his back. It also allows him to scratch areas he can't reach. It is very therapeutic and healthy for him!

Rolling helps Horses stretch and scratch their Backs!

Equipment

Introducing New or Different Equipment

When trying new equipment, don't spring it on the horse the day of the race. Have him get used to it in the comfort of his stall or paddock. Blinkers, for example, are a very strange piece of equipment for the horse. When the horse wears them for the first time, he usually tries to back out of them. He seems to think that if he backs up, he'll be able to see. Eventually, he accepts that something mystical is not allowing him to see properly and settles down. If you put them on for a few hours while the horse is in his own paddock, he won't try to run through a fence he can't see. In their confusion horses who have gotten loose with blinkers on have been known to crash into things.

It is easier for an animal to learn the limitations of new equipment in his own territory. When breaking two-year-olds, they wear a head stall with a D bit all day. They must eat with the bit on and endure it for hours. They learn how to keep it comfortable in their mouths and don't fret when confronted with a complete bridle for the real training. Bandages, bell boots, vet wrap . . . all should be presented to the animal first in his own environment under non-stressful conditions.

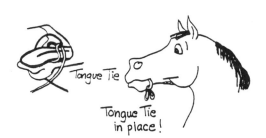

Tongue Tie

Tongue Tie in place!

Tongue Ties

Panty hose can be cut and made into very comfortable tongue ties. An idea from Jess Cloud.

EXPECT THE UNEXPECTED . . .

HORSES are UNPREDICTABLE

In handling young untrained horses, there is always an element of risk. As I have mentioned previously, I use Thoroughbreds in the example of the worst possible scenario. They can be the most volatile, high strung, over reactionary animals in the horse family.

One Easter Sunday stands out in my mind . . . I share it with you to **make you aware of the kind of risks you could encounter when working with horses.**

The horses were loaded and I was ready to head for the track. I had left Alex, my oldest son who was home for Easter with some Navy buddies, in charge of taking the saddles off some two-year-olds that were in the "getting used to the saddle" phase of training. Each horse was strolling around his paddock wearing the new equipment.

One particularly flighty filly caught my eye, and I decided to supervise her unsaddling as she was hypersensitive to being handled. I stopped the truck, jumped out and called Alex. Six foot four, two hundred and twenty pounds, Alex has always been very calm and kind around the horses . . . a steadying influence.

We both entered the small paddock, walking slowly toward the filly. I waited as Alex went quietly toward her head. She saw him coming and stood apprehensively. He spoke reassuringly to her. She seemed to be fine . . . then suddenly she whirled around and nailed Alex squarely, right under the chest with both rear hooves.

Alex stopped . . . turned around, took three steps, dropped to his knees and keeled over backwards . . . laying still as death. I ran to him. Only the whites of his eyes were visible. He was not breathing and had no pulse. "Alex," I shouted. "Wake up!" Dropping to my knees, I grasped him around the waist and shook him. It was like shaking a lifeless rag doll . . . his arms flopped and his head lolled back. No response . . . none. "My God," I thought, "My son. He's dead. He stopped breathing. He can't die . . . not like this . . . not here in this dirty corral." Such thoughts flashed through my mind as I tried pumping his chest and breathing life into him.

"Quick," I shouted to his friends who came running. "Call 911." I continued the CPR (Cardio Vascular Resuscitation) pumping and pounding with rhythm on his chest . . . sitting him up . . . jiggling him . . . anything to restore life. He had no pulse, no respiration, "Please God, don't let him die!"

I vowed that I would never, ever have anything to do with horses, if my son died. Other thoughts flashed inexplicably through my mind, as I mentally pleaded with Alex to respond while I continued the CPR. Suddenly, he started trembling and shaking all over - a convulsion. Paramount in my mind was a sick mare I tended once that convulsed and then died. In a panic, I kept working on him. Finally his eyes fluttered . . . he looked at me . .

Realize that any undertaking with horses should be done with caution and care.

. he recognized me. "Gosh," he said, "That was strange!" On my knees, I hugged and held Alex. He seem embarrassed . . . this huge hunk of a man being cradled in my arms like a baby. "Are you all right? Are you all right?," I kept asking while silently praying that his mind and intellect would be intact. There had been no pulse or heartbeat for what seemed like an eternity. It was probably only a few minutes.

He knew the day, the time, his name, and answered my questions coherently . . . albeit sheepishly. "How strange", he recounted, "I was there, somewhere, and I felt I had to do something. I couldn't remember what it was. Then it occurred to me . . . I had to breathe . . . that was it . . . I started, and there you were!"

I was just coming to the realization that my son was not dead . . . that he was okay . . . thank God, when I looked up and remembered that the truck was still running and the horses in the trailer were fretting and stomping. I had horses entered in two races in Tampa Bay Downs that Easter Sunday. Alex assured me that he was fine. I insisted that he go to the emergency room. He promised me that his friends would take him and insisted that I should not miss the races because of him. CPR certainly saved his life. I encourage all of you to learn how to use it. You never know . . . you may save someone's life!

I headed down the road and marvelled at how much we can appreciate life when faced with the threat of death. The horses ran miserably, but that was secondary to the fact that my first born was still alive and well!

Just another day at the farm!

Useful information and <u>Track Terminology</u>

insight into the
Front side
and
Back side !

Track Publications
Official Track Personnel
Backside Personnel
Racing Entities

INSIGHT INTO THE FRONTSIDE AND THE BACKSIDE

Before ever owning a racehorse. I had only been to the racetrack once in my life. I never bet. and my first day at the track was spent admiring the beautiful horses. the color, and pageantry of the races. I knew nothing about races, bettors or the politics that go into racing and nothing about the logistics on the backside.

The following information should help the uninitiated familiarize themselves without undergoing some of the painful lessons that come from learning along the way.

The BACKSIDE is the stable area of the racetrack. The FRONTSIDE includes the grandstand and clubhouse. It is where patrons go to see the races and bet. The following information describes the role of some of the people you will deal with at the track. Much of the information has been taken from the *Appaloosa Club Racing Handbook*

Depending on the layout of the track, certain offices are on the backside, within easy access of trainers. The RACING OFFICE is where trainers handle all the business of entering horses and filing ownership papers, turning in Coggins, etc.

Owning a racehorse should be a pleasure. Saturday afternoon television flashes ecstatic owners winning thousands of dollars for a minute and half of work on the part of their horses. Some of the winners cost millions in a sale . . . others as little as $2,500. It looks easy. Go to a sale, buy a horse with your spare change, and win the Derby. Why not! These are not unreasonable goals. People on television do it all the time. It looks easy? However, when you get involved, you will learn that centuries of effort and experience are involved.

Keep in mind that the BEST expert advice and millions of dollars DO NOT GUARANTEE that the horse will make it to the races . . . let alone win a race. Perhaps this is why we all have a chance. The most obscure breeding may relate to great bloodlines and throw a winner. Around 40,000 foals are registered with the Jockey Club every year. Only a small percentage ever win a race.

This is not intended to discourage you, it is to prepare you for the reality of racing. An educated owner is a great asset to the racing industry.

If you believe that nothing of value comes easily, you are ready to be a racehorse owner.

Condition Book Page

SIXTY-SECOND DAY - Calder Race Course

SIXTH RACE   **ALLOWANCE**
Purse $14,000 (Plus $1,500 FOA). For Fillies Two Years Old which have
net won a race other than Maiden or Claiming......................................118 lbs.
Non-winners of a race other than claiming since June 15 allowed.. 3 lbs.
                                             SIX FURLONGS

SEVENTH RACE   **ALLOWANCE**
Purse $15,000 (Plus $1,800 FOA). For Three-Year-Olds and Upward
which have net won a race other than Claiming, or Starter.
Three year olds......................117 lbs.   Older.............................122 lbs.
Non-winners of a race other than claiming since June 15 allowed.. 3 lbs.
                                             ONE MILE

EIGHTH RACE   **OVERNIGHT HANDICAP**
THE SOLO HAINA
$20,000
* (Plus $2,100 For Owners Award)
A HANDICAP FOR FILLIES AND MARES THREE YEARS OLD AND
UPWARD. WEIGHTS: SATURDAY, AUGUST 14.
Nominations Close Friday, August 13, 1993.
                          ONE MILE AND A SIXTEENTH (Turf)

NINTH RACE   **CLAIMING**
Purse $7,000. For Fillies and Mares Three Years Old and Upward
which have never won two races.
Three year olds..................114 lbs.   Older.........................119 lbs.
Claiming Price $10,000; if for $9,000.............................. 3 lbs.
                                ONE MILE AND A SIXTEENTH

TENTH RACE   **CLAIMING**
Purse $12,000 (Plus $1,300 FOA). For Fillies Three Years Old
(Condition Eligibility). ....122 lbs.
Non-winners of two races at one mile or over
since June 15 allowed.. 3 lbs.
One such race since then.. 5 lbs.
Claiming Price $25,000; if for $22,500............................. 2 lbs.
(Maiden races, claiming and starter races for $20,000 or less not
considered.)
                          ABT. ONE MILE AND A FURLONG (Turf)

Closing Sunday, August 15
THE PRIVATE SECRETARY - $20,000
For Fillies & Mares 3 YO & Upward, SIX FURLONGS
To be run Friday, August 20
THE CATCHER LANE - $12,000
For 3 YO & Upward, ONE MILE & 1 FUR. (Turf)
To be run Friday, August 20

19

← This is really a
difficult Race !
← A horse could have
won **many** high
claiming races and
still be eligible
here !

← This race is
limited to winners
of <u>only</u> <u>one</u> <u>race</u>
... of <u>any</u> <u>kind</u> !

Hmm!
which
one
for
me!

Notice the difference
in purses between
Claiming and Allowance Races

TRACK PUBLICATIONS

The Condition Book

Tracks conducting a live meet put out their Condition Book about every two weeks. It lists all of the races the track hopes to fill for that time period. Usually 8 to 14 different races are offered each day. Those attracting most entries are run. Some tracks write extras every day to accommodate fluctuations in the equine population at any given time. The goal of the Racing Secretary is to have competitive fields for the betting public.

Many trainers moan and groan when owners learn about the Condition Book. Owners overestimate the potential of their horse. They want him running in allowance races with big purses and tough competition. Trainers, on the other hand, want to put the horse with the easiest company. They want him to win and gain confidence as he begins his career. Trainers want to work the horse up the ladder and make purses as he rises to his level of competence. The saying on the backside is "Keep yourself in the best company and your horses in the worst company." An owner who paid $40,000 dollars or so to get a horse to his first race, has nightmares when the trainer wants to run the horse for a $12,000 purse. Much communication is necessary for both parties to be comfortable.

The maiden race and the non-winners of one and the non-winners of two races are going to be the easiest races the horse runs. Depending on whether the horse is running in claiming or in allowance races, soft spots may be found by reading the conditions of a race very carefully.

In the section on types of races, the differences between NW (non-winners) of two races lifetime allowance versus NW (non-winners) of two races other than claiming or maiden is described. If a horse is a NW of two races other than claiming or maiden, he probably has broken his maiden and may have won many claiming races. On the other hand, a NW of two races lifetime has only won one race. Big difference. Purses and competition may vary greatly even though they sound similar. Learning the subtleties of the *Condition Book* is a great help.

Trainers have a name for owners who decide they should choose the races for the horse: "Owners from hell". One of my owners fit the category. He would call me and inform that he had entered his horse in thus and such a race . . . without even asking me about the horse's condition. Maybe the horse hadn't recovered from his last race. Maybe he wasn't quite right. Maybe he was off his feed. When the owner was told that the horse wasn't ready or the race didn't suit him, he would say, "Well, if it really won't do you can scratch tomorrow."

Scratching a horse frivolously is not good policy. As a trainer, you can get a reputation for entering and scratching. You can also be "stuck" in a race, when the field is short and your horse is needed for the race to go. If you are stuck, you must have a vet scratch (meaning a vet must state that your horse has a physical reason for not being able to run). Depending on the ground rules at the track, a vet scratch may put you on the vet's list for 14 days. Then you might miss the race you really need. Be aware of all of the repercussions ahead of time. The racing office is trying to fill races in a competent manner. Don't waste their time with games.

The Condition Book is the trainer's bible.

The Daily Racing Form

Each day after the entries are drawn for the next day's races. the information goes to the printer, and daily programs are printed.

Some tracks include the past performances on each horse along with post position, distance and other pertinent information in their daily programs. Other tracks print only the essential information (horse's name and breeding, post position, distance, jockey, weight, owner, trainer, etc.). At tracks where past performance lines are not printed in the program, the spectator can find the information on each horse in the *Daily Racing Form*.

Equibase Company

Equibase Company was formed to establish and maintain an accurate and reliable industry-owned central data base of historical racing records, Full-scale operation of Equibase began on January 1, 1991. The company is a partnership between the Thoroughbred Racing Associations of North America (TRA) and The Jockey Club. Speed pace and class ratings have now been added to the basic past performance information, and Equibase has become the dominant provider of information to handicapping services, thereby playing a major role in the expanded availability and affordability of such service. The Equibase performance database continues to grow, and now contains some 3 million starts, representing every race track in North America as well as most major foreign races. With the re-engineering of computer systems. major priorities continue to remain operational improvements in efficiency, and timeliness and accuracy of information. which began charting every race in North America.

OFFICIAL TRACK PERSONNEL

The Clerk of Scales

At most tracks, the clerk of scales has complete control of the jockeys' room and all who work there, as well as all equipment. At the larger racetracks, he normally has a crew including an assistant clerk of scales, a supervisor of the jockey room, a color man who cares for and stores the racing colors, a number cloth and equipment custodian, security men and numerous valets.

It is the clerk's responsibility to ensure that the weight carried by the jockey is the weight assigned. He weighs all jockeys with their tack before and after the race. A jockey's weight includes his riding clothing, saddle and pad. Before the results of a race are declared official by the stewards, all jockeys must weigh in, in full view of the stewards and the public. If underweight after the race by more than two pounds, their mount may be disqualified.

The clerk of scales posts all overweights. He calls weight changes to the announcer, the jockey's room, the mutuels, *The Daily Racing Form*, stewards, and officials in full view of the stewards and the public. He does not allow a jockey to pass the scale at more than five pounds overweight except under conditions where the trainer may waive allowance previously claimed. The sex or age allowance generally cannot be waived. In most areas, two-year-old fillies are allowed three to five pounds. The clerk of scales is also responsible for providing the paymaster an accounting of riding fees due each jockey.

Clocker

The official timer hired by the race-track to record timed workouts. All official work times are given to the racing office and the racing form, so that they can be posted publicly.

CLOCKER
Times the workouts of Horses

The CLOCKER

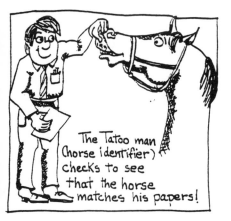

The Tatoo man (horse identifier) checks to see that the horse matches his papers!

Horse Identifier

Every horse entered in a race is positively identified to be the horse that appears on its registration certificate. Every horse which is racing at approved tracks must be tattooed on the inside of the upper lip with an official identification number. This number is placed on the horse's registration certificate and becomes part of its identifying features along with the natural markings and characteristics.

Each horse is definitely identified prior to his race by the official **track identifier** and

Respect all track personnel.
They work for you!

thoroughly examined by the track veterinarian to assure that he is in fit physical racing condition. If there is any discrepancy in identification or a sign of any physical disability, the horse will be withdrawn, or scratched, from the race.

I'd like to share a story about Buddy Hatcher, the Track Identifier at Calder. He gives a dollar to the owner of each horse he tattoos and says, "I hope this is the first of many dollars your horse will earn." He is one of the track characters that brighten our lives on the backside. Can you imagine how many dollars he has given away?

Licenses

All persons actively involved in racing must be licensed. This includes racing officials, all track employees, jockeys, owners, trainers and their employees. Licenses are obtained from the racing commission office at the track. Anyone wishing to obtain a license must fill out an application supplied by the state racing commission and return it to the racing commission office at the track. A photograph and fingerprints are included for identification. The application is given to the stewards for review. In most cases, the stewards speak with the applicant or, in the case of a trainer, give a test.

Licenses must be held for each state in which the licensee races. The application procedure is repeated each year.

The Paddock Judge

Approximately 25 minutes before the race, the horses are taken to the paddock where they are saddled under the supervision of the paddock judge. The saddling is done by the trainer with assistance from the jockey's valet.

The paddock judge is in charge of the area where the horses are saddled for a race. He has control over the individuals who may be admitted into that area. He verifies the racing equipment of each horse and verifies the use of special equipment, such as blinkers. He signals the saddling of the horses in the paddock area, directs them to parade around the walking ring, and signals the jockeys when to mount. While they are in the walking ring, the public can view each horse from all sides and the state veterinarian can inspect them. If a horse is deemed unsound, the horse is scratched from the field and put on the veterinary list. The stewards are notified immediately as is the mutuel department. The paddock judge starts the parade to the post. If he is serving as a patrol judge at the same time, he leaves the paddock with the horses and proceeds to the tower or stand assigned to him.

Patrol Judges

Patrol judges supervise every race and assist the stewards in enforcing the rules and regulations. Patrol judges observe the races from elevated platforms situated at the clubhouse turn, finish line and the 1/2 and 1/4 poles at a typical mile track. Along the straightaway, generally two patrol judges are used, with one being stationed approximately at the half-way mark of the race and the other at the finish line. Their primary responsibility is to watch the race closely from their particular vantage point. They use binoculars to look for rule violations such as reckless riding, interferences, lack of jockey effort, and other practices which could affect the outcome of the race.

 The video tape patrol is so efficient, some tracks are trying to eliminate patrol judges.

Viewing the race from their assigned stand, the patrol judges report findings to the stewards via intercom.

Placing Judges

Three placing judges assist the stewards in determining the order of finish of each race. The placing judges post the official finish after the race according to the photo finish camera. It is advisable to have three judges. As the horses cross the finish line, the judges write down the complete order of finish. They have a small board with numbers on it so they can post the order during the race and race fans can check the board if they lose track of their horses. The placing judges and stewards are aided in their decisions by photo-finish pictures if the finish is close.

Although the order of finish may be hardly perceptible by the spectators or even the stewards, the photo-finish pictures are accurate, and the placing judges and stewards can distinguish in fractions of inches the order of finish. Photo finish pictures are always posted in various places around the grandstand area in order for spectators to satisfy themselves about the finish of any race. The placing judges post the official finish after the race according to the photo finish camera.

When the finish of a race is close and a photo is called for, the word "photo" will flash on the tote board. One of the most unique systems ever conceived to provide the placing judges with absolute proof of the results of horse racing is the photo-finish camera. The camera system was developed in 1937 through the efforts of three key people: Bing Crosby, Buddy Fogelson and Bogart Rogers. With the photo-finish camera, the placing judges, in making close decisions, have as their ultimate reference a permanent photographic record of the finish of every race accurate to within 1/100th of a second.

It should be kept in mind that in any instance where the pictures furnished are not adequate or usable, the decision of the stewards will be final.

The Racing Secretary

The racing secretary has perhaps the hardest job in racing. His duties are many and important because he is directly responsible for the end result . . . the horses competing on the track in races which he first created on paper.

Although the racing secretary is employed by the racing association or management, he has an unrelenting responsibility to:

1) The Public - Under the rules of racing, the racing secretary must provide the public

with the best and most entertaining races he can provide with the horses available.

2) The Management - It is his duty to create a stakes program and write a condition book that will attract the best quality horses that are available.

Bing Crosby, Buddy Fogelson and Bogart Rogers were key people in the development of photo-finish cameras.

3) The Owners and Trainers - When the racing secretary approves stalls for a stable of horses, he obligates himself to the owner and trainer of the horses because in accepting them, he implies they will fit into his scheduled program at the race meeting. He must be fair to them without compromising his responsibility to the public or management.

No single racing official can contribute more to the success or failure of a race meeting than the racing secretary. He must bear all of his obligations in mind at all times and uphold them, being dignified and impartial but firm in his attitude.

The Starter

The starter takes charge of the horses once they leave the paddock and summons them to the starting gate. The horses and jockeys parade past the stands. Everyone can see them and make their final selection for wagering. Ponies may be used to lead a horse to the start.

Post time is the specified time horses are to enter the starting gate. It also notifies patrons of the time remaining for wagering. Following the parade, the starter may excuse horses because of injury or incorrigibility.

He gives the orders and takes the necessary measures to ensure a fair start. Most starters stand on a platform slightly in front of the gate so they can see all of the horses.

The job of loading the horses into the gate can be dangerous. The dangers can be greatly reduced by thorough training and practice. The gate is towed to the various starting positions by a tractor-type truck and is pulled off the track after the start of the race. As a safeguard system, the gate truck is backed up by a regular tractor.

Along with actual loading of the horses, the crew is responsible for maintenance of the gate. The individual gates are operated by electromagnets and must be checked periodically as a precautionary measure. All moving parts must be lubricated on a weekly basis.

The Stewards

The stewards are like the umpires or judges at the track. They have complete jurisdiction over the race meeting. Problems between individuals . . . owners, trainers, grooms . . . may be aired in front of them. Infractions of ground rules at the track , smoking under the shedrow, fighting, horses arriving late in the paddock for the race . . . are all aired before the stewards. The stewards may fine, suspend, or do both, depending on the severity of the problem. They may take purse money back, after the fact, if the medication tests show signs of overdoses or banned substances.

 Stewards have complete jurisdiction over the race meeting.

The stewards' most visual job, in relation to the public, is settling disputes in the actual races. If a jockey claims a foul or interference during the race, the stewards review the films and judge the incident. There are cameras all the way around the track. If there is an objection or inquiry, the stewards review the films. If they can't see the infraction on the film, they will not recognize that it happened. Film replays have improved their ability to discern infractions tremendously.

They report all suspensions and fines to the state racing commission and in turn to the Association of Racing Commissioners International so that offenders will be barred from taking part in all race meetings during the period of suspension.

The stewards have the most delicate position in racing. It requires a combination of attributes which one individual rarely possesses. In addition to integrity and knowledge of the sport, a steward must have some cognizance of the law, an ability to handle people and an understanding of psychology. Three stewards preside over the racing at all tracks, one of whom is a representative of the respective state racing commission. A board of three is appointed to provide a tie-breaking vote.

Track Bookkeeper

The track bookkeeper manages track disbursements. Keeping the expenses of stables, corporations, syndicates, jockey's fees, trainer's fees, and other track expenses can be a very complex job.

Make sure you disburse your Earnings!

Track and Commission Veterinarians

The track veterinarian is responsible for examining each horse to ensure that all entries are in "racing sound" condition. This includes pre-race morning examinations and close observation during the parade to the post, at the starting gate and during and after the race. He is responsible for the inspection of all horses registered with the racing secretary and for maintaining the veterinary list of all horses officially scratched from a race. He is also responsible for control of all communicable animal diseases, insect control and inhumane acts against horses including neglect in feeding, watering and care.

The commission veterinarian is in charge of all sample collections and must be available for stewards at scratch time and any time they desire identification of drugs or examination of a horse for tampering. He may not practice medicine on the racehorse; he may not wager nor may he sell drug supplies. It is his responsibility to study new medications and to disseminate this information to the practicing veterinarians and trainers.

The Track Superintendent

It is the job of the track superintendent to maintain the racetrack surface. A racing surface is composed of a 10-to-12 inch firm base with a 3-to-3 1/2 inch cushion. Each of these layers is composed of sand and clay to varying degrees. Track conditions are rated as follows:

Try to understand all of your obligations and the worst case scenario in order to survive unscathed!

STANDARD DISTANCES
(one mile track)

220 to 440 yards
4 furlongs
4½ furlongs
5 furlongs
5½ furlongs
6 furlongs

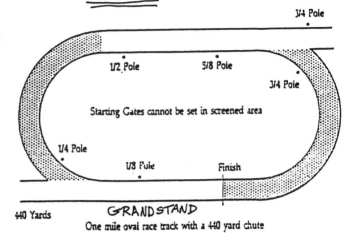

Starting Gates cannot be set in screened area

¾ Pole
½ Pole
5/8 Pole
¾ Pole
¼ Pole
1/8 Pole
Finish

440 Yards

GRANDSTAND

One mile oval race track with a 440 yard chute

STANDARD DISTANCES
(1/2 mile track with 440 yard chute)

220 to 440 yards
2½ furlongs
3 furlongs
½ Mile plus 70 yards
4½ furlongs
5 furlongs
5½ furlongs
6 furlongs

3/8 Pole
¼ Pole
2 1/2 Furlongs Pole
3/8 Pole

Starting Gates cannot be set in screened area

1/8 Pole
1/16 Pole   1/2 Mile plus 70 yards

440 yards   330 yards   220 yards

Finish

One half mile oval race track with a 440 yard chute

Typical Race Track Distances

Fast (f): Footing at its best, dry and even.
Good (gd): Rated between fast and slow.
Slow (sl): Damp and clinging, between heavy and good.
Heavy (hy): A drying track, between muddy and slow.
Sloppy (sy): Condition immediately after a rain, usually has firm footing beneath its surface. Footing is splashy but even.
Muddy (m): Soft and wet.

Valets

The valet is a track employee who takes care of a jockey's equipment, sees to it that the correct silks are at his locker, that the rider has the proper weight in his lead pad, carries the saddle and equipment to the paddock, helps the trainer saddle the horse, meets the rider after the race, and carries the saddle and equipment back to the jockey's room.

Video Tape Patrol

Video tapes are generally made of each race for the stewards, patrol judges and placing judges and are usually taken from two positions, head-on and from the side. This enables the stewards to immediately view the race from every aspect in the case of an inquiry. The tapes eliminate any conflict of opinion as to what may have happened. Any reported incident can be carefully analyzed.

These tapes are replayed for the spectators over monitors at many tracks and are also available for reviewing by trainers and jockeys for training purposes, or by horse owners who may have missed seeing the actual running of the race.

The tapes of all races are reviewed by the board of stewards the following day. At this time, they look for any infractions and assess any fines or suspensions they deem necessary.

Be mature and realistic enough to understand the term "out run". It means that other horses in the race were faster than yours.

BACKSIDE PERSONNEL

The Authorized Agent

If you sign and notarize an authorized agent form, the person named on the form may conduct your horse business for you. Often, the trainer is the authorized agent for the owner. He may buy, sell, or claim a horse for you. He may take money out of your account or put it in. Needless to say, trust is paramount in this kind of relationship.

Farriers

Every track has a colony of farriers who understand the idiosyncrasies of the track and who should be able to guide you. Remember that changing styles of shoes is considered a change of equipment and must be OK'd by the stewards.

Jockeys

The jockey is another important member of the racing team. I do not like to hear disparaging remarks about them, or hear them referred to as pinheads, idiots, etc. Good jockeys do a difficult job well. Not only do they have a knack for knowing where to be when, they can give the horse the courage and the desire to run. Great jockeys are artists. They take horses that are nervous, fractious and insecure, and mold them into willing partners of a racing team. Poor jockeys can lose the race with a fleeting instant of bad judgement.

Horses have completely changed their losing form when coupled with a sensitive, gifted rider. To win, a horse must want to run. A good jockey knows how to channel the horse's energies into that goal.

Of course, the great jockeys are usually the leading riders at major tracks. As small time players in the learning process of horse racing, you, as an owner and/or trainer, must strive to find the best jockey available. Don't expect a leading jockey to choose your untried two-year-old maiden, first time out. Understand that the jockey's agent is hustling to get his rider the best mount in any given race.

If the jockey hasn't been named on a better horse, he might try to pick up a ride on an unknown, on the theory that any horse can win. However, if the form on your horse is miserable, don't be offended if the jockey declines your mount. A well known jockey wants to ride better horses and earn as much money as possible. The jockey won't want to risk his health, safety, and reputation on a horse that looks green, unpredictable or unsound.

Some of the jockeys at our local track are good friends. One year, I was running a bunch of "duds". I didn't even ask my regular jockeys to ride. They had much better chances on almost any other horse. I found a jockey who was an excellent rider, eager for experience and willing to work with quirky horses. He was learning the trade and willing to ride anything.

This does not imply that you settle for less than the best jockey you can find. It means that you should not take it personally if the jockey refuses to accept your mount until the horse shows some talent and is controllable. Remember, all jockeys charge the same for the ride, plus 10 percent of the purse, if they win.

 **Great jockeys are gifted, instinctive riders.**

Be sure to discuss the idiosyncrasies of your horse with the jockey. Share all the information on whether the horse likes to run in front, on the inside, the outside, etc. Then leave the running of the race to the jockey. Many trainers give very specific instructions as to where the horse should be every minute of the race. They become angry if the jockey doesn't follow these instructions to the letter. My feeling is that trainers should discuss their goals for the horse, but allow the jockey to use his judgement in attaining them.

Be sure to listen carefully to the jockey after the race. You must assume jockeys are the competent experts in race riding. As an owner, you have the right to accompany the trainer, horse and jockey after the race. At the moment of dismounting, your jockey makes the freshest and most informative comments about the horse and how he performed. The jockey will tell you about the horse. He knows whether the horse was frightened, intimidated, tired, fit, impressive, tried to bear out or in, if his teeth bothered him, if he was sore, lame, etc. You learn about your horse if you listen to your rider. I am offended by enraged trainers screaming at jockeys as they ride in to dismount after the race. This is an embarrassment to the Great Sport of Racing.

Many trainers joke that when the jockeys bring the horses back to the finish line after the race, they are frantically trying to come up with some excuse as to why the horse didn't win.

Respect the jockey and assume he is trying his best to win. If your jockey is blatantly not following your orders or if you see a pattern of riding that you find suspect, change jockeys. Be aware that there are jockeys that don't play by the rules. One usually hears about such things on the backside. Be all ears, but take all comments with a grain of salt.

As you learn more about the business, both on the frontside and the backside, you will be able to choose your jockey wisely. Try to understand all of your obligations and the worst case scenario in order to survive unscathed!

The Jockey's Agent

This is usually the middle-man between the jockey and the trainer. A jockey agent must be a real hustler. He should be up early in the morning and help his jockey get to all the morning works. While the jockey is riding one horse, his agent should advise the next trainer to prepare the next mount. Since so much work must be done in so little time at the track, it is imperative that a popular jockey have coordination between his commitments. If a jockey "hangs up" a trainer and misses riding the horse, it can throw the trainer's schedule off terribly.

A good agent keeps the trainer happy and the jock busy. If his jock is named on more than one horse in a race, he should follow-up and notify the trainer that he needs another rider. The agent must smooth feathers if he chooses one horse over another one. He wants his jock to ride the horse with the most chance of winning. However, sometimes he is committed to a big stable and is obligated to ride all of their horses, regardless of the chance to win. **Top jockeys can almost choose their mounts... the others take what they can get.**

Agents scout riders in much the same way baseball or football scouts find players. They make trips to smaller tracks and try to find raw talent. Many riders come from Latin America. The agent may teach the rider how to shake hands, say, "Yes sir," and most

A good agent keeps the trainer happy and the jock busy.

importantly, "I understand"... even when he doesn't. They often share an apartment, and the jock is molded and advised by his mentor agent. Certain agents are famous for developing talent. Many agents are retired from "real" jobs and have this as a second career. Since the agent's pay is a slice of what the jockey makes, he may need his pension to live on.

Owners

As the owner of a racehorse, you have many responsibilities and should be aware of the following:

Horses must be registered in your correct name.

Fees must be paid or arrangements made with the trainer to pay all fees, such as entry fees, jockey mounts, tattooing, etc.

In most cases the owner must provide jockey silks. Colors are registered when the owner applies for a license in each and every state in which he will race.

If an owner changes trainers, he must notify the racing secretary and have the new trainer sign his name on said owner's registration.

The personnel of every stable must be registered.

After horses have been registered and owners listed with the racing secretary, no horse will be transferred (unless claimed at the meet) without permission of the stewards. The stewards will require a notarized bill of sale from the registered owner.

The purchase or transfer of any horse on the grounds at any track, whether by private sale, claiming, or public auction, does not guarantee the new owner a stall for such horse unless approved by the racing secretary and/or the stewards. The management has the right to allocate stalls only to those horses which fit the racing program and those horses which are healthy.

Horses sold to any person or stable not registered for racing must be removed from the grounds within 24 hours unless approved by the racing secretary and/or the stewards.

Before a horse may be entered in a race, its owner must secure an owner's license from the racing commission. The stewards may grant a reasonable delay in the case of absentee owners.

Trainers

As the trainer of a race horse, you have many responsibilities and should be aware of the following:

No horse shall be qualified to start in any race unless he is in the hands of a licensed trainer.

No trainer shall practice his profession except under his own name.

A trainer shall attend his horse in the paddock and shall be present to supervise his saddling unless he has obtained the permission of a steward to send another licensed trainer as a substitute.

Each trainer shall register with the racing secretary every person in his employ.

A trainer is responsible for the condition of each horse trained by him.

A trainer shall not have in charge or under his supervision any horse owned, in whole or in part, by a disqualified person.

If owner and trainer are philosophically in tune, you won't have these problems. You will work together

In some states when a trainer is to be absent for a period of more than two racing days from his stable or the grounds when his horses are racing, and his horses are entered or are to be entered, he must provide a licensed trainer to assume the complete responsibility of the horses he is entering or running. Such licensed trainer shall sign in the presence of the stewards a form furnished by the State Racing Commission accepting complete responsibility of the horses entered or running.

Only the trainer is authorized to withdraw the registration certificate from the racing secretary's office.

Pony Horses

Pony horses are not ponies. They "pony" racehorses. To pony a horse means that the pony rider exercises the racehorse, taking him on a lead rope at the side of the pony. The racehorse carries no weight. He is expected to move at the speed of the pony. Racehorses can be so rambunctious that they want to run away with a rider. The trainer has such a horse ponied so that he won't burn up too much energy but will get exercise. Sometimes, when a racehorse is young and insecure, a pony rider will accompany the racehorse and rider to the track. The older horse steadies and comforts the young inexperienced animal. He may gallop at his side to get him going and then drop off as the racehorse gains confidence.

The pony is also very useful on race day. Many racehorses become over excited and ready to run when they see the track. The pony will accompany horse and rider and help control the racehorse as he warms up before the race. Some jockeys worry about the horse getting away from them in the warm up . . . and will not allow the horse to gallop unless accompanied by a pony and lead shank. After a few races, as the horse becomes accustomed to the routine of racing, the pony is no longer necessary. Some trainers always use a pony. Others never use one.

If a horse gets away from a rider before the race and runs hard, the stewards may scratch him, on the grounds that the horse has already run his race and the betting public must be protected. That was frustrating for me. After hauling into the track to run, I wanted my horses to run. A mile gallop is a warm-up for most of my horses.

Older horses can become very professional and workman-like. For the young and high strung animals, the pony and his experienced rider are a great asset.

We're easy going steady horses!

Pony horses are not ponies. They "pony" racehorses.

RACING ENTITIES

Horse Racing Boards or Racing Commissions

These are government appointed bodies which act on behalf of the state, provincial or local governments to regulate the pari-mutuel horse (or other) racing within their jurisdiction.

State Racing Commissions

The various state racing commissions, by law, supervise the implementation of their rules and regulations regarding the operation of all racing within the state. The commission which governs each state is authorized by law to prescribe the rules of racing, grant the franchise for racetrack operations, determine how many tracks may operate within the state, limit the number of days of racing, approve purse schedules, pass the appointment of officials for meetings and supervise the strict licensing of all racetrack personnel. Licenses are issued only after thorough investigation. You must be licensed in each state you are going to race. State rules and regulations supersede breed registry or association rules.

State racing commissions are also responsible for testing each winning horse to see that no drugs which may have affected his condition were in his system. After every race, the winner and any other horse designated by the stewards are taken to the state racing commission's testing enclosure where urine, saliva and/or blood samples are taken. (The first three horses in stakes races normally are tested.) The state veterinarian seals, tags and delivers the specimens to the laboratory. Most labs are members of the Association of Official Racing Chemists. The labs run an extensive series of chemical tests on each sample to ensure that no drugs or prohibited medications appear which may have affected the racing condition and performance of the horse.

Although their problems and ways of dealing with them vary greatly from state to state, the commissions, through the Association of Racing Commissioners International, are able to act as one body on important issues and establish precedents concerning racing matters.

Keep informed of the regulations of your racing jurisdiction.

Hotwalkers — popular
on the Backside of the
Race Track

AS
WE
SAY
GOOD-BYE

In the previous pages, I hope to have given to you the ESSENCE of my horse training methods. **You must adapt them to your circumstances and that which suits you. A trainer's role is to develop the PERSONAL BEST of each animal... without breaking him down in the process.** People think I'm naive when I say good training can be done without medications and chemical enhancements. If I had not had the joy of a somewhat talented horse, I might have followed the advice of so many. Use the stuff or be at a disadvantage. But I had a decent horse . . . I kept her sound enough to run for more than four years and earn over $300,000. Though she was not brilliant, she was wonderfully game and useful. She ran over one hundred times, and she only had problems when I couldn't get enough races to keep her fit. She was eligible for very few races and needed to run every ten to fourteen days to be at her tightest. The joy of having a stakes class filly who never ran on medication, was never unsound, and who was turned out every day of her life to be a horse, has given me the courage to write this manual. I want others to have and achieve the same goals.

A few newspaper articles are included to give you an idea of what a game mare FIRST PREDICTION was.

Talented and truly gifted horses are few and far between. Most horses are lucky to win bottom of the barrel claiming races. But even this kind of racing can be fun . . . and your horse may last many years. If you run off the farm, the expenses are minimal and the horse has a better chance of paying his way.

Enter the Racing Industry cautiously . . . one horse at time . . . and invest your money carefully. If you start out with a reasonably priced horse . . . the horse doesn't know what he cost . . . and follow this program, you can be successful. Be patient and do your homework well. Learn everything you can about the Anatomy and Physiology of the horse. Read, study, and attend instructional seminars. Always follow your instincts about your animal. Above all - use your common sense.

Beware of trainers and veterinarians who want to "give your horse a little something" to help him when he has an injury . . . and thus keep him running when he should rest. Bute is fine occasionally. It helps a lot of horses "warm out" of certain aches and pains. Remember, injecting ankles and knees with cortisone, administering steroids and continuing to race is setting your horse up for breakdown. Read the vet bills from your trainer at the track. Learn the names of drugs that are legitimately helping your animal, and learn those which are painkillers given a day or two before a race. Banamine, Ketofen, steroids, etc., may "help" a horse get through a race, but are short term fixes that cause long term damage.

**Enter the business cautiously . . .
one horse at a time.**

Some of you will feel my suggestions are impractical in the "real life" atmosphere of horse racing. So be it. **I am in this for the long run ... for the long term good of the horse and racing. WE MUST CLEAN UP OUR OWN ACT OR IT WILL BE DONE FOR US.** What better way to improve our image than by example ... by running sound, useful, horses year in and year out. Horses are not disposable items to be weeded through in search of the good horse. I must train each and every animal with the proper foundation. That takes time ... time that most owners are not willing to spend. Believe me, they will spend time later, with chips in young joints, bowed tendons, etc. Spend it early or spend it late. My program allows you to raise and develop your animal easily, with no real pressure until the animal is mature and physically and mentally more able to withstand the rigors of racing.

Doesn't that make sense? A good foundation for horses (and children) is best done while they are young and growing. **What they become, once fit, healthy, and sound, will depend upon their inherent genetic ability ... their own individual "gift" of speed. Understand that all the training and galloping and drugging in the world will not make a horse run faster than he is meant to run. Give him the necessary time to develop the guts to withstand his own speed.**

I have enjoyed having this dialogue with you. If any of you have been inspired to pursue the great sport of horse racing with an attitude of fair play, I have achieved my goal. **Each and everyone of you that starts racing sound, fit horses and wins, is a solid reinforcement that the little guy can win!** That's a great message for everyone. I hope our relationship doesn't end here. The *Backyard Racehorse Newsletter* is now being published. I would appreciate input from all of you out in the field. The names of trainers willing to work with our style of training are listed in the newsletter. The newsletter is a forum ... a network for backyard owners and trainers to share, to exchange ideas, and to encourage and support each other. Racing varies drastically from one end of the country to the other. Working together we can have a positive impact on racing and win races!

GOOD LUCK AND GOD BLESS YOU!

GLOSSARY

Firing?

BLISTER?

Maiden?

CRIBBING?

Sesamoiditis?

Bog Spavin?

DAM?

SIRE?

GLOSSARY
The following are terms common, sometimes unique, to the racetrack environment.

ACEY DEUCY - A style of riding in which the right stirrup is shorter than the left enabling the jockey to balance more easily on turns.

ACTH - Adrenocorticotropic hormone. It stimulates the adrenal glands to produce their own steroids. If used over a long period of time, it will suppress the horse's own adrenal glands. It is very harmful long term. Make sure you know what is being given to your horse. The accumulation of all of these medications definitely affect the overall structure and health of your horse.

AEROBIC - (With air.) The phase of training where your horse gallops within himself, comfortably and for miles without going into oxygen debt.

ALLOWANCE RACE - A race where horses run without a claiming price. Every track has a limit on the price of claiming races. Allowance races are a step above the highest claiming races. In allowance races certain conditions (non-winners of two races in a lifetime, for example) are met. A good allowance horse is a very valuable commodity.

ALSO ELIGIBLE - An entered horse that will race only if a scratch occurs (at or prior to scratch time) in the body of the field.

ANABOLIC STEROIDS - The steroids you hear so much about in human sports. They create more muscle mass on the animal and make fillies and geldings aggressive. They produce an "Arnold Schwartzenhorse" according to Dr. Ruth James. Long term use of this on fillies can impair their ability to reproduce. It is contraindicated in colts. Muscle can become hyper developed and tear itself from the bone.

ANAEROBIC - (Without air.) When the horse is galloping hard and is going into oxygen debt he is in an anaerobic state. He will be huffing and puffing after the run to repay the oxygen debt to his muscle. The further he can go before running out of oxygen, the better the race horse he will be.

ANHIDROSIS - A non-sweater. Horses with the inability to sweat.

ANTHELMINTIC - A drug for killing worms or parasites.

APPRENTICE - Rookie jockey who receives weight allowances.

ARTHROCENTESIS - Puncture and aspiration of joint fluid.

ARTHROCHONDRITIS - Inflamed joint cartilage.

ARTHRODESIS - Surgically induced fusion of a joint.

AUSCULATION - The act of listening for sounds within the body, chiefly for determining the condition of the lungs, heart, pleura, abdomen, and intestines.

AZOTURIA - "Tying-up" (Monday Morning Sickness) - Severe painful cramping of large muscle masses, resulting in discoloration of the urine with the by-products of muscle destruction. Commonly triggered in fit horses who resume heavy exercise after a few days of rest without any reduction in grain ration. According to *The Merck Veterinary Manual, Seventh Edition* relates to excess total feed energy consumption.

BACKSIDE - Stable side of the racetrack.

BACK-UP TO THE WIRE - Take the horse in the wrong direction to the finish line.

BASE-NARROW - The distance between the center lines of the limbs at their origin is greater than the center lines of the feet on the ground: will be broad-chested.

BASED-WIDE - Opposite of base-narrow.

BEAN - A firm bean shaped mass formed from dried secretions and urine salts in the pouch at the end of the penis of a male horse.

BEARING IN (OR OUT) - A horse that moves or lugs inward (to its left toward the inside rail) or outward while racing. May be due to weariness, infirmity, whip use by rider or rider's inability to control mount.

BETAMETHASONE - The generic name for one of the most potent corticosteroids. Regulates carbohydrate and protein use and acts as an anti-inflammatory.

BLACK TYPE - Used in a sale catalogue to designate a horse who has won or placed in a stakes. The name of a stakes winner is printed in boldface uppercase letters (i.e., **FIRST PREDICTION**), while the name of stakes-placed horse in is boldface upper- and lower-case letters (i.e. **First Prediction**).

BLEEDER - A term used for horses suffering from Exercise-Induced Pulmonary Hemorrhaging, a predisposition to hemorrhaging from the nostrils either during a work, in a race or immediately following such exertion.

BLINKERS - A hood placed over a horse's head with cups sewn onto the eye openings. The cups prevent a horse from seeing anywhere but straight ahead, thus preventing distractions. The size of the cups are varied to allow a horse more or less peripheral vision.

BLISTER - A chemical ointment or liquid which, when applied to a limb, causes an acute inflammation. It is used to treat chronic conditions such as an osselet, ring bone, bowed tendon, etc. When a trainer says he is going to "blister" a particular area of the leg, it means he is going to apply a caustic chemical that will cause severe inflammation to the area. The theory is that the inflammatory reaction will bring increased blood supply to the area and hasten healing. Aggressive massages might do the same with a fraction of the trauma to the animal. Ask trusted vets what they think.

BLOW OUT - A very short (220 to 250 yard) workout at full speed. Used to put a horse on its toes before a race

BOG SPAVIN - A chronic distention of the joint capsule of the hock that causes a swelling of the front-inside aspect of the hock joint.

BONE SPAVIN - Osteoarthritis or osteitis of the hock joint. Can be caused by conformation, concussion and mineral imbalance.

BOOKKEEPER - The person who manages track disbursements.

BOWED TENDON - A traumatic injury to the flexor tendons behind the cannon bone as a result of severe strain in which there is tearing and stretching of tendon fibers. This gives a bowed appearance to the tendons externally. A Bow keeps a horse from ever running to his best ability.

BREAK MAIDEN - When a horse gets his first win.

BREEZE - To encourage a horse to gallop out to his full speed, usually without whipping. That's saved for the "work".

BROOD MARE - A female horse that has been bred and is used to produce foals.

BUCKED SHIN - A painful swelling on the front surface of the cannon bone, associated with microscopic stress fracture or periostitis. Caused by concussion in young horses in which bones are not fully conditioned. Rest from training is important until soreness and inflammation have disappeared.

BURR - A leather or rubber disc with protruding bristles. It is added to the bit to aid the rider in keeping the horse from running wide on turns.

BUTE - Trade name for Phenylbutazone, a frequently used nonsteroidal anti-inflammatory drug (NSAID).

CALCIUM-PHOSPHORUS RATIO (CaP Ratio) - The dietary balance of these minerals; needs to be between 2:1 and 1:1 for normal bone and teeth formation..

CALF-KNEED or BACK AT THE KNEE - A conformational fault of the forelegs where the knee is seen to bend backwards when viewed from the side.

CAPILLARIES - Smallest of blood vessels; connect arteries with veins.

CAPILLARY REFILL TIME - The amount of time required for blood to return to the gums after application of pressure. One to two seconds is normal; slower refill time may indicate low blood pressure, shock or dehydration.

CAPPED HOCK - A swelling found at the point of the hock and caused by a bruise. It usually stems from kicking in horse vans or stalls.

CASLICK'S OPERATION - An operation to correct pneumovagina and/or windsucking that involves suturing the upper vulvar lips together.

CAST - A horse that has laid down or fallen and is unable to rise.

CAULKS - Small cleats on the back end of a horse shoe or racing plate. Used frequently when track becomes muddy to increase the grip, avoid slipping, and provide better footing.

CHEAP SPEED - A horse that can run the first two furlongs in 22 seconds, but then peters out and finishes the race poorly has "cheap speed". He has the mechanical ability to run 11 second furlongs - but lungs, structure, or something doesn't allow him to carry his speed the distance.

CLAIMING RACES - Races that have evolved so that horses of equal ability may have a chance to win. A horse that is more talented than the rest of the field will stand the risk of being claimed if put in a race he can win easily. If he is put where he belongs, any horse in that particular race could be the winner. These races came about to give the public a fair chance at betting and to give less than great horses a place to run. Even if it is at the "bottom", they still have an opportunity to be useful for their owners and trainers. I don't like claiming races. If I put my horse where he can be useful, and he is, he may be claimed, and all my work is lost. Our dream is allowance horses that don't risk being claimed in every race. Unfortunately, good allowance horses are few and far between.

COGGINS TEST - A laboratory blood test for the presence of antibodies against the Equine Infectious Anemia (EIA) virus.

COLIC - A term used to describe any abdominal pain in the horse. Most often such pain is associated with digestive upsets.

COLORS - The jockey's silk or nylon jacket and cap provided by the owner.

COLT - A male horse under the age of five.

COMEBACK TO THE RIDER - Allowing the horse to choose his own pace when slowing down from high speed.

CONDITION - The qualifications or eligibility rules for horses to be entered in a race.

CONDITION BOOK - The track publication for horsemen listing conditions of upcoming races.

231

CONSIGNOR - The person who executes the consignment contract, offering a horse for sale through the auction.

CONTRACTED FEET - Abnormal contractions of the heel. Can be caused by improper shoeing or excessive dryness.

CORD- UP - A term used at the track to describe the tightening of the muscle along the spinal column that you see when a horse comes back from a strenuous work. It is not as severe as tie-up (Azoturia).

CORTICOSTEROIDS - Any of a number of hormonal steroid substances obtained from the cortex of the adrenal gland. Therapeutically they may be injected into joints to decrease inflammation. Rest is a must when used this way. If used systemically, many trainers believe they enhance the horse's overall performance and make him more aggressive. Beware of the ramifications of long term use.

COUPLED ENTRY - Two or more horses belonging to the same owner or trained by the same person. They run as an entry comprising a single betting unit. Their program number regardless of position would be 1 and 1A. A bet on one of these horses is a bet on both.

COW HOCKS - A conformation fault where the hocks are very close together while the lower portion of the rear legs are widely separated and toed out.

CRACKED HEELS (GREASED HEELS/SCRATCHES) - A weeping, moist dermatitis found on the back of the pastern and fetlock just above the quarters; often associated with poor stable hygiene.

CRIBBING (STUMPSUCKING) - An incurable vice or habit often learned by imitation. The cribber closes his teeth on any convenient surface (manger, gate, part of the stall partition, etc.), continuously extending his neck to swallow deep drafts of air with a grunting sound.

CRYPTORCHID - A male horse in which one or both testicles are retained in the abdomen.

CUPPY - A description of a dirt track surface which is loose and dry, therefore tending to break away from the horses as they run.

CURB - A hard swelling on back surface or rear cannon about four inches below the point of hock.

DAM - A female parent (mother)

DARK DAY - A day that the track is closed to racing.

DEAD HEAT - A tie occurring when the photo-finish camera shows two or more horses crossing the finish line simultaneously.

DEAD WEIGHT - Tack and lead slabs that bring the rider up to the horse's assigned weight.

DEHYDRATION - The excessive loss of body fluids such as would occur in severe diarrhea.

DERBY - A stakes exclusively for three-year-olds.

DEXAMETHASONE - A generic name for a potent corticosteroid often used to control inflammation.

DMSO - (Dimethylsulfoxide.) An oxygen-free radical scavenger used as an anti-inflammatory. It is often mixed with other concoctions, such as steroids, because it opens the pores and allows the medications to be absorbed into the bloodstream.

DOGS - Rubber cones placed away from the inner rail on the turf course during morning workouts in order to prevent wear and tear on the main portion of the course. Also used on dirt tracks when they are muddy or sloppy.

ELECTROLYTES - Salts that maintain proper blood balance. These are usually found in a well balanced feed program. However, if a horse is over stressed, he may need short-term supplementation after hard races.

ELIGIBILITY - Current qualification to a stakes race or incentive program.

EDEMA - An abnormal collection of fluids in body tissue. Congestion. Most apparent in the legs.

ENDORPHINS - Morphinelike proteins produced by nerve tissue to suppress pain and regulate emotional state.

ENDOSCOPE - A flexible tube with an optical attachment on the end, enabling the vet to inspect the horse internally. It is the instrument vets use when scoping a horse.

EPIPHYSITIS - An abnormal enlargement of the epiphysis (the horizontal growth line at the end of long bones) in young horses. It is often called big knees because of an enlargement over the knees. Can be a component of osteochondrosis.

EQUINE INFECTIOUS ANEMIA (EIA swamp fever) - An extremely contagious infectious disease of horses. It occurs in acute, chronic or inapparent forms, characterized in the acute or chronic stage by intermittent fever, depression, progressive weakness, weight loss, edema and anemia. Persists in white blood cells of all infected horses for life. See Coggins Test.)

FADE IN THE LANE - Tire in the homestretch.

FARRIER - Blacksmith.

FIGURE EIGHT - A leather strap used to keep the horse's mouth closed and keep the tongue from being put over the bit.

FIRING - The terrible custom of burning the front of the cannon bone, generally because of bucked shins. (See Setback Section.)

FILLY - A female horse under five years of age.

FLOAT - A heavy flat piece of equipment used to seal and remove water from the racetrack surface. To file down the sharp edges of a horse's teeth.

FLUNIXIN MEGLUMINE - The generic name for Banamine, a nonsteroidal anti-inflammatory pain reliever.

FOAL - A young horse of any sex in its first year of life.

FORGING - A fault in the gait in which the toe of the hind foot strikes the bottom of the front foot on the same side.

FOUNDER - See laminitis.

FREE ROUNDPEN - A Backyard Racehorse term for exercising without a lunge line in an area no smaller than 100' x 100', never in a typical roundpen, which is too small and puts too much torque on the legs of a young racehorse. A buggy whip is used to keep the horse at the desired speed, usually a steady gallop.

FURLONG: Eight of these make a mile. One is 220 yards.

GATE CARD - The official permission from the Starter, stating that your horse has been schooled and has broken from the gate in an acceptable manner.

GELDING - An altered, or castrated, male horse of any age.

HAND - A unit of measurement (four inches) by which a horse's height is measured from the ground to the withers. A horse that stands 15 hands is five feet tall at the withers.

HANDICAP - A race in which the weights are assigned depending on a horse's past performance and present form. The racing secretary or handicapper assigns a range of weights which would theoretically cause horses to finish in a dead-heat.

HANDICAPPER - The racing secretary or other official who assigns weights, handicaps, and races. Also the journalist who handicaps for a day's racing card and reports his selections for the wagering public.

HANDILY - Said of a horse winning a race easily. In a workout, a pace which is a bit slower than driving but faster than breezing.

HANDLE - The amount of money wagered on each race by the betting public.

HANG - A horse that hangs holds back to run with the horse next to him instead of passing and forging ahead.

HEAD - A margin between horses which describes one horse leading another by the length of his head.

HOMEBRED - A horse bred by his owner.

HORSE - A stallion five years of age or older.

HORSE'S BIRTHDAY - All horses become one year or older on January 1 of each year for purposes of competition.

HORSING - A filly or mare in heat.

HOTWALKER - The person who cools out the horse after exercise. A mechanical device with four 40 foot arms. Commonly used on backside to cool horses after exercise.

IDENTIFICATION - Of horses, involves a system of recognition of several types of markings by the horse identifier. Markings are noted on animal's breed registry papers and usually includes from coat color, lip tattoos, hair whorls, cowlicks, white markings, night eyes, scars and brands.

INFIELD - The are within the inner racing surface.

INQUIRY - The stewards immediate investigation into interference in the running of a race which may result in the disqualification of one or more horses.

IRONS - Stirrups.

JAIL - Signifying the 30 days after a horse has been claimed, in which it must run for a 25% higher claiming price than for what it was claimed. Some tracks may differ in their regulations.

JOINT CAPSULE - A sac-like membrane that encloses a joint space and secretes joint (synovial) fluid.

JOINT MOUSE - A small chip of bone enclosed in the joint space.

JOURNEYMAN - A licensed jockey who has completed his apprenticeship.

JUG - A mixture of fluids with vitamins and electrolytes (and who knows what). It is administered to horses by V by vets at the racetrack.

LAMINITIS - A disturbance of the sensitive plates of soft tissue, or laminae, in the horse's foot which leads to breakdown and degeneration of the union between the horny and sensitive laminae. Acute laminitis refers to a disturbance with rapid onset and brief duration, while chronic laminitis is a persistent, long-term disturbance. In severe cases, either one may result in **founder** and internal deformity of the hoof. According to *The Merck Veterinary Manual, Seventh Edition*, usually caused by ingestion of excess carbohydrates, grazing lush pastures,

and excess exercise and concussion in an unfit horse. Can also be caused by colic, postparturient metritis, or administration of an excess of corticosteroid or other medications.

LANE - Homestretch. The track in front of grandstand before the finish line.

LASIX - A brand name drug for furosemide, a diuretic.

LEAD PAD - A piece of equipment under the saddle in which thin slabs of lead may be inserted to bring a rider's weight up to the weight assigned the horse in a specific race.

LEAD PONY - A horse used specifically to lead the racehorses from the paddock to the starting gate.

LENGTH - Unit of measurement in racing and charting terminology. One length is equal to the length of one horse. Five lengths are equal to the distance covered in one second at racing speed.

LIVE WEIGHT - The weight of a jockey that a horse carries.

LUGGING IN - A term used to describe a horse which is pulling strongly to the inside or outside while running. (See Bearing in and out.)

MAIDEN - A horse that has never won a race. ''To break the maiden'' means to win his first race.

MAIDEN RACE - A race for non-winners.

MARE - A female horse five years of age or older.

MORNING GLORY - A horse known for phenomenal morning workout times, but is a disappointment when raced in the afternoons.

MUDDER -A horse which races well on a muddy track.

NAPROXIN - The generic name for a non-steroidal, non-psychotropic anti-inflammatory pain reliever.

NAVICULAR APPARATUS - The small boat-shaped bone and saclike bursa located behind the coffin joint in the hoof. Together they regulate the angle at which the deep digital flexor tendon and the coffin bone meet.

NAVICULAR DISEASE - Insidious and degenerative pathology of the navicular bone, bursa and deep flexor tendon, with both circulatory and mechanical (upright conformation of the forefoot) cause.

NECK - Unit of measurement the length of a horse's neck; a quarter of a length.

NEURECTOMY - An operation in which the sensory nerve is severed with the idea of permanently eliminating pain that arises from that area.

NERVED - A horse that has had an operation or manipulation in which the sensory nerve is blocked or severed to temporarily or permanently eliminate pain in that area.

NOSE - Smallest advantage by which a horse can win.

OBJECTION - A complaint filed by an owner, trainer, or jockey.

OFFICIAL - The designation given to the result of a race by the stewards when any occurrences that affected the actual order of finish have been decided in terms of pari-mutuel payoffs to winning bettors.

OSSELETS - A swelling of the front part of the fetlock joint. The swelling may be due to arthritis of the fetlock joint or to a bony growth. According to *The Merck Veterinary Manual, Seventh Edition*, "It may progress to degenerative joint disease. The exciting cause is the strain and repeated trauma of hard training in young animals. It has come to be recognized as an occupational hazard of the young Thoroughbred."

OSTEOCHONDROSIS - A bone disease possibly caused by severe over feeding and/or too much calcium supplementation. May also be caused by overuse of drugs, especially steroids. Anti-inflammatory drugs are not indicated since they promote physical activity, and thus aggravate the condition.

OUTRIDER - The track employee who leads the post parade and who, along with his/her fellow outriders, keeps all horses and jockeys in line and gets them to the starting gate on time; also catches any loose or runaway horses. In the morning they are the "traffic cops" who make everybody follow the correct traffic patternhs on the track.

OVERNIGHT - A race for which entries close 72 hours or less before post time for the first race on the day the race is to be run. Also, the mimeographed sheet available to horsemen at the racing secretary's office showing the entries for the following day.

OVER-REACHING - When the rear toe strikes the quarter of the front foot on the same side while the horse is in motion, another name for grabbing his quarters. This usually happens when a horse stumbles upon breaking out of the starting gate.

OVERWEIGHT - Pounds that a horse carries in excess of his officially assigned weight, because the jockey is too heavy.

OWNER - The name recorded on the back of the foal certificate. In most states, one is not permitted to race with an application for transfer attached to the foal certificate.

PADDOCK - The area where the horses are saddled and viewed prior to a race. The paddock is always adjacent to the jockeys' quarters.

PEDIGREE - Lineage or parentage.

POLES - Markers around the track indicating the distance to the finish line.

PONY - The good old faithful horse, usually an Appaloosa, Paint or Quarter Horse that helps the young, inexperienced horse.

POPPED A SPLINT - When a lump suddenly appears on a leg. See Splint. According to *The Merck Veterinary Manual, Seventh Edition*, "A periostitis with production of new bone caused by trauma from concussion or injury, strain from excess training (especially in the immature horse), faulty conformation, or improper shoeing. Complete rest is indicated. Local use of steroids delays the consolidation process and is contraindicated. In Thoroughbred practice, it has been traditional to point-fire a splint, the aim being to accelerate the ossification of the interosseous ligament. However, in most cases irritant treatments are contraindicated."

POST - The starting point for the race.

POST PARADE - The time period prior to the race when the horses leave the paddock, come on the racetrack, and walk in front of the stands where they break off and jog to the starting gate. The duration of the post parade is usually 10 minutes.

POST POSITION - A horse's position in the starting gate from the inside rail outward, decided by a drawing at the close of entries prior to the race, with the approval of the starter.

PREFERENCE LIST - A system which makes entering a horse to race more fair; horses with the longest time since last racing or having a chance to race, have the higher preference for the next race entered.

PUBLIC TRAINER - One whose services are available to the public and who expects to train a number of horses from a number or owners.

PURSE - The prize monies offered in a race. generally made up of the added money based on handle and/or sponsor's contribution. and any nomination sustaining or entry fees.

QUARTER CRACK - A crack found in the wall of the hoof in the area of the quarter. It often runs from the bottom of the wall up to the coronet.

QUITTOR - A chronic purulent inflammation of the cartilage of the coffin bone that drains through tracts at the level of the coronet band.

RACING BOARD/COMMISSION - A state-appointed body charged with the duty of regulating and supervising the conduct of racing in that state.

RACING PLATE - A type of horseshoe which is very light. made of aluminum, with a toe grab or cleat for better traction.

RACING SECRETARY - The person who puts together the Condition Book at the track.

RATED - To control the horse's speed.

REBUILD-DAY - A *Backyard Racehorse* term for days the horse is not saddled. He is turned out and given time to rest and rebuild from stresses. If he needs exercise, you can swim. roundpen. teach loading or any lessons he needs.

RECEIVING BARN - The horse hotel, so to speak, at the racetrack. The barn for ship-in horses.

REDLINE - A *Backyard Racehorse* term used frequently in this manual. It means that the horse is doing his ultimate best, trying his hardest, giving you all he's got, stressing every fiber of his body to his own personal best. This should really only be done under race circumstances. The horse will need time to rebuild from such a workout.

REGISTRATION CERTIFICATE - The document forwarded by the breed registry that certifies that the horse is duly registered.

RHINOPNEUMONITIS - A contagious disease caused by a virus of the herpes group, characterized by fever. mild upper respiratory infection and, in mares, abortion. May trigger an "abortion storm" in brood mare bands.

RIDDEN OUT - Winning a race without rider urging horse to do his utmost because he has a wide margin over the second-place horse.

RIDGLING - A male equine with one testicle.

RING BONE - A bony enlargement seen in front and on both sides of the pastern. If it is under the top of the hoof. it is called a low ring bone. If it is found halfway up the pastern, it is call a high ring bone. Caused by faulty conformation, improper shoeing, or repeated concussion through working on hard ground.

ROARER - A horse with paralyzed vocal chords. The condition causes fluttering noise when the horse makes a quick move. It interferes with the horse's ability to race, especially in distance races.

RUN-OUT BIT - A special type of bit to prevent a horse from bearing in or out.

RUNDOWN BANDAGES (WRAPS) - Bandages on the hind legs, usually with a pad inside. to keep a horse from burning or scraping his heels or fetlocks when he races.

SADDLE CLOTH (TOWEL) - Cloth under the saddle on which program numbers and sometimes horse's name are displayed. On many tracks, color coded as to position.

SCALPING - The toe of the front hoof hits the pastern of the rear foot on the same side, when the horse is in motion.

SCOPING - Inserting a fiber optic tube through the nostril and down into the throat. Enables the vet to see breathing problems such as paralyzed flap, loose palate, entrapped epiglotis. This procedure may also confirm bleeding lungs and is an absolute necessity when purchasing a horse.

SCRATCH - The act of withdrawing an entered horse from a race after the closing of overnight entries.

SCRATCH TIME - The deadline established by the race office for horses to be scratched prior to the printing of the official program. Generally, races are drawn 72 to 48 hours before race day and scratch time will be 24 hours before race day; for stakes races, scratch time can be up to 15 minutes before post time.

SESAMOID BONES - The sesamoids are two pyramid-shaped bones found at the rear of the fetlock joint and act as a pulley for the flexor tendons. They are attached to the cannon bone and long pastern bone by ligaments and form the back of the fetlock joint, beneath the flexor tendons.

SESAMOIDITIS - The tearing of the sesamoidean ligaments due to the great stress placed on the fetlock during fast exercise. Also an arthritic condition or mineral deposits on the sesamoid bones.

SEX ALLOWANCE - Fillies and mares, according to their age and time of year, are allowed to carry three to five pounds less when racing against males.

SHADOW ROLL - Sheepskin or cloth cylinder strapped across a horse's nose to bar its vision of the ground, preventing the horse from shying from shadows.

SHEDROW - The aisle in front of stalls at the track barn. Stable area with barns and walkways under a roof.

SHOE BOIL - A soft swelling at the point of the elbow caused by bruising with a long-heeled shoe when the horse is lying down or by lack of sufficient bedding to prevent the elbow from being in contact with the hard floor of the stall.

SILKS - Jockey's racing shirt displaying the owner's colors.

SIRE - A male parent; father.

SKIN PINCH TEST - Time test used to determine horse's hydration level. The longer it takes for a fold of skin on the horse's neck or shoulder to return to normal, the more dehydrated he is. One to two seconds signifies adequate hydration; six to 10 seconds represents severe dehydration.

SPEEDY CUT - Occurs when the front foot hits the inside of the hock or the rear foot hits the outside of the front cannon bone. It is caused by poor conformation and/or poor shoeing.

SPIT BOX - The State Barn where the horses go to be tested for drugs.

SPLINTS - Bony enlargements occurring on the cannon or splint bones, characterized by swelling, heat and sometimes lameness. Most common in young, strenuously worked horses. See **POPPED A SPLINT**.

SPRINTER - A horse than can run fast at 6 furlongs or less.

STAKES - Races that have paid entry fees. A horse's winnings will pay his entry into the Stakes. If he can't earn enough to pay his own way, he shouldn't be competing at that level. A horse that runs in Stakes is a better than the average allowance horse. Remember, the horse's winnings tell you how good he is.

STALLMAN - Person in charge of putting horses in their assigned stalls in the receiving barn.

STALLION - A male horse that is used to breed mares.

STAR LIST - A list of horses posted in the racing secretary's office which are given credit because they have been excluded due to too many entries. The more stars a horse has, the more likely it is to be accepted as an entry in a race since preference is given according to the number of stars a horse has.

STARTER - The official in charge of starting the race and head of the gate crew. He gives the okay for the horse to get his gate card. No horse may start racing without an official gate card.

STARTER (HORSE) - A horse is recognized as a starter when the stall door of the starting gate opens in front of it at the time the official starter dispatches the horse in the race. When the stall door of the starting gate does not open in front of the horse due to mechanical failure, the horse is not considered a starter.

STARTER'S ALLOWANCE - An allowance or handicap race restricted to horses who have started for a specific claiming price.

STARTER'S LIST - A list of horses that cannot be raced or entered until they have been schooled in the gates and approved by the Starter. The official Track Starter maintains this list.

STEWARD - Racetrack official who presides over the race meeting.

STEWARD'S LIST - A list of horses that perform poorly or have problems concerning their ownership, etc. They cannot be entered in a race until the matter is cleared by the Stewards. This list is maintained by the official track stewards.

STRONGYLES - Large strongyles are a common equine parasite sometimes known as "red or blood worms".

SUPERFICIAL FLEXOR TENDON - The outer tendon connecting the superficial muscles of the upper leg to the back of the pastern bones.

SUSPENSORY LIGAMENTS - The strip of fibrous tissue running from the upper cannon bone over the fetlock joint to the pastern bones. Supports the fetlock joint, preventing it from sinking to the ground.

STICK - The jockey's whip; bat.

TATTOO - A form of identification in which racehorses are marked under the upper lip with a letter/number combination, which is also reflected on the registration certificate.

THOROUGHPIN - Puffy swelling which appears on upper part of hock and in front of the large tendon.

THRUSH - A chronic, moist deterioration of the frog of the hoof. Most frequently seen in horses that stand in bedding soaked with urine and feces or mud, and whose feet do not receive regular attention.

TONGUE TIE - Strap or strip of cloth used to tie down a horse's tongue to prevent choking in a race or workout.

TRACE MINERALS - Minerals found in small quantities in feedstuffs and required in small quantities by the body.

TURF - Term used for infield grass course on which some races are run.

TWO-YEAR-OLD - Every Thoroughbred becomes a "two-year-old" on January 1 of the second year following the date of its birth.

TYING-UP - See Azoturia.

UPSET PRICE - The minimum acceptable price to open the bidding on a horse offered for sale in the auction.

VALET - A track employee who takes care of a jockey's equipment.

VETERINARIAN'S LIST - A list maintained by the official racetrack vet of horses that may not be entered in a race until approved by the official racetrack vet.

VIDEO PATROL - The system by which video cameras are strategically placed around a racing oval in order to broadcast and record the running of each race from each possible angle.

WARM UP - A slow gallop or canter to the starting point of a race.

WASHY - Horse breaking out in a nervous sweat before a race.

WEANLING - A foal being weaned and until he becomes a yearling on January 1 of the following year.

WEIGH-IN - The procedure where the Clerk of Scales, prior to the race, checks the weights of jockeys and their riding equipment against the officially assigned weight for each horse in the race.

WEIGH-OUT - The procedure where the Clerk of Scales, after the race, checks the weights of jockey and their riding equipment against the officially assigned weight for each horse in the race.

WEIGHT-FOR-AGE - A fixed scale of weights to be carried by horses according to age, sex, distance of the race, and season of the year.

WINDSUCKING - Occurs when a filly, while running hard, sucks wind in through the vagina. Even when cooling out, you may hear the intake and expelling of the air under her tail. It sounds like she is passing gas. It can be painful! It is usually caused by conformation where the tail is set high and the opening to the vagina is at a particular angle. It is easily remedied by a Caslick's operation (having the vet take a few stitches at the top of the entrance to the vagina).

WIRE - Finish line.

WOLF TEETH - Extra teeth found just forward of the first upper molar. They must be extracted because they are tender and interfere with the bit of the bridle.

WORK - One step up from a breeze and a tad below a real race. This is the timed tryout on the racetrack that gives you an idea of your horse's true ability. When a horse is "worked" he is generally pushed to the limit, against another horse or alone. The rider will use the whip on him and ride him hard.

YEARLING - Every Thoroughbred becomes a "yearling" on January 1 of the first year following the date of its birth.

Note - These terms are taken from *The Merck Veterinary Manual, Seventh Edition, EQUUS Magazine, The Daily Racing Form, How to Speak Thoroughbred, Veterinary Treatments & Medications for Horsemen,* and various other sources. Many thanks to them.

WINNER'S CIRCLE - Where we'd like to be.

Rancho Del Castillo ~ 3708 Crystal Beach Road ~ Winter Haven, Florida 33880
Phone 863 299 8448 ~ Fax 863 294 9401

SEMINARS

Hands on seminars are held at Rancho Del Castillo continually. The seminars are usually held on the weekends with the participants arriving Friday night and leaving Sunday night . But they can be held anytime...depending on the racing schedule. Janet always tries to have a race or a workout at the local track so that the participants may see the logical transition from the farm to the race track.

Horses are horses, being turned out and grazing for a portion of every day at the farm.   Then they are loaded in the van and off to the track to gallop, work, or race.

By doing every part of the process, you can see how you can adapt your circumstances to racing off the farm. Janet is (ahem) over fifty five, no longer rides her own two year olds, and still manages to usefully race and train. There's hope for all of us!

If you are a competent horseman, you too, can do a great deal of the early prep work in your own environment.

Call up and find out about where the next seminar is going to be held or when the next one will be at the farm in Winter Haven Florida.

The cost is $350.00 each (partner or significant other $150.00).

Staying at the farm is $25.00 per night including breakfast.

Lunch the first day is supplied to all attendees at the farm. Each person purchases his own lunch and dinner at the race track. If the trip is overnight to the Miami tracks then there will be a regular hotel room charge.

If you would like to stay at a local motel and rent a car, price lists will be sent to you. We are located in Central Florida, less than one hour from Tampa, (Busch Gardens etc,) and Orlando, (Disneyworld).

There are many other activities in the area...Water Skiing, Scuba Diving, etc.

Consider a Vacation here in Central Florida

delcastilo@aol.com   *http://www.backyardracehorse.com*

RECOMMENDED

READING

Books, Magazines, References

**Books
hold the
answers**

**Magazines
keep you
up to date**

**References
for infor-
mation
in the book**

BOOKS

My philosophy is to read everything possible about horses and racing. Some books stand out in my mind. Their authors show a great sensitivity to the horse. This is a list of a few that should help you. Several of these publications provided invaluable information in our research.

ADAMS' LAMENESS IN HORSES, by Ted S. Stashak, published by Lea & Febiger, Philadelphia, PA.

AINSLIE'S COMPLETE GUIDE TO THOROUGHBRED RACING, by Tom Ainslie. We understand that Ainslie's books are out of print. Look for them in used book stores.

THE BODY LANGUAGE OF HORSES, by Tom Ainslie and Bonnie Ledbetter

COLOR ATLAS OF VETERINARY ANATOMY, published by J. B. Lippincott Company, Gower Medical Publishing.

CONDITIONING SPORT HORSES , by Hilary M. Clayton, published by Sport Horse Publications, Box 355 RPO, University Saskatoon, Saskatchewan, Canada 57N4J8

CONSIDERING THE HORSE, by Mark Rashid, published by Johnson Printing, 1880 South 57th Court, Boulder, CO 80301.

DRUGS AND THE PERFORMANCE HORSE, by Thomas Tobin, published by Charles C. Thomas & Co.

EQUINE INJURY, THERAPY AND REHABILITATION, by Mary Bromiley, published by Blackwell Science, Cambridge, MA.

EQUINE MEDICINE AND SURGERY published by American Veterinary Publications.

THE FIT RACEHORSE II, by Tom Ivers, published by Equine Research.

HOW TO BE YOUR OWN VETERINARIAN (sometimes), by Ruth B. James, DVM, published by Alpine Press, PO Box 1930, Mills, WY 82644. You can order this book through Alpine Press for $19.95 plus $2.50 postage and handling.

IMPRINT TRAINING OF THE NEWBORN FOAL, a 60 minute video by Robert M. Miller, DVM.

HORSEMAN'S GUIDE TO LAMENESS, by Ted Stashak and Cherry Hill, published by Williams & Wilkins.

Books hold the answers.

THE LAME HORSE, by James R. Rooney, DVM, Wilshire Book Co., 12015 Sherman Road, North Hollywood, CA 91605, 1 (215) 875-1711.

TRAINING THOROUGHBRED HORSES, by Preston M. Burch, published by The Russell Meerdink Company.

EQUINE DRUGS AND VACCINES, by Eleanor M. Kellon, VMD, in consultation with Thomas Tobin, MVB, MRCVS, published by Breakthrough Publications.

RACEHORSES AT RISK, by Lennert Krook and George A. Maylin, published by the authors, Ithica, NY 14850.

SPECIFICATIONS FOR SPEED IN THE RACEHORSE: THE AIRFLOW FACTORS, by Dr. W. Robert Cook, published by The Russell Meerdink Company.

SELECTING RACEHORSES USING THE AIRFLOW FACTORS, a 90 minute video by Dr. W. Robert Cook, produced by The Russell Meerdink Company.

SPORTS MEDICINE FOR THE RACEHORSE, 2nd Edition, by William E. Jones, DVM, PhD, published by Veterinary Data, P.O. Box 1209, Wildomar, CA 92595.

TRAITS OF A WINNER, by Carl A. Nafzger, published by The Russell Meerdink Co., Ltd., Neenah, WI 54956.

For hard-to-find equine and racing related publications contact The Russell Meerdink Co., Inc. Call them at 1 (800) 635-6499 to order a copy of their catalogue.

MAGAZINES

THE BACKSTRETCH is the magazine published by the United Thoroughbred Trainers Association. You don't have to belong to subscribe. It has good articles that will keep you abreast of the racing situation . . . generally from the trainers viewpoint. Call 1 (800) 325-3487 for subscriptions.

THE BLOODHORSE is the magazine of the Thoroughbred Owners and Breeders Association. It comes out weekly and keeps you informed about what is going on where in the Thoroughbred racing world. Call 1 (800) 582-5604 for subscriptions.

THE DAILY RACING FORM is the state of the art, best newspaper around to get a history and form on the horses running. The articles are current and there are daily editions at every major track every racing day. It is the best money you can spend to get racing information.

There are many other fine books.
Read as many as you can.

EQUUS MAGAZINE provides excellent and well written articles. Many of them explain complex subjects in layman's terms. There are also good articles on equine sports physiology and training. Back issues are available by calling 1 (301) 977-3900 Ext. 100 or call 1 (303) 678-0439 for subscriptions.

THE FLORIDA HORSE is the voice of the Florida Thoroughbred Owners and Breeders Association. Call 1 (352) 732-8858 for subscriptions.

THE FINISH LINE provides complete information on Arabian racing. Call 1 (352) 620-8069 for subscriptions.

THE HORSEPLAYER MAGAZINE is a bi-monthly four color publication that caters to racing fans nationwide. Often referred to as the *Time* or *Newsweek* for horsemen. Call 1 (800) 334-6560 for subscriptions.

QUARTER RACING JOURNAL is a monthly publication dedicated to Quarter Horse racing. Call 1 (806) 376-4811 for subscriptions.

QUARTER WEEK is a bi-monthly publication dedicated to Quarter Horse racing. Call 1 (714) 826-4195 for subscriptions.

RACING NORTHEAST - The official publication of the Horsemen's Benevolent & Protective Associations in New England and New York, and the Massachusetts Thorough-bred Breeders Association. Call 1 (800) 672-2464 for subscriptions.

SPEED HORSE - RACING REPORT is a weekly tabloid for Quarter Horse racing. Call 1 (405) 573-1050.

THE THOROUGHBRED TIMES is an excellent magazine to keep you updated on what's going on in Thoroughbred racing. Subscription Dept., PO Box 420235, Palm Coast, FL 32142-0235.

***BACKYARD RACEHORSE NEWSLETTER* provides networking and information for hands-on owners and trainers. Call 1 (941) 299-8448 for subscriptions.**

Arabian, Appaloosa, Paint and Quarter Horses are raced throughout the country. Contact the Racing Division of the Breed Registry to receive more information about their publications.

Include magazines in your reading. They will keep you abreast of new developments in the industry.

REFERENCES

Over the years, I have made it a practice to save outstanding magazine articles for future reference. Some of these as well as the text from several books have been quoted throughout the manual. The following list will help you find and refer to this information. Many thanks to the publications for allowing these reprints.

Text from *A 10-point Plan for Equine Worm Control*, by Rupert P. Herd, MVSc, PhD, Department of Veterinary Preventive Medicine, College of Veterinary Medicine, Ohio State University, *Veterinary Medicine*, May 1995, is quoted in *Farm Layout and Friends - A visit from the Vet.*

Text from *A Hoof-care Primer*, by Emily Kilby and Celia Strain, *EQUUS Magazine*,©1995, Issue 219, (Reprinted with permission of Fleet Street Publishing Corporation) is quoted in *Legs, Bandages, and Shoeing.*

Text from *Balanced Hooves*, by Barbara Robbins, *EQUUS Magazine*©1992, Issue 170, (Reprinted with permission of Fleet Street Publishing Corporation) is referred to in *Legs, Bandages, and Shoeing - The Duck Foot.*

Drawings appear in *Legs, Bandages, and Shoeing*, from **Hoof Balance and Lameness: Improper Toe Length, Hoof Angle, and Mediolateral Balance**, by Olin Balch, DVCM, PhD, Karl White. DVM, Doug Butler, PhD, CJF, FWCF and Sarah Metcalf, DVM, from the **Compendium of Continuing Education, Practical Veterinarian 17 610: 1276-1283, 1995**. Reproduced with permission.

Drawings and text from **Land Flat, Fly True**, by Matthew P. Mackay-Smith, DVM, with Emily Kilby, *EQUUS Magazine*,©1994, Issue 197, (Reprinted with permission of Fleet Street Publishing Corporation) appear in *Legs, Bandages, and Shoeing.*

Alleviating Surface Transit Stress on Horses, by Sue Creiger, PhD, is referred to in *Hauling.*

The Fit Racehorse and **The Racehorse Owner's Manual**, by Tom Ivers, were referred to in *Training Aids - Heart Rate Monitor and Interval Training.*

Text from *A Marvel of Design*, by Karen Kopp Du Teil, *EQUUS Magazine*,©1992, Issue 180, (Reprinted with permission of Fleet Street Publishing Corporation) is quoted in *Training Aids - Heart Rate Monitor and Interval Training.*

The Compendium of Veterinary Products, published by North American Compendiums, Inc., Port Huron. MI, was a source of information for *Medications at the Racetrack.*

 **Keep a file of your favorite articles for future reference.**

The Complete Guide to Prescription & Non-Prescription DRUGS, 1995 Edition by H. Winter Griffith, M.D. published by The Body Press/Perigee Books, The Berkeley Publishing Group, 200 Madison Ave., New York, NY 10016, was a source of information for *Medications at the Racetrack*.

Text from *Good Steroids, Bad Steroids*, by Laura Hillenbrand, *EQUUS Magazine* ©1991, Issue 166, (Reprinted with permission of Fleet Street Publishing Corporation) is quoted in the *Medications at the Racetrack - Another Real Vet Bill*.

Text from *How to be Your Own Veterinarian (sometimes)*, by Ruth B. James, published by Alpine Press, Mills, WY, is quoted in the *Medications at the Racetrack - Common Medications at the Racetrack: What They Are and What They Do;* and *Basic Training*. You can order her book through Alpine Press, PO Box 1930, Mills, WY 82644, for $19.95 plus $2.50 postage and handling.

Text from *Unlocking Sticky Stifles* by Matthew Mackay-Smith, DVM, Medical Editor of *EQUUS Magazine* ©1992, Issue 180 (Reprinted with permission of Fleet Street Publishing Corporation) is quoted in the *Bag of Tricks* on *Sore Stifles/Locked Stifles*

Text from *The Merck Veterinary Manual, 7th Edition* is quoted in the *Glossary; Medications at the Racetrack;* and *Feeds - When and How to Feed*.

Veterinary Treatments & Medications for Horsemen published by Equine Research, Inc., PO Box 535547, Grand Prairie, TX 75053, was the source for various medical definitions in the Glossary.

Read, Read, Read!

Don't forget videos. They are excellent learning tools.

Thought Provoking Letters to Editor!

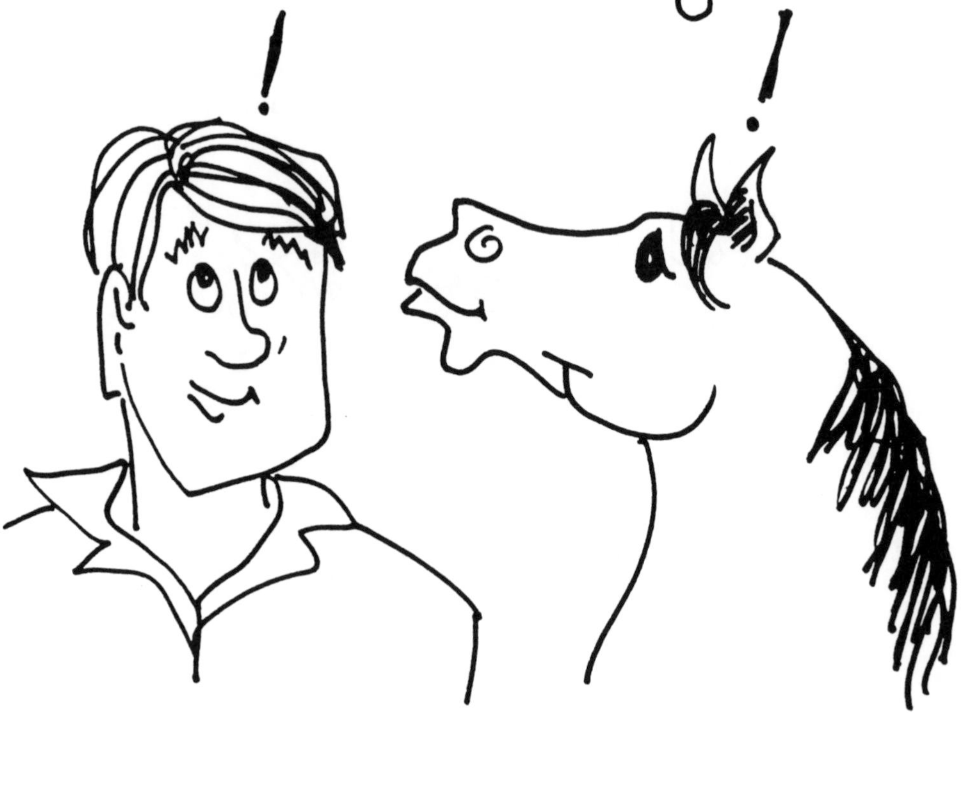

In defense of jockey Luis Collazo

To the Editor:

It was interesting to read that the stewards at Philadelphia Park slapped a $250 fine on jockey Luis Collazo for not doing a very good job of riding a horse named North Branch Kid. Now, if we could only fine the stewards, the owner and trainer of the horse and, yes, let us not forget the track veterinarians. All of these people are far more guilty of wrongdoing that is jockey Collazo.

What we have here is official racing's traditional response to one of its most basic problems: the sport is being surreptitiously conducted under one set of rules, while the public has been deceived into betting it under another set.

An uninformed racing public — and that unfortunately includes most of the people who bet their money every day — probably assumes Collazo is some kind of a three-headed villain — a little "pinhead muck sack" who, on purpose, did them in and robbed them of their right to win. Nothing could be further from the truth.

The truth needs to be told, probably for the first time, that those in horse racing really do play by one set of rules — many of them unwritten and unspoken, but quite understood — while the public bets horses under "official rules," which are that in name and perception only.

The scenario that got Collazo in trouble plays itself out over and over almost every day at every race track in the country. Dozens of injured, sore and bad legged horses are permitted to run. Racetracks desperately need them to fill those nine or 10 races each day, and they need them to insure full fields in all those gimmick races, where higher payoffs are the desired attraction.

The problem with letting horses such as North Branch Kid be entered in races is not that jockeys won't let them run, but that trainers are permitted to keep entering them and track veterinarians become conveniently distracted as the horses limp through their race-day health inspections.

Every day, trainers are coerced into running such horses, with that being demanded by racing secretaries who are under tremendous pressure to fill a card. Even when trainers tell the racing office the horse is not fit to run and might not "get by the vet," nobody cares to listen. The horse is needed, "so put 'em in."

When these horses are entered, a jockey, out of loyalty to the trainer, will accept the mount and then make some effort to get them around the course. The trainer knows the public is getting robbed; the jockey knows the public is getting robbed; the track vets know the public is getting robbed; the general manager of the racetrack knows the public is getting robbed. And nobody cares as the racing fan is robbed.

The real responsibility of stopping sore and lame horses from running rests with the track veterinarians, who examine each of the horses on race day, as is required by the "official" rules. But these vets know early in their employment they will not be on the payroll for long if they scratch too many of them.

Joe Abbey, the chief steward at Philadelphia Park, sounded somewhat the fool when he explained to Daily Racing Form the Collazo fine.

"This horse was obviously in distress," said Abbey. "The rider said the horse was making all kinds of noises during the race and when questioned, the outrider confirmed this. We also found out this horse had been on the vet's list in New Jersey last year. The trainer stated he did not want to run the horse, that he was going to turn him out, but the owner wanted to run him one more time."

And Collazo was fined?

And then Abbey said the most ridiculous thing of all: "We have told these riders repeatedly, if they think a horse is in distress and he can't be ridden in a fitting manner, then the horse should be pulled up."

Wait a big minute here. Why pull the horse up during the race? Since 99 percent of all these horses show these very negative signs during their pre-race warmup, why not simply scratch them before they run? And, herein lies the big catch, and it is something those of us who have been in racing for many years are not supposed to discuss.

Those official rules of racing say that once the gates open, the horse is a starter. This means that the race track gets its big commission on all the money bet. If the horse was scratched before the race, there would be a refund and the track would not get anything but aggravation.

Needless to say, this certainly puts stewards such as Abbey in a real ethical dilemma themselves. Unfortunately, money usually wins out over ethics, and the public keeps getting robbed.

It is my fantasy wish that one day, when the field is made up of sore horses — as is quite often the case — that the jockeys at Philadelphia Park will do just what Abbey suggests, and ease them all. Will Abbey and his fellow stewards declare the race "no contest," or will they declare them all starters and let the track keep the money?

It is absolutely shameful to fine Collazo, who is an innocent victim, while horseracing hides behind those unwritten and unspoken rules. He is the innocent party in all of this and we would suggest the stewards take another look at the situation, fine themselves $250 each and then go after the owner and trainer.

Kelso Sturgeon
Bel Air, Md.

Masking drugs need investigating now

I have more than a 50-year association with horseracing. I have heard most all of the criticisms of the Triple Crown format that have been raised since the latest disaster. The only possible exception is the Chrysler Triple Crown bonus. As Mark Simon noted (Daily Racing Form, June 20), this bonus is an obscenity which should be eliminated.

My view is that if you take immature horses and run them three times in five weeks at distances that most have never tackled and are not likely to try again, while putting 126 pounds (121 pounds for fillies) on them in dangerously large fields, you are going to have serious trouble for the horse.

This is not anything new – the criticism is obvious and has been around as long as I have. So I doubt anything will be done to correct it.

However, in all the verbiage, why has the possibility of masking drugs being a contributing factor not been mentioned? If, for example, a joint is injected with cortisone at the optimal time prior to a race, it may become impossible for the jockey, the track vet, the stewards or Ross Perot to determine that the horse is unfit to run.

I am not pointing the finger at anyone, nor do I imply that cortisone is the only such drug available. There may be others of choice. All I am saying is that I believe that a masking drug, injected into the joint, is not discoverable by a blood test. Truesdail Lab and all their science be damned, because the drug is not likely to enter the blood stream. The most thorough exam – pre-race – is not apt to discover the fitness problem being masked because of the effectiveness of the drug being used.

Why has this possible contributing factor to the problem not been discussed?

Charles E. Samuel
Stockton, Calif.

A sample of letters to the Racing Form and Bloodhorse Magazine

These are caring people - looking for Solutions

THE OLDER, THE BETTER

Editor:

As the industry prepares for the coming technology of DirecTv (*The Blood-Horse* of April 17, page 1865), be forewarned that we may find horse racing going the way of fur coats. The all-too-common occurrence of horses breaking down simply will not withstand the public scrutiny.

Perhaps it's time for a new vision—racing horses older, sounder, and therefore longer. Could Arazi have been our much-needed superstar had he not needed surgery at the tender age of two? Or A.P. Indy, had he been able to run longer than just enough to prove himself? I see little use in 2-year-old racing and wouldn't mind if the Triple Crown was for 4-year-olds.

From a business point of view, isn't it sensible to run your investment sounder and stronger? From a humane point of view, don't we owe it to these beautiful creatures that have served us so well?

Tori Keith
Knightdale, N.C.

The BloodHorse

Editor:

Racing isn't fun anymore. It used to be, and it could be again, but not without a complete overhaul. Every horse I ever owned got injured. After my best and favorite horse fractured a cannon bone, resulting in an 18-month lay up, it became a test of nerves just to watch him run.

And now the best horses are going down. Despite undoubted expert care and love, it happened to Go for Wand, Union City, and Prairie Bayou. It is happening too much, and the hard part is that it often happens unexpectedly to horses who have never had a problem before.

But that is not entirely true. Very often, catastrophic breakdowns are not a sudden event. Just like a paper-clip that is bent back and forth over and over, a series of micro-fractures accumulate until suddenly the whole thing gives way. That is what happens to overworked bone. The bottom line is that we race horses too young and too much.

It is time for some big changes. Every racing event in a horse's life should be pushed back one full year. The lightest training should start no earlier than age two. Maiden races should start no earlier than age three. Yes, all the great races such as the Champagne Stakes (gr. I) and the Hopeful Stakes (gr. I) should be for 3-year olds. Horses should run in the classics at age four. The extra time will be good not only for the horses, it will help horse racing too. Tragedies will occur less frequently. Horses will have longer healthier careers, allowing horse lovers to follow their favorite horse. That develops the kind of good will that the sport desperately needs.

Next, horses should not race year round. Every horse needs some time off. We humans, with the bills to pay, will not do that unless it is mandated. We keep running horses until they are injured or worse. If we don't change our ways, animal rights groups will do it for us, and rightfully so.

Donald A. Cocquyt
Simi Valley, Calif.

WHAT do YOU THINK?

By the way . . .

My newsletter is being published quarterly.
It contains an evergrowing list of trainers who will
be willing to work with you Readers.

If you are a Trainer and would like to be on the
list, call or write!

If you are interested in the Newsletter or the
Trainers' List, send a self addressed and
stamped envelope to:

Janet Del Castillo
3708 Crystal Beach Road
Winter Haven, FL 33880

If you would like to share
your experience with the newsletter
readers - send me an article or a
letter.

If you would like a farm
consultation call
863 299-8448
FAX 863 294-9401
web site :
BACKYARDRACEHORSE.com

email-
DELCAStilo.com

Racing Organizations and Information

THE
JOCKEY CLUB
1894-1994

821 Corporate Drive
Lexington, KY 40503-2794
Telephone (606) 224-2700
Fax (606) 224-2710
Telex 856599

Every Thoroughbred which races in the United States, Canada and Puerto Rico must be registered in The American Stud Book.

This Thoroughbred Registry is maintained by The Jockey Club, an organization established in 1894, which issues all Certificates of Registration.

Registration in the Stud Book ensures the correct identification of every Thoroughbred and, as such, is essential to the integrity of Thoroughbred racing.

A new owner should always compare the markings on their horse with its description on the Certificate of Foal Registration at the time of purchase and when the horse reaches its final destination. If the horse and its description do not match, the sooner this is discovered, the better.

For racing and breeding purposes, any transfer of ownership must be endorsed by the seller or their agent on the back of the Certificate of Foal Registration. But the Certificate is not a deed of ownership and should never be relied upon as such.

The Jockey Club's Registration Department is based in Lexington, Kentucky, where a group of dedicated staff which understands the Thoroughbred business is ready to help with any problems.

Dedicated to the improvement of Thoroughbred breeding and racing, The Jockey Club is also involved in numerous subsidiary and affiliate organizations.

These include The Jockey Club Information Systems, Inc., a computerized on-line information and sales catalogue production service; Equibase, racing's central performance database; the news and sports media service, Thoroughbred Racing Communications, Inc.; the Grayson-Jockey Club Research Foundation, which raises funds for equine veterinary research; and The Jockey Club Foundation, providing relief of poverty and distress among indigent members of the Thoroughbred industry and their families.

The Jockey Club has also started a new Registry, the Performance Horse Registry, Inc. (PHR™), which, for the first time, links pedigrees and performance records of Thoroughbreds and half-Thoroughbreds in competition other than racing. PHR™ horses are eligible for wide-ranging annual awards covering all the major disciplines of show-jumping, hunter/jumpers, combined training and dressage.

EXECUTIVE OFFICES - 40 EAST 52ND STREET, NEW YORK, NEW YORK 10022
DEDICATED TO THE IMPROVEMENT OF THOROUGHBRED BREEDING AND RACING FOR OVER A CENTURY

U.S. DEPT. OF AGRICULTURE - Animal & Plant Health Inspection Services:

Administrator	Washington, D.C.	(202) 720-3668
Veterinary Services	Washington, D.C.	(202) 720-5193
Animal Care (Horse Protection Act)	Hyattsville, MD	(301) 436-7586
Equine & Miscellaneous Diseases	Hyattsville, MD	(301) 436-5913

FOOD & DRUG ADMINISTRATION - Center for Veterinary Medicine:

Veterinary Equine Specialist	Rockville, MD	(301) 594-1740

INDUSTRY:

The Jockey Club Executive Office	New York, NY	(212) 371-5970
The Jockey Club Registry Office	Lexington, KY	(606) 224-2700
Performance Horse Registry, Inc.	Lexington, KY	(606) 224-2880
The Jockey Club Information Systems, Inc.	Lexington, KY	(606) 224-2800
The Jockey Club Racing Services, Inc.	Lexington, KY	(606) 224-2860

HORSE COUNCIL:

American Horse Council	Washington, D.C.	(202) 296-4031

RACING ORGANIZATIONS:

Association of Official Racing Chemists	Portland, OR	(503) 644-9224
Association of Racing Commissioners International	Lexington, KY	(606) 254-4060
Breeders' Cup Limited	Lexington, KY	(606) 223-5444
Equibase Company	Lexington, KY	(606) 224-2860
Horsemen's Benevolent & Protective Association	New Orleans, LA	(504) 945-4500
International Racing Bureau	Lexington, KY	(606) 276-5228
Jockey Agents' Benevolent Association	Pembroke Pines, FL	(305) 433-3288
Jockey's Guild	Lexington, KY	(606) 259-3211
National Museum of Racing	Saratoga Springs, NY	(518) 584-0400
National Steeplechase Association	Elkton, MD	(410) 392-0700
National Turf Writers Association	Louisville, KY	(502) 245-3809
Racing Advisory Committee	Washington, D.C.	(202) 296-4031
Thoroughbred Horsemen's Associations, Inc.	Columbia, MD	(410) 740-4900
Thoroughbred Owners & Breeders Association	Lexington, KY	(606) 276-2291
Thoroughbred Racing Associations of North America	Fair Hill, MD	(410) 392-9200
Thoroughbred Racing Protective Bureau	Fair Hill, MD	(410) 398-2261
Triple Crown Productions	Louisville, KY	(502) 635-2494
Turf Publicists of America	Lexington, KY	(606) 224-2717
United Thoroughbred Trainers of America	Southfield, MI	(313) 354-3232

EQUINE HEALTH & RESEARCH:

American Association of Equine Practitioners	Lexington, KY	(606) 233-0147
American Farrier's Association	Lexington, KY	(606) 233-7411
American Veterinary Medical Association	Schaumburg, IL	(708) 925-8070
Grayson-Jockey Club Research Foundation	Lexington, KY	(606) 224-2850
Maxwell H. Gluck Equine Research Center	Lexington, KY	(606) 257-1531
Morris Animal Foundation	Englewood, CO	(303) 790-2345
RCI Quality Assurance Program	Lexington, KY	(606) 253-1145

PUBLICATIONS:

The Blood-Horse	Lexington, KY	(606) 278-2361
The Daily Racing Form	Phoenix, AZ	(602) 468-6500
Thoroughbred Racing Communications	New York, NY	(212) 371-5910
Thoroughbred Times	Lexington, KY	(606) 260-9800

ALABAMA

Birmingham Racing Commission	Birmingham	(205) 328-7223
Birmingham Race Course	Birmingham	(205) 838-7500
Alabama Thoroughbred Association	Birmingham	(205) 877-8510

ARIZONA

Arizona Department of Racing	Phoenix	(602) 542-5151
Arizona Racing Commission	Phoenix	(602) 542-5151
Horsemen's Benevolent & Protective Association	Phoenix	(602) 942-3336
Apache County Fair	St. Johns	(602) 337-4364
Cochise County Fair	Douglas	(602) 364-7701
Coconino Fair	Flagstaff	(602) 774-5139
Graham County Fair	Safford	(602) 428-6240
Prescott Downs	Prescott	(602) 445-7820
Rillito Park	Tucson	(602) 293-5011
Santa Cruz County Fair	Sonoita	(602) 455-5553
Turf Paradise	Phoenix	(602) 942-1101
Yuma County Fair	Yuma	(602) 726-4655
Arizona Thoroughbred Breeders Association	Phoenix	(602) 942-1310
Arizona State Horsemen's Association	Phoenix	(602) 258-2708
Race Track Industry Program	Tucson, AZ	(602) 621-5660

ARKANSAS

Arkansas State Racing Commission	Little Rock	(501) 682-1467
Horsemen's Benevolent & Protective Association	Hot Springs	(501) 623-7641
Oaklawn Park	Hot Springs	(501) 623-4411
Arkansas Thoroughbred Breeders' Association	Hot Springs	(501) 624-6328
Arkansas Breeders' Sales Co.	Hot Springs	(501) 624-6336
Arkansas Horse Council	Texarkana	(501) 774-8822

CALIFORNIA

California Horse Racing Board	Sacramento	(916) 263-6000
Federation of California Racing Associations	Sacramento	(916) 449-6820
Horsemen's Benevolent & Protective Association	Arcadia	(818) 447-0169
Bay Meadows	San Mateo	(415) 574-7223
Del Mar	Del Mar	(619) 755-1141
Fairplex Park	Pomona	(714) 623-3111
Ferndale/Humboldt	Ferndale	(707) 786-9511
Fresno	Fresno	(209) 453-3247
Golden Gate Fields	Albany	(415) 526-3020
Hollywood Park	Inglewood	(310) 419-1500
Los Alamitos	Los Alamitos	(714) 751-3247
Pleasanton/Alameda	Pleasanton	(415) 846-2881
Sacramento/Cal Expo	Sacramento	(916) 924-2088
Santa Anita Park	Arcadia	(818) 574-7223
Santa Rosa/Sonoma	Santa Rosa	(707) 545-4200
Solano/Vallejo	Vallejo	(707) 644-4401
Stockton/San Joaquin	Stockton	(209) 466-5041
California Thoroughbred Breeders Association	Arcadia	(818) 445-7800
Barretts Equine Sales	Pomona	(909) 629-3099
California Thoroughbred Sales	Del Mar	(818) 445-7753
California State Horsemen's Association	Santa Rosa	(707) 544-2250

COLORADO

Colorado Racing Commission	Denver	(303) 894-2990
Horsemen's Benevolent & Protective Association	Lafayette	(303) 688-9020
Arapahoe Park	Aurora	(303) 690-2400
Gateway Downs	Holly	(303) 537-6866
Colorado Thoroughbred Breeders Association	Littleton	(303) 798-5548
Colorado Horsemen's Council	Denver	(303) 429-9739

CONNECTICUT

Connecticut Division of Special Revenue	Newington	(203) 566-2756
Connecticut Horse Council	Bethany	(203) 393-3665

DELAWARE

Delaware Thoroughbred Racing Commission	Wilmington	(302) 739-4811
Delaware Park	Stanton	(302) 994-2521

FLORIDA

Florida Division of Pari-Mutuel Wagering	Tallahassee	(904) 488-9130
Florida Pari-Mutuel Commission	Miami	(305) 470-5675
Horsemen's Benevolent & Protective Association	Opa Locka	(305) 625-4591
Calder Race Course - Tropical Park	Miami	(305) 625-1311
Gulfstream Park	Hallandale	(305) 454-7000
Hialeah Park	Hialeah	(305) 885-8000
Tampa Bay Downs	Oldsmar	(813) 855-4401
Florida Thoroughbred Breeders & Owners Association	Ocala	(904) 629-2160
Fasig-Tipton Florida	Lexington, KY	(606) 255-1555
Horsemen's Blookstock-Florida, LC	Ocala	(904) 237-9113
Ocala Breeders' Sales Co.	Ocala	(904) 237-2154
Sunshine State Horse Council, Inc.	Arcadia	(813) 494-1408

GEORGIA

Georgia Thoroughbred Owners & Breeders Association	Atlanta	(404) 365-1878
Georgia Horse Foundation	Alpharetta	(404) 740-8413

IDAHO

Idaho State Horse Racing Commission	Boise	(208) 884-7080
Horsemen's Benevolent & Protective Association	Meridian	(208) 888-4519
Cassia County Fair	Burley	(208) 678-7985
Eastern Idaho Fair	Blackfoot	(208) 785-2480
Gem County	Emmett	(208) 365-6144
Jerome County Fair	Jerome	(208) 324-7209
Les Bois Park	Boise	(208) 376-7223
Oneida County Fair	Malad	(208) 766-2247
Pocatello Downs	Pocatello	(208) 234-0181
Rupert Fairgrounds	Rupert	(208) 436-4793
Sandy Downs - Teton Racing	Idaho Falls	(208) 529-8722
Idaho Thoroughbred Breeders Association	Boise	(208) 375-5930
Idaho Horse Council	Boise	(208) 323-8148

ILLINOIS

Illinois Racing Board	Chicago	(312) 814-2600
Horsemen's Benevolent & Protective Assn. (Chicago)	Cicero	(708) 577-6464
Horsemen's Benevolent & Protective Assn. (Illinois)	Caseyville	(618) 345-7724

ILLINOIS *(continued)*

Illinois Dept. of Agriculture - Horse Racing Programs	Springfield	(217) 782-4231
Arlington International Racecourse Ltd.	Arlington Heights	(708) 255-4300
Balmoral	Crete	(708) 672-7544
Fairmount Park	Collinsville	(618) 345-4300
Hawthorne Race Course	Cicero	(708) 780-3700
Sportman's Park	Cicero	(312) 242-1121
Illinois Thoroughbred Breeders & Owners Foundation	Fairview Heights	(618) 344-3427
Illinois Thoroughbred Breeders & Owners Foundation Sales	Fairview Heights	(618) 344-3427
Horsemen's Council of Illinois	Villa Grove	(217) 832-8419

INDIANA

Indiana Horse Racing Commission	Indianapolis	(317) 233-3119
Horsemen's Benevolent & Protective Association	Guilford	(812) 576-2073
Indiana Thoroughbred Association, Inc.	Indianapolis	(317) 375-6406
Indiana Horse Council	Indianapolis	(317) 692-7115

IOWA

Iowa Racing & Gaming Commission	Des Moines	(515) 281-7352
Horsemen's Benevolent & Protective Association	Altoona	(515) 276-5533
Prairie Meadows	Altoona	(515) 967-1000
Iowa Horse Industry Council	Des Moines	(515) 266-4734

KANSAS

Kansas Racing Commission	Topeka	(913) 296-5800
Horsemen's Benevolent & Protective Association	Zenda	(316) 243-6641
Eureka Downs	Eureka	(316) 583-5528
The Woodlands	Kansas City	(913) 299-9797
Kansas Thoroughbred Association	Medicine Lodge	(316) 886-9824
Kansas Thoroughbred Association/Sales	Beloit	(913) 738-3749
Kansas Horse Council	Lecompton	(913) 887-6422

KENTUCKY

Kentucky State Racing Commission	Lexington	(606) 254-7021
Horsemen's Benevolent & Protective Association	Louisville	(502) 363-1077
Churchill Downs	Louisville	(502) 636-4400
Ellis Park	Henderson	(812) 425-1456
Keeneland Association, Inc.	Lexington	(606) 254-3412
Turfway Park Race Course	Florence	(606) 371-0200
Kentucky Thoroughbred Association	Lexington	(606) 278-6004
Kentucky Thoroughbred Owners & Breeders	Lexington	(606) 277-1122
Fasig-Tipton Company, Inc.	Lexington	(606) 255-1555
Lexington Breeders' Sales	Lexington	(606) 269-0695
Keeneland Association, Inc.	Lexington	(606) 254-3412
Stallion Access/Fasig-Tipton	Lexington	(606) 255-1555
Kentucky Derby Museum	Louisville	(502) 637-1111
Kentucky Horse Park	Lexington	(606) 233-4303

LOUISIANA

Louisiana State Racing Commission	New Orleans	(504) 483-4000
Horsemen's Benevolent & Protective Association	New Orleans	(504) 945-1555
Delta Downs	Vinton	(318) 589-7441

LOUISIANA *(continued)*

Evangeline Downs	Lafayette	(318) 896-7223
Fair Grounds	New Orleans	(504) 944-5515
Louisiana Downs	Bossier City	(318) 742-5555
Louisiana Thoroughbred Breeders Association	New Orleans	(504) 943-7556
Breeders Sales Co. of Louisiana	New Orleans	(504) 947-4676
Fasig-Tipton Louisiana	Lexington, KY	(606) 255-1555
Louisiana Thoroughbred Breeders Sales Co.	Carencro	(318) 896-6152

MARYLAND

Maryland Million, Ltd.	Timonium	(410) 252-2100
Maryland Racing Commission	Baltimore	(410) 333-6267
Laurel Race Course	Laurel	(410) 792-7775
Marlboro	Upper Marlboro	(301) 952-4740
Pimlico Race Course	Baltimore	(410) 542-9400
Timonium	Timonium	(410) 252-0200
Maryland Horse Breeders Association	Timonium	(410) 252-2100
Maryland Horse Breeders Foundation	Timonium	(410) 252-2100
Maryland Thoroughbred Horsemen's Association	Baltimore	(410) 265-6842
Fasig-Tipton Midlantic, Inc.	Elkton	(410) 392-5555
Horsemen's Bloodstock Services, LLC	Hunt Valley	(410) 771-0900
Maryland Horse Council, Inc.	Timonium	(410) 252-2100

MASSACHUSETTS

Massachusetts State Racing Commission	Boston	(617) 727-2581
Northampton	Northampton	(413) 584-2237
Suffolk Downs	East Boston	(617) 567-3900
Massachusetts Thoroughbred Breeders Association, Inc.	Boston	(617) 492-7217

MICHIGAN

Michigan - Office of the Racing Commissioner	Livonia	(313) 462-2400
Horsemen's Benevolent & Protective Association	Livonia	(313) 261-5700
Ladbroke - Detroit Racing Corporation	Livonia	(313) 525-7300
Mount Pleasant Meadows	Mt. Pleasant	(517) 773-0012
Michigan United Thoroughbred Breeders & Owners Assn.	Livonia	(313) 422-2044
Michigan Horse Council	Lansing	(517) 468-3684

MINNESOTA

Minnesota Racing Commission	Eden Prairie	(612) 341-7555
Horsemen's Benevolent & Protective Association	Shakopee	(612) 496-6442
Minnesota Thoroughbred Association	Shakopee	(612) 496-3770
Minnesota Thoroughbred Association/Sales	Hamel	(612) 477-4829
Minnesota Horse Council	Roseville	(612) 644-7849

MISSISSIPPI

Mississippi Thoroughbred Breeders & Owners Association	Madison	(601) 856-8293
Mississippi Equine Association	Batesville	(601) 372-8801

MISSOURI

Missouri Horse Racing Commission	Jefferson City	(314) 751-3565
Missouri Thoroughbred Owners & Breeders Association	Willard	(417) 742-2624
Missouri Equine Council	Brookline	(417) 882-1727

MONTANA

State of Montana Board of Horse Racing	Helena	(406) 444-4287
Horsemen's Benevolent & Protective Association	Billings	(406) 256-8364
Cow Capital Turf Club	Miles City	(406) 232-3758
Flathead Fairgrounds	Kalispell	(406) 756-5628
Great Falls	Great Falls	(406) 727-8900
Helena	Helena	(406) 443-7210
Marias Fair	Shelby	(406) 434-2692
MetraPark Race Track	Billings	(406) 256-2400
Ravalli County Fairgrounds	Hamilton	(406) 363-3411
Western Montana Fair	Missoula	(406) 721-3247
Montana Horse Council	Helena	(406) 449-8775

NEBRASKA

Nebraska State Racing Commission	Lincoln	(402) 471-2577
Horsemen's Benevolent & Protective Association	Grand Island	(308) 389-3073
Ak-Sar-Ben	Omaha	(402) 556-2305
Atokad Park	South Sioux City	(402) 494-3611
Columbus	Columbus	(402) 564-0133
Fonner Park	Grand Island	(308) 382-4515
Lincoln	Lincoln	(402) 474-5371
Nebraska Thoroughbred Breeders' Association	Grand Island	(308) 384-4683

NEVADA

Nevada Gaming Control Board	Las Vegas	(702) 486-6400

NEW HAMPSHIRE

New Hampshire Pari-Mutuel Commission	Concord	(603) 271-2158
Rockingham Park	Salem	(603) 898-2311
New Hampshire Horse Council	Brookfield	(603) 522-6018

NEW JERSEY

New Jersey Racing Commission	Trenton	(609) 292-0613
New Jersey Thoroughbred Horseman's Benevolent Assoc.	Colt's Neck	(908) 389-0804
Atlantic City Racing Association	Atlantic City	(609) 641-2190
Garden State Park	Cherry Hill	(609) 488-8400
The Meadowlands	East Rutherford	(201) 935-8500
Monmouth Park	Oceanport	(908) 222-5100
Thoroughbred Breeders' Association of New Jersey	Bordentown	(609) 298-6401
New Jersey Horse Council	Quakertown	(908) 735-2682

NEW MEXICO

New Mexico Racing Commission	Albuquerque	(505) 841-6400
The Downs at Albuquerque	Albuquerque	(505) 262-1188
The Downs at Santa Fe	Santa Fe	(505) 471-3311
Ruidoso Downs	Ruidoso	(505) 378-4431
San Juan Downs	Farmington	(505) 326-4551
Sunland Park	Sunland Park	(505) 589-1131
New Mexico Horse Breeders' Association	Albuquerque	(505) 262-0224
Ruidoso Horse Sales Co.	Glencoe	(505) 653-4242
New Mexico Horse Council	Albuquerque	(505) 344-8548

State Organizations *(continued)*

NEW YORK

New York State Racing Commission	New York	(212) 219-4230
New York State Racing & Wagering Board	New York	(212) 417-4200
Horsemen's Benevolent & Protective Assn. (Finger Lakes)	Canandaigua	(716) 924-3004
Horsemen's Benevolent & Protective Assn. (New York)	Jamaica	(718) 641-4700
New York City Off-Track Betting Corp.	New York	(212) 704-5000
New York State Regional OTB Corporations:		
Catskill Regional OTB	Pomona	(914) 362-0400
Capital Regional OTB	Schenectady	(518) 370-5151
Nassau County Regional OTB	Hempstead	(516) 292-8300
Suffolk Regional OTB	Hauppauge	(516) 853-1000
Western Regional OTB	Batavia	(716) 343-1423
Aqueduct	Queens	(718) 641-4700
Belmont	Elmont	(516) 488-6000
Finger Lakes	Farmington	(716) 924-3232
Saratoga	Saratoga	(518) 584-2110
New York State Thoroughbred Breeding & Dev. Fund Corp.	New York	(212) 832-3700
New York Thoroughbred Breeders	Elmont	(516) 354-7600
Fasig-Tipton New York	Elmont	(516) 328-1800
New York State Horse Council	Churchville	(716) 293-2561

NORTH CAROLINA

North Carolina Thoroughbred Breeders Association	Hillsborough	(919) 929-3226
North Carolina Horse Council	Raleigh	(919) 552-3536

NORTH DAKOTA

North Dakota Racing Commission	Bismark	(701) 224-4290

OHIO

Ohio State Racing Commission	Columbus	(614) 466-2757
Horsemen's Benevolent & Protective Association	Grove City	(614) 875-1269
Beulah Park	Grove City	(614) 871-9600
River Downs	Cincinnati	(513) 232-8000
Thistledown	North Randall	(216) 662-8600
Ohio Thoroughbred Breeders & Owners	Cincinnati	(513) 241-4589
National Equine Sales	Springfield	(513) 324-5558
Ohio Horseman's Council	Miamitown	(614) 833-1211

OKLAHOMA

Oklahoma Horse Racing Commission	Oklahoma City	(405) 848-0404
Horsemen's Benevolent and Protective Association	Oklahoma City	(405) 427-8753
Blue Ribbon Downs	Sallisaw	(918) 775-7771
Fair Meadows at Tulsa	Tulsa	(918) 743-7223
Remington Park	Oklahoma City	(405) 424-1000
Will Rogers Downs	Claremore	(918) 341-4720
Oklahoma Horsemen's Association	Oklahoma City	(405) 843-8333
Oklahoma Thoroughbred Association	Oklahoma City	(405) 840-3712
Heritage Place Sales Company	Oklahoma City	(405) 682-4551
Oklahoma Horse Council	Stillwater	(405) 744-6060

OREGON

Oregon Racing Commission	Portland	(503) 731-4052
Horsemen's Benevolent & Protective Association	Portland	(503) 285-4941

OREGON *(continued)*

Eastern Oregon Livestock Show	Union	(503) 562-5828
Grants Pass	Grants Pass	(503) 476-3215
Harney County Fairgrounds	Burns	(503) 573-2326
Klamath County Fairgrounds	Klamath Falls	(503) 883-3796
Lone Oak Park/Salem	Salem	(503) 378-3247
Portland Meadows	Portland	(503) 285-9144
Oregon Horsemen's Association	Springfield	(503) 746-6564
Oregon Thoroughbred Breeders' Association	Portland	(503) 285-0658

PENNSYLVANIA

Pennsylvania State Horse Racing Commission	Harrisburg	(717) 787-1942
Horsemen's Benevolent & Protective Association	Grantville	(717) 469-2970
Horsemen's Benevolent & Protective Assn (Philadelphia Pk)	Bensalem	(215) 638-2012
Penn National	Grantville	(717) 469-2211
Philadelphia Park	Bensalem	(215) 639-9000
Pennsylvania Horse Breeders' Association	Kennett Square	(610) 444-1050
Fasig-Tipton Midlantic	Kennett Square	(610) 444-9000
Pennsylvania Equine Council	Noxen	(717) 624-4263

RHODE ISLAND

R.I. Dept. of Business Reg., Div. of Racing & Athletics	Providence	(401) 277-6541

SOUTH CAROLINA

South Carolina Department of Agriculture	Columbia	(803) 734-2210
Thoroughbred Association of South Carolina	Camden	(803) 432-4190
South Carolina Horsemen's Council	Columbia	(803) 734-2210

SOUTH DAKOTA

South Dakota Commission of Gaming	Pierre	(605) 773-6050
South Dakota Horse Council	Colton	(605) 339-1203

TENNESSEE

Tennessee State Racing Commission	Nashville	(615) 741-1952
Tennessee Department of Agriculture, Marketing Division	Nashville	(615) 360-0160
Tennessee Thoroughbred Owners & Breeders Association	Nashville	(615) 254-3376
Tennessee Breeders Sales Co.	Nashville	(615) 373-8197
Tennessee Horse Council	Brentwood	(615) 297-3200

TEXAS

Texas Racing Commission	Austin	(512) 794-8461
Horsemen's Benevolent & Protective Association	Austin	(512) 467-9799
Bandera Downs	Bandera	(210) 796-7781
Grand Prairie's Lone Star Park	Grand Prairie	(214) 720-7820
Retama Park	Selma	(210) 229-0119
Sam Houston Race Track	Houston	(713) 807-8700
Trinity Meadows	Weatherford	(817) 441-9240
Texas Thoroughbred Breeders' Association	Austin	(512) 458-6133
Texas Thoroughbred Breeders Sales Co.	Austin	(512) 458-6133
Thoroughbred Horsemen's Association of Texas	Bryan	(409) 823-1911
Texas Horse Council	Lancaster	(214) 227-7372

VERMONT
Vermont Racing Commission	Rutland	(802) 786-5050

VIRGINIA
Virginia Racing Commission	Richmond	(804) 371-7363
Virginia Thoroughbred Association	Warrenton	(703) 347-4313
Virginia Horse Council	Newport	(703) 552-9010

WASHINGTON
Washington Horse Racing Commission	Olympia	(206) 459-6462
Horsemen's Benevolent & Protective Association	Renton	(206) 228-3340
Harbor Park	Elma	(206) 482-2651
Playfair Race Course	Spokane	(509) 534-0505
Sun Downs	Kennewick	(509) 582-5434
Yakima Meadows	Yakima	(509) 248-3920
Washington Thoroughbred Breeders Association	Seattle	(206) 226-2620
Washington Thoroughbred Breeders Sales Cooperative	Seattle	(206) 226-2620
Washington State Horse Council	Olympia	(206) 352-5883

WEST VIRGINIA
West Virginia Racing Commission	Charleston	(304) 558-2150
Horsemen's Benevolent & Protective Assn. (Charles Town)	Charles Town	(304) 725-7001
Horsemen's Benevolent & Protective Assn. (Mountaineer Pk)	New Cumberland	(304) 387-9772
Charles Town	Charles Town	(304) 725-7001
Mountaineer Park	Chester	(304) 387-2400
West Virginia Thoroughbred Breeders Association	Charles Town	(304) 725-5274

WISCONSIN
Wisconsin Gaming Commission	Madison	(608) 264-6607
Wisconsin State Horse Council	Oostburg	(414) 564-3621

WYOMING
Wyoming State Pari-Mutuel Commission	Cheyenne	(307) 777-5887
Central Wyoming	Casper	(307) 235-5775
Energy Downs	Gillette	(307) 682-0552
Wyoming Downs	Evanston	(307) 789-0511
Wyoming Horse Council	Laramie	(307) 766-6855

PUERTO RICO
Puerto Rico Racing Sport Administration	Rio Pedras	(809) 768-2005
El Comandante	San Juan	(809) 724-6060
Puerto Rico Thoroughbred Breeders Association	Hato Rey	(809) 759-9941

CANADA
The Jockey Club of Canada	Rexdale, Ont.	(416) 675-7756
Racetracks of Canada	Ottawa, Ont.	(905) 821-7795

ALBERTA
Alberta Racing Commission	Calgary	(403) 297-6551
Northlands	Edmonton	(403) 471-7379
Stampede Park	Calgary	(403) 261-0214
Canadian Thoroughbred Horse Society	Calgary	(403) 266-2248

BRITISH COLUMBIA
British Columbia Racing Commission	Burnaby	(604) 660-7400
Horsemen's Benevolent & Protective Association	Vancouver	(604) 984-4311
Hastings Park	Vancouver	(604) 254-1631
Sandown Park	Sidney	(604) 386-2261
Canadian Thoroughbred Horse Society	Surrey	(604) 574-0145

MANITOBA
Horsemen's Benevolent & Protective Association	Winnipeg	(204) 832-4949
Manitoba Horse Racing Commission	Winnipeg	(204) 885-7770
Assiniboia Downs	Winnipeg	(204) 885-3330
Canadian Thoroughbred Horse Society	Winnipeg	(204) 832-1702

ONTARIO
Ontario Racing Commission	Toronto	(416) 327-0520
Horsemen's Benevolent & Protective Association	Inglewood	(416) 675-3805
Horsemen's Benevolent & Protective Association (Eastern)	Rexdale	(416) 675-3805
Ontario Jockey Club	Rexdale	(416) 675-6110
Fort Erie	Fort Erie	(416) 871-3200
Greenwood	Toronto	(416) 698-3131
Woodbine	Toronto	(416) 675-6110
Canadian Thoroughbred Horse Society	Rexdale	(416) 675-3602
Woodbine Sales	Rexdale	(416) 674-1460

QUEBEC
Quebec Racing Commission	Montreal	(514) 873-5000
Canadian Thoroughbred Horse Society	Dunham	(514) 538-8172

SASKATCHEWAN
Saskatchewan Horse Racing Commission	Saskatoon	(306) 933-5999
Marquis Downs	Saskatoon	(306) 242-6100
Canadian Thoroughbred Horse Society	Saskatoon	(306) 374-7777

International Organizations

	Country Code	Telephone	Fax
AUSTRALIA			
Australian Jockey Club (New South Wales)	(61)	2 663 8400	2 662 1447
BRITAIN			
The Jockey Club (London)	(44)	71486 4921	71935 8703
Weatherbys (Northants)	(44)	93344 0077	93344 0807
Tattersalls (Newmarket)	(44)	63866 5931	63866 0850
British Horseracing Board (London)	(44)	71396 0011	71935 3626
FRANCE			
Societe d'Encouragement (Paris)	(33)	1 49 10 20 30	1 47 61 93 32
Union Pour la Galop (Paris)	(33)	1 49 10 20 02	1 47 61 93 32
GERMANY			
Direktorium Fur Vollblutzucht und Rennen (Cologne)	(49)	221 7498 113	221 7498 116
HONG KONG			
The Royal Hong Kong Jockey Club (Happy Valley)	(852)	2966 8111	2577 9036
IRELAND			
The Turf Club (Co. Kildare)	(353)	45-41455	45-41116
Goffs Bloodstock Sales Ltd. (Co. Kildare)	(353)	45-77211	45-77119
Tattersalls (Ireland - Co. Meath)	(353)	1 8256777	1 8256789
ITALY			
Jockey Club Italiano (Rome)	(39)	6 58.33.09.05	6 58.33.09.21
JAPAN			
Japan Racing Association (Tokyo)	(81)	3 3591 5251	3 3438 4893
NEW ZEALAND			
New Zealand Racing Conference (Wellington)	(64)	4 385-3988	4 384-5867

There are many good Horsemans
Associations related to Racing
  CHECK for the Nearest HBPA
office in your state - They can
give good information about
Racing and it's current issues
Call the National Office in
MIAMi Florida -
to find the nearest
chapter

305 935 4700

HBPA NATIONAL OFFICE
    Bill Walmsley - President
    Scott Savin - Ex. Director } 1995
    ED HAGEN - CHAIRMAN OF
                        BOARD
    Don Sturgill - GENERAL
                        counsel

HERE
TO HELP
HORSEMEN!

USEFUL RACING ASSOCIATIONS

AMERICAN ASSOCIATION OF EQUINE PRACTITIONERS
4075 Iron Works Pike
Lexington, KY 40511
1 (606) 233-0147
The association of veterinarians similar to the AMA.

AMERICAN HORSE COUNCIL
1700 K Street, NW
Washington, DC 20006-3805
1 (202) 296-4031   FAX 1 (202) 296-1970
The lobby group that represents all horse interests. They are also the clearing house for the horse industry.

APPALOOSA RACING
5070 Highway 8 West
Moscow, Idaho 83843
1 (208) 882-5578   FAX 1(208) 882-8150

NATIONAL ASSOCIATION OF THOROUGHBRED OWNERS, INC. (NATO)
Post Office Box 878
Unionville, PA 19375
1 (800) 545-7777
An association of licensed 40,000 Thoroughbred owners.

THOROUGHBRED OWNERS AND BREEDERS ASSOCIATION (TOBA)
Post Office Box 4367
Lexington, KY 40544
1 (606) 276-2291   FAX 1 (606) 276-2462
The TOBA is a national non-profit association founded in 1961. Its 3,116 individual members, essentially owners and breeders, include association memberships of 35 state breeders associations, whose constituency of licensed owners encompass and other 28,000 persons.

THOROUGHBRED RACING COMMUNICATIONS, INC. (TRC)
Tom Merrit, Executive Director
40 East 52nd Street
New York, NY 10022
1 (212) 371-5910   FAX 1 (212) 371-5917
A New York-based national media relations office that was formed in July 1987 to expand awareness of Thoroughbred racing. It is funded by founding organizations The Jockey Club, Breeders' Cup Ltd., and the Thoroughbred Racing Associations. (TRA).

THOROUGHBRED RACING ASSOCIATIONS (TRA)
Chris Scherf, Executive Vice President
420 Fair Hill Drive, No. 1
Elkton, MD 21921-2573
1 (410) 392-9200   FAX 1 (410) 398-1366
The organization of racetracks and racetrack owners.

UNITED THOROUGHBRED TRAINERS OF AMERICA, INC.

P.O. Box 7065 • Louisville, KY 40257-0065
Phone: (502) 893-0025 • Fax: (502) 893-0026
Toll Free: (800) 325-3487

United Thoroughbred Trainers of America, Inc., 40 years old in 1996, is an organization that exists to serve the interests of Thoroughbred trainers and Thoroughbred racing. Among its goals are: to elevate the standards of the vocation of professional training; to promote the sport of Thoroughbred racing and the ownership of Thoroughbred horses; and to work with track management, state Racing Commissions, the HBPA, Jockeys' Guild and all other racing bodies to protect the concerns of its members and to assist them in matters affecting the practice of their profession. UTTA offers reasonably priced workers' compensation and has made available a business development program for trainers and a presentation on thoroughbred ownership for prospective owners.

The organization honors excellence in its field with an annual Outstanding Trainer award. Past recipients include Warren A. 'Jimmy' Croll, Claude R. 'Shug' McGaughey, H. Allen Jerkens and Frank L. Brothers.

Since 1962, UTTA has published THE BACKSTRETCH. This award-winning bi-monthly magazine is read on the backside of every major Thoroughbred track in the United States and, in its focus on matters of interest to trainers, makes fascinating reading for owners and fans as well. Subscriptions, included in membership, are $21 a year for non-members.

For information on membership in UTTA and its benefits, or to subscribe to THE BACKSTRETCH, call (502) 893-0025.

AMERICAN QUARTER HORSE RACING

The AQHA Racing Department is the official record keeper for American Quarter Horse racing. They compile the results of recognized races from the United States, Canada and Mexico, maintain all official statistics, oversee the racing tattoo program and handle awards. The department also provides an extensive marketing and promotional program to assist tracks that race American Quarter Horses.

Some of AQHA's helpful materials available for potential racehorse owners:

• "A Guide To Owning America's Fastest Athlete." This guide gives a new owner information on buying a horse at auction, claiming a racehorse, choosing a trainer and figuring costs, plus, interviews with American Quarter Horse owners. Free.

• *The Quarter Racing Journal.* An award-winning monthly magazine with accounts of major races, commentary from industry leaders, articles on racehorse health and management, profiles of notable owners, breeders, jockeys and trainers, and more. A one-year subscription is $25. To subscribe call the *Journal* Circulation Department at (806) 372-1192.

• "Owning America's Fastest Athlete" This 12-minute video explains acquiring a racing American Quarter Horse, choosing a trainer and the opportunities available in the industry. The video ends with the award-winning music video "Running Blood" by Michael Martin Murphy. $10.00.

To order the above materials, call the AQHA Racing Department at (806) 376-4888, ext. 357 or write AQHA, Racing Dept., P.O. Box 200, Amarillo, TX 79168.

ARABIAN JOCKEY CLUB

12000 Zuni Street   Westminster, CO 80234
303-450-4714 or 4712   fax 303-450-2841   e-mail AJCAJCAJC@aol.com

A RABIAN racing was organized around 1959. Today, pure-bred Arabian horses have carved out a niche in the racing industry sharing race cards with Thoroughbreds, Quarter Horses and other breeds. Purses and handles are at an all-time high and new and exciting opportunities abound for competitive Arabian racehorses at major racetracks across the country.

To ensure that opportunities for owners of Arabian horses continue, the Arabian Jockey Club—a national organization dedicated to the promotion, education and professional management of the Arabian racing industry—has developed a number of promotional and educational resources to help reach this goal.

- *The Original Racehorse*—this free educational video offers the racing newcomer a professional, evenhanded look at getting involved in the sport.
- **Arabian Race Source**—this online data base gives users 24-hour access to over 30 different racing reports from a personal computer. The information contained in the reports is generated from the AJC's racing data base—the official data base of Arabian racing.
- *Arabian Jockey Club Stallion Directory*—every year, the AJC publishes a directory of racing stallions featuring reliable, complete racing statistics.
- **Arabian Racing Cup**—in 1996, the AJC began administering the 13-year-old breeders' incentive program. Nominators of Arabian Cup Sires and Runners reap the rewards of this lucrative program.

For additional information, please contact the AJC.

American Paint Horse Association

Paint Racing

The mission of the American Paint Horse Association is to collect, record and preserve the pedigrees of American Paint Horses and to stimulate and regulate all matters that pertain to the promotion, history, breeding and exhibition of the breed.

With its roots firmly grounded in American Quarter Horse and Thoroughbred bloodlines, the American Paint is a formidable speed horse. Paints are generally considered to be sprinters – horses that run at distances ranging from 220 to 870 yards. However, the most common distance for Paints to race is 350 yards. Paint racers contend for nearly $1 million in purses each year on recognized pari-mutuel tracks.

APHA Racing Department

The Racing Department is responsible for race approval, recording race results, maintaining racing standings, and overseeing the racing tattoo program. The department also furnishes information on the racing records of American Paints, and co-produces the bi-monthly APHA racing newsletter, *Down the Backstretch*, with the Marketing and Communications Department.

Paint Horse Journal

The monthly breed publication, the *Paint Horse Journal*, reports on major races during the year, and provides monthly updates on standings and race results.

Incentives and Awards Programs

Champion Running Paint Horses are honored each year during the annual APHA Workshop. Official Paint Racing awards are presented to the World Champion Running Paint Horse and Champion Running Paint 2-Year-Old, 3-Year-Old and Aged Horse. These horses are selected by a point system, with more competitive races being worth more points than less competitive races.

Racing Honor Roll Awards are issued annually to the horse in each sex category earning the most points in racing. The horse with the most points receives an engraved trophy or plaque, while horses placing second through 10th receive certificates.

APHA annually awards Register of Merit (ROM) designations to Paint Horses who qualify. ROMs are awarded to horses earning an official speed index rating of 80 or better, or who earn 10 racing points. Points are awarded based on the speed index ratings at any of the 11 recognized distances. Superior Awards are awarded to Paint Horses earning 50 or more points in racing. Register of Merit and Superior earners' are published annually in the *Paint Horse Journal*.

NCBRC Stakes Book and Directory

The APHA and the Appaloosa Horse Club co-produce the National Color Breeds Racing Council (NCBRC) Stakes Book and Directory. Distributed free of charge, the directory is a guide for Paint and Appaloosa owners, trainers, breeders, racing officials and the media. Information includes the name of the race and track, scheduled running date, purse or added money, age and state-bred restrictions, distance, nomination fee, and the date nominations are due. The directory includes addresses and phone numbers of trainers, breeders, farms and ranches, race tracks, state racing associations and state-bred registries.

For more information, contact the APHA Racing Department, P.O. Box 961023, Fort Worth, Texas 76161, or call (817) 439-3400, extension 247.

POST OFFICE BOX 961023 FORT WORTH, TEXAS 76161-0023
PHYSICAL ADDRESS: 10405 N. I-35 W FORT WORTH, TEXAS 76177
(817) 439-3400 FAX (817) 439-3484

Pacific Coast
Quarter Horse Racing Association

Helping California's Quarter Horse Horsemen

- **Administration of 7 major California Futurities & Derbies:**

  (1) Ed Burke Memorial Futurity [Gr 1]   (5) California Sires Cup Futurity [R3]
  (2) Governor's Cup Derby [R1]   (6) California Sires Cup Derby [R3]
  (3) PCQHRA Breeders Futurity [R2]   (7) PCQHRA Breeders Derby [R3]
  (4) Governor's Cup Futurity [R2]

- **Full-time legislative advocacy in Sacramento**
- **Administration of Cal-Bred Awards Program for breeders, race horse owners & stallion owners**
- **Administration of PCQHRA Annual Yearling & Mixed Stock Sale**
- **Contract representation for horsemen at all California race meets with Quarter Horse participation**
- **Providing the only recognized representation of Quarter Horse interests before the California Horse Racing Board**
- **Promotion of California racing opportunities for Quarter Horsemen across the United States**
- **Publication of the only regular California Quarter Horse newsletter to keep horsemen informed on racing issues**
- **Publication of the most complete directory of Quarter Horse racing interests in California**
- **Membership and participation in national organizations working to develop & improve the economic future of the Quarter horse industry**

Representing California's Quarter Horse Horsemen Since 1951

PACIFIC COAST QUARTER HORSE RACING ASSOCIATION

P.C.Q.H.R.A.

For More Information On Quarter Horse Breeding & Racing Opportunities In California

call 714 236 1755
FAX 714 236 1761

To MR. GREEN!

Rest, done
soon enough,
Heals most problems!

Remember . . .

Haynets
cause the wrong
Kind of motion

DAYS of GLORY...
My Favorite Newspaper Articles

Dave Joseph

■■■■ HORSE RACING

'Prediction' making fond memories for trainer and charity

There are fond memories, Janet DelCastillo says, but not many of victory.

Between bushtrack racing and bad breeding, DelCastillo, 40, has had little luck and fewer winners with the thoroughbreds she has trained.

After eight years, she can't recall any of her horses as "noteworthy. It seems they've always been bottom-of-the-line claimers."

In Winter Haven, where DelCastillo lives with her three children, the locals don't care a lot about horse racing. In February they turn their attention to the Boston Red Sox, headquartered there for spring training. The rest of the year Winter Haven is known as the home of Cypress Gardens.

But DelCastillo may yet change the way they think. In the middle of Winter Haven, on 12 acres, DelCastillo has what seems to be a legitimate stakes horse in First Prediction.

The horse has been in the money six of her 10 races, and in her last start finished second in a division of Calder's Gloxinia Stakes.

DelCastillo isn't the only one profiting from First Prediction's success. The Florida Horsemen's Children's Home in Ocala for "problem" boys and girls shares.

When Ed MacClellan of the children's home offered to sell DelCastillo the filly and another horse in March for a bargain-basement $5,000, DelCastillo didn't have the money.

"I was helping them with artwork at the school, and Ed asked if I wanted the two," DelCastillo said.

The horses had been donated to the school, and "he said that I could pay him when I had the money."

When First Prediction began earning some purse money, DelCastillo didn't forget. Now, every time First Prediction earns a check, the children's home gets a donation.

DelCastillo's odyssey began 10 years ago. Born and reared in San Francisco, she trained polo ponies until she joined the Peace Corps and went to Colombia, where she met her husband.

After living in Buffalo and Staten Island, the DelCastillos moved to Winter Haven and started racing horses.

"One day my husband said that we should get some race horses, so we got a few mares and we bred them," DelCastillo said.

"We raced [quarter horses] at Pompano, then we got thoroughbreds. But after putting around $16,000 into the horses we were lucky if they were running in $2,500 races at Tampa [Bay Downs]."

Finally, along came First Prediction, a 3-year-old by On To Glory-Around The Bend.

First Prediction is not a large filly, but she has showed enough to be considered a runner.

After breaking her maiden at Tampa Bay Downs in March, the filly has continued to improve.

After running respectably in two allowance races at Hialeah, the filly moved to Calder and finished second to C'Mon Liz in the Gloxinia two weeks ago.

Appearing to weaken after C'Mon Liz passed her entering the stretch over Calder's turf coure, First Prediction made a run at the victor in the closing yards to place.

In lieu of a track, DelCastillo has used her back yard. She builds her horses up with slow five-mile gallops through orange groves

"It's really more like a trail," mostly heavy sand, which DelCastillo says builds up stamina.

"I think it's like a child," she said. "If you expose a horse to a lot of things, then it's only a question of speed. I think my training builds up a horse and makes it a stronger piece of equipment."

After building up the endurance and then testing her horses with intervals of speed workouts, she swims them in a mile lake behind her house, "sometimes two times a day if it's hot."

The rest of the time, DelCastillo quarters her horses in her eight-stall barn as little as possible.

"I think a horse needs sun and vitamin D," she said.

"Sure, mine have a few problems with some cuts and nicks they get on our fences, and their coats always look bleached, but their bodies are much more solid, and I've never had any tendon problems because of the long, slow foundation."

The foundation has been laid for Saturday's $50,000 Office Queen Stakes for 3-year-old fillies over Calder's 1 1/16-mile turf course.

"I really think we've got a chance," DelCastillo said. "All I've ever really wanted all these years was a horse I could throw in the van to race that I wasn't afraid was going to get claimed.

"I've waited a lifetime for this, and I may not get another chance."

So Friday Janet DelCastillo will van First Prediction the 4½ hours from Winter Haven to Miami in hope of winning the Office Queen.

There will be a lot of people pulling for DelCastillo, but none more than the boys and girls at the Florida Horsemen's Children's Home.

We didn't win the Office Queen Stakes — But we had fun trying!

275

Can nice girls finish first? Calder race tells the story

By LUTHER EVANS
Herald Turf Writer

First Prediction held only a head advantage over charging Truly when they reached the eighth pole in Saturday's $47,650 Black Velvet Handicap before 9,884 fans at Calder.

On which filly would you have bet your money at that point?

Truly was the 2.20-1 favorite. She is is a daughter of the great stallion In Reality, bred by the eminently successful Frances A. Genter. She is trained by Frank Gomez, Calder's all-time-leading winner of stakes with 58. She was being ridden by Jose Velez Jr., Calder's 1985 riding champion with 109 winners.

First Prediction went off as a 15.30-1 long shot. She is a daughter of On to Glory and was bred by Paul Marriott, who culled her from his yearlings as being too small and gave her to the Florida Horsemen Childrens' Home in Citra, Fla. Later, Janet Del Castillo bought her on credit as part of a two-filly package for $5,000.

The primary training of First Prediction consists of Del Castillo, admittedly "a large woman," galloping her through a Winter Haven orange grove and also swimming the filly in a nearby lake. Saturday, First Prediction was being ridden as usual by Benny Green, a nice guy who has to scuffle to make a living ... unfortunate for a jockey with his ability.

At the sixteenth pole, First Prediction and Truly had swept past front-runner Merry Cathy and C'mon Liz and still were at each other's throats. Now, by all logic, you would have bet 'on Truly. Right?

Wrong.

First Prediction, under a super ride by Green, refused to yield more than a few inches in the drive and outgamed Truly by a nose to earn her first stakes victory.

"I knew she had the guts to do it," said Del Castillo.

But the first female owner-trainer to win a Calder stakes this season didn't come down to earth to analyze 4-year-old First Prediction's unexpected added-money triumph until 10 minutes after it had been accomplished. She had rushed onto the track, leaping high with every other stride, to hug Green and his mount before they got to the winner's circle. And all the time, she was whooping in sheer ecstacy.

Del Castillo was entitled. When Ed McClellan, the children's home director, decided that the home couldn't care for the fillies and offered to sell them to her, she tried to say no. "I was in the middle of a divorce, had four kids, and no money," she said. "But I couldn't resist buying them, if on credit."

The other filly never panned out, but before Saturday, First Prediction had earned $94,241 in 35 starts with a 6-8-7 record. And that had alowed Del Castillo to, pay off the $5,000 debt last year. But she didn't stop there. Since then, every time First Prediction earns a check, the home gets a donation from her. The next contribution will be the biggest — First Prediction collected $29,790 in the Black Velvet.

First Prediction carried 114 pounds over the mile and 70 yards in 1:45 3/5 and paid $32.60, $10.20 and $5.20. Truly returned $3.60 and $2.60 and Hail The Lady $3.60.

End of an improbable — but heartwarming — report on a horse race.

23 in Desert Vixen

The six-furlong Desert Vixen, the opening test in the fifth annual Florida Stallion Stakes series, headlines the card at Calder today. It has been split into two divisions because of 23 entries.

Twelve 2-year-old fillies will compete in the first division and 11 in the second.

Ocali Gal, Rapturous and My Nicole are expected to be among contenders in the first division.

Allaise, a winner at Belmont Park, and Calder victors Blues Court and Jill Of All Trades head the second division.

Words Cannot describe The joy of this = Win!

At Calder, 'Prediction' turns dream to reality

By DAVE JOSEPH
Racing Writer

MIAMI — Against all odds, dreams can still come true. Just ask Janet Del-Castillo.

Two years ago while visiting the Florida Horsemen's Children's Home in Citra, DelCastillo bought two horses on loan from the home's administrator Ed MacClellan for $5,000. One, an On To Glory filly named First Prediction, had been donated by breeder Paul Marriott so the home's neglected children could ride her for recreational purposes and later breed her, not to become a stakes-winning filly at Calder Race Course.

"I remember having no money at the time," DelCastillo recalled. "I didn't even know if I would be able to keep my farm (in Winter Haven) at that point. But a voice from heaven said, 'Take a shot.' I figured once she started winning I could pay the $5,000 off."

That's how sure DelCastillo was that First Prediction would not only become a winner, but a stakes winner. Some called her a dreamer, but DelCastillo wouldn't give in.

On her Winter Haven farm, she trained First Prediction through sandy trails of orange groves and took her for swims every day in a lake behind her farm.

Despite everyone telling her that she had wasted her money — that you couldn't expect to win when you ship in overnight from a tiny farm to a major racetrack — DelCastillo dreamed on. And Saturday at Calder, her dream came true.

Racing third down the backstretch, First Prediction and jockey Benjamin Green came driving down the middle of the stretch to nose out Frances A. Genter's Truly to win the $47,650 Black Velvet Handicap.

A 15-1 longshot, 4-year-old First Prediction took the lead just past the eighth pole and held game while favorite Truly and jockey Jose Velez Jr., battled with her neck-and-neck to the wire. First Prediction covered the mile and 70 yards in 1:45 3/5.

First Prediction was second in an allowance race Aug. 15 at Calder. Instead of preparing her for the Black Velvet by galloping her as she usually does through the groves, DelCastillo prepped the filly with daily swims on the farm. During the day, DelCastillo turns First Prediction out in a pasture.

"It's a dream come true," said DelCastillo, who danced for joy in the winner's circle after the race. "Today she

SEE **CALDER** / 14C

CALDER

FROM **PAGE 1C**

First Prediction turns dream to reality at Calder

just wouldn't give up.

"Everyone always told me you couldn't ship a horse in like this and win. But in this particular case, it's all worked."

DelCastillo's good fortune has also helped the children's home. After First Prediction's prior victories — she has won seven races and placed in 22 of 36 — DelCastillo has donated $1,000 to the home. "And you can bet they'll be getting another check tonight," she said.

Breaking fifth in the nine-horse field, Green moved First Prediction up along the rail around the first turn and settled into third going down the backstretch behind C'Mon Liz and Merry Cathy. It was an unusual move, because First Prediction's best running style is usually to close from well off the pace.

"I was closer than I expected to be today," Green said. "But she was running strong so I let her run."

While C'Mon Liz was setting fractions of 24, :48 2 5. First Prediction continued inching closer to the front. By the time Green hit the 3/8th pole, First Prediction was full of run, as was Truly, closing from sixth.

DelCastillo

"As we came around the 3/8th pole she was picking up horses and they weren't really moving away from her too much," Green said. "She just kept on going."

Two-wide entering the stretch, First Prediction took the lead from Merry Cathy at the eighth pole. A neck behind on the outside Truly was closing. But First Prediction would not give in. The filly continued on strongly in the last sixteenth and to the wire.

"I am so glad she is a legitimate horse," DelCastillo said. "I am so glad."

So is the Florida horsemen's Children's Home.

First Prediction paid $32.60, $10.20 and $5.20. Truly paid $3 60 and $2.60 and Hail The Lady, who closed from eighth, returned $3.60 to show.

Commoner almost dethrones royalty

By LUTHER EVANS
Herald Turf Writer

First Prediction, a racing commoner who works out in a Winter Haven orange grove, almost put the squeeze on aristocratic Fragrant Princess in Calder's $52,030 New Year Handicap before 12,267 fans Thursday.

First Prediction, purchased in a two-horse package for a mere $5,000 from the Florida Horsemen Children's School near Ocala two years ago, charged between horses in the final furlong but just missed catching winner Fragrant Princess by a head. But her rally from last place in the early going did enable her to finish one length ahead of Greentree Stable's Perfect Point, who had been expected by many to deprive Harper Stables' Fragrant Princess of her third consecutive victory.

Trainer Luis Olivares sprinted down from the fourth floor just in time to make the winner's circle. "I told you to expect me here because I was here after Powder Break won the La Prevoyante last Jan. 1," he said. "I like to start every year in a big way. And I think my Flying Pidgeon will win the W.L. McKnight Handicap at 1½ miles on Wednesday, closing day."

Olivares has gone on from such January success to earn the title as South Florida's outstanding trainer of the past two winter seasons. "I believe that three is an even better number," he said.

Fragrant Princess carried 116 pounds over the nine furlongs in 1:55 and paid $8.60, $5 and $4.60. First Prediction (113 pounds) returned $6 and $3.60. Regal Prin-

third-place Regal Princess.

Julio Pezua, who rode First Prediction for the first time for trainer Janet Del Castillo, thought that jockey Heriberto Valdivieso had allowed Fragrant Princess to drift in and shut off his gray mount late in the drive. Stewards studied race films and decided that the winner had been clear when she lugged in and did not force Pezua to check the runner-up.

It was a good horse race. And it probably would have been even better except for heavy early-morning rain bringing five scratches after the 1¼-mile test had been taken off the turf course. Included among the defectors was cess, whom trainer Jose "Pepe" Mendez had sharp enough to lead most of the way under Walter Guerra, paid $3.80.

Fragrant Princess disposed of Regal Princess and Donna's Dolly inside the eighth pole and seemed to have matters in hand when First Prediction began her powerful bid that made the finish exciting.

There is financial parity today between Fragrant Princess, a 4-year-old Diplomat Way filly, and First Prediction, a 5-year-old On To Glory mare. Fragrant Princess' $34,150 purse increased her earnings to $163,531. First Prediction's $9,050 second-place money increased her winnings to $152,464.

And who, you may ask, is nervy enough to get aboard First Prediction and gallop her through an orange grove? Owner-trainer Janet Del Castillo, that's who.

The Jan. 1 crowd wagered $1,722,256.

This was amusing!

The story covered the horse that lost more than the horse that won!

Tale of Gift Horse And Home for Kids

Lew Zagnit / *TAMPA BAY*

OLDSMAR, Fla.—You take a horse with a broken leg, add a trainer, a divorcee trying to make it on her own, and tie in a home for dependent children, and what have you got? No, not a remake of "Annie Meets National Velvet." You have the Gold Coup—Janet del Castillo—Florida Horsemen's Children Home story, which is being played out at this meeting. You can catch the latest installment of this real life melodrama on Saturday, when del Castillo runs Gold Coup in a $5,000 claiming race here.

Now a little background on the cast.

"The Florida Horsemen's Children's Home offers long-term residential care for neglected and dependent children; children from families with problems or whose parents are divorced," explained director Ed Mac-Clellan, when contacted by phone at the Florida facility.

MacClellan had for 12 years served as the director of the Rodeheaver Home, a boys ranch in Putnam. Thus he was an obvious selection when people within the horse industry here, particularly Joe Durkin of the Florida Horse Magazine, decided there was a need for a similar facility in Marion County.

"We started raising money four years ago, and George Steinbrenner, through his New York Yankee Foundation, gave us a grant for one half of the land purchase. We raised the other half by donations. We do not receive any government funds. We are supported entirely by donations.

"We turned 1-year-old in November," said MacClellan. "We have one cottage for 12 kids, 60 acres of land, and 15 head of horses. Our staff consists of one set of cottage parents and a relief set of cottage parents, one of whom doubles as a secretary. We also have a thrift store in Ocala.

"We have paddocks for the horses, but no barns, but we are trying to raise funds to build barns."

Part of the support the horsemen contribute comes in the form of horses who are donated for the children to take care of or, if possible, are sold to race, which is how del Castillo became involved.

A couple of years ago, she paid $5,000 for two thoroughbreds who had been donated to the home. One of them just recently broke his maiden, but the other one turned out to be a pretty good runner. He name is First Prediction, and the 5-year-old On to Glory mare just went over the $170,000 mark in earnings with a second in an allowance race at Hialeah last Saturday.

First Prediction, who was donated by breeder Paul Marriott, has been a steady and useful campaigner partly by design, and possibly partly due to a mistake by del Castillo, who took out her trainer's license three years ago after she and her husband were divorced.

"I think part of the reason she's so strong," said del Castillo, the mother of three teenaged children, "is that I never start my horses until they're 3-years-old. And, when I was galloping First Prediction around the orange grove I thought I was going three miles a day, but I was actually going closer to five and a half.

"She was the first one I got from the children's home. They've gotten wonderful support from the horse community, certainly from Clayton O'Quinn, and Helmuth Schmidt. I've worked with them the most at picking up the horses that were donated, trying them out and either getting rid of them, or trying to run them. And Gold Coup, who was donated by Evelyn Poole, was the first one good enough to run in the childrens home's name.

"I got him sometime in the middle of last summer "continued del Castillo, who spent time serving in the peace corps." He had a fractured cannon bone, and was very body sore. The first thing I did was bring him home, geld him, and turn him out. Then I started long slow gallops. I tried him a few times in Miami, but I think he was just tuning up, and he's gotten better since. He's been on the board or won every race he's been in since."

Gold Coup is owned in partnership with the children's home, (even through the children, who are of course minors, are not allowed at the track due to state law) and del Castillo's mother and stepfather. Thus half the money the 5-year-old Gold Stage gelding makes, which totals about $4,000 so far, goes to support the home.

And the best thing about this story is there's no happy ending, just a happy continuation.

C. V. B. Cushman Dead; Rode in '30 Carolina Cup

RANCHO PALOS VERDES, Cal.—Charles V. B. Cushman, who rode in the inaugural running of the Carolina Cup Steeplechase in 1930, died here on January 13 at the age of 84, it was learned Thursday. He was one of four generations of the Cushman family to participate as amateur and professional riders.

Mr. Cushman, whose grandson, John, won the Carolina Cup in 1982 aboard Quiet Bay, operated Eastland Farm Stable and campaigned stakes winners. In 1928 he paid a then record yearling price of $75,000 for New Broom, a Whisk Broom II colt.

He is survived by his widow, Elizabeth; two sons, two daughters, 14 grandchildren and eight great-grandchildren.

Leading Filly and Mare Earners

(Includes horses who have started at least once in North America. Lifetime earnings of horses who have raced in foreign countries are included through the date of last start in North America.)

(Includes Racing of January 18)

This was another horse I got from the Childrens' Home

He went to Canada and I lost track of him!

Daily Racing Form Jan 31, 1987

Art Grace

Horse racing

Gulfstream announcer and his memorable goof

I have listened to a lot of track announcers (Hialeah's Tom Durkin, a notable exception) mangle a lot of pronunciations, but my favorite is the most recent, by Gulfstream's Ross Morton.

As far as I know, there is only one way to pronounce "be-nign." It has to rhyme with fine. Unless it is Morton's interpretation of the 4-year-old filly Benign Begum.

When she ran at Gulfstream the first time on March 20, I thought I must have been fantasizing when I heard Morton refer to her, throughout the race, as, so help me, "Benijgan Begum." (He also mispronounced "Begum," but that's understandable.)

Nah, it couldn't be, I decided to wait until Benign Begum ran back in order to make sure I had not been hallucinating. She finally showed up again in the first race last Sunday. And sure enough,

Grace

Morton called her "Benijgan Begum" with every rundown as the field plodded its way through the mile and a sixteenth.

I think I'll go out for dinner tonight. . . . for a hamburger and fries at that popular restaurant on 163rd street. You know the one I'm referring to: Benign's.

*   *   *

Apparently, I am not the only race track person, to have been smitten by Patty Smyth's new solo album, and especially the title song, "Never Enough."

Janet Del Castillo, a very nice lady who owns and trains First Prediction, has decided that "never enough" is the way to handle her horse. A more appropriate theme would be "enough is enough."

First Prediction, a 5-year-old mare, has been one of my favorites for a long time. She is, or rather was, a stone closer who made a big run virtually every time.

I liked her a lot when Bennie Green was riding her at Calder last year and positively loved her when Julio Pezua got the mount beginning Jan. 1 this year. It was a perfect marriage, a closer with a

great finishing rider.

She just missed in the New Year's eight days later in the Suwanee River Handicap at Calder, at 7-1, and won at 8-1 at Hialeah nine days later. She then finished second in the Bal Harbour and third, beaten a neck and a nose to Anka Germania and Chaldea, in the Columbiana. Next time out she closed big again to finish second in the Key Largo.

At that point she had to be considered an iron horse, the Margaret Thatcher of Florida racing. She already had run five times in six weeks in 1987 after a very rigorous campaign in 1986.

She was back in one week later at Tampa Bay and finally the regimen caught up with her. She finished fifth, beaten 14½ lengths.

Undiscouraged, DelCastillo vanned her back to Hialeah for the Black Helen two weeks later. First Prediction never got out of a gallop, finishing 11th.

I got the message loud and clear two weeks later at Gulfstream when First Prediction turned back to seven furlongs and finished a weak fifth. When she failed to fire going short I knew the romance was over between us.

When she showed up still again, just eight days later in the Suwanee River Handicap, I wasn't about to bet on her.

Surely Del Castillo would give her a rest now? Yeah, three whole days. Four days later First Prediction was in the December, finishing seventh, 15 lengths behind Spindle City.

How sad it was to see him running for a $5,000 claiming price at Tampa last

Surely Del Castillo would give her a rest now? Yeah, three whole days. Four days later First Prediction was in the Rampart Handicap, in body but not in spirit. She was last all the way, finishing 16 lengths behind the next to last horse.

First Prediction is nominated for Saturday's mile-and-a-half Orchid Handicap and next Wednesday's seven-furlong Old Hat Handicap. She will warm up for those stakes today in the ninth race, an allowance feature at a mile and a sixteenth on the grass. Unless 20 races in 29 weeks prove a mite debilitating I'm sure she will be able to make the Orchid and Old Hat.

I went through the same depressing experience with another personal favorite, Command Attention, owned and trained by Nathan Kelly. Command Attention hasn't been around much lately but his last start, at Gulfstream March 26, was the 140th of his career. The 9-year-old gelding was running in

stakes races two years ago. I will never forget the afternoon in October, 1985, when he won an allowance race on grass at Calder by a nose and paid $59.80.

How sad it was to see him running for a $5,000 claiming price at Tampa last December, finishing seventh, 15 lengths behind Spindle City.

He raced only 16 times last year because he had to laid up from July to December. But if he could make it to the paddock he didn't miss any dances in previous four years. He ran only nine times as a 2-year-old and only 13 times at 3. But from 1982 through 1985, he maintained a twice-a-month schedule without buckling.

If he was a cat I'd take him home and let him enjoy the good life.

First Prediction already has matched Command Attention's busiest year — 27 starts in 1983. She equalled that total last year and is well on her to surpassing it this year.

More's the pity. Horses are not machines, but sometimes they are treated as though they were.

This article was a complete surprise to me — & I had arrived at the track the night before and Grace never interviewed. Read on → the next day's article tells "The Rest of the Story!"

This was the following day! What joy to prove them wrong!

Art Grace

Horse racing

Del Castillo has a right to feel wonderful

April 17, 1987

In this column, yesterday, I excoriated owner-trainer Janet Del Castillo for what I considered poor, and possibly abusive, management of her horse First Prediction. After running extremely well against top competition all winter, the 5-year-old mare appeared to have been ground down by an exhausting schedule — 20 races in 28 weeks.

I was moved to voice my displeasure when First Prediction ran three times in 12 days at Gulfstream, twice in major stakes, and had run five very poor races in a row. Immediately before going off form, First Prediction had finished third, beaten a neck and a nose, to top filles Ankle Germain and Chaldea in the Columbiana at Hialeah Feb. 1 and two weeks later came from last to finish second to Singular Bequest in the Key Largo.

Then came five terrible races, the most recent in the Rampart Handicap April 5. But there are two sides to most stories and Miss Del Castillo surely was entitled to present a defense. She came to see me yesterday and did so, an hour before First Prediction ran still again in the ninth race which, to Janet's discomfort, had been switched from grass to dirt.

"I know it looks terrible on paper," she said. "All people see is that she ran on March 24 and April 1 and April 5. What they don't realize is that I can't ever work this mare like a normal horse.

"Every time I try to work her, she ties up (suffer severe cramping). If I let that happen, it takes two months to get her ready to run again. So I never work her. She has to get fit by running, and in order to stay fit she has to run at least every 10 to 14 days. If she's off longer than that I have to start from scratch again.

"If I ever felt she had a physical problem, if she ever went off her feed, I'd stop on her immediately. She's like a part of my family ... she's in our yard (Del Castillo lives in Winter Haven) when she's not running. I could never abuse her. She's absolutely sound.

"She's been running poorly, but I've been trying to get her back into her rhythm. I know it looks bad when she runs in a tough race like the Rampart with only three days rest. What they'd never understand is that I needed that race to get her back to her optimum form. Not many people use a $125,000 15-horse field into the first turn. She didn't have a stakes as a work, but I did. I never was able to be very subtle.

"She's been acting just fine; I expect she'll run really like her ... she doesn't seem to like dirt. But I still expect her to run a whole lot better.

"After what you wrote in the paper today, I hope the people don't throw rocks at me when I go to the paddock. If she runs bad again, I'd consider resting her until Calder opens (in six weeks)... which would mean it would take me four races to get her ready again. That's something I can't really afford to do.

"If I had to choose yesterday to lambaste Miss Del Castillo, at least my timing was exquisite. First Prediction was so utterly worn out that she came from next to last on the backstretch and wore down from-running Bereavement in the last 50 yards to win the mile and a sixteenth allowance feature by a length. Julio Pezua, of course, rode her flawlessly.

After the race, Miss Del Castillo could not resist rushing to the press box and to tell me "I told you so."

Well, indeed she had. Practically everyone except everybody in the afternoons. She doesn't do well in a stall. She has to get her one who went public with it. She had a right to rub it in. It was the least she could do.

"I feel wonderful, it's such a relief to know I

wasn't wrong," she said. "For a while I was starting to doubt myself."

Before the race Janet had felt First Prediction could not run well on dirt 'except for Calder (which has a unique racing strip). She was running super on two years; she's never refused to eat up. She's like a working man who puts on his hard hat and goes to work every day. 'Another day, another dollar.'

"If the race sets up right (with early speed) she'll be there. If it doesn't, she won't. If I can run her with no more than 10 to 14 days between races, I don't have to be concerned about not working her. If it's 20 days I fall two races behind with her.

"She didn't like the track and didn't fire (finishing a bad fifth). When she ran back in the Black Helen it was against killers and she was widest of all in a chance.

"At that point, I had to try and get her back into her rhythm. I ran her seven furlongs and she did close ground. But she couldn't handle those fractions:22, :44 and change, 1:10. And she didn't like the dirt. The only place to run her next was the grass stake at Gulfstream (Suwanee River) and the fractions were so slow she couldn't make up ground.

"With a horse like her, who comes from way out of it, things have to break right (a realistic early pace by the speed horses) for her to run well. But I felt she needed that race, and one more, to reach her level of competence.

"The reason I ran her back four days later (in the $125,000 Rampart Handicap) is that I got suckered into it. Just before the entries closed, they called me and said only four horses were entered. It turned out to be seven.

"I told Pezua not to abuse her if she didn't have a shot. The pace was slow again and he realized there was no point beating on her.

"It's no fun to have to train her in front of everybody in the afternoons. She doesn't do well in a stall, works in her races. She has to get her exercise that way.

"I have her in a normal environment at Winter Haven, in cycle with nature. She's out in the pasture

every day, in the sunshine, not locked in a stall. She swims every day. That's it.

"A horse can't talk to you; you have to go by your perceptions. I can tell you she hasn't gotten sour in two years; she's never refused to eat up. She's like a working man who puts on his hard hat and goes to work every day. 'Another day, another dollar.'

"If the race sets up right (with early speed) she'll be there. If it doesn't, she won't. If I can run her with no more than 10 to 14 days between races, I don't have to be concerned about not working her. If it's 20 days I fall two races behind with her.

"It's tough when I have to keep running her in stakes but it's the only way to keep her in her rhythm.

"Most people have no idea how tough this game can be. They've never had to load a hysterical 2-year-old filly on a van at 5 in the morning and take her to Tampa to work."

First Prediction ran 19 times in 1985, 24 times last year, and already has run 11 times this year. She has finished in the money in 32 of those 54 starts, winning nine. She went over the $200,000 mark in earnings with a $13,200 winner's purse yesterday.

While I still have reservations with Miss Del Castillo's handling of First Prediction, she aced me in straight sets yesterday and the overall results have been good.

Last year at Hialeah First Prediction ran twice in five days and finished second both times. She ran at Calder Aug. 2, 15 and 23 and won twice and finished second once.

Before the slump hit late in February this year the mare ran eight times in 2½ months and every race was a corker. After her performance yesterday, I doubt she ever will break down. Her career will end when the iron starts to rust.

Racing *Daily* Form

Copyright © 1987 by Daily Racing Form, Inc. All rights reserved

VOL. 17, No. 130   HIGHTSTOWN, N.J., SUNDAY, MAY 10, 1987   PRICE $2.00

Fieldy Heads Gulf's Very One

HEADLINES and Front Page on Racing FORM! Guess WHo WoN? ...Not Fieldy!

By WILLIAM C. PHILLIPS

GULFSTREAM PARK, Hallandale, Fla.—Arriola and Seltzter's Fieldy, an Irish-bred 4-year-old who dead-heated for win with Fama in a division of the Grade III Suwannee River Handicap on turf April 1 and then was unplaced in the Grade II Orchid 'Cap on grass April 18, heads a field of 11 fillies and mares entered for the inaugural running of the $62,700 The Very One Handicap, which features a Mother's Day card here Sunday.

The race will be decided at a mile on the turf for a winner's prize of $37,620.

Craig Perret will return from the North to ride Fieldy at topweight of 115 pounds.

Janet del Castillo's First Prediction, a winner of her last two starts, is next in the weights at 114, with leading jockey Julio Pezua back in the saddle.

The field is completed by J. Robert Harris Jr.'s Thirty Zip, 113, Earlie Fires; J. C. Dudley's Tri Argo, 112, Robert Lester; Barbara Hunter's Duckweed, 111, Jose Velez Jr.; Mike J. Doyle and Sherry Farm's Miss Enchanted, 111, Steve Gaffalione; Southlake Stable's Lady of the North, 110, Pezua on another call; Dana S. Bray Jr.'s Evening Bid, 110, Santiago Soto; Buckram Oak Farm's Royal Infatuation, 110, Constantino Hernandez; Joanne and R. Thornton's Tuscadoon, 108, Mike Lee, and Mrs. Henry D. Paxson's Lustrous Reason, 108, James Reed.

Fieldy showed her class in France as a 2-year-old by winning the Group I Marcel Boussac at Longchamp. She was off form for three other races in France as a 3-year-old, but trainer Steve W. Young reports that whatever her problem

was, it no longer exists. His statement is supported by her two winning races and a close second in her United States race this year. Fieldy was not a factor in the Orchid, but that race was at a mile and a half, and Young described the race as "an experiment" to see whether she could handle the distance.

"She couldn't," he said, "but the mile will suit her fine."

First Prediction has gained a large following on the story how she was a yearling purchase from an orphanage home near Ocala and is trained by her owner in an orange grove next to a lake in Winter Haven. The attractive 5-year-old gray mare by Or to Glory has come from off the pace for a number of top efforts on the turf, including a third in a three-way photo finish at Hialeah this past winter with Anka Germania and Chaldea in the Grade III Columbiana Handicap, and a rousing two and one-half length tally on the grass her last start, beating Truly.

larry Geiger has found Thirty Zip performs best when her races are spaced a month apart and this event fits the schedule perfectly. She was fourth behind the crack filly Life at the Top in the Grade III Rampart Handicap that was run on the main track on April 5. Three weeks before that, she finished strongly at a mile on the turf and just missed catching Small Virtue in a division of the Joe Namath Handicap.

The 4-year-old Tri Jet filly also ran well on the grass at Calder last fall when third behind Anka Germania and Slew's Exceller in the Calder Breeders' Cup Handicap.

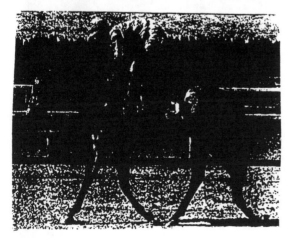

Prominent

First Prediction seeks third straight Florida win Sunday.

HORSE RACING

Thirty Zip (2) doesn't have enough zip to catch Julio Pezua and First Prediction Sunday.

First Prediction has enough gas to capture third straight victory

By FRAN LaBELLE
Staff Writer

HALLANDALE — The photos had been taken, horse and jockey dutifully kissed and Janet Del Castillo was about to answer any questions about First Prediction's 2½-length victory in Sunday's $62,700 Very One Handicap at Gulfstream.

"Do you think we can tell her how we ran out of gas on the turnpike now?," said her son, Alex.

"Don't tell me any more," Del Castillo said.

As it turns out, Alex and his brother, Hernando, ran out of gas near the Pompano Beach exit of the turnpike Friday while shipping in First Prediction for Sunday's 1-mile turf test for older fillies and mares. After a 20-minute wait, the van was back on the road.

Fortunately, Del Castillo left the driving to Julio Pezua Sunday. This time, no one ran out of gas.

Pezua, whose victory was his second of the day and increased his record season's total to 75, got something extra from First Prediction in the stretch to get by J.R. Harris Jr.'s Thirty Zip. It was First Prediction's third straight victory, and it came before a Mother's Day crowd of 10,752.

"I had to lay up closer to the pace than usual because the race was only a flat mile," said Pezua, who stayed fourth behind Tri Argo, favored Fieldy and Tuscadoon until the stretch. "I saved all the ground I could and was able to get through inside. My horse made the lead in the stretch, but then the [Thirty Zip] went by here. When my horse saw that, she dug in and went ahead to win the race."

Del Castillo said her main worry was that the early fractions of :23 4/5, :41 1/5 and 1:11 1/5 would mean Pezua would have to use his mount earlier than he would like.

"It was a wild race," said Del Castillo, whose charge turned in a winning time of 1:35 1/5 for her second stakes victory. "But First Prediction's been knocking at the door. She's a game little thing, and God bless Pezua. He knew enough to keep her close."

First Prediction, a 5-year-old daughter of On To Glory-Around The Bend by Hagley, returned $7.80, $4.20 and $3.00.

It is also thought that Del Castillo will use part of the winner's purse of $37,620 to gas all of her vehicles.

NOTES: Pezua has been named on another stakes contender. He will ride Easter Mary for trainer **Sonny Hine** in Wednesday's $41,195 Honey Fox Stakes for 3-year-old fillies at a mile and a sixteenth... Gulfstream will offer simulcasting of the Preakness next Saturday.

Breeding Business: Romance and Glory

Bill Giauque / *FLORIDA*

OCALA, Fla.—Imagine, just to test your business sense, a smallish, late, gray 2-year-old filly. Consider also the parentage of this filly. She came into this world as the daughter of a modest but successful Florida sire and a more or less undistinguished dam.

Further imagine that the breeder, a man of means, donated the filly to a home for children, who, for one reason or another, need supervision from other than their parents.

The supervisor of this home, unable to get an offer of more than $500 for the filly and another horse of similar origin and condition, finally sells the horses to a woman trainer for $5,000, to be paid whenever.

The new owner runs her horse operation with her three children. She is in the middle of a divorce, trains her horses in an orange grove and ships from the farm to the track to race, a four-and-a-half-hour trip, if the traffic is light.

Based on this scenario, would you predict success for the principals involved? If you said yes, you have the business sense of the man who bought a share in John Henry, the heart of a Hollywood movie producer and your address is the Magic Kingdom ... but you are right.

The stakes-winning filly, First Prediction, has earned owner-trainer Janet Del Castillo more than $200,000. She paid the Florida Horsemen's Children's Home for the two horses long ago, and according to Children's Home president Ed Mac Clellan, Del Castillo sends a check for $1,000 every time First Prediction wins a race. Not only that but breeder Paul Marriot got his tax writeoff for the donation, and he continues to receive Florida breeders' awards every time the filly wins.

"The most anybody offered was $500 apiece," MacClellan recalled. "I knew they were worth more than that, so I sold the package (to Del Castillo) for $5,000, but she didn't have to pay anything up front."

On the buying end of the transaction, Del Castillo remembered, "Ed McClellan called me, said he had two horses for sale. One was a May filly 14-months old. The Florida Horsemen's Children's Home didn't even have fences up yet. In the middle of trying to say, 'No,' this voice from above said. 'Shut up and take the horses'."

Because Del Castillo trains her horses long and slowly in the deep sand of the nearby orange grove, First Prediction was not rushed to the track at 2. Still, her training performance did not give rise to any burst of confidence in the trainer.

"She absolutely trained like a very, very ordinary horse," said the Winter Haven trainer. "I would never have said this one is going to be great. In fact, I offered another trainer a half-interest in her for $2,500. He didn't have any money, either."

Two years ago in February after First Prediction rolled up a couple of seconds and a third, an agent offered $25,000 for the filly. "When you get a horse for $2,500, and someone offers you $25,000, that is a lot of money," the owner said. "I went to the kids and everyone said, 'Oh, Mom, don't sell the filly'."

After the daughter of On to Glory broke her maiden at Tampa Bay Downs, Del Castillo snipped to South Florida for a crack at the big time.

"I was so stupid I didn't know you couldn't ship in and win," the unorthodox trainer said. "But she was fit and had a tremendous stretch run to win a $25,000 claiming race.

"I was going to put her back in a $35,000 claimer, but Roger McElhiney told me not to run for $35,000 or she'd get claimed. First Prediction ran third in an allowance race, and afterward someone offered me $50,000 so she probably would have been claimed away at the lower price. Every time I was going to lose her someone always helped me."

In all First Prediction has started 59 times with 11 wins and 14 seconds and earnings of more than $250,000.

In the latest chapter of this movie-like story, the gray filly defeated Thirty Zip in a thrilling stretch run in The Very One Handicap. "She was passed by Thirty Zip in deep stretch, and she came again to win," said Del Castillo with excitement still in her voice.

The owner's three helpers and children are Alex, 19; Hernando, 18; and Victoria, 15. The Very One Handicap was the first time the boys had been allowed to transport a horse five hours down the Florida Turnpike for a race. They made the trip the night before the race.

"In the winner's circle, my son turned to me and said he ran out of gas on the turnpike," Del Castillo revealed. "The gas gauge was not working right. Here the poor little filly is coming down to run in one of the biggest races of her life, and she is stuck on the side of the Turnpike."

First Prediction has given the woman from Winter Haven credibility and a belief in dreams.

"You must not ever forget," she explained, "there is serendipity in life. Getting this wonderful horse is the greatest thing that ever happened to me. She has made so much that it would be awful not to remember."

And the checks continue to arrive at the Florida Horsemen's Children's Home.

This is my favorite story!

URF AUTHORITY

Daily Form

Daily Racing Form, Inc. All rights reserved.

WEDNESDAY, MAY 20, 1987

'Prediction' Risks Skein In Gulf 'Cap

By WILLIAM C. PHILLIPS

GULFSTREAM PARK, Hallandale, Fla.—Janet del Castillo's First Prediction, who has become a favorite of Florida racing fans, seeks her fourth straight triumph in the second running of the $39,620 Candy Eclair Handicap here Wednesday. Six fillies and mares are entered to compete at a mile and a sixteenth for a winner's purse of $23,772.

The public has become enraptured with First Prediction's background: a yearling purchase from a home for orphans and wayward children near Ocala, trained in her owner's orange grove next to a lake in Winter Haven, and brought to the racetrack for her afternoon engagements in a van driven by Castillo.

The fans have been impressed, too, by Del Castillo's display of joyful emotions after she has saddled her mare for a winning race, and the apparent comaradarie she shares with Julio Pezua, the mare's regular rider this season.

First Prediction began her skein by beating Bereavement by a length in a mile and a sixteenth allowance race on April 16. She defeated Truly by two and a half lengths in a mile race on the grass May 1, and outgamed Thirty Zip by a nose in a dramatic stretch duel to capture The Very One Handicap at a mile on the turf nine days later.

A winner of 11 races in a career of 59 races, accruing $255,520 in purses, the 5-year-old gray daughter of On to Glory will carry 115 pounds.

Mr. and Mrs. Cleo Hall's 4-year-old Judy's Red Shoes, a multiple stakes winner, whose earnings total $269,349, is topweighted at 116 pounds. Santiago Soto will ride.

Ross Heritage Farm & Baird's Lady Vernalee, a winner of three straight, including the Sweetest Chant and Lady in Waiting handicaps, will carry 114 and Robert Lester will ride.

The field is completed by Frances A. Genter's Truly, 114, Jose Velez Jr.; R. & J. Thornton's Tuscadoon, 108, Mike Lee, and C. & E. R. Dixon's Warm and Soft, 107, Norberto J. Palavencino.

This will be the first race for Judy's Red Shoes since she was third in a division of the Joe Namath Handicap here at a mile on the grass March 15. She was the winner of a mile and a furlong overnight race on dirt in three starts at Hialeah this winter and won seven of 19 outings last season.

Lady Vernalee has been raced as a sprinter but the 4-year-old Hold Your Peace filly's recent performances have been so strong the stable decided to give her a shot at the longer distance. Tuscadoon is the only rival in this race with the speed to challenge her early, and if Lady Vernalee steals off to a long lead she could be hard to catch.

Santiago Soto

Has Mount in Gulf 'Cap

This is the day my filly came down with a virus, foundered and almost Died!

It was a full year before she returned to race!

Racing *Daily* Form

Nine Clash at Gulf In F-M Turf Event

By WILLIAM C. PHILLIPS

GULFSTREAM PARK, Hallandale, Fla.—Cynthia Phipps' For Kicks, who was a good third behind a pair of stakes-winning rivals on the turf in her only race at the meeting, will be solidly supported in the wide-open betting field of nine older fillies and mares named to compete at a mile on the turf in the allowance feature here Thursday.

For Kicks was the pacesetter in a mile and a sixteenth race on the grass the opening day of the meeting, January 8, and held on gamely in the drive to be third behind Without Feathers and Vana Turns. Both of those fillies won on the grass in their next starts.

For Kicks was still a maiden and she tired after showing speed and finished unplaced when she first tried the grass in the third start of her career at Belmont Park last spring. The 4-year-old Topsider filly since then has won four of six races at distances from seven furlongs to a mile and a sixteenth on the dirt at Belmont Park, Aqueduct and Calder. She is trained by Angel Penna Jr. and is to be ridden by Jorge Chavez at 119 pounds.

She is oposed by Holly Ricon's Ana T., 122, Earlie Fires; D. E. Hager 2d's Stop and Smile, 119, no rider; and six contenders who are each to carry 115 pounds. They are M. Miller's Luckie's Girl, Jorge Duarte; Stanley M. Ersoff's Miss K. L. Taylor, Doug Valiente; Janet del Castillo's First Prediction, no rider; Firmanento Farm's Kalerre, also Valiente; T. Asbury's Bug Bug, no rider, and

Big Bucks Racing Stable's Lost Weekend, no rider.

Two of the rivals to For Kicks have shown sreed on ne grass at the meeting and can be expected to challenge ier for the early lead.

Stop and Smile came back after tiring in ter first sart to lead from the start and to widen her margn to bette than two lengths over a good allowance fiel< in a mile and a sixteenth race on January 19. Incidentaly, she was he first to win on the turf at Gulfstream th's winter b leading from the start. The 6-year-old daugfter of Libres Rib apperaed to be overmatched in the first division of Saturday's Grade III Suwannee River and dropped hack after showing early speed to finish last.

This will be the fifth race fr First Predictbn since she resumed racing in the fall. The 7-year-old On t Glory mare is a stretch runner and the class of the field going back a couple of years when she won two stakes on grass over this course.

Bug Bug was in from into the stretch run of a mile and a sixteenth race captured by the stakes filly Orange Motiff on grass here on January 29. She lost by a little more than four lengths and finished fifth. The 4-year-old Ginistrelii filly similarly held the early lead in the Atlantic City Oaks on turf last summer at Atlantic City and in the Tropical Park Oaks at Calder in the spring

Edge? First Prediction (middle), a stakes winner, may be the class of the filly-mare turf feature at Gulfstream.

Mixing oranges and horses

The dew glistens atop the oranges as the sun rises. Suddenly, the birds stop chirping and the ground starts to shake. From around the bend come three thundering thoroughbreds in a race down the narrow lanes between the rows of heavenly laden trees.

For three miles, the horses maneuver the tight curves and straightaways through the groves around Winter Haven, Fla. Then, it's everyone in the lake for a cool dip.

Is this anyway to train thoroughbreds?

According to Janet Del Castillo, it's the best way.

"I raise them like I raised my three children, by using good old fashioned common sense," said Del Castillo, 43, a former Peace Corps volunteer who began training thoroughbreds full-time four years ago. "I allow them to be horses, to do what comes natural. I put them in their natural environment so that they can frolic together, eat grass and definitely talk to each other.

"I tell them that I'll give them two weeks of devotion on the farm if they will give me two minutes of devotion on the horse track."

Del Castillo realizes most trainers and many owners laughed at her unorthodox training methods. "I would say the first couple years I was like the Country Bumpkin coming to the big city. I had no money at all and had to do everything myself.

"I know some veteran trainers were laughing and snickering. But I didn't care. When I was in the Peace Corps in Colombia, I taught the poor natives that they had to make do with what they had. I was in the same boat. I didn't look for excuses."

On her 14-acre farm outside Winter Haven, she built barns, a mini-paddock and make-shift starting gates. She did it all — training the horses, riding them, feeding them, swimming them, bathing them and doctoring them like her own children — with the help of her three children.

In 1976, all the hard work started to pay off. First Prediction, a $2,500 castoff who had been given to a children's home in Central Florida, proved that Del Castillo's methods worked during a Cinderella racing career that produced $270,000 in earnings. "First Prediction saved my farm, she was a heavenly gift,"

said Del Castillo. "When I was first galloping First Prediction through the orange groves, I thought I was going three miles a day, but I was actually going closer to 5½ miles."

Little wonder First Prediction went on to become known as the "Iron Maiden" with more than 70 career starts.

Make no mistake, Del Castillo trains her eight to 14 thoroughbreds each year to run forever.

"I like to have a solid foundation in my horses before I take them to a race track," said Del Castillo, who was born in Oregon but raised in San Francisco where she worked with polo ponies before joining the Peace Corps. "By working them three miles through heavy sand, up and down hills and around tight turns, I am building a racing machine. I don't believe in drugs, so when my horses reach a point where they want to tear through the three-mile course, then I know they're ready to go to the race track."

That presents another problem, getting them to the tracks in South Florida. And, often, it's not to race, but just to get work out of a real starting gate. "I don't mind the drive down," she says of the 220-mile trip. "It's something that has to be done."

It can seem a short trip home if her horse wins. "Nothing beats winning, nothing." It can be a very long trip home if her horse loses, or maybe doesn't even get into the race.

But the long and short of it is that Del Castillo believes in her method.

"I train a lot of young fillies, and some are hyper and delicate and tend to tie up or get nervous when they run. But when they are home, they are with their friends and can talk and play together. It's not their natural life style to be cooped up at a track 24 hours a day. God meant for them to graze and be moving all the time. I know it may sound silly, but I think it's important to let horses be horses."

Asked if she would like to become a conventional-type trainer, Del Castillo was quick with an emphatic "NO."

"But I would," she added, "like for owners to have enough confidence in me and my training methods to let me have their horses from age 18 months to 2½ for what I think is solid progressive type training. I also would love for an owner come to me and say, 'Here is $20,000 or $30,000, go out and buy me a good horse.'"

There is one point to her training methods that can not be overlooked. Even if her horses do not make the grade on race tracks, they do as family horses/pets. "They are raised in such a placid setting, they can do something else other than be race horses. So I always try to find them a nice home," she said.

And there is a personal benefit that would make her reluctant to trade places even with Hall of Fame trainer Woody Stephens.

"The best part of the day is working the horses," she said. "Tearing through orange groves is a fantastic ride through nature. It's thrilling, a natural high without doing drugs."

SEPTEMBER 1988
THE MIAMI HERALD

Del Castillo's training style unorthodox

By Lisa A. Hammond
The Ledger

EAGLE LAKE — Most racehorses learn to run during one-mile jaunts within the confines of a racetrack. Janet Del Castillo's thoroughbreds train by galloping for three miles in the deep sand of an orange grove on her Rancho Del Castillo.

Her methods, including swimming the horses in Eagle Lake, are considered unorthodox.

"People feel sorry for me when I have to train on the farm and not at the track, but I wouldn't trade them," she said.

Her horses negotiate the sharp turns of the orange grove which, she says, makes the gradual curves of the race track a breeze.

"People say the sand will bow the horses' tendons, but my horses are very sound. Galloping through the deep sand and up the hills strengthens all of their muscles, and going around the sharp turns makes them surefooted," Del Castillo said.

The grove and ranch are located off of State Road 540 on Crystal Beach Road.

"I love the orange grove," she said. "To be able to support my family doing this is just heavenly."

She often treats herself to an orange plucked off a tree after she rides.

Del Castillo, 43, is a tall, stocky woman, who radiates strength. She has shoulder-length brown hair with a few streaks of gray. She seems very motherly and kind, especially to the horses, which she strokes with her large hands and calls her "little babies."

She began by training polo ponies when she was in high school.

"I started cleaning stalls so I would be allowed to gallop the polo ponies," she said.

Later her uncle, who owned a quarter horse ranch in Virginia, got her family involved with quarter horses, which she took to the Green Swamp for match races.

Her association with thoroughbreds began when her ex-husband, Dr. Hernando Del Castillo, acquired some.

"I watched how the trainer trained these horses and I couldn't believe that the horses could run. I think they really damage them structurally," she said. "I think they need a better foundation, which is why I train the way I do.

"I want to put guts in them," she said.

Trainer Dwaine Glenn of K-ville said Del Castillo's practices are based on a sound theory.

"Anytime you run a horse in deep sand like that, you're going to leg them up real well," Glenn said. "It's an endurance program — it does help them. I see nothing wrong with it."

Glenn said more orthodox methods are often used because the trainers don't have the facilities to train the horses any other way.

Del Castillo's horses do not get drugs, liniments, or leg wraps, all common practices in horse racing.

"If a 2-year-old needs leg wraps, he shouldn't be training," she said.

She has been training thoroughbreds for about 10 years and says experience has been a great teacher.

"I used to gallop them all the time," she said. "But I learned that no matter how fit they are, they won't run any faster than God will allow them to run. They won't run faster than their natural ability."

The proof, of course, is in the race results, and Del Castillo's evidence is First Prediction, a horse she refers to as "sweetness and light."

First Prediction, owned and trained by Del Castillo, is a 7-year-old gray mare who has won two stakes races. Only 3 percent of thoroughbreds ever win a stakes race.

"She is a dream come true. People wait for years for a stakes horse, and I never knew what I had," Del Castillo said. She bought the delicate mare, which is gray with dark flecks, from a children's home for $2,500. First Prediction has won more than $270,000.

First Prediction has displayed heart, a racehorse's most elusive quality, in both her racing style and in coming back from injuries.

"One time she started at 26 lengths behind, and ended up losing by three lengths," Del Castillo said.

First Prediction has also had to recover from physical setbacks.

"She had a bone chip in her knee from being kicked in the pasture, and then she got a virus and foundered (an inflammation of the tissue that attaches foot to hoof)," Del Castillo said. "People said she would never race again."

First Prediction's rehabilitation took place in Eagle Lake. Del Castillo would attach a long lead to the horse's halter and stand on a dock while the horse paddled around in the lake. Swimming exercised the horse without straining her sore feet and legs.

"She loves to swim now. Sometimes she'll lay over on her side and just float," Del Castillo said.

First Prediction returned to dry land to win several races at Gulfstream Park, including a stakes race, the Very One Handicap, which took place on Mother's Day of 1988. Del Castillo said that race was especially meaningful to her.

"She is really my baby, and it was wonderful to win a stake on Mother's Day," she said.

First Prediction now is trained almost exclusively by swimming because galloping causes her muscles to "tie up." The small, sprightly mare, who looks more like a pet than a racehorse, has won 12 races in her long career, including a $30,000 allowance race on Feb. 21 at Gulfstream.

She races most often at Gulfstream, Calder and Hialeah, where she is viewed as an underdog.

"Whenever I haul this horse down to Miami, they think she's a pony horse," Del Castillo said.

Del Castillo uses a chart to keep track of the 12 to 15 horses she trains. Assistant Eric Low, two exercise riders, and Del Castillo's children, Nando, 20, and Victoria, 17, help out at the ranch.

Most of the other horses Del Castillo trains run in claiming races at Tampa Bay Downs.

"First Prediction is the only big-league horse I've had," she said.

Lisa Hammond was an intern for The Ledger during the winter months. She is a student at Northwestern University in Evanston, Ill.

Janet Del Castillo, right, and Vicki Portlock, an exercise girl, run some horses through an orange grove on Del Castillo's ranch near Eagle Lake.

a nice Background story!

First Prediction Tops F-M Feature On Grass at Gulf

By WILLIAM C. PHILLIPS

GULFSTREAM PARK, Hallandale, Fla.—First Prediction, a dappled gray 5-year-old who is owned and trained by Janet del Castillo, will attract the most attention when 10 fillies and mares go postward in the mile allowance feature on the turf here Friday. Another four are listed as also eligibles.

Del Castillo, who trains her horses under the orange trees at Winter Haven in the central part of the state and vans them to the track to race, entered her stakes-winning earner of $204,700 to carry 122 pounds. The mare will be piloted by her regular rider, Julio Pezua.

First Prediction, who obviously thrives on the unorthodox method of training, closed with characteristic speed in the final run and won a mile and a sixteenth race by a length last out on April 16. The race was transferred from the grass to the main track.

But she is also adept on the grass. This past winter at Hialeah she got up approaching the wire for a neck victory over Christmas Dancer, who will be one of her main rivals on Friday. She was beaten by the same short margin in a three-way photo with Anka Germania and Chaldea over the Hialeah turf course in a division of the Grade III Columbiana Handicap, and in her last start at that meeting she took second behind Singular Bequest on the grass in the Key Largo.

The others who drew into the field are J.S. Carrion's Christmas Dancer, 117, Earlie Fires; Dr. Keith C. Wold's Opera Diva, 122, Robert Lester; Cam M. Gambolatti's Stuttering Sarah, 122, no rider; Gladys Ross' Frau Agustina, 115, no rider; W.P. Sise's Lycka Dancer, 110, apprentice Jorge Milian; Gray and Yingling's Betsy Mack, 115, Robert Breen; Horse Haven's Social Occasion, 108, apprentice Jorge Santos; Virginia K. Payson's Imprudent Love, 117, Lester, and Frances A. Gen-

<hr>

Special Kentucky Derby Edition on Saturday

Saturday's issue of Daily Racing Form will be the annual Kentucky Derby Edition, featuring complete Past Performances of all the entrants, including latest workouts, plus special articles on their owners, trainers, jockeys. Pedigree Profiles and many other features about the race and the people associated with it.

Included in Saturday's issue with the Past Performances will be a graded handicap, probable odds, expert selections, a handicapping analysis of the race and consensus.

<hr>

ter's Truly, 117, Jose Velez Jr.

The also eligibles are Wimborne Farm's Grande Couture, coupled as an entry with Imprudent Love, 115, Earlie Fires; Knoll Lane Farm's Tea for Top, 119, Mile Gonzalez; Peter Barbarino's Lucky Touch, 117, no rider, and Hardesty and Walden's Bereavement, 117, Fires.

Christmas Dancer, third and fourth in a couple of other turf races at Hialeah, comes off a sharp second to True Chompion at a mile on the grass here March 22. She held a daylight lead before she was overtaken by First Prediction in their previous meeting at Hialeah and she has the speed to either take the lead or be near the pace in this event. She is a 5-year-old daughter of Sovereign Dancer and trained by J. Bert Sonnier.

This will be the first race for Truly since the 5-year-old In Reality mare was second behind Algenib in a race taken off the turf and run at seven furlongs on a sloppy track March 24. She won four of 16 races in 1986, including the Impatiens and Vizcaya handicaps and lost the Black Velvet Handicap on the main track there to First Prediction by a nose in August

Training in the Orange Groves

Imagine this scenario, if you will:

You're sitting on a beautiful bass lake in central Florida, casting artificial worms and crank baits against the cattails while in search of that trophy large-mouth. The lake is all but deserted.

You're 90 miles from Ocala, 50 miles from Tampa Bay Downs and more than 200 miles from Miami. The furthest thing from your mind is horses and horse racing.

But suddenly you hear a sound, a familiar sound you've heard a hundred times before. It starts as just a murmur, but in a matter of moments it grows louder and more distinct.

It's the sound of horse's hooves, and from the pattern of the sound, it's obvious these horses are in a strong gallop or are working. You look around for a training track, for some sign of a racing strip, but all you see are orange trees.

JANET DEL CASTILLO
An off-beat trainer

After some investigation you find out that you had indeed heard race horses at work and that those charges came from the Rancho Del Castillo, a unique training facility located high on a hill overlooking Eagle Lake and the surrounding rolling landscape of central Florida.

The story of Rancho Del Castillo and it's master, Janet Del Castillo is one well worth repeating.

From the Peace Corps to the Race Track

It seems that many years ago a young Peace Corps volunteer found herself in the wilds of Columbia. While working with the natives there, she met a doctor who she later married. The couple eventually settled in Winter Haven. The husband wanted some race horses so they went into business the usual way, by contacting a trainer and buying some stock.

"To make a long story short," continues Janet Del Castillo, "the horses were soon beat up and injured from racing and wound up on the farm here. My husband wanted to get rid of them but I persisted, stalling him for a time.

"After he went to work I would work with the horses, learning as I went along. I snuck them over to the track to work once they were recovered, hurrying back before my husband got home."

Although the marrriage failed to survive, Del Castillo's interest and love for thoroughbreds not only lived, it blossomed. Using training methods and philosophies considered radical and outlandish by many of her peers, Del Castillo went about training and developing horses the way she wanted to, with only a modicum of success.

Then along came First Prediction. "I got her from the Children's Home, believe it or not," the trainer recalled. "They had two fillies they couldn't keep and I took them both for $5,000 on the cuff."

That modest purchase went on to become a top stakes and handicap distaffer for Del Castillo, earning more than $260,000 during her career and recently came back from a bout with founder to race again with top grass company at Gulfstream Park.

Developing Sound, Healthy Horses

And where did the pounding hooves come from?

"I gallop my horses through an orange grove," Del Castillo explained. "It's exactly one mile around, with a half mile stretch where we cluck 'em and let them work."

Del Castillo calls her training style the "Montessori school of horse training" and her horses are permitted to develop at their own individual pace. She doesn't race horses at two and admits it takes her charges several races to acclimate themselves to racing once their careers start.

"Because I'm here on the farm I can take my time with my horses. I don't believe in pushing young horses and I believe the results speak for themselves. I rarely use medications, hardly ever have a horse on Lasix and I don't believe I've ever had a horse of mine bow a tendon.

"Here at the farm they're allowed to graze in the paddocks, we swim them in the lake after training and we do everything to give them a natural environment.

"I substitute time, patience and healing powers Mother Nature has given the horse over speed, medications and shortcuts. I know one thing: I develop sound, healthy race horses. We may train in the groves but it's training all the same."

— **Doug McCoy**

Doug McCoy is RACING ACTION's Tampa Bay correspondent.

First Prediction Makes Grade

This is the tale of a woman and a horse.

It is also the tale of good things coming to those who do things, "my way" and the "hard way."

Best of all, it is the story of charity, the good side of horse racing, the nice people involved and their rewards.

The woman raised in San Francisco during the 1950s always loved horses. She cared for and trained polo ponies in Northern California while growing up. She joined the Peace Corps in the mid-1960's, served in the poverty of South America doing whatever she could.

In fact, it was while there that she met her husband and aided him delivering babies by candlelight in Columbia. Her name is Janet Del Castillo.

The horse is a mare. A gray mare foaled in 1982 by On To Glory out of the Hagley mare Around The Bend. She was just another one of the

JANET DE CASTILLO
Trains in groves

yearlings in breeder Paul Marriott's large operation and when the herd was culled, her destiny was to be donated as a yearling to the Florida Children's Home in Cintra, Florida. Her name is First Prediction.

Dr. Hernando Del Castillo and his family returned to the United States and bought a farm, Rancho Del Castillo, in Winter Haven, Florida and went into the thoroughbred business with the expectations of raising a champion. Janet took out a trainer's license but there were no champions.

"When the horses (they were just cheap claimers) did not win the Kentucky Derby right away, my husband lost interest in racing," she said. "But we had over $25,000 invested and I didn't want to give up just like that."

Then she got a break.

While working at the Florida Children's Home, still helping others, she spotted a gray yearling filly that she thought might have some ability on the race track and invested in her and took her back to her farm in Winter Haven. The filly was First Prediction.

First Prediction's road to success has not been traditional, unconventional would be more apt.

"I can train horses in an orange grove," Janet said, "and have them as fit as any that train at the race track."

First Prediction's success story on the track is just as unbelievable. She could really be called the "Iron Mare," for in nearly 60 starts, she has earned over $250,000 and done it the hard way—on the rubber-based strip at Calder, the main tracks at Gulfstream and Hialeah, and the grass courses of all three South Florida race tracks.

Her most recent string of wins began in an even more bizarre manner. It seems Gulfstream Racing Secretary Tommy Trotter was having a tough time filling the Rampart Handicap because no one wanted to challenge Wayne Lukas' Life At The Top and Woody Stephens' I'm Sweets. He approached Del Castillo, and though she had another race in mind for First Prediction, she said that she would be there.

When we questioned her on why she accepted this spot she responded, "Did you ever hear of a trainer using a handicap race as a tightener for an allowance race?"

Unfortunately, everything did not go right, as First Prediction did not reach a contending position for her patented late charge and trailed throughout.

But 11 days later, she made the six-hour van trip from Winter Haven down to Gulfstream and won an allowance race.

Then on Mother's Day, after a lengthy van trip, First Prediction—under the brilliant handling of Julio Pezua—was up to win The Very One Handicap by a nose at one mile on the turf.

As First Prediction came back to the winner's circle, hundreds of fans circled around and cheered the winning horse, jockey and owner in a display of emotion most befitting the holiday.

Oh yes, in a story with a happy ending such as this, what began as a charitable venture continues on that way. That's because Janet Del Castillo makes a donation to the Florida Children's Home after every win.

■ **Derk Ackerman**

Racing Action Contributing Writer

Peace Corps Service In Trainer's Past

By Graham Ross

OLDSMAR — The first thing that Tampa Bay Downs trainer Janet Del Castillo projects is a free spirit. She is a happy soul but one with a sense of adventure — a trait perhaps first noted on Nov. 18, 1963, when she left her San Francisco upbringing on a trip to Kansas City as a Peace Corps volunteer.

Four days later President John F. Kennedy was shot, and a lot of dreams died for a lot of other children of the '60s, but Del Castillo was one of those who kept the flame burning — serving honorably in the most rural area of Colombia, dependent on villagers for all human contact and existence itself.

"You learned to depend on others — and they on you — for everything that kept us all alive. If you didn't learn to speak the language you didn't eat, so you learned quickly, but you also learned to deal with things at their simplest level," Del Castillo now recalls. "Basically it was the 'in-order-to-make-lemonade-you-start-with-lemons' kind of lesson in life repeated throughout the two years I was there.

"But I also learned not to be so quick to judge other people's way of doing things while I was in Colombia. You'd start to build a roof on a hut and the villagers would tell you to wait until the moon was right — and if you resisted the temptation to scoff, you could learn that sap flows better when the moon is right, and would help hold the roof in place."

But while in Colombia Del Castillo met and married a doc-tor, returned to this country, and mostly through her husband's initiative, became involved with thoroughbreds at their farm in Winter Haven. When the marriage failed, Del Castillo became a horse trainer by default, using training methods as unorthodox as her Peace Corps past and her life with the villagers.

"I take my horses on three-mile gallops through the orange groves overlooking Eagle Lake," Del Castillo offers, as one of her training exercises, and I find that the middle mile is the hardest. That middle mile pretty much tells me a lot about each horse — whether or not they are going to want to go that third mile."

Mercedes Won In Beam Stakes

OLDSMAR — Florida Derby winner Mercedes Won, owned locally by Oldsmar resident Christopher Spencer, came out of his third-place finish in the Tampa Bay Derby "better than he went into it," according to Spencer, and will be in northern Kentucky for a planned next engagement in the upcoming Jim Beam Stakes at Turfway Park on Saturday, April 1.

"He came back bouncing," Spencer said of Mercedes Won following the Tampa Bay Derby on March 19. "He just had too much to overcome. It would have been nice to win one in front of the home folks, but that's racing luck and it wasn't meant to be."

Spencer plans to remain in the northern Kentucky area until after the Jim Beam.

Another somewhat unusual training regimen — swimming her horse in Eagle Lake after training — led to an unusual experience for one of her three children, who range in age from 21 to 17 years old. "My kids always helped with the training of the horses from the time they were 14. They did everything. No matter what, they pitched in," Del Castillo now recalls.

"For some reason, my son always wanted to be one of those smiling, happy kids you always see on television commercials for soft drinks, and I've always tried to teach my kids the power of imagery: the ability to make things come true by thinking positively about them and working to make them happen.

"One day a television camera crew came to town, and ended up filming a Mountain Dew commercial at our farm, with my son riding one of our horses around Eagle Lake towing a water skier in the lake itself. It was a great commercial, and a dream come true for my son."

And what of her own dreams — this child of Camelot — beyond the usual fantasies of horse trainers? "I'd like to have my cartoon strip, that I call 'Mulliken Stu,'" become syndicated," Del Castillo says. "It's centered around thoroughbreds being raised on our farm by kids, and the idea is to present my world of thoroughbreds as a fun thing, full of family involvement, not as a threat to families.

"That's how we all need to project thoroughbred racing —

Trainer Janet Del Castillo shows a condition book to one of her thoroughbreds running at Tampa Bay Downs.

Photo by Bob Cicero

showing its health and its basic communication with nature," Del Castillo concluded.

She explained all that following a guest apperance on the Tampa Bay Downs' Saturday Morning Glory Club recently, on

a day when she had no horses entered and no real reason to make the hour-long drive from her farm to the race course, other than to help promote the sport which she initially inherited by default.

2, 'Horses need to romp on grass.
They need each other's company.'

It's a strictly down-home operation

JANET DEL CASTILLO

Del Castillo believes in her methods despite skeptics

By TOM AINSLIE

In a 11-acre orange grove on the sandy shore of Eagle Lake, near Winter Haven, Fla., a non-conformist named Janet Del Castillo raises, schools and trains thoroughbreds in unusual ways.

Even when racing, her horses live at home, 60 miles from Tampa Bay Downs, 220 from the eastern Florida tracks. They van to the track on race day. That evening they come home to recuperate in grassy paddocks, swim in the lake and gallop every few days on the trails among the orange trees.

"It is important to treat horses as horses," says Del Castillo. "They need to romp on grass. They need each other's company, individual confinement in practical stalls for 23 hours a day is unnatural."

She asks no horse for speed until he is almost 3. Her horses race on food and water, unmedicated.

These attitudes arouse skepticism, but her horses dispel it. They win their share. None has broken a tendon or broken down in a race. They last for season after season. She never pays more than $2,500 for a yearling. But she has — so states —

Her best buy was First Prediction, a 2-year-old filly that had been donated to a children's home where Janet was a volunteer worker. The tiny gray was by On to Glory, a half-brother to Ruffian. Lecuyade and Buckfinder. In a six-year career, she competed in more than 100 races, winning or placing in 34 stakes and earning $331,200.

The Janet Del Castillo approach is novel but not new. Before racing

was urbanized in enclosed stadiums, horses trained at home. Some harness races, quarter horses and thoroughbreds still do. What sets this woman apart is her sense of bounden duty to advance an idea that might benefit fellow horsefolk, the breed and racing itself.

To encourage experimentation by others, she is writing an instruction manual called, "The Backyard Racehorse." She also conducts seminars. She recently regaled a two-day gathering of enthusiastic horsefolk at the New Jersey farm of a friend and fellow Slower, owner-trainer Ann Cain. She was interviewed there.

"Thousands of Americans already have horses on their own property," said Janet. "Not only thoroughbreds, but horses of all kinds — pleasure horses, cutting horses, draft horses, you name it. When these horse-lovers learn how gratifying it is to school and care for an actual racehorse, and how practical it is, we'll recruit new stable owners to our sport. Matter of fact, we already have."

Obviously, not everyone with a horse has enough acreage for serious conditioning. But many do, says Del Castillo, and others have access to useful trails, hills and bridle paths. If shipping back and forth between home and track is not feasible, horses are welcome in schooled at home and return home for furloughs.

Before its first start, a horse needs to be at the track a few times to become acclimated to the environment and accustomed to producing speed on a dirt oval. Del

Castillo points out. "But, before and after those workouts and all the races that follow, home is the best place.

As the reader may have surmised, these ideas come from no shrinking violet. Janet Helene Mulgannon Del Castillo is a strapping, strong-minded individual who speaks her mind. She is 40-something, with three grown children and a divorce from the Colombian physician whose family name she retains.

She grew up in San Francisco, where she was a federal narcotics agent. She became a major at San Francisco State, she opted for real life, joined the Peace Corps and spend two years of privation in a Colombian village. She nursed the sick, struggled to establish rudimentary sanitation and warmed to the dignity and generosity of the poor.

The young Colombian doctor whom she married and assisted in the village. He revived her interest in horses when he decided to all seriousness that they should buy an inexpensive yearling, run it in the Kentucky Derby. When that failed, they dropped the project. But she was hooked and has had racehorses ever since.

All right now. What exactly are the advantages of "backyard" schooling and conditioning? And what does it take to develop a winner's who go the track only to race?

"The purpose of training," says Janet Del Castillo, "is to fulfill a horse's potential without breaking him down. At home you give your

horses the natural environment in which their bodies and spirits thrive. Frolicking and grazing with each other makes them more resilient, less hectic, less frightened

"But the main factor is the severe disadvantage of trying to strengthen equine bone, muscle and attitude at a track. Conditioning is a cycle of stress-recovery stress recovery. At a track, the horse stressed by a hard race or workout is confined to a stall, sometimes walked under the shed a few minutes a day until asked once again to strain himself, at high speed. The program, combined with the frequent ills, the effects of medication, can hasten the onset of physical problem. But a horse conditioned at home recovers naturally from routine trauma, free to walk and jog his way through the discomfort.

"Another major advantage is economic. The expense of shipping to and from the track is far less than the cost of keeping a horse in training there. And the cost is in the joy of having your horse around and knowing that no other arrangement could be more constructive."

As to the Know-how, she describes it in loving detail, explains it as I love for horses plus technique that is gradually increased exercise that begins before age 2. At her own place, Del Castillo has cut a trail that winds up and down grades, with many slow turns. She gallops young horses slowly for three miles every three or four days, monitoring their reactions. After a year, at the track's birthday approaches, they are rippling, rugged animals, ready for truck.

JANET DEL CASTILLO has been training in Florida from her home base.

THE
FILE

The Road Less Traveled

Racehorse trainer Janet Del Castillo
says at-home conditioning is the best route
to the winner's circle.

By Laura Hillenbrand

Angie Draper

Janet Del Castillo's multiple stakes winner First Prediction thrived under her
owner's unconventional "backyard race-training" regimen. Del Castillo (right)
conditioned the mare through swimming and long gallops on her farm.

From the moment she first visited a racetrack backstretch, Janet Del Castillo was uneasy about the physical and mental demands placed on conventionally trained racehorses. Kept in their stalls 23 hours a day, pushed to increase their speeds early in their lives and oftentimes plied with medication to add a competitive edge, most equine athletes are not allowed enough time to be horses in Del Castillo's view.

Nonetheless, it wasn't until the former polo pony trainer faced a personal dilemma that she discovered that a completely different training style was feasible—and profitable.

In 1986, a divorce left Del Cas-tillo with three children to raise on her own and a barn full of race horses to train. Complicating matters was the fact that her home, an orange farm located in Winter Haven, Florida, was a 4½-hour drive from the nearest racetrack. But the solved her problem by drawing on her experience as a Peace Corps volunteer and the maxim she had once taught to others.

"In the Peace Corps, my mission was to teach people to look at their problems and cope with what they have," she says. "If you have lemons, make lemonade."

In surveying her lemons—a 14-acre orange grove and a small barn miles from the nearest racetrack—it

occurred to Del Castillo that her horses might train just as well, or even better, on the heavy sand trails between her orange trees. Then, to the scorn of many trainers, owners and journalists, she packed up her horses, shipped them to her farm and began making lemonade. With the help of her children, she galloped her horses into condition on the meandering trails of her orange groves and swam them in a nearby lake. By ferrying them to the track only for races and occasional timed workouts.

More than a decade later, a brilliant, multiple-stakes-winning mare and a matchless record of training sound, durable horses have silenced the naysayers. And Del Castillo is spreading the word about her concept of a "backyard racehorse."

Del Castillo's offbeat training approach does not consist of simply keeping racehorses on the farm. Blending practical experience with common sense, her program is designed to engender the endurance, strength and physical maturity needed to withstand the breakneck speeds of racing.

"Horses have a capacity to do more than what is good for them," she explains. "On the track, [trainers] go straight to speed. The horses start pulling themselves apart. That's damage you can't undo. You have to follow them so certain amounts of growth time before they are three years old. In-stead, the trainer uses swimming and long gallops at graduated distances and weights to give them the "substructure to allow them to hold up to their own speed." And, once horses are fit, Del Castillo gallops them only every three to four days.

"All you have to do is keep their wheels greased," she says.

The trainer also takes a com-monsense approach to her horses' stabling arrangements. Unlike track-dwelling athletes, who are usually out of their stalls only for training or racing, Del Castillo's horses are turned out for much of the day, an arrangement that allows them to stretch, graze and so-cialize at will. "I try to inhibit the horse as little as possible," she says. "Horses are very social animals. When they are emotionally undernourished, they develop

neurotic habits to cope with their boredom.

"People think a horse has to be pumping out of its stall and acting like an idiot to be a good runner. Those things don't go hand in hand," she continues. "My horses are relaxed, but to keep them fit for the racetrack, they know what they're doing."

While one set of unusual circumstances spurred the development of Del Castillo's unique training approach, another led to her greatest triumphs—as well as the long-awaited vindication of her methods.

In 1984, a Florida breeder donated two Thoroughbred fillies as pleasure horses to Del Castillo's teen's home where Del Castillo was a volunteer. The home's director soon determined that she could not house the fillies, and asked Del Castillo if she was interested in them. Although in such a precarious financial position that she feared losing her home, Del Castillo saw enough potential in the fillies to buy them, on credit, for the bargain-basement price of $5,000.

One of the fillies did indeed prove to be best suited to life as a riding horse, but the other, a little gray named First Prediction, proved to be a first-rate prospect. Dubbed the "Iron Maiden," the mare was phenomenally sound, racing more than 100 times be-tween ages three and eight, while sometimes competing as often as three times in two weeks.

So far, First Prediction is the only stakes-class campaigner to emerge from Del Castillo's barn, but her success with her less celebrated charges—though she has been able to afford only obscurely bred runners, almost every one of her horses has made it to the winner's circle during its racing career—an extraordinary statistic for any rac-ing stable.

In addition, Del Castillo has managed to avoid the soundness troubles that frequently plague rac-ing operations. She reports, for ex-ample, that none of her horses has

several stakes races and earned more than $300,000, almost single-hand-edly put her trainer on the map and proved the legitimacy of her once-maligned training approach.

First Prediction, who won sev-eral stakes races and earned more than $300,000, almost single-hand-edly put her trainer on the map and proved the legitimacy of her once-maligned training approach.

Currently at work on a track-side training manual, Del Castillo is also planning a se-ries of seminars for those interested in learning more about her philoso-phy and techniques.

While admitting that backyard training is not for just anyone with a horse, barn and pasture, Del Cas-tillo believes that her program can bring much-needed new blood to racing. "I'm trying to appeal to people who want to be a positive, competent horseperson. I want to encourage racing to be a positive force," she says. "People have illu-sions that only the rich and the criminals are involved, but there are many, many people like me in the sport."

A strong selling point is the comparative cost of backyard train-ing as opposed to conventional race training. On-track training can cost as much as $100 per day; Del Cas-tillo's a $100-per-day racehorse at home costs no more than keep-ing a pleasure horse. Thus, she points out, racehorses normally spend months at the track running up bills before they are even old enough to have their talent gauged. In contrast, her program calls for a horse to be shipped to a profes-sional trainer at the track only when the animal is ready to begin speed training and racing. If a prospect, for whatever reason, never turns out to be a poor racing horse would have, Del Castillo says, and his related upbringing will make him an excellent pleasure horse.

Basically, the trainer says, she wants to share some of the enjoy-ment she has derived from racing. Looking out the window of her home, but Del Castillo's eyes rest on her Cinderella horse, First Predic-tion, now in foal to Preakness win-ner Fate Dancer. "The joy I've had with this could never be bought.

For information, training seminars
contact Janet Del Castillo, Winter
Haven, FL 33881, (813)
299-8448.

Trainer's Dialog

Backyard Racehorse: Hands-On Training

Janet Del Castillo
Winter Haven, Florida

The logistics of training a horse at the racetrack work against both the trainer and the horse. The track closes at 10:00 a.m., so any significant work must be done by that time. The daily cost and maintenance at the track forces trainers to come up quickly with answers for impatient owners. Trainers are trying to develop athletes and this is not done overnight – a great deal of patience and guidance are necessary. While an idea that I have to alleviate some of these problems may not be for everyone, it may prove to be a solution to limited training time and some of the other pressures trainers experience. What I'm talking about is called hands-on training, which allows the competitive horse owner (who owns horses from other disciplines, i.e., jumpers, rodeo competitors, endurance riders), to consider training their own racehorse up to a certain point. By my own experience and observation, I know that a racehorse can be trained in other than racetrack circumstances until it is about 28 to 32 months of age. Trainers should be happy to receive horses with a sound foundation as they will be fairly fit and ready to go into speedwork at the racetrack.

What's Involved?

Being turned out daily is an important part of the training of the young horse. Common practice of "benevolent neglect" is essential; I advise saddling and riding a young horse no more frequently than every 3 days. This allows the hands-on trainer to be aware of any stress or overwork done in the early training of a young horse. One can differentiate 'stocking up,' typical of horses adapting to the progressive stress being put upon them, from overstress to joints and tendons. There are many signs the hands-on trainer should be aware of that will warn him or her well in advance of problems to joints and tendons. Given proper rest between 'stresses' is what allows the horse to build a system that can withstand its own high speed.

No speed work whatsoever should be done until the horse is 30 to 32 months of age. Up to that point, the backyard trainer's (owner's) goal should be a horse with a good foundation achieved by slow, steady progressive training. Ideally, a 2- to 5-mile route over hill and dale is the best way to establish this. The horses that I train in this manner must achieve certain goals within this route

before I allow them to go on to more work and/or speed. Riding a horse every 3rd day allows the body rebuild time for any slight pulls or strains the trainer might not be aware of. Having the horse out a good portion of the day allows it to walk out naturally from any stiffness and lets the trainer observe the animal's movement. If swelling is a result of a strain, it will persist.

Janet Del Castillo off the track. In the hands-on training process she recommends saddling and riding the young horse no more than once every 3 days.

At the track it is easy to be fooled about the status of legs and joints. Common practices of poulticing and wrapping legs may hide whether or not there is talent to pursue in the animal. If no gift of speed is apparent, the horse may go back home to be a hunter jumper or whatever else the owner had in mind. If, however, the horse keep their horses comfortable, but hide heat and/or strains and stresses. If the horse is not obviously lame, then it goes out to the track again and perhaps be comes too severely injured. I don't think a 2-year-old should be wrapped during its normal training regime. If this type of horse has swellings or strains, it should be turned out until the swelling and/or strains are gone, at which time training may resume (it may only be a couple of days until the limb is normal again). Obviously, this is difficult for trainers to do at the track as most backsides do not have paddocks to turn out horses in.

Letting the Owner Take Over

If owners have been competitive in showing, rodeo, and/or hunter jumping – and have been successful in those fields – they might consider buying a yearling (Thoroughbred, Arabian, Appaloosa, or other racehorse) that they could do a great deal of preliminary training with themselves. By doing most of the work at home, these owners will initially save thousands of dollars in training fees and when their horse goes to a track trainer, it will be a little older than most and will have been well handled and used to a great many more circumstances than the typical track-trained animal. Most trainers will be happy to get a 32-month-old animal that hopefully has already been through the flux and colts suffered during its first 2 years of life and, after a few days

of getting adapted to the racetrack routine, is ready to breeze. Within about 2 months at the track, the trainer should have an idea of whether or not there is talent to pursue in the animal. If no gift of speed is apparent, the horse may go back home to be a hunter jumper or whatever else the owner had in mind. If, however, the horse shows racing ability (remember, many Thoroughbreds start racing, only a small percentage win and/or pay their way), then it will start bringing in checks to help defray its costs. The track trainers should be glad to have sound horses to hone into speed. No one really likes to "hold a horse together" for one more race.

Running to Win

A good trainer is one who manages to allow the horse to develop into its natural ability without breaking the horse down in the process. Many horses are capable of pulling themselves apart long before they are mature enough and sound enough to run. That is why a good trainer is tuned into how much stress the horse is enduring. The trainer should allow the horse to evolve comfortably and naturally into its speed. When its mind grows into having the concentration necessary to run full out 6 furlongs to a mile-and-a-half and likes what it's doing, then you have a runner. Defining a horse's personal best at that point is important so that it is not put in competition that is over its head. Keep the horse happy and run it at a level where it is capable of winning.

Racing is a challenging, difficult business. The hands-on training methods I suggest will allow some owners a more active role with their horses, cost them less money, and give the horses a better chance of making it to the races. Racing can utilize the energies and

economic about of pleasure horse owners to give a boost to the industry, and we all win. ∎

The Equine ATHLETE encourages trainers and others to send us their opinions and ideas for this feature in our newsjournal. All readers are invited to respond to the comments printed here. Please address your materials to: *The Equine ATHLETE*, P.O. Box 457, Santa Barbara, CA 93140-4457.

Janet Del Castillo is currently holding training seminars at her farm in Winter Haven, Florida, while working on a "Backyard Race Horse" training manual. For information about seminars and/or manual please write: Janet Del Castillo, 3708 Crystal Beach Rd., Winter Haven, FL 33880, (813) 299-8448.

Continued

Country People

SECTION

Horses Benefit from Fruits of Her Labor

JANET DEL CASTILLO of Winter Haven, Florida has bucked the odds when it comes to training Thoroughbreds.

Most trainers run their horses at the closest racetrack. Not Janet. She works her horses in the orange groves on the family farm.

"It's the perfect environment for them to build up muscle and stamina," Janet says. "Galloping through the deep sand and up the rolling hills of the groves gives strength to all their muscles."

Makes sense — especially when you consider Janet got the idea from raising her own children. "I thought about raising strong, healthy kids and applied the same thinking to horses. The best place for them to develop and grow is right in their own backyard!"

Horsing Around

At the farm, the horses are turned out early in the morning and given the freedom to frolic in the pasture.

Janet only works them every 3 or 4 days, and often includes a swim in a nearby lake as part of the routine. "I found that it's good therapy, especially if a horse has an injury."

GALLOPING GROVES. Janet Del Castillo chooses to train her Thoroughbreds at home instead of at the racetrack. She runs them through the orange groves on the family's Winter Haven, Florida farm.

To support her claim, she points out one of her Thoroughbreds that had a bone chip in its knee and suffered from inflammation. "People said she'd never race again," Janet recalls.

"Sometimes she'll lay on her side and float in the water!"

She took the horse to the lake, attached a long lead rope to the halter and let the horse paddle around, getting exercise without stressing the injury. "She really loves to go

to the lake and swim now," Janet affirms. "Sometimes she'll actually roll over on her side and just float!"

Proof's in Pace

When her horses aren't floating or frisking in the orange groves, they're often winning races. "First Prediction", a gray mare Janet bought on credit in 1984, is a prime example.

A Florida breeder had donated First Prediction and another filly to a children's home where Janet was a volunteer. The director of the home decided that he couldn't house the horses and asked Janet if she was interested in them.

The other filly turned out to be best suited for pleasure riding. But First Prediction went on to win dozens of races, earning over $300,000. Not bad for a "backyard" horse!

"My horses get to run free and act like horses every day, and I think that gives them an edge," Janet informs. "There are many ways to train Thoroughbreds, but I think my 'backyard regimen' will soon become more popular with other trainers."

No doubt. Why buck a winning trend?

EQUUS Magazine Nov '93 HORSE TRENDS

"Restoring a Tarnished Image"

A Voice In The Wilderness

Janet Del Castillo is on a mission. She's a Thoroughbred trainer who believes that the flagging industry can be revitalized by returning the focus of the sport to the welfare of the animal athlete. The current American way of keeping racehorses "incarcerated" 23 hours a day, of undertraining them and then using legal, painkilling drugs to control body soreness is a recipe for the horses' eventual self-destruction, she says.

Del Castillo trains her stable on the home farm in Winter Haven, Florida, conditioning the runners with gallops through the orange groves and swimming them in the pond, and ships to regional tracks on race days. She shares her do-it-yourself training principles and practices in booklet and seminar forms under the title "Backyard Racehorse."

She also writes letters to the movers and shakers of the Thoroughbred industry, letters that have gotten no positive response but which have, with uncanny accuracy, foretold rude awakenings to come. From a letter dated December 3, 1992 to the Animal Welfare Committee of the American Association of Equine Practitioners (AAEP):

"The spectacle of horses snapping their legs in front of the grandstand and jockeys going down on them is not good. The standard comment when breakdown occurs is that it is a tough business...high speed...fast horses...accidents happen. That is true; however, we know that if we look at the history of the majority of the horses that break down, we see warnings all along the way. The vet bills tell a story of a horse with problems. Potent painkillers used when the horse runs, injections of cortisone in knees and ankles, an abundance of short- and long-term steroids given persistently over a period of time—these are not indications of a fit and healthy racehorse."

In September 1992, Del Castillo wrote to the head of the Arizona Race Track Industry Program, hoping she might be included in the annual symposium. She wasn't, but her calls for better owner relations, reduced dependence on drugs, more rational conditioning and greater fair play and honesty in the industry are just now being uttered by some of the recognized leaders.

"I am fully aware of the pressures put to the trainers and vets by the owners and tracks," she wrote in her letter to the AAEP Animal Welfare Committee. "I realize that everyone is struggling to survive, but the decisions made for short-term gain are long-term disaster. From within the industry, we must encourage change."

"Backyard" trainer Janet Del Castillo and First Prediction, the castoff filly who ran 100 races, some in stakes company, and earned over $300,000 while being conditioned on the home farm.

Karen Del Castillo

ORDER FORM

Backyard Racehorse
3708 Crystal Beach Road
Winter Haven, Florida 33880
Tel 863 299-8448 FAX 863 294-9401

SEND TO:

_____

_____

_____

Telephone:_____

Backyard Racehorse - $24.95 per copy

Number of Copies: ___ x $24.95 = _____

Florida Residents add 6%   _____

Shipping - Priority Mail $3.00

Total Enclosed   _____

For information regarding The Backyard Race Horse Newsletter, or seminars at Rancho Del Castillo or in your area, contact Prediction Publications at the above address.

I am interested in The Newsletter   _____

I am interested in Seminars   _____

website:
BACKYARDRACEHORSE.com
email- DELCASTILO@aol.com

Drop me a Line!